The Letters of
MATTHEW
ARNOLD

This photograph probably dates from mid-1884. (Courtesy Special Collections Department, University of Virginia Library)

The Letters of
MATTHEW
ARNOLD

Edited by

Cecil Y. Lang

VOLUME 6

1885–1888

THE UNIVERSITY PRESS OF VIRGINIA

Charlottesville and London

VICTORIAN LITERATURE AND CULTURE SERIES
Karen Chase, Jerome J. McGann, *and* Herbert Tucker, *General Editors*

This volume has been published with support from the series endowment

THE UNIVERSITY PRESS OF VIRGINIA
Copyright © 2001 by the Rector and Visitors
of the University of Virginia
All rights reserved

Printed in the United States of America

First published 2001

Library of Congress Cataloging-in-Publication Data

Arnold, Matthew, 1822–1888.
  [Correspondence]
  The letters of Matthew Arnold / edited by Cecil Y. Lang.
    p. cm. — (Victorian literature and culture series)
  Includes index.
  Contents: v. 6. 1885–1888.
  ISBN 0-8139-2028-0 (v. 6: Cloth: alk. paper)
  1. Arnold, Matthew, 1822–1888 — Correspondence. 2. Poets,
English — 19th century — Correspondence. 3. Critics — Great
Britain — Correspondence. I. Lang, Cecil Y. II. Title. III. Series.
PR4023.A44 1996
821'.8 — dc20   95–50448
[B]   CIP

∞ The paper used in this publication meets the minimum requirements
of the American National Standard for Information Sciences —
Permanence of Paper for Printed Library Materials, ANSI Z39.48–1984.

To Violette
and
In Memoriam
Amanda Stewart Bryan Kane

Contents

Acknowledgments

This edition of letters was made possible by the cooperation and support of Matthew Arnold's grandson, the late Arnold Whitridge (1891–1989), and it remains pain and grief to me that he did not live to see it completed. *His* son, Frederick Whitridge, extending the cooperation and support and friendship begun by his father far beyond the imperatives of duty, has transfused them all with new meaning and renewed vitality. In these volumes their name probably occurs more often than that of any other except the writer of the letters.

This edition was made feasible by a five-year grant from the National Endowment for the Humanities, without which it could not have been undertaken. I acknowledge the support with heartfelt gratitude.

Five close friends imprint every page of the work—Beverly Kirsch, Paul Barolsky, Jerome McGann, Marjorie Wynne, and Kathleen Tillotson. Three works also impress every page of this edition, which in a well-ordered world would have preceded them all, and to these works mine is heavily indebted: R. H. Super's edition of *The Complete Prose Works of Matthew Arnold,* Kenneth Allott's and Miriam Allott's editions of *The Poems of Matthew Arnold,* and Park Honan's biography, *Matthew Arnold: A Life.* All three are acknowledged over and over again in these volumes, and each reference rests on a silent gratitude at once personal, admiring, and profound.

Librarians—warders, in Swinburne's happy phrase, of the "sevenfold shield of memory"—are the unsung heroes and heroines of civilization as we would like to know it, and they have all, everywhere, given evidence repeatedly of devotion to an ideal of work and learning that the writer of the letters collected here would have admired as much as the writer of this sentence appreciates it. A librarian in Paris once telephoned me in Charlottesville about a comma in an Arnold letter, one in Ottawa telephoned to give me an address that I needed, one in Leeds to say that an item I was looking for was indeed there, one in New York to call my attention to some special information, one in San Marino (California) to answer a question, one in New Haven to reassure me that my patience (!) was paying off. One in Oxford pulled himself away from the Oxford-Cambridge boat race, then in a dead heat, to let me know that I was pursuing a dead end. Baron Coleridge, not a librarian but a man with all the good qualities of one, telephoned to make sure an invitation to visit his library had not gone astray. The curator of the Spoelberch de Louvenjoul collection (then) in Chantilly deposited the album of Arnold's letters to Sainte-Beuve in the library of the chateau, where it was wonderfully taken for granted by all the *gardiens* that I was a connection of Jack Lang, the minister of culture. The Acting Director General of the Educational Advising Center, in Moscow (Felicity, thy name is Glasnost!), Ekaterina U. Genieva, moving mountains that neither the post office nor the American State Department, working through the Embassy, had budged, sent me a fax and caused faxes to be sent me from the State Museum of L. N. Tolstoi in Moscow and the Pushkin House in St Petersburg.

I owe a massive, long-standing, and continuing debt to the staff of the Library of the University of Virginia, especially to Kendon L. Stubbs, Associate Librarian (himself an Arnoldian figure in all the essentials), Michael Plunkett, Curator of Manuscripts, James Campbell, North Europe Bibliographer, Linda Lester, Director of Reference Services, and her admirable staff, including Bryson Clevenger, Martin Davis, Susan Marcell, Karen Marshall, Francis Mooney, Mohammad Yusuf. Some others have taken a personal interest in this work and made Arnold's cause and my cause their cause. Penelope Bulloch, Librarian of Balliol College, Oxford University; Vincent Giroud, Curator of Modern Books and Manuscripts, Beinecke Library, Yale University; Christopher Sheppard, Librarian of the Brotherton Collection, Leeds University; and John Bell, Archivist, National Archives, Ottawa, have all repeatedly gone far beyond the call of professional duty. The letters to Henry Bence Jones are printed by courtesy of the Royal Institution.

Two notable groups of letters would have remained unknown to me without the intervention of (as it seems to me) providence. Christopher Stray, Department of Sociology and Anthropology, University College of Swansea, called my attention to Arnold's letters to Henry John Roby, Secretary of the Taunton Commission (belonging to Roby's grandson, John King, who gave me permission to publish them) and sent me photocopies of them as well of Roby's *Reminiscences of My Life and Work* ("For My Own Family Only") from the unique copy in the library of St John's College, Cambridge. John Bell wrote to A. K. Davis, Jr, drawing his attention to the Arnold letters in the (then) Public Archives of Canada, at a time when Davis was already beyond the reach of mortal communication, and Wilma MacDonald then telephoned and wrote to me about them. Margaret L. Evans, Laurier House, Ottawa, sent me lists of Arnold books, bookplates, and inscriptions there.

Among those whose learning and generosity have supported me specifically as well as generally are Raúl Balin, Peter Beal, William Bell, Georgiana Blakiston, T. A. J. Burnett, Manfred Dietrich, Pauline Dower, Shiela Sokolov Grant Duff, Katherine Duff, Charlotte Fisher, Alastair and Jenny Fowler, Eeyan Hartley, Patrick Jackson, Roger Lonsdale, Jennifer Macrory, A. C. W. Mitford-Slade, Vanda Morton, Richard and Leonée Ormond, Tim Procter,

John Spedding, Virginia Surtees, Alan Tadiello, Peter Thwaites, Raleigh Trevelyan, Clive Wainwright, H. B. Walrond, C. D. Watkinson, Martin Williams, Timothy Wilson, Robert Woof. Also, Mildred Abraham, Edmund Berkeley, Jr, Staige Blackford, Sidney Burris, John Clubbe, Morton N. Cohen, Philip K. Cohen, Betty A. Coley, Ann C. Colley, Lowell W. Coolidge, Sidney Coulling, A. Dwight Culler, Kenneth Curry, David DeLaura, Robert T. Denommé, Leo M. Dolenski, Donald H. Dyal, William E. Fredeman, Donald Gallup, William Godshalk, Jennifer Hamilton, Martin J. Havran, the late Walter Houghton, Ann Hyde, Philip Kelley, Karen Lang, Mark Samuels Lasner, Larry Mazzeno, Patrick McCarthy, Mark Morford, John Powell, Mark Reed, Elizabeth Richardson, Harold Ridley, David Riede, Clyde Ryals, Nicholas Scheetz, Bernard Schilling, Alexander Sedgewick, H. L. Seneviratne, Vincent Tollers, Sue Surgeson, Aram Vartanian, John Unsworth, John O. Waller. Also, Lucien Carrive, Annie Chassagne, Jean Favier, G. Laflaquière, and (what a pleasure to conclude with these two names!) Georges Lubin and Christiane Sand.

"Grâce à l'exorbitance de mes années," as Chateaubriand wrote at the conclusion of *Mémoires d'Outre-Tombe,* "mon monument est achevé." Mine has been a privileged life, a thesaurus of experiences, of sensations and ideas. Who else, on a train from Waterloo Station to Devonshire to see Coleridges, has been picked up and engaged in conversation by a Dickens? Who else identifies as the very pleasure principle the satisfaction of editing Swinburne's letters, Tennyson's, Arnold's, and, with it, of meeting and knowing personally Swinburnes and Trevelyans, Capheaton and Wallington, Rossettis and Cheyne Walk, Speddings and Tennysons, Mirehouse and Farringford and Aldworth, Coleridges and Ottery St Mary, Wordsworths and Arnolds, Rugby School and Oxford, Grasmere and Fox How? "Thou hast forgotten, O summer swallow, But the world shall end when I forget."

Cecil Y. Lang
Charlottesville, 2000

Editorial Principles

In all letters the date, return address, salutation, and closing have been normalized, with most abbreviations spelled out; square brackets indicate that an *essential* part of the date is an editorial addition.

Letterheads (and seals) are centered; handwritten return addresses are printed flush right.

Angle brackets, in letterheads or in letters, indicate cancellations.

In the texts of letters printed from manuscript, ampersands have been preserved, superior letters lowered, abbreviations retained or, occasionally, expanded in square brackets. A period is used when the last letter is not the last letter of the word. Numbers, punctuation, and capitalization follow the source.

Printed texts follow the source, except that the hyphen is omitted in *tomorrow, today, tonight,* in conformity with Arnold's invariable practice.

In general, previous publication has not been recorded, except that all letters or parts of letters included in Russell's *The Letters of Matthew Arnold 1848–1888* are indicated by an asterisk after the name of the addressee in the heading.

Reviews of Arnold's works and books and articles referred to by him have been identified whenever possible.

All contemporaries referred to, even unto wives and children, have been identified whenever possible—to the verge of scrupulosity. Perfection here, perhaps happily, is unrealizable, but no halfway house seems defensible.

Cartoons (usually caricatures) of persons formally identified in these letters as they appeared weekly in *Vanity Fair* magazine from Jan. 30, 1869, to Jan. 14, 1914—2,358 in all, typically with a biographical sketch, leading off with Disraeli and then Gladstone—have been noted, usually with this formula: (*VF,* 1/30/69). The excellent book *In "Vanity Fair"* by Roy T. Matthews and Peter Mellini is definitive—occasionally supplemented in the annotations by quotations from the cartoons or biographical sketches in the collection of the editor.

Arnold, regarded by many as England's foremost French writer, wrote a French that, though very good indeed, was less than perfect—inferior to Swinburne's, superior to Tennyson's, superior to the editor's, inferior to the editor's wife's—and his occasional breaches of idiom are noted throughout.

Short Titles and Abbreviations

Album	*An Arnold Family Album,* ed. Cecil Y. Lang, *The Arnoldian,* 15. no. 3 (Special Issue 1989–1990)
Allibone	Samuel Austin Allibone, *A Critical Dictionary of English Literature and British and American Authors,* and J. F. Kirk, *Supplement,* 5 vols (Philadelphia: J. B. Lippincott)
Allott	*The Poems of Matthew Arnold,* ed. Kenneth Allott; 2d edn ed. Miriam Allott (London and New York: Longman, 1979)
Allott-Super	*Matthew Arnold* (The Oxford Authors), ed. Miriam Allott and Robert H. Super (Oxford and New York: Oxford University Press, 1986)
Annual Register	*The Annual Register; A Review of Public Events at Home and Abroad* (London: Rivingtons, 1758–)
Arnold-Forster	*Florence Arnold-Forster's Irish Journal,* ed. T. W. Moody and Richard Hawkins with Margaret Moody (Oxford: Clarendon Press, 1988)
Baldwin	A. B. Baldwin, *The Penroses of Fledborough Parsonage* (Hull: A. Brown & Sons, 1933)
Bertram	*New Zealand Letters of Thomas Arnold the Younger,* ed. James Bertram (University of Auckland, 1966)
Boase	Frederic Boase, *Modern English Biography,* 6 vols (London: Cass, 1965)
Bonnerot	Louis Bonnerot, *Matthew Arnold Poète* (Paris: Librairie Marcel Didier, 1947)
Buckler	William E. Buckler, *Matthew Arnold's Books: Toward a Publishing Diary* (Geneva, Paris: Librairie Droz, Librairie Minard, 1958)
Cohen	Lucy Cohen, *Lady de Rothschild and Her Daughters, 1821–1931* (London: John Murray, 1935)
Coleridge	Ernest Hartley Coleridge, *Life and Correspondence of John Duke Lord Coleridge, Lord Chief Justice of England,* 2 vols (London: William Heinemann, 1906).
Connell	W. F. Connell, *The Educational Thought and Influence of Matthew Arnold* (London: Routledge and Kegan Paul, 1950)

Coulling	Sidney Coulling, *Matthew Arnold and His Critics* (Athens: Ohio University Press, 1974)
County	*Walford's County Families of the United Kingdom* (London: Robert Hardwicke, 1871, Chatto and Windus, 1904)
Critical Heritage	*Matthew Arnold's Prose Writings: The Critical Heritage,* ed. Carl Dawson and John Pfordresher (London: Routledge and Kegan Paul, 1979)
Crockford	*Crockford's Clerical Directory,* 15th edn (London: Horace Cox, 1883)
DNB	*The Compact Edition of The Dictionary of National Biography,* 2 vols (Oxford University Press, 1975)
Foster	Joseph Foster, *Alumni Oxonienses,* 2 vols (Oxford: Parker, 1887)
Graham	Edward Graham, *The Harrow Life of Henry Montagu Butler, D.D.* (London: Longmans, Green, 1920)
Guthrie	William Bell Guthrie, *Matthew Arnold's Diaries, The Unpublished Items: A Transcription and Commentary,* A Dissertation Presented to the Graduate Faculty of the University of Virginia for the Degree of Doctor of Philosophy 1957, 4 vols (University Microfilms International)
Harding	Joan N. Harding, *From Fox How to Fairy Hill* (Cowbridge and Bridgend: D. Brown and Sons, 1896)
Harrow	*Harrow School Register,* 1st edn ed. R. Courtenay Welch 1894, 2d edn ed. M. G. Dauglish 1901 (London: Longmans Green and Co. 1901)
Hillairet	Jacques Hillairet, *Dictionnaire historique des rues de Paris,* 2 vols (Paris: Editions de Minuit, 1963)
Honan	Park Honan, *Matthew Arnold: A Life* (London: Weidenfield; New York, McGraw Hill, 1981)
Hopkinson	David Hopkinson, *Edward Penrose Arnold: A Victorian Family Portrait* (Penzance: Alison Hodge, 1981)
Jowett	Evelyn Abbott and Lewis Campbell, *The Life and Letters of Benjamin Jowett,* 2 vols (London: Murray, 1897)
Kelly	*Kelly's Handbook to the Titled, Landed & Official Classes for 1896* (London: Kelly, 1896)
Kenny	Anthony Kenny, *The Oxford Diaries of Arthur Hugh Clough* (Oxford: Clarendon Press, 1990)

Landed	*Burke's Landed Gentry* (London: Burke's Peerage Limited, 1939)
Leichman	Howard Bernard Leichman, *Matthew Arnold's Correspondence: The American Visits* (Ann Arbor, Mich.: University Microfilms International, 1980 [dissertation, University of Washington]).
Leonard	Chilson Hathaway Leonard, *Arnold in America: A Study of Matthew Arnold's Literary Relations with America and of His Visits to This Country in 1883 and 1886* (New Haven, Conn.: 1932 [dissertation])
Lowry	Howard Foster Lowry, ed. *The Letters of Matthew Arnold to Arthur Hugh Clough* (London: Oxford University Press, 1932)
Lyonnet	Henry Lyonnet, *Dictionnaire des comédiens français* (Geneva: Slatkine Reprints, 1969)
Martineau	*Harriet Martineau's Directory of the Lake District 1855.* An Alphabetical Index Compiled by R. Grigg (Beewood Coldell, 1989)
McCalmont	*McCalmont's Parliamentary Poll Book, British Election Results 1832–1918,* 8th edn by J. Vincent and M. Stenton (Brighton: Harvester Press, 1971)
Mulhauser	*The Correspondence of Arthur Hugh Clough,* 2 vols, ed. Frederick L. Mulhauser (Oxford: Clarendon Press, 1957)
OCAL	James D. Hart, *The Oxford Companion to American Literature* (London: Oxford University Press, 1941)
OCFL	Paul Harvey and H. E. Heseltine, *The Oxford Companion to French Literature* (Oxford: Clarendon Press, 1959, 1961)
OCGL	*The Oxford Companion to German Literature,* ed. Henry and Mary Garland, 2d edn (Oxford and New York: Oxford University Press, 1986)
OED	*The Oxford English Dictionary*
Petit Robert	Le Petit Robert. Dictionnaire universel des noms propres (Paris: S.E.P.R.E.T., 1974)
POLD	*Post Office London Directory* (London: Kelly)
Reid	T. Wemyss Reid, *Life of the Rt. Hon. W. W. Forster,* 3d edn (London: Chapman and Hall, 1888; rptd Bath: Adams and Dart, 1970)
Rugby	*Rugby School Register,* 2 vols, rev. A. T. Mitchell (Rugby: Printed for Subscribers, 1901, 1902)

Russell | George W. E. Russell, ed., *Letters of Matthew Arnold, 1848–1888,* 2 vols in one (London: Macmillan, 1895)

Senior | Nassau William Senior, *Conversations with M. Thiers, M. Guizot, and Other Distinguished Persons during the Second Empire* (London: Hurst and Blackett, 1878)

Spoelberch | Vicomte Spoelberch de Louvenjoul, *George Sand: étude bibliographique sur ses œuvres* (1914; rptd New York: Burt Franklin, 1971)

Stanley | Arthur Penrhyn Stanley, *The Life and Correspondence of Thomas Arnold, D.D.* (London: B. Fellowes, 1844)

Super | R. H. Super, ed., *The Complete Prose Works of Matthew Arnold,* 11 vols (Ann Arbor: University of Michigan Press, 1960–77)

Swinburne | Algernon Charles Swinburne, *The Swinburne Letters,* ed. Cecil Y. Lang, 6 vols (New Haven: Yale University Press, 1959–62)

Tennyson | *The Letters of Alfred Lord Tennyson,* ed. Cecil Y. Lang and Edgar F. Shannon, Jr, 3 vols (Oxford: Clarendon Press, 1981–90)

Tinker and Lowry | C. B. Tinker and H. F. Lowry, *The Poetry of Matthew Arnold: A Commentary* (London: Geoffrey Cumberlege, Oxford University Press, 1940, 1950)

Tuckwell | William Tuckwell, *Reminiscences of Oxford* (London: Smith, Elder, 1907)

Upper Ten Thousand | *Kelly's Handbook to the Upper Ten Thousand for 1878* (London: Kelly, 1878)

Venn | John Venn and J. A. Venn, *Alumni Cantabrigienses,* 6 vols (Cambridge: Cambridge University Press, 1922–54)

VF | *Vanity Fair: A Weekly Show of Political, Social, and Literary Wares,* 1869–1914

Ward | Mrs. Humphry Ward, *A Writer's Recollections,* 2 vols (New York and London: Harper & Brothers, 1918)

Wellesley | Walter E. Houghton and others, *The Wellesley Index to Victorian Periodicals 1824–1900,* 5 vols (Toronto: University of Toronto Press, 1966–89)

Whitaker | *Whitaker's Naval and Military Directory and Indian Army List* (London: J. Whitaker & Sons, 1900)

Whitridge	Arnold Whitridge, *Dr Arnold of Rugby* (London: Constable, 1928)
Woodward	Frances J. Woodward, *The Doctor's Disciples* (London, New York, Toronto: Geoffrey Cumberlege, Oxford University Press, 1954)
WWW	*Who Was Who* (London: A. & C. Black; New York: Macmillan)
WWWA	*Who Was Who in America* (Chicago: Marquis Who's Who, 1896–)
Wymer	Norman Wymer, *Dr Arnold of Rugby* (London: Robert Hale, 1953; rptd Greenwood Press, 1970)

Chronology

1822   (Dec. 24) Matthew Arnold born at Laleham-on-Thames, oldest son and second of the nine surviving children of the Rev. Thomas Arnold and Mary Penrose Arnold.

1828   Rev. Thomas Arnold appointed headmaster of Rugby School.

1834   Fox How, in the Lake Country, built and occupied by the Arnolds as a holiday home and later as permanent home of the family.

1836   Matthew Arnold and his brother Tom enter Winchester College.

1837   Arnold enters Rugby School in September.

1841   Dr Thomas Arnold appointed Regius Professor of Modern History at Oxford, and Matthew Arnold enters Balliol College on an open scholarship.

1842   (June 12) Dr Thomas Arnold dies of a heart attack at Rugby.

1844   (Nov.) Matthew Arnold takes the degree of B.A., Oxford.

1845   (Feb.–Apr.) Substitutes as assistant master at Rugby.
(Mar.) Elected fellow of Oriel College, Oxford.

1847   (Apr.) Appointed private secretary to the marquis of Lansdowne, Lord President of the Council.

1849   (Feb. 26) Publishes *The Strayed Reveller, and Other Poems*.

1851   (Apr. 15) Appointed inspector of schools by Lord Lansdowne.
(June 10) Marries Frances Lucy Wightman.
(Sept.–Oct.) Honeymoon, France, Switzerland, Italy.
(Oct.) Takes up duties as school inspector.

1852   (Oct.) Publishes *Empedocles on Etna, and Other Poems*.
Thomas Arnold born July 6 (d. Nov. 23, 1868).
Inspectorial Districts: "'The midland district in which these schools are situated is a new district, formed in 1851'—for British Wesleyan and other Non-Conformist Schools, included the English counties of Lincoln, Notts, Derby, Stafford, Salop, Hereford, Worcester, Warwick, Leicester, Rutland, Northamptonshire, Gloucester, and Monmouth together with all of North Wales except Flintshire and Derbyshire [*for* Denbighshire], and all of South Wales" (Connell, p. 229n).

1853   (Nov.) *Poems. A New Edition*.
Trevenen William ("Budge") born Oct. 15 (d. Feb. 16, 1872).
Inspectorial Districts: "Gloucester, Hereford, Worcester, Monmouthshire, and South Wales withdrawn. Middlesex, Hertford,

Bedford, Essex, Huntington, Cambridge, Suffolk, Norfolk added" (Connell).

1854   (Dec.) *Poems, Second Series.*
Inspectorial Districts: "4 counties in North Wales and 7 North Midland and Eastern counties withdrawn. Kent, Sussex, Bucks, Oxford, and Worcester added. Many of the schools of his district were in London" (Connell).

1855   Richard Penrose Arnold born Nov. 14 (d. 1908).
Inspectorial Districts: "The title of the district became 'Midland Metropolitan and S. Eastern Division of England'" (Connell).

1856   Inspectorial Districts: "Arnold referred to the extent to which his district had changed by speaking of South Staffordshire as 'the nucleus of my original district but which forms nearly the remotest portion of my present district, the centre of which is London'" (Connell).

1857   (May 5) Elected Professor of Poetry, Oxford.
Inspectorial Districts: "The district originally 'extended from Milford Haven to the Humber' now consists of Middlesex, Kent, Essex, Hertford, Buckingham, Oxford, and Berks" (Connell).

1858   Lucy Charlotte Arnold born Dec. 15 (d. 1934). Married Frederick W. Whitridge of New York in 1884. Their three children married, and there are many, many Arnold descendants of several generations and names in the United States as well as in England.

1859   (Mar.–Aug.) In France, Holland, Belgium, Switzerland as assistant commissioner to Newcastle Commission.
(Aug.) *England and the Italian Question.*

1861   (Jan.) *On Translating Homer.*
(May) *The Popular Education of France.*
Eleanor Mary Caroline Arnold born Feb. 11, 1861. She married (1) Armine Wodehouse (3d son of the earl of Kimberley) in 1889 (d. 1901) and (2) William Mansfield, Baron (later, Viscount) Sandhurst, in 1909.

1864   (June) *A French Eton.*

1865   (Feb.) *Essays in Criticism.*
(Apr.–Nov.) In France, Italy, Germany, Austria, Switzerland as assistant commissioner to Taunton Commission (Schools Enquiry Commission).

1866   Basil Francis Arnold born Aug. 19 (d. 1868).

1867   (June) *On the Study of Celtic Literature.*
(July) *New Poems.*

1868   (Mar.) Left Chester Square, the Arnold home for ten years, and moved to Harrow, their home for five years.

Inspectorial Districts: "District restricted to Middlesex, Herts, Essex, Suffolk, and Norfolk" (Connell).

1869   (Jan.) *Culture and Anarchy.*

Inspectorial Districts: "Lost the counties of Suffolk and Norfolk, and gained Bucks" (Connell).

1870   (May) *Saint Paul and Protestantism.*

1871   (Feb.) *Friendship's Garland.*

Inspectorial Districts: "Reduced to the Metropolitan district only of Westminster with Hendon and Barnet and Edmonton districts of Middlesex, also designated one of the eight new Senior Inspectors with general responsibility for Essex, Middlesex, and London districts north of the Thames" (Connell).

1873   (Feb.) *Literature and Dogma.*

(June) Moves to Pains Hill Cottage, Cobham, Surrey, his permanent home.

1875   (Nov.) *God and the Bible.*

Inspectorial Districts: "Lost the districts of Hendon and Barnet" (Connell).

1877   (Mar.) *Last Essays on Church and Religion.*

1878   (June) *Selected Poems of Matthew Arnold.*

1879   (Jan.) *Mixed Essays.*

(Sept.) *Poems of Wordsworth.*

Inspectorial Districts: "Lost Edmonton" (Connell).

1881   (June) *Poetry of Byron.*

1882   (Mar.) *Irish Essays.*

1883   (Oct.) First American tour.

Inspectorial Districts: "Retained Westminster and was made Senior Inspector for the whole Metropolitan District consisting of the District of the London School Board, Middlesex (extra-metropolitan), and Essex" (Connell).

1884   Inspectorial Districts: "Title changed to Chief Inspector, lost part of Essex. England and Wales in this year divided into 10 chief Inspectorates" (Connell).

1885   (June) *Discourses in America.*

1886   (May–Aug.) Second American visit.

(Nov.–Dec.) In Germany for Royal Commission on Education.

1887   (Feb.–Mar.) In France, Switzerland, Germany for Royal Commission on Education.

(Apr. 30) Retires as Inspector of Schools.

1888   (Apr. 15) Matthew Arnold dies of a heart attack at Liverpool.

(Nov.) *Essays in Criticism (Second Series).*

The prints on this page and facing are from the studio of Allesandro Bassano, probably dating from 1884 (by courtesy of the National Portrait Gallery, London). Compare similar photographs in Nicholas Murray, A Life of Matthew Arnold, *between pages 274 and 275.*

The Letters of
MATTHEW ARNOLD
VOLUME 6
1885–1888

To Miss Galloway [1]

Miss Galloway   Pains Hill Cottage, Cobham, Surrey
Dear Madam   January 2, 1885
    I am sincerely interested by what you tell me of the foundation and
scope of your College, and I thank you for your invitation, but my engagements are such that it is really impossible for me to be at Glasgow on the 16th
instant. Believe me,   Faithfully yours

                                                        Matthew Arnold.—

MS. Glasgow University.

    1. Probably not the one alluded to on Feb. 13, 1866.

To Arthur Howard Galton

                    Pains Hill Cottage, Cobham, Surrey
Dear Mr Galton   January 5, 1885
    I shall be in London from the end of this month till Easter, and in the
course of that time I hope you will be coming up there. You will always hear
at the Athenæum where I am. I assure you I feel the kindness of your words.
Truly yours

                                                        Matthew Arnold.—

MS. The College of Wooster.

To Council Office, Education Department

C. O.   January 6, 1885
    I am sending out my February notices. May I not announce a Pupil
Teacher Exam[inati]on for the last Saturday in Jan[uar]y? I spoke to Mr Cumin
on this point.

                                                                M. A.—

MS. Public Record Office, London.

To Charles Myhill

Education Department, Whitehall

Cobham

Dear Mr Myhill—   January 7, 1885

I am very glad to have your beautifully neat Form 8. I will see that you have additional copies of that Form.

Did Ellen Stocker, Candidate in St Peter's Inf[an]t S[chool], pass? Ever yours truly

M. A.—

MS. Yale University.

To Charles Myhill

Education Department, Whitehall

Dear Mr Myhill   January 9, 1885

The entry is just. If altered it must run: "Part of Mr G.'s division does but moderately in arithmetic, the rest of the work in his division is good." He had better be content with the entry he has.

I send you some more Schedules, and some more Forms 7 and xxiii. Truly yours

Matthew Arnold.—

MS. Yale University.

To Charles Myhill

Education Department, Whitehall

Cobham

Dear Mr Myhill   January 12, [?1885]

Mrs Arnold has just found the enclosed in a portfolio of hers. I hasten to send it.   Truly yours

Matthew Arnold.—

MS. Pierpont Morgan Library.

To Lucy Charlotte Arnold Whitridge

Education Department, Whitehall

Cobham

My darling child   January 12, 1885

This is my first letter to you, and the first time that I write *Mrs Whitridge*! I said I should write to you once a fortnight, but I shall write every Monday, you are so far off, and so dear to my heart. You will not expect long letters, but I shall just scribble a sheet like this every Monday. Your letter from Queenstown was delightful, and so was Flu's [*for* Flo's] account of you—then you went off into the unknown. Today we turned eagerly to the Times for news of your safe arrival, but there is nothing yet. I suspect you will arrive on the Monday morning, just as we did.

All goes on here in the way you so well remember. A bright, cold windy morning was this morning; after breakfast I went out as usual with the two dear boys, who found the front gate open and escaped into the village; I brought them back from Lee's yard. Then I pottered in the shrubberies and marked the things that wanting moving; then I came in and worked till lunch. I am writing a long promised thing for Knowles—"A word more about America"; I often think of you, as I write it, and that it would be unpleasant for you if it gave offence over there; but I do not think it will. Mamma, however, is in a thousand agonies, I need not say. She and I are going to call at the Helmes', who have a child ill; then I meet Nelly at Downside, where she is gone to join Mrs Deacon at her mothers' meeting, and Nelly and I and the darlings return by the Poynters Corner and Kough Lane. Then tea, work again, dinner, Mansfield Park, the Times, and bed. Mansfield Park is a great success—I have only read them the first two chapters, but every sentence tells. What a contrast to Miss Bretherton, which I am reading honestly through, a chapter a night, after they are all gone to bed![1] I can read it, but there is no human life to it, only criticism. It reminds me of Ranthorpe, a novel written by George Lewes, the man who married George Eliot, which had much the same merits and defects. Mary has more delicacy than Lewes, but not so much cleverness and knowledge; neither of them could create men and women. We have no dinner engagements this week: on Saturday we were starved with cold at the Buxtons'.[2] Mamma's new maid is frightened at the prospect of having to wait at dinner, and thinks she had rather go—to the annoyance of Mamma and Nelly, who like her. I myself think she is too much used to be one of a great household to take to a little place like this, but we shall see. The waiting has been given up by Mamma, and Lydia is to think the matter over again. Lola is just moved across the window, with the sun shining on her back; I wish you could see her; I looked up from my writing, and her dear little figure caught my eye. We have excellent accounts from the Dicks, and I think their stay here has made an improvement in their affairs. Ella says that since they went back they have been able to fully settle all their debts. Ask your husband with my love to try and get me at his leisure the number of the *Manhattan* which contained my *Literature & Science*;[3] I want to print from it—it is a little different from the Cambridge version which I keep by me. I wonder if you are actually on terra firma and in your own house at this moment; I hope so. Give my particular love to Fannie Coddington, the Butlers, and Bessy Marbury;[4] I do love to think of you having such friends over there to welcome you. My own darling child, goodbye for the present. Never mind writing to me in particular; the letters to Mamma and Nelly quite satisfy me.   Your own tenderly loving

                                                        Papa—

MS. Frederick Whitridge.

1. *Mansfield Park* is of course Jane Austen's novel, *Miss Bretherton*, Mrs. Humphry Ward's.

2. Two passages (eighteen lines, all recoverable) have been inked over: "What a contrast . . . at the Buxtons'" and, below, "and I think . . . all their debts."

3. *Manhattan*, 3 (Apr. 1884): 323–32.

4. Elizabeth Marbury (1856–1933: *WWWA*), author, translator, and play-agent for Oscar Wilde and others.

To William Parsons Warburton

Education Department, Whitehall

                                                        Cobham

My dear Warburton   January 15, 1885

I must send you one word of congratulation. The preferment has come late, and you well deserved more: still I can imagine few pleasanter things for you, with your habits and associations of the last ten years and more, than a Canonry at Winchester.

Believe me that I sincerely rejoice in whatever can give you pleasure, and that I am always, my dear Warburton,   most cordially yours

                                                        Matthew Arnold.—

Mrs Arnold and my remaining daughter wish to add their congratulations.

MS. Yale University.

To C. E. Swinerton[1]

Education Department, Whitehall

Mr Swinerton

My dear Sir   January 24, 1885

I can sincerely assure you that your letter has given me very keen pleasure. What I have written about religion is so perpetually misunderstood, that to find it turned to good account and all the main points in it taken rightly is as satisfactory as it is rare. In time I cannot but hope that the utility of the books will become apparent to many; but those who were the first to recognise it will always have a special claim upon my good will.

The poem about which you enquire (The New Sirens) was composed when I was only twenty four, and the meaning is not brought out with sufficient distinctness. The mythological Sirens were, as you know, beautiful and charming creatures, whose charm and song allured men to their ruin. The idea of the poem is to consider as their successors Beauty and Pleasure as they meet us in actual life, and distract us from spiritual Beauty, although in themselves transitory and unsatisfying. Believe me, my dear Sir,   most truly yours,

Matthew Arnold.—

MS. New York University.

1. Unidentified. The envelope is addressed to him at 149–51, Front Street, New York City.

To Thomas Hay Sweet Escott

Athenæum Club, Pall Mall, S. W.

My dear Escott   January 29, 1885

I cannot accept Mr Rice's handsome offer,[1] because I have nothing ready which would suit him, and to "prepare" three [*or* these?] poems for the occasion is an impossibility to me.

You are one of my "real good" readers, and I shall like you to see what I have said about America in fulfilment of an old promise to Knowles.

If I live to return again from America I will do something for the Fortnightly.   Ever yours most truly

Matthew Arnold.—

MS. British Library.

1. Rice has not been identified.

To Lucy Charlotte Arnold Whitridge

Athenæum Club, Pall Mall

My darling   February 2, 1885

I saw and shook hands yesterday at Lady Ellermere's lodge with Bertram Buxton who sails for New York on Thursday, and will come to see you as soon as he arrives.[1] He brings a box containing a pillow which the Rates have sent you (very handsome), the writing paper, the suits for your sister in law's boys, and other things. How I like to think of the pleasure you will have in seeing some one who saw Nelly, and me, and both the dear men, Miss Lu, as lately as 4 in the afternoon on February 1st. And I think you will hear of us again very soon afterwards from Marie Coddington, who proposes to come to us on Wednesday for the night. It is our last day at Cobham, and Nelly will be gone—she goes to Manchester tomorrow—but we certainly shall accept the offered visit and do as well for Marie as we can. Dick sent us your delightful long letter to him, and Mamma read it aloud to me—she reads all your letters aloud to me, it is the way in which I like best hearing them. You must really take care of yourself, and the Darkie's reproof as to the perils of fashionable evening dress in that horrible New York climate was very judicious. You do not mention the Carnegies; it is said here that he is bothered by the embarrassment of the iron trade in Philadelphia. Mind you let us know how this is, and at any rate you should not fail to be attentive in going to see Mrs Carnegie. The news of your Uncle Walter is not good, though he has not had another stroke; but he has pain in the head, and the eye gets worse instead of better. Your Aunt Forster has gone to him, and your Aunt Fan has gone back to Fox How for a few days. We have offered your Uncle Walter the Cottage as soon as he can be moved—he would be in a good climate and near an excellent doctor; your Aunt Fan says that Morecambe is gloomy and wretched to the last degree, and she does not care for either of their doctors. But I sometimes doubt whether your poor Uncle Walter will ever leave Morecambe. The weather has changed, and we have had torrents of rain and a flood; Admiral Egerton told me they were to have a meeting at Weybridge to discuss remedies for the scarity of water, and they say at Cobham Mill that for years there has not been such a want of water there as this year; however the rain has come at last. It is quite warm, the first snowdrops are showing, the points of the crocuses and daffodils are coming up everywhere, and in the shrubbery yesterday I found three primroses out. Lola is so pleased with the mildness that I saw her yesterday rolling on her back in the paddock, and then starting up and gallopping about, kicking up her heels. Mamma goes up to London tomorrow to make arrangements about the new house; it is a very pretty one and I myself like the situation; she and Nelly

would of course have preferred Belgravia. We go up on Thursday and this is
Monday. I stay down at Cobham tomorrow and Wednesday, then I shall not
go down there again till Saturday week, the 14th; by that time the spring will
really have started, unless the frost returns which is not likely. The new railroad is opened, and I came up by it today; the country between Stoke and
Surbiton is very pretty, and we kept excellent time. Now I must stop—my
love to your husband— always your fondly loving

Papa

My kindest regards and remembrances to Eliza; tell her I miss her very much.

MS. Frederick Whitridge.

1. Bertram Henry Buxton (b. 1852), son and heir of Charles Buxton and older
brother of Sidney Charles, was a near neighbor, at Fox Warren, Cobham (*County*). Rear-
admiral Hon. Francis Egerton, below, was also a neighbor, at Weybridge, here and below,
and Liberal Member for E. Derbyshire since 1868 (*Upper Ten Thousand*).

To Percy William Bunting

Athenæum Club, Pall Mall

Percy W. Bunting Esq.
My dear Sir   February 9, 1885
    I hope to perform my promise this month, but I should like to have till
the latest day compatible with seeing a Revise. My manuscript is not troublesome to printers, and I am not a great alterer. Perhaps I had better send the
copy straight to the printers, if you will tell me who they are.   Most truly
yours

Matthew Arnold.—

MS. University of Chicago.

To Edmund William Gosse

Athenæum Club, Pall Mall

My dear Mr Gosse   February 9, 1885
    When you announced your Gray, you were just going, and when it
arrived you were gone; so I waited for your return to thank you, which I
now do most heartily. I am gratified for the world that it has this excellent
new edition, and for myself that I have your dedication.
    We had heard from my daughter of her meeting you at Mr Carnegie's,
and from American friends of the interest with which your lectures were

followed—It is very much on my mind to arrange a meeting with you during the next few weeks which I am to pass in London.

As soon as I get my Scandinavian friend[1] I will hand him over to Dasent who has promised to put me in a way of writing a proper acknowledgment. I wish I knew Danish and Dutch—but the hours of life which can remain to me are too few for that, or for many other of the acquirements which tempt me.   Ever sincerely yours

Matthew Arnold.—

MS. Rutgers University.

1. Probably, Alfred Ipsen, Milo'ske Boghandels Forlag Odense, listed, with other addresses, at the beginning of the 1885 Diary (Guthrie, p. 1659). See below, letter to Edmund William Gosse of Mar. 3, 1885, n. 1.

To Council Office, Education Department

February 10, 1885

C. O.

Please remind my colleagues Messrs *Alderson, Danby, Faber,*[1] *Renouf,* and *Sharpe,* that they have still to send me their Forms 7 for the Quarter ending Decr 31st, 1884.

M. A.—

MS. Public Record Office, London.

1. J. D. B. Faber, School Inspector (*POLD*).

To Aubrey Thomas De Vere

Athenæum

My dear Aubrey de Vere   February 10, 1885

I have read your pamphlet with interest, and others, too, will read it with interest—but if you look at what I have said about Ireland in the last number of the Nineteenth Century, you will see I do not believe in government of Ireland by the "Loyalists." The "Loyalists" have had their chance, and they have missed it; I see no solution now but self-government for Ireland, imperial matters being reserved.

I do not believe the landed class will retain power even in Scotland and England, nor do I wish them to retain power, for their virtue, as a political force, is used up. But it is in Ireland that this class will first disappear. Ten thousand perils and difficulties beset the future of Ireland and of England's relations with her; but the remedy for them is to be found, I think, in courses not yet tried—hardly even suggested.   Most truly yours

Matthew Arnold.—

MS. National Library of Ireland.

To Percy William Bunting

Athenæum Club, Pall Mall, S. W.

Percy William Bunting Esq.

My dear Sir   February 12, 1885

I have received no answer to my enquiry, what is the latest day you can give me for sending my article? Pray let me have a line at once to 7a Manchester Square, where I am at present staying.   Very truly yours

Matthew Arnold.—

MS. University of Chicago.

To Percy William Bunting

Education Department, Whitehall

Percy William Bunting Esq.   7a, Manchester Square

My dear Sir   February 12, 1885

Your note to Cobham has just reached me. April will be *far* better, if you can wait for me till then;—as I shall have but two articles this year, they had better not follow one another closely; and I am so pressed with school-inspecting that it would have been a great strain upon me to get my article finished by Wednesday night.—Many thanks.   Most truly yours

Matthew Arnold.—

MS. University of Chicago.

To Lucy Charlotte Arnold Whitridge

London

My darling child   February 17, 1885

I have just come in with Max who has been his usual round by the Marble Arch, the Magazine the Serpentine round to Grosvenor Gate, and home by the Marble Arch and Portman Square again. He likes this walk extremely, Miss Lu, and today he was so good that I let him come home

through the streets from the Marble Arch without his collar; but this is rather
dangerous, Miss Lu, he is such a nervous boy at the crossings. I took him to
Cobham on Saturday and he enjoyed the return home wonderfully: but it
was too sad to hear the moans of Kai when we went away and left him shut
up poor boy. Mamma and Nelly are gone out driving in Dolly Thompson's
brougham: she is very kind in lending it; they are gone to see Mrs Lushington
at Grey's.[1] We dine tonight with the Rates, quite quietly. On Sunday I dined
with Sir Richard Morier, the newly appointed ambassador to St Petersburg,
and met the Russian ambassador, M. de Staal,[2] who told me that his wife
delighted in my essays on the Guérins. She is a daughter of the Field Marshall
Gortschakoff, who commanded in the Crimea. Does it not show how books
get about? We have left very few cards as yet and people are only just beginning to come to town; but nearly all the dinners to which we are asked Nelly
is asked to also, which pleases her and us much. I have been asked to stand
for the Kensington division of London in the New Parliament, and to receive
a deputation and make an address: I have declined the whole thing. You will
be glad to hear that a new edition of my Poems is wanted, which will make
our coming to America quite easy, even if the lecturing came to nothing. I
hear Brandram has come back quite disgusted, saying that the whole thing—
readings and recitations more especially—has been overdone, and people do
not care about it any longer; he has barely paid his expenses, though his
reading is certainly remarkable. Irving does well, but that is another matter;
theatre going is all the fashion. I shall ask the Gosses to dinner that we may
hear of you from them by word of mouth, and he will tell me, also, how he
got on with his lecturing. Flo arrives at the end of this week and the Forsters
themselves arrive tomorrow; we are a long way from them, but in every
other respect this situation is excellent: a shilling fare, as Stopford Brooke said
to me the other day, from every place in London to which one wants to go.
We heard yesterday of the safe arrival of your poor uncle Walter at Wharfeside; your uncle John Cropper went with them and everything that was possible was done by the railway people; the Fisons sent their omnibus carriage
to the station for him and he was in bed again at Wharfeside within three or
four hours after leaving his bed at Morecombe. But I fancy he is terribly
changed, and that they fear a gradual weakening of the brain, even if he lives.
His strength just lasted out the journey, and that was all. Your aunt Fan is
worn out and depressed: but now she will be able to go back to Fox How
for a time, as the Walters are to be joined at Wharfeside by their own servants.
It is said that Dr Butler has been offered and has accepted the Deanery of
Gloucester; it is a poor deanery, but still I think the news likely; he was so
tired of Harrow. We dine with Fanny du Quaire on Wednesday in next
week—she is dying to hear of "that sweet Lucy," she says. If you see the
Adamses say every thing kind from us to them.[3] Nelly had an excellent letter

from Eliza—remember me to her. I hope you are not forgetting to send me the Manhattan, with my lecture on "Literature and Science." Now my own darling, I must stop—but whether I stop or go on I am always my Lucy's fondly loving

Papa.

MS. Frederick Whitridge.

1. Among the hordes of possibilities, she was probably the wife of Edward Harboard Lushington (1822–1904), of Brackenhurst, Cobham. Grey has not been identified.

2. Baron de Staal (1822–1907: *WWW*), a career diplomat, remained at his London post till 1902, effectively refuting the patronising notice in *VF*, 12/5/85: "Should there ever arise an English Minister disposed to resist a Russian Cabinet, M. de Staal will be replaced or supplemented by another man."

3. Henry Adams (whose wife committed suicide in 1885).

To ?

Athenæum Club, Pall Mall, S. W.

Dear Sir   February 25, [?1885]

You are quite welcome to print the pieces you mention. I remain Faithfully yours

Matthew Arnold.—

MS. Pierpont Morgan Library.

To Richard Penrose Arnold

London

My dearest Dick   February 24, 1885

On Sunday I was unable to write either to your Aunt Fan or you, for in the afternoon, my time for writing, I was making calls, and was kept so long that I could write no letters afterwards. Tonight I am going to dine with Lord Rosebery, and shall perhaps hear something about the Australian offers of help, as he is so great a friend to the colonists. I do not wonder that you and Ella have been pleased at the offers and at the notice of them by the newspapers. Every one is blaming Lord Derby's stupid way of treating them, though it is said he does not really mean to decline them, but only to ask for a little time to see exactly what will be wanted. I am afraid that as the hot weather comes on, the force in Egypt will waste very fast, and we shall want all the men we can get. About Herat and the Russian advance people today seem to be reassured. But the times are very anxious, and I do not think the present Government are good people for dealing with them.[1]

Mamma and Nelly make constant expeditions together, sallying out generally on foot, and returning in a hansom. This is the most convenient situation we have ever been in; Eccleston Square is our only difficulty; in general, every place one wants to go to seems quite at hand. The other day at Grill[i]on's I sate next Lord Northbrook,[2] who has excellent fishing on the upper Itchen. He asked me if I would come down there with him some day and try it; so, unless he forgets his proposal, there is some more Hampshire fishing for me—the best trout-fishing, I think, in the world. Mamma will perhaps have told you that a new edition of my poems is called for. My love to Ella, and I am always, my dear old Dick,   your loving

Papa

Text. Russell, 2:317–18.

1. A very complex situation centering in Egypt and involving all the great powers that culminated in the fall of Khartoum and the slaying of General Gordon in Jan. 1885. In a few days Australia would volunteer troop support.

Archibald Philip Primrose (1847–1929: *DNB*; *VF*, 6/3/76, 3/14/01), fifth Earl of Rosebery, later (1894) prime minister, who was taken into Gladstone's cabinet as Lord Privy Seal in March (just in time to witness its defeat by Salisbury in June), was associated with "a commonwealth of nations" as a result of visits to New Zealand and Australia in 1883–84. (His wife, Hannah de Rothschild, who did not "care" for Arnold, was a niece of Arnold's good friend.) Derby was colonial secretary.

Herat, Afghanistan, regarded as the "Key to India," was crucial to the containment of Russia.

2. Thomas George Baring (1826–1904: *DNB*), earl of Northbrook, holder of many high government positions before and after this date, was now First Lord of the Admiralty, under Gladstone.

To Hallam Tennyson

My dear Tennyson   February 24, 1885

It is not quite convenient to me to attend on the 13th of March, but Mr Bhownaggree's subject is so important, that, if he wishes me to take the chair at his lecture, I do not like to refuse, and I will therefore put myself at his disposition for that evening.[1]   Most truly yours

Matthew Arnold.—

MS. Tennyson Research Centre.

1. Mancherjee Merwanjee Bhownaggree (1851–1933: *DNB*), who came to be regarded as "the leading Indian permanently resident in Great Britain," was called to the bar (Lincoln's Inn) in 1885 and was an important legal reformer in India; later M.P. for

North-East Bethnal Green. He lectured on Mar. 13 at the Society of Arts on "The Present Condition and Future Prospects of Female Education in India," with Arnold present (Guthrie).

To Lucy Charlotte Arnold Whitridge*

Athenæum Club, Pall Mall, S. W.

My darling child   February 24, 1885

A beautiful day with a bright sun and a south-west wind; what an awful spell of weather they seem to be having in America! We thought much of you yesterday—it was your afternoon—I wish I could have looked in at it. But we rather pity you for your incessant luncheons and *dining* business; it is a sign of real civilisation when the *world* does not begin till 8 P.M. and goes on from that to 1 A.M.—not later. I hope you will gradually form your own habits, and that you will neither give up walking nor give up reading. Keep always something going besides the mere novel of the hour; you know what pleasure your turn for reading always gave me, and you will find the resource more and more precious. They are bringing out "Junius" at Wilson Barrett's theatre,[1] and I need not say I have been asked to attend the first representation and to write a page of "old Play-Goer" about it. I have refused; in the first place we dine out that night; in the second the play cannot be very good or Bulwer would have brought it out in his lifetime; if it is poor I should not like to do execution upon it as Bulwer was always so studiously kind to me. Mamma and I are put off by Fanny du Quaire, with whom we were to have dined; Nelly dines with the Buxtons, and I meant to have quietly taken Mamma to see Jane May in Niniche; but Knowles has just stepped in and asked us to dine with him to meet Lord Acton, and I have accepted; Ld Acton is here so little and I like him so much. Tonight I dine with Lord Rosebery. On Sunday at Lady Reay's I was introduced to Lady Garvagh and talked to her a long while; she made herself very pleasant.[2] I also met there Margot Tennant,[3] who is a dear little thing, and very preferable to Laura in my judgment; she is coming to see us in Manchester Square. Lady Reay spoke sweetly of you, my darling. Dr Talbot[4] told me that his sister in law, Lady Emma Talbot, could not say enough in Nelly's praise; you know she went to a ball there without Mamma. She enjoys London very much; last night we dined with Lord Coleridge and met Lord & Lady Feilding you remember her as that pretty Miss Clifford, and she is as sweet mannered as she is pretty. Nearly every day, Miss Lu, I go home to luncheon and take the dear man his round in Hyde Park afterwards; he quite expects it and is the best of boys. I did not take him to Cobham last Saturday, but all the coming Saturdays I shall take him; next Saturday Mamma is coming with me. The graciousness of the Leafs has no bounds, and they send to the station to meet us, give us luncheon and tea, and send us back to the station if we will; but it is a pleasant walk to the Cobham Station for the 5.7 train. You will find it makes quite a change as to the labour of getting to and from London. I am to be painted by Weigall[5] for Mr Knowles, who is making a collection of his chief contributors; there will at last be as many portraits of me as of Rubens's wife. Do not forget the Delafields. Are you not much pleased with the offers of service made by the Colonies? It is pretty to see Ella's pride and delight in them. Now I must stop, and go and pay Dent for that chain for which you paid so faithfully.[6] Your letters are delightful, my child; I always cry when they are read to me, but it is a happy cry.   Your own loving

Papa.

MS. *National Archives of Canada.*

    1. Lytton's "Junius Brutus" opened at the Princess on Feb. 26; below, Jane May was playing in *Niniche* with a French group at the Royalty Theatre.
    2. Dowager Lady Garvagh (d. 1898) was the widow of second Baron Garvagh (1826–1871), captain, 10th Hussars, J.P. and D.L.
    3. Emma Alice Margaret (1864–1945: *DNB*), daughter of Charles Tennant, later first baronet (*VF*, 6/9/83), married in 1894 as his second wife Herbert Henry Asquith (1852–1928: *DNB*; cr. earl of Oxford and Asquith 1925; *VF*, 8/1/91, 7/14/04, 3/17/10). At this point, however, they were both on the verge of their remarkable careers, she as a famous wit and political hostess, he as a statesman, with almost every conceivable honor, including the prime ministry, 1908–16. (Margot's older sister Laura married Alfred Lyttelton in May and died in the following April.)
    4. The Rev. George Augustus Chetwynd-Talbot (1810–1896), rector of Withington, Gloucs., brother-in-law of the long widowed Lady Emma Charlotte Chetwynd-Talbot (daughter of the fourteenth earl of Derby); in the next sentence, Viscount (later ninth earl) and Lady Feilding (d. 1919), the former Cecilia Mary Clifford, daughter of eighth Baron Clifford of Chudleigh.
    5. Henry Weigall (1829–1925: *WWW*), prominent artist (his wife was a daughter of the eleventh earl of Westmorland and sister of Julian Fane). The painting (if it exists) remains untraced.
    6. Possibly, E. Dent and Co., Strand, watchmakers.

To James Russell Lowell

7*a*, Manchester Square

My dear Lowell   February 25, 1885

    Of course this requires no answer, but I cannot let these sad days pass without one line to say how we are thinking of you and feeling for you.[1] Most sincerely yours

Matthew Arnold.—

MS. *Harvard University.*

    1. His second wife, the former Frances Dunlop, died Feb. 19.

To Thomas Arnold

Athenæum Club, Pall Mall

My dear old boy   February 26, 1885

Lucy's address is 12, West Tenth Street, New York City. The book-post will take your charming present—the rates are not at all high.

I do most strongly think that the Catholics ought to have one of the Dublin cathedrals, and I hope they will some day have it. It is only sentiment which makes for leaving one to the Anglicans, but perhaps it would be felt that a church which had once had so great a position ought to be treated tenderly. Of course if the Imperial Parliament tried to do a thing of this kind there would be endless opposition and delay; this is why I am for local *Moots*; the question is a Leinster one, not one for Evangelical congregations in Liverpool or Presbyterian congregations in Edinburgh to settle. Ulster should in like manner deal with its own religious endowments and cathedrals, without the interference of Catholic provinces. A far more burning question than Church is land; the temptation to interfere in land questions would be very strong with the landlord class in the English Parliament; but the locality, the provinces, is the best authority for settling the matter.

I am glad to have said something in favour of America, something which I think ought to be said in its favour; there are plenty of things to be said against it, and some of them, in a last article, I shall have to say.

The accounts of Walter are very sad.   Your ever most affectionate brother

Matthew Arnold.—

MS. Balliol College.

To D. Boulger[1]

Education Department, Whitehall

D. Boulger Esq.   7a, Manchester Square

Dear Sir   March 2, [1885]

I shall be happy to take the Chair at the reading of Mr Bhownaggree's paper on Friday evening the 13th of March.   Your faithful servant,

Matthew Arnold.—

MS. Yale University.

1. Demetrius Charles Boulger (1853–1928: *WWW*), "has contributed to all the leading journals on questions connected with our Indian Empire, China, Egypt, and Turkey, since 1876."

To John Morley *

7a Manchester Square

My dear Morley   March 2, 1885

I am losing sight of you, which is very bad. But we are here for a few weeks, and I don't know when we may be here again. Can you come and dine with us next Monday, the 9th, at eight, to meet a Montrealer[1] who was very kind to me in Canada, and who is all with you and Goldwin Smith, and against Forster, on the Federation Question? You will also meet Browning and the Gosses. Do snatch two or three hours from the "Thyestëan banquet" in Palace Yard, and give us all the great pleasure of seeing you again.   Ever yours,

Matthew Arnold

Text. Russell, 2:320–21.

1. Unidentified. Guthrie: "Morley Burney &c at home."

To Percy William Bunting

⟨Athenæum Club, Pall Mall⟩

Percy Wm Bunting Esq.   7a, Manchester Square, W.
My dear Sir   March 3, [1885]

March has begun, and now I want to know the extent of my tether— what is the latest day on which I may send my manuscript to the printer? Very truly yours

Matthew Arnold.—

MS. University of Chicago.

To Edmund William Gosse

7a, Manchester Square

My dear Mr Gosse   March 3, [1885]

Sir George Dasent, an excellent judge, had read Dr Ipsen's translation of "Balder Dead" and has compared it in several places with the original. He thinks the poem very well rendered; and he is greatly pleased, too, with the prefatory notice.

When I retire, and get some leisure, I hope to master Danish myself and to read what Dr Ipsen has written.[1] Meanwhile I shall think it very kind of you if you will convey to him my cordial acknowledgments and thanks, and if you will add that I hope he will allow me to send him the new and complete edition of my poems which is now being printed, and which will appear in the course of the spring.

I am very glad we shall see you here next Monday.   Most truly yours
Matthew Arnold.—

MS. Rutgers University.

1. Alfred Ipsen (1856–1922) also translated Byron and Kipling.

To Lucy Charlotte Arnold Whitridge

Athenæum Club, Pall Mall

My darling   March 3, 1885

I had your sweet letter yesterday. Of course we will stop and see you on our way to the Windsor. I don't like to hear of these colds, I am afraid you take too much out of your dear little self. We are doing more than I like socially over here too, but then it is only for a few weeks and the climate is not so trying. Last night I dined at Grillion's—very pleasant. Gibson and Plunket the two Irishmen, the Abp of Canterbury, Sir Stafford Northcote, Ld Sherbrooke, Ld Rosebery, Ld John Manners, Ld George Hamilton, Ld Acton, W. H. Smith and W. E. Forster.[1] Tonight we dine, all three, with the Lockers, and go to Lady Brassey's afterwards. Tomorrow we have the Forsters and Flo and Ld Coleridge and Gilbert, at dinner at home. On Thursday we dine with the Walronds, on Friday with the Arthur Russells. On Saturday we go to the Private Secretary, and to Lady Hayter's afterwards.[2] On Sunday I go to Aston Clinton, to meet the Roseberys and Arthur Balfour. Lord Rosebery is very much to my taste; we walked home together last night from Grillion's. I have had a kind letter from Mr Carnegie; he has been blackballed at the Reform—20 black-balls; it is said, the cause is in his account to the American interviewer of the motives which had made him buy up a number of newspapers here; I am afraid he will be annoyed, as an active political club, like the Reform, is just the sort of place he would enjoy. I must write to him. Wilson Barrett sent me tickets for Junius, but I could not go, and, if I had gone could not have written about it; I hear it was very stupid, though Wilson Barrett had got a wonderful house together. On Sunday in Grosvenor Square I came upon Bodley[3] walking with a young lady with yellow hair and glowing cheeks, and very much of the period; I nodded to him and passed on when he ran after me and asked if I would allow him to introduce me to Miss Fortescue the actress. I said, oh certainly: we were introduced and walked together along one side of the Square and through

Grosvenor St. to the Park St. turning, shaking hands at parting. I do not think her fascinating, but she talks pleasantly. I have promised to dine with Bryce to meet Parnell in order to talk about Ireland—which will be interesting.[4] I have determined, after all, to go and see Mildred Coleridge; at any rate, to write to her and ask her if she will see me. Things are so bad they cannot possibly be made worse, and I have the advantage of being in my own real feelings a friend to her, and of being so thought by her, I believe. Did I tell you that Mr Knowles is going to have me painted by Weigall, and I am to begin sitting immediately. I have also an article to write—not the final one about America which I reserve until I come back next year—but to fulfil an old promise. What you say about my recent article is very sweet; people here have taken it very well, but then this is certainly the most tolerant country in the world as to criticism upon institutions and classes, if the thing is done without ill-temper. Nelly is enjoying herself much, though both she and Mamma say they have difficulties about clothes, which difficulties must to you at present be unknown. The accounts of your poor Uncle Walter are slightly better. I wonder if you have remembered about getting me the *Manhattan* with my lecture in it. My love to your husband, and I am always, my darling child—   your own

Papa

Kindest remembrances to Eliza.

MS. National Archives of Canada.

1. Three nonmembers: John Thomas Manners (1852–1927), third baron, had been a lieutenant in the Grenadier Guards, married 1885 and bred sons and daughters, was D.L. Southampton, and apparently not much else; Edward Gibson (1837–1913: *DNB*), solidly Conservative and critical of Gladstone, was cr. Baron Ashbourne in 1885 and appointed Lord Chancellor of Ireland with a seat in the cabinet by Salisbury; Plunket was perhaps Henry Patrick Coghill (b. 1845), fifth son of third Baron Plunket (Kelly).

Lady Brassey, in the next sentence, the former Anna Allnutt (d. 1887), was the wife of Thomas Brassey (1836–1915: *DNB*; *VF*, 10/6/77; later, baron, then earl), K.C.B., Member for Hastings and parliamentary secretary to the Admiralty.

2. "The Private Secretary," Charles H. Hawtrey's English adaptation of Gustav von Moser's "Der Bibliothekar," at the Globe with Beerbohm Tree. Lady Hayter, the former Henrietta Hope, was the wife of Sir Arthur Divett Hayter (b. 1835), second baronet, an old Balliol man, formerly of the Grenadier Guards, and now financial secretary of the War Office.

3. John Edward Courtney Bodley (1853–1925: *WWW*), an old Balliol man and a barrister, was private secretary to the president of the Local Government Board and also secretary to the Royal Commission on Housing of the Working Classes and (later) an author of note.

In a letter (MS. Balliol) to Tennyson, Feb. 6, 1890, Bodley wrote: "I am a complete stranger to your Lordship, but I have known some who are and have been dear to you. Your much loved son [Lionel] who lies at rest in the Red Sea I had the pleasure of meeting at the house of my good friend Matthew Arnold." Probably, he met Lionel Tennyson on Apr. 14 when "The Tennysons dine" but perhaps at Frederick Locker's, where Arnold dined on Mar. 3 (Guthrie).

4. Neither Guthrie nor these letters reveal whether this meeting took place.

To Mountstuart Elphinstone Grant Duff

Education Department, Whitehall

London

My dear Grant Duff   March 4, 1885

I promised Canon Fleming,[1] a very popular and very estimable Belgravian clergyman, to mention to you his son-in law, the Rev. Charles Gib, who has just been appointed to a chaplaincy at Madras and has gone out there with his newly married wife.

It was a great pleasure to see Mrs Grant Duff in the summer—and looking so well too. Again and again it was in my mind to write to you when I was in America, but I led a driven life and hardly wrote a letter except on business matters or to my family at home. I was greatly struck with the easy and natural working of institutions in America, whereas ours here begin to strain and creak so formidably—but I have said enough of this in an article in the Nineteenth Century, which I daresay you will read. You will come back to an England where thoughts are current and things are discussed which were not current or discussed when you went away; and perhaps in our present difficulties we are paying the inevitable penalty for our inhospitality to ideas, while they are still ideas only. Our astonishing middle class remains as occupied as ever with questions of Church and Dissent and of getting institutions opened by the Prince and Princess of Wales; our intelligent rulers were misled into thinking that the Prince and Princess might be applied with effect in Ireland, but it seems doubtful whether they will not have to own that they were mistaken and to withdraw their specific. But I will not go on writing about these matters. I must tell you what you will sympathise with me in, I know. I have a passion for the true cypress, the *cupressus sempervirens* which is such a feature of the Italian landscape; you cannot get it of people like Waterer or Veitch,[2] they say it does not succeed here; but I knew from two grand specimens at Pains Hill that in our soil it would do, and now Mr Leaf has procured me two plants which promise beautifully, and which it will console my remaining years to watch, I hope; prospering amid the crash of States. I have also succeeded in establishing the wild daffodil from Westmorland at the bottom of our shrubbery; and this is a great pleasure. To pass from this poetry of nature to my own poor productions; you will be glad to hear that my poems sell better than ever, though they have now been before the world some thirty years. I am just bringing out a new edition with *Geist* and *Matthias* in it, which you must let me give you to celebrate your return.³ Coleridge dines with us tonight; he always speaks of you most cordially. He dines nowhere except in the quietest way, and is sorely troubled by this odious lawsuit. I am going to make a desperate effort to get Mildred to agree to a reconciliation and settlement.⁴   Ever yours,

                                                                    Matthew Arnold.

Kindest regards to Mrs Grant Duff—tell her we have good news of Lucy from New York. I must be allowed to send my love to Clara.

MS. British Library Oriental and India House Collections.

1. James Fleming (1830–1908: *DNB*; *VF*, 6/29/99), canon of York and a strongly Protestant chaplain to the royal family (for whom, like Tennyson, he prostituted his talents, with a famous sermon in 1892 on the death of a ludicrously unworthy subject, the duke of Clarence).

2. James Veitch & Sons, nurseryman, King's Road and Fulham Road. Both Veitch and Waterer appear occasionally in Guthrie.

3. *Poems* (3 vols, 1885).

4. Arnold or somebody achieved exactly that, and the matter was settled in court in June, when the action was stayed without a judgment, Bernard Coleridge unreservedly withdrew his charges, and his father restored to his daughter her £600 a year (*The Times*, June 10, 1885).

To Percy William Bunting

Athenæum Club, Pall Mall, S. W.

Percy Wm Bunting Esq.

Dear Sir   March 5, 1885

I will send my manuscript to the printer on the 18th, so that he shall have it on the morning of the 19th. I hope this will do. It is hard to get a thing of this sort accomplished when one is daily inspecting schools, as at this season I am.   Most truly yours

                                                                    Matthew Arnold.—

MS. University of Chicago.

To Andrew Carnegie

My dear Mr Carnegie   March 5, 1885

Often and often, as I was writing my "Word more about America," I thought of you, and had pleasure in believing that I should give you satisfaction by it. I am not sure that the final "Word" will please you quite so well, but I shall take plenty of time for consideration over it; I quite agree with you that any one who is listened to in America incurs a great responsibility in uttering criticism which is sure to be taken as English criticism upon America, and to touch international feelings accordingly.

I was glad to hear from Lucy that the people whom she sees had been pleased by what I have written. Here some of the newspapers have shown indignation at my praising so much that is American and censuring so much that is English; but the real public of London for things literary—the most liberal public, perhaps, in the world—has been favourable.

You may be sure that we will gladly come to you for our first week or ten days in New York next October, if it then suits you to have us. But I wish Lucy gave us a better account of your mother. I suppose her state of health will very much determine whether or no you come over to England this summer. I was talking to Lord Rosebery about you the other day, and he spoke of you most cordially. I think he has an important career before him, but the real set of things and the real future of public men will not appear till Mr Gladstone disappears from the stage.

If Mrs Arnold and Nelly were by my side they would send their love to you; and also, with mine to your mother.   Ever affectionately yours
Matthew Arnold.—

MS. New York Public Library.

To Lucy Charlotte Arnold Whitridge

Athenæum Club, Pall Mall

My darling Lucy   March 11, 1885

First as to what I have several times asked you to do but you have paid no attention: getting Mr Whitridge to ask the Manhattan people to send me that number of their Magazine which contained my *Literature and Science*. I cannot write to them, for I do not know their address—I think *Temple* comes into it. Now do pray attend to this, for the press is stopped over here for want of the copy which this Magazine must furnish, and if there is much more delay it will be too late to publish my American lectures this season.

My darling if I had had any notion that you would have liked a copy of the Nineteenth Century, you should have had it. But I knew the article would be instantly reprinted over there. However, if you would like the Nineteenth Century even so, you shall have it—only don't forget to tell me. You have been sweet in all you have said about the article and its reception over there. I have just been to see Lady Derby,[1] who is always interested about my visiting America. On Sunday I was at Aston Clinton; Henry James had been there and had given them great pleasure by the character he drew of Mr Whitridge. I am going there again next Sunday; Lady de Rothschild gets dearer and dearer, and I am very fond of Constance too. And I like Cyril; your friend his sister has given up the house in Charles Street and taken one in Eaton Place; the house in Charles Street stood them at £1200 a year, and they could not afford it. But did you ever hear of such a rent—it is beyond New York. Mamma and Nelly accompanied me across the Park today in a bitter east wind to Albert Gate on my way to Weigall's; the darling was with us; you know Miss Lucy, how he likes to take as many of his [?]fam. out with him as possible. They took him home from the Albert Gate; it is the best walk possible for him. I thought Weigall's picture of me was going to be good, but now I doubt. He wants to see Sarony's photographs,[2] but I have none left: I wish you would tell him to send me some. We are filling up entirely with engagements, and shall soon not have a single free night till Passion Week. Has Nelly told you the news about Oakeley? he is engaged to Mary Maskelyne; it is just settled. The Forsters are delighted, and it is a very nice marriage. She is pretty, quite pretty, though without a particle of style, or *chic*, or whatever it is to be called; but I like her, and her father I like very much indeed. The Forsters were down in Wiltshire with the Maskelynes on Sunday, and this morning we had a letter from your Aunt Forster to announce the news. The Maskelyne girls will be co-heiresses, as they have no brothers. Oakeley has £400 a year from Cassell, the firm in which he is, and about £250 a year of his own; they are to start with £1000 to £1100 a year, Flo says. Flo is in great force, and delighted to have got lodgings in Ebury St, where they will be quite independent. Nelly is asked out to dinner with us a great deal, which is charming. Tonight she dines with the Lingens, while we dine with the Stewart Hodgsons; but she joins us there after dinner, and we go to a party at Lady Victoria Buxton's together.[3] Very good accounts of Dick and Ella—Dick is in full work, and very important. Now I must go home to dress for dinner, but this will go with an extra halfpenny. My darling, darling Lucy,   I am your ever loving

Papa.

MS. *Frederick Whitridge.*

  1. Mentioned earlier, she was the former Mary Catherine Sackville (d. 1900), daughter of fifth Earl De La Warr, widow of the second marquis of Salisbury, married now to the fifteenth earl of Derby, Gladstone's colonial secretary.
  2. Napoleon Sarony (*c.* 1836–1896: *WWWA*) artist and photographer at Union Square, to whom Arnold sat four days after arriving in New York, Oct. 26 (Guthrie); reproduced in Russell's *Portraits of the Seventies*, facing p. 294.

3. Born Noel, she was a daughter of the first earl of Gainsborough (by his fourth wife), sister of Roden Noel, the poet, and wife (d. 1916) of Sir Thomas Fowell Buxton, who lived in Grosvenor Crescent.

To Lucy Charlotte Arnold Whitridge*

Education Department, Whitehall

London

My darling child   March 17, 1885

This morning I have your letter to console me for being left alone—Mamma and Nelly having gone down yesterday to East Grinstead. They come back today and your dear letter will delight their eyes when they come in. Thank you for telling me about the Manhattan, and thank Mr Whitridge for the trouble he has taken—I must now set to work to correct the copy I lectured from, but as I had remodelled the thing a good deal for the Manhattan it is a bore having to go over the ground again. I hope the £50 Mr Forman paid me for that article did not hasten his catastrophe.[1] I am pressed by an article which I am now preparing for the Contemporary—you know how these things worry me and upset me, and I am more pressed than usual; but somehow I am not quite so much worried, as I know pretty well what I want to say and feel as if it would come easily within the limits proposed. The article will not particularly interest people, but I had promised it. I think we dine out more than ever; we have not a single free evening till Passion Week. Yesterday we had four invitations to dinner arrive in the course of the day, not one of which we could accept. Of course it is a great pleasure to take Nelly about, she enjoys it so much. Mamma and I constantly say to each other: Lucy would be pleased with her dress tonight; and then we add: And if we could have seen Lucy herself come into the room! Nelly dined with us at the Pascoe Glyns on Saturday, and went to the Ripons afterwards,[2] looking her very best and making herself her very pleasantest. On Sunday I went to Aston Clinton; they always ask much about you there. It was a large party this time: Sir Nathaniel, the Roseberys, the Marjoribankses (she is Lord Randolph Churchill's sister) Arthur Balfour and Reginald Brett, and a young Ferguson, member for Rossshire.[3] Lord Rosebery is very gay and "smart" and I like him much. I have promised to go to the Durdans near Epsom which he likes much the best of all his places—it is very small. Lady Rosebery does not care for me by nature, but makes herself civil because she sees her husband so. She is devoted to him. She produced, for me to write in, an interesting autograph-book she has just set up, beginning with the Queen, who has written Tennyson's stanza "Tis better to have loved and lost" in her very best and boldest hand. Then the Prince of Wales has written a long rigmarole out of a French author about l'amour: the Princess, Plus penser que dire, and, Plutôt mourir que changer; each of the Princesses a sentiment and the two Princes—that of Prince George being—"Little things on little wings bear little souls to heaven.["] Gladstone has written a verse from Wordsworth: Ld Salisbury, Ich bin der Geist der stets verneint,[4] (Mr Whitridge will tell you what it means, but learn German), from Faust. Tennyson has written a passage from Locksley Hall which he says is his best couplet—I do not think so, but it is interesting to have what he thinks his best. Ld Granville some very poor verses—Millais a capital impromptu. Altogether the book much amused everybody. I dined at the Coleridges last night: your uncle W. E. F. failed, having to go to a meeting, and Mrs Bernard [Coleridge] was suffering so badly from headache that it saddened my spirits to see her. Your Aunt Forster was not in force; the best company there was Gilbert. Tonight we dine with Admiral Maxse. Tomorrow we have a young party here, the Star Bensons for chief; but I have asked Pigott the Licenser as a second old death's head beside mine. On Saturday we dine at the Arthur Hobhouses, and have Lady Hayter's second party afterwards; Nelly likes these crushes better than any thing; I don't, and I think you did'nt. I have just taken the sweet man a turn in Portman Square as I can't take him out this afternoon; I have to sit for my portrait, which is going to be quite bad. He has just heard the doorbell, Miss Lu.—I think it is Mademoiselle coming to lunch; he is barking furiously. But I have given him your kiss, and he sends you his very best love. He gets on so much better in London now than he did in the summer. Tell us if you did not like hearing of Marie Coddington's visit to Cobham. Now I must stop—always, my own precious child,   your most loving

Papa—

MS. Frederick Whitridge.

1. Allan Forman (b. 1860), now editor and proprietor of *The Journalist*.

2. Son of the first Lord Wolverton, Pascoe Charles Glyn (1833–1904) and his second wife, the former Caroline Henrietta Hale, of Eaton Square. He was commissioner of lieutenancy for London, Liberal Member for Eastern Division of Dorset briefly 1885–86. The marquis and marchioness of Ripon, of the Chelsea Embankment, had returned recently from the viceroyship of India (1880–84).

3. Arnold himself, now well past fifty, was senior to them all: Edward Marjoribanks (1849–1909: *DNB*; *VF*, 7/12/94), second Baron Tweedmouth and his wife, a daughter of the seventh duke of Marlborough; Arthur James Balfour (1848–1930: *DNB*; cr. earl 1922; *VF*, 9/24/87, 1/27/10), philosopher and one of the most influential statesmen of modern times (prime minister 1902–5), now Member for Hertford and merely on the edge of political distinction; Reginald Baliol Brett (1852–1930: *DNB*; succ. as second Viscount Esher 1899); Ronald Crauford Munro-Ferguson (1860–1934: *DNB*; cr. viscount 1920), formerly a Grenadier Guardsman, now Liberal Member for Ross and Cromarty, later governor-general of Australia.

4. Mephistopheles on first meeting Faust: "I am the spirit that negates" (*Faust*, 1.1338).

To [?Arthur Naylor] Wollaston[1]

7a, Manchester Square

Dear Mr Wollaston   March 22, [1885]

Of course I put down my name for you, and I was both sorry and surprised at your not getting in. There is a report that you were mistaken for another man.   Very truly yours

Matthew Arnold.—

MS. Fitzwilliam Museum.

1. Arthur Naylor Wollaston (1842–1922: *WWW*, K.C.I.E. 1908), orientalist, author of an English-Persian dictionary and other works, superintendent of translation of oriental inscriptions in the South Kensington Museum from 1881, later registrar and superintendent of records in the India Office.

To Lucy Charlotte Arnold Whitridge

London

My darling child   March 24, 1885

Nearly always, when I am going to write to you comes a charming letter from you to acknowledge—and now we have this morning had one of your very most charming letters. First let me tell you that there is a decidedly better account of your uncle Walter; your aunt Fan has had a letter from him, written with his own hand—his first letter since his attack. He has a good deal of discomfort still, but the actual bad pain is gone; I think he is going to make a recovery, however slow a one. I have been lunching with Lady Dorothy Nevill—there were Justin McCarthy, Blumenthal and Lord Wharncliffe.[1] There are two new things Mikado at the Savoy and The Magistrate by Pinero, which are said to be *simply* irresistible; we have not a single evening, or we should go to see them: after Easter I shall remind D'Oyly Carte that he promised me a box at any time I wanted them—Wilson Barrett is taking off Junius, and going back to the Silver King. I have been going through Merope for my new edition, and am convinced that if it were well put on the stage it would be very striking; but every one in it ought to be well-bred, and the expense of mounting it would be great. But it will be put on the stage some day by a royal or wealthy amateur, after I am dead. Last night we dined with the Colliers and had Count Münster and his two daughters, Wyke who was Minister in Mexico, Lord & Lady Saltoun, Sir Henry &

Lady Layard and the Reeves; it *was* pleasant. After dinner we went into John Collier's studio, which was lighted up, and saw his pictures. Mamma was within sight and earshot of me at dinner, and I was particularly struck by her resources of conversation. She was between Reeve and old Lord Saltoun. John Collier was away; his wife is too hysterical to be in London and has to live at Norwood.² Tonight we were asked to dine with the Goschens, and one or two other people asked us besides, but I have been obliged to keep today for "The Club," though dining there is not very amusing. Tomorrow we dine with the Fitzjames Stephens, and there is a concert at Mrs Eustace Smith's afterwards.³ They say it is to be a very good one, and Nelly likes the idea of it; but I shall drop them at the door and go on home. What I do like the thought of for tomorrow is going down home; it is more than a fortnight since I was at Cobham; I was going on Sunday but there was a snowstorm that morning, the only snow we have had this year. I shall take the dear Yellowsweet,⁴ Miss Lu, and I think he knows already he is going. Next Saturday we have a conference at the office, and on Sunday I must pay calls, so tomorrow will be my last visit to Cobham before our return home. I expect to find much progress, in spite of the cold East wind—but the camelias will be out in the Greenhouse, at any rate. The Leafs are gone to Gloucester, to see the place where their dear Dr Butler is going to live. What devotion! Mr Farmer is going to leave Harrow; he does not want to try another headmaster after Dr Butler.⁵ He has been made organist of Balliol, and will live at Oxford. His salary is but £100 a year, whereas at Harrow he had £200: but he thinks he will get all the pupils he wants at Oxford, and at any rate Harrow was wearing him out. I have been sitting to Weigall, but my picture will be a horror. I sit looking at his portraits of Cardinal Manning, Miss Halkett, and Ethel Fane, Julian Fane's daughter; they are all excellent, I am the exception. I long to hear of the weather changing at New York; mind you tell me about the change. Ever my own darling Lucy,   your fondly and tenderly loving

Papa—

MS. *Frederick Whitridge.*

    1. Dorothy Fanny Nevill (d. 1913; *VF*, 11/18/08, 6/11/12), daughter of the third earl of Orford and widow of Reginald Henry Nevill (d. 1878, grandson of first earl of Abergavenny), who lived in Charles Street, Berkeley Square. Justin McCarthy (1830–1912: *DNB*; *VF*, 5/23/85), Irish politician, journalist, essayist, historian, and novelist; George Russell, acknowledging indebtedness to McCarthy's *Portraits of the Sixties*, used him to lead off *Portraits of the Seventies*. Jacques Blumenthal (1828–1908: *DNB*), composer of songs, pianist to the queen, music teacher to aristocratic ladies. Edward Montagu Stuart Granville Montagu Stuart Wortley Mackenzie (1827–99: *WWW*), first earl of Wharncliff, large landowner and collector of pictures.
    2. Count Münster Derneburg (1820–1908: *WWW*; *VF*, 12/23/76), German ambassador in London 1873–85 and then in Paris. Charles Lennox Wyke (1815–1897: *DNB*; *VF*, 2/9/84; K.C.B. 1859) had been more recently minister to Portugal but he

retired in 1884. Alexander William Frederick Fraser (1851–1933), eighteenth Lord Saltoun and his wife, the former Mary Grattan-Bellew. John Collier (1850–1934), the painter, son of Lord Monkswell (Robert Porrier Collier) was married first to Huxley's daughter, Marian (d. 1887), and then to her younger sister, Ethel.

3. Katherine Isabella, *née* Place, wife of Eustace Smith (d. 1914), physician and author, of Queen Anne Street, Marylebone.

4. Yellowsweet: not clear, not misread, and not in *OED*.

5. John Farmer (1836–1901) had been at Harrow since 1862.

To Frederic William Farrar

Cobham, Surrey
My dear Farrar   March 25, 1885

If you put yourself into the hands of the Boston bureau, they will arrange for you to lecture all over the Eastern states. For this you have no inclination, you say; and I suspect you have not time for it either. The best way will be for your friends to arrange a lecture for you in all the principal places you visit; this was done for Tom Hughes, I believe. Phillips Brooks would arrange it for you in Boston no doubt, and you would find friends in all the great cities who would do it. The only thing against this is, that it is well to make a longer stay in each city than you are contemplating, if your friends are to get up a thoroughly paying audience for you. But perhaps you will stay longer than I suppose.

But you had much better write at once to Phillips Brooks and ask his advice. Do not rely on mine, for I was so entirely in my agent's hands that I am no good authority as to ways of proceeding without one. D'Oyly Carte is, I believe, going to send over Justin McCarthy, but any way you would not like, I suppose, to be managed by an "impresario" over here.

I am glad one of your boys takes orders.   Ever yours affectionately
Matthew Arnold.—

If you apply to the bureau, direct:
The Redpath Lyceum Bureau,
Boston, U. S. A.

MS. Bodleian Library.

To Morris Hudson [1]

Education Department, Whitehall
Morris Hudson Esq.   London
Dear Sir   March 25, 1885

I have again to thank you for telling me of *Errata* in my volume of Selections from Wordsworth.

As the book is stereotyped, I must not now attempt an addition so considerable as that insertion of dates you recommend.   Faithfully yours

Matthew Arnold.—

MS. *Texas A&M University.*

 1. Hudson has not been identified.

To John Hall Gladstone[1]

Athenæum Club, Pall Mall, S. W.

Dear Dr Gladstone   March 28, [?1885]

 I have not yet heard anything from Mr Sharpe about the Memorial, but I am glad to have it, and shall venture to keep it if I do not hear from you that you want it returned.   Very truly yours,

Matthew Arnold.—

 1. John Hall Gladstone (1829–1902: *DNB*), a chemist, was a member of the London School Board, the Rev. Thomas Wetherherd Sharpe (1829–1905: *WWW*) a Chief Inspector of Schools.

To Lucy Charlotte Arnold Whitridge

Education Department, Whitehall

London

My darling child   March 31, 1885

 I have been taking out dear Max in the Park; he rather depends upon his old master, as his Mrs Arnold and his Miss Nell have both of them got colds and have been confined to the house for some days. Mamma has gone out today, but we would not let her take Max, for fear she should have to loiter about. But his delight when he sees me putting on my coat after lunch is something pretty to see. Mamma was finished on Thursday last, when a really bad cold on her chest declared itself; she has not again been out in the evening, and not in the day time till today—Tuesday. On Friday Nelly dined with me at Annie Yorke's—a pleasant party—Cyril Flower, Capt. Montagu and Lady Agneta, Mr Moreton whose wife is with the Duchess of Connaught, Mr Reginald Brett and the Duke and Duchess of St Albans.[1] I took Nelly afterwards to Lady Goldsmid's—a magnificent house with a great many foreigners and a great deal of music. By this time Nelly had a cold beginning; next day, Saturday, she dined with me at Mrs Jeune's[2]—a large dinner and an evening party afterwards—by 11 Nelly was quite voiceless, and I took her home soon after. She passed next day in bed, and shared with Mamma the attentions of Dr Hutton. In the afternoon I was obliged to call on old Lady Monteagle and one or two others; Jane had to take Max out, and then occurred a terrible incident, Miss Lu. A horrid little Skye terrier flew at Max and pinned him by the ear. Max cried, but could not get at his adversary—his adversary's owner[,] a lady, was quite helpless; Jane could not part them; a gentleman came to the rescue, two hansoms stopped and the occupants got out—quite a crowd Miss Lu round the poor little sufferer— and at last the gentleman, by forcing his stick into the terrier's mouth and twisting it round, forced him to let go his hold. Max returned home rather forlorn, but his ear was well washed and will soon heal. He was bitten in the flap of the ear and nowhere else. On Sunday I lunched with the Prince, who has had to go to Berlin to congratulate the Emperor on his birthday, and who stopped one day in London on his way back to Newcastle. The Italian Minister was at lunch—a pleasant man.[3] The Prince came to tea with Mamma and Nelly in the afternoon, and in the evening dined with the Prince of Wales. Yesterday I dined out by myself; it was at the George Howards: there was Lady Airlie, Henry James, and Burne Jones and his wife—It was lively and pleasant. Today I sate to Weigall, who is improving his portrait of me but it will be never good. Then I took Nelly to lunch with me at the Duchess of St Albans—a delightful woman with sweet manners. You will be grieved to hear that Nelly has not yet accomplished her wish of shaking hands with a Duke, as the Duke of St Albans came in to luncheon late, and left for Newmarket before it was over. Tonight we have the Forsters, Willy Wood, Frank Arnold[4] and Walter Leaf to dinner here—and with that our dinings end. I am delighted to think that it is so; but it has been a pleasure to see Nelly enjoy herself. I am so very glad that you saw Mrs Fields, as she is sure to write to Mamma about you, and to give us far more notion of your habitation and your dear self in it than the Coddingtons give us when they write. But your own letters are so long and natural and charming, that they make us live with you.   Ever, my darling love, your own

Papa

MS. Frederick Whitridge.

1. Victor Alexander Montagu (1841–1915), later rear admiral, second son of the seventh earl of Sandwich and his wife, Lady Agneta (1838–1919), *née* Royston, daughter of the fourth earl of Hardwicke and lady of the bedchamber to Princess Christian; Richard Charles Reynolds Moreton (1846–1928; knt 1913) and his wife Jane, *née* Ralli, lady of the bedchamber to the duchess of Albany—not Connaught, as Arnold has it, in a slip that may be unique; William Amelius Aubrey De Vere St Albans (1840–1898; *VF*, 1/4/73), tenth duke, and his second wife, Grace, daughter of Bernal Osborne.

2. Susan Mary Elizabeth Jeune, a widow, wife of Francis Henry Jeune (1843–1905: cr. Lord St Helier 1905, the year of his death; *VF*, 4/11/91), son of bishop of Peterborough and former master of Pembroke College, Oxford, an old Balliol man, a prominent barrister (Q.C. 1888), and later a judge. She has an agreeable page on Arnold in her book *Memories of Fifty Years.*

3. A revenant, Prince Tommaso, duke of Genoa, who had lived with the Arnolds for two years while a schoolboy at Harrow. The Italian minister was Count Nigra (*VF*, 3/6/86).

4. Francis Arnold (1850–1927), Tom Arnold's youngest son and seventh child.

To Emily Talbot[1]

Athenæum Club, Pall Mall

Mrs Emily Talbot
Dear Madam   April 3, 1885
    I thank you for your invitation, but I shall not be in America when your Association meets in September.   Your faithful servant,

Matthew Arnold.—

MS. University of Virginia.

1. Unidentified. The envelope is addressed to 66, Marlborough Street, Boston Mass., U.S.A.

To Percy William Bunting

Percy Wm Bunting Esqre   Cobham, Surrey
My dear Sir   April 4, 1885
    I have just arrived here, and find your kind note and cheque. I doubted about the article suiting you, but its tone and temper make it possible for a public such as we have at present; vicious attacks on the orthodox position do nothing but harm in every direction. I cannot but hope that the line taken by me will prove, in the times upon which we are entering, to be of use; I feel myself really in sympathy with the religious world far more than with its assistants—even with the religious world as it is at present.

    I am afraid I must stick to my self-denying ordinance as to article-writing. I have already refused a request from America for an article on the revised version. Believe me, my dear Sir,   most truly yours

Matthew Arnold.—

MS. University of Chicago.

To Thomas Arnold

Cobham
My dear Tom   Easter Sunday, [April 5], 1885
    You may be very sure I would gladly have stood aside for your sake, even had I meant to compete; but I never did. How can a poor old man

"faire son salut" while he is giving 42 lectures a year—trying to make them probably the sort of show lectures that a wicked and adulterous generation [1] demands, and that Ruskin gratifies them with? No, nothing would induce me to become a professor now; I had a kindly feeling to the Portuguese Minister at Vienna who entirely refused to believe Lady Bloomfield when she told him that I was one, years ago. The métier of a school-inspector is not one to rejoice the heart perhaps, but I prefer it to that of a professor.

But I spoke to Jowett last autumn about *you*. You would give the right sort of lectures—substantial lectures for real students. However, he was clear that you were impossible.

If you really wish it, I must manage to come to the wedding [2] by throwing over my school. But I must return the same day, I am so busy at present. We will take, two of us, the 8 o'clock A.M. train from Weybridge to Reading on the 16th; that will bring us in time for the marriage, Nelly says.　　Your ever affectionate

M. A.—

MS. Balliol College.

1. Matthew 16:4.
2. Tom's daughter Julia (1862–1908) married Leonard Huxley (1860–1933) on Apr. 16.

To George Lillie Craik

Education Department, Whitehall

Cobham, Surrey

My dear Craik　　　　　　　　　　　　　　　　April 9, 1885

You were away when I called last week, but I was told that you would be back in a few days.

As it is better to settle these things beforehand, I should like to know what you propose to give for this new edition of the Poems, with which Clark is getting on very much to my satisfaction. I want the "Discourses in America" to appear at Whitsuntide; of those I think we should print 1200, and I should like to sell you the edition.

Of the Poems we should print, of course, 2000, as before.

Bain thinks there will be a demand for the "Merope" volume amongst people who have bought the previous editions, and that the volume should, therefore, have at the end a second title and half title, without the words *Third Volume*—for the benefit of such people when they bind it. He thought this of importance, and I promised to mention it to you.

If you have a bound copy of the expiring edition of my Poems, will you kindly send it in my name to

Miss Julia Arnold
29, Norham Road
Oxford—

my niece, who is to be married to young Huxley next week.   Most truly yours

Matthew Arnold.—

You know you yourself wished I should get through the Poems before taking up the Johnson notes—but now I am really going to get these done.

MS. British Library.

To John Duke Lord Coleridge

Education Department, Whitehall

Cobham

My dear Coleridge   April 11, [1885]
    I send the Toronto letter; return it, and tell me whether or no you would answer it, if in my place.
    What Lawley says is this: (he has been saying that several of our old friends in Devonshire are gone)—"Any connexion one may ever have had with Coleridge, one would naturally feel inclined to make the most of *now*, in his great family troubles. I have never seen him since old Balliol days, but am intensely sorry for him."   Ever your affectionate

M. A.—

MS. Lord Coleridge.

To George Lillie Craik

Education Department, Whitehall

Cobham, Surrey

My dear Craik   April 12, 1885
    Your offer for the Poems was above what I expected—an unusual avowal, I suppose, for an author to have to make to a publisher. I am more than satisfied with it, I am very much pleased.
    With regard to the "Discourses in America" I suppose you will sell them at 4s/, not less. In that case £50 for the sale here is a small sum for an edition of 1250, if the edition goes off at once. If the edition slowly dribbles

itself away, the £50 beforehand is a fair price enough: but I think if the edition is sold out, say, before Christmas, I ought to have £25 more. For the next edition we would make a new bargain.

I leave you to settle the title page question for the Poems as you like. I dislike "The First Volume" at length—I prefer Volume I, or Vol. I.

I am very glad you had a copy of the Poems for my niece.

I have been very busy with new Notes to this edition, but this is done now, and Clark will not send me proofs, I suppose, of what he has in stereotype. He is getting on fast with the "Discourses" now.

I should like to say about May 20th for the payment of the money into Twinings. Both books will be ready by that time, I think.   Most truly yours

Matthew Arnold.—

MS. British Library.

To George Smith

Cobham
Sunday, [? April 12, 1885][1]

Going to throw me over tomorrow? Let me find a frank avowal at the Athenæum.   Ever yours

M. A.—

MS. National Library of Scotland.

1. My date is groundless, except that the words *avowal* and *throw over* occur in 1884–86 only in letters on Apr. 5 and 12.

To [?]Martin Joseph Griffin

Cobham, Surrey
Dear Sir   April 19, 1885

I quite well remember meeting you at Toronto. You tell me not to answer your letter about Goldwin Smith,[2] but I have been reading it again, and it is so kind and sensible that I must send you a few lines of answer. I do not think we shall now move him from Canada; and indeed his favourable moment for action here is now, perhaps, passed. He will stay in Canada, and the thing is for him to make the best of himself there, and for you to make the best of him. No doubt he is inclined to be too high-wrought, severe, and scornful; and whoever has lived in the centre of the life of the old world

cannot but find the life of the new—that of the States just as much as that of
Canada or Australia—wanting in many things. Marcus Aurelius says, indeed
that "he who sees one set of men and events, sees as much as if he saw all
men and all events—for all things are of one kind and one pattern."³ But he
was a sage of the first water. Goldwin Smith in Toronto will always miss
Oxford and London; but his friends may do something in recommending
to him hopefulness of view and gentleness of tone. I have myself urged him
to mitigate his severity of both view and tone as regards the Irish.⁴ On the
other hand, I think it important that the literary class in Canada should not
be withheld by any fear of being misunderstood from showing their regard
for him and their sympathy with him. They can easily do it, while keeping
their independence of judgment; and I am sure it would do good; much of
his acerbity comes from his sense of isolation. Believe me,   very truly
yours

Matthew Arnold.—

MS. National Archives of Canada.

1. Martin Joseph Griffin (1847–1921), literary critic and historian, was for four
years (1881–85) editor of the Toronto *Mail* (Leichman).
2. Arnold had a paragraph (Super, 11:215–16) on Smith in "A Word More about
America," which may in fact have occasioned this letter.
3. *Communings with Himself*, 6:37 (Leichman).
4. Smith's severity was nearly indistinguishable from bigotry.

To Charles Thomas Mitchell

Athenæum Club, Pall Mall

C. T. Mitchell Esq.
Dear Sir   April 20, 1885
It is out of my line to attend meetings, and I think I am of more use by
abstaining: but you are right in thinking that the object of your meeting
interests me, and I will give myself the pleasure soon of sending you what I
said in America on the general question, in relation to France.   Truly
yours

Matthew Arnold.—

MS. Cheltenham Ladies' College.

1. Charles Thomas Mitchell (b. 1842), from Gonville and Caius College, Cambridge, had been called to the bar in 1868; the envelope (with an Official Paid postmark
and bearing the handwritten name P. Cumin) is addressed to Mitchell at 3, New Court,
Lincoln's Inn (*Men-at-the-Bar*).

To Ernest Hartley Coleridge

Pains Hill Cottage, Cobham, Surrey

Dear Mr Coleridge   April 22, 1885

Surely I answered your previous note? If I did not, pray accept all my apologies! It will be impossible for me to be present on the 7th of May;[1] I must be at Exeter on that day, for the inspection of a Training College. Most truly yours,

Matthew Arnold.—

P. S. I think you will like a word I have said about S. T. C. in the last number of the Contemp. Review.

MS. University of Texas at Austin.

1. See 5:468.

To Patrick Cumin

Mr Cumin.   April 26, 1885

No X. P. hitherto issued is provided with the new scale, and the reading, recitation, practical teaching and needlework of all cases taken from Feb. 1 up to present date, are already marked on the old scale. It will be extremely inconvenient to use the new scale for earlier cases than *May* ones; and where is the advantage?

M. A.—

MS. Public Record Office, London.

To Lucy Charlotte Arnold Whitridge*

Cobham

My darling Lucy   April 28, 1885

I had your long letter, and as sweet as it was long, yesterday evening; never imagine that I mind about your not writing direct to me, but still this was a beautiful letter. I have a letter from Major Pond to ask what I am going to do; I am waiting to hear from you, but I think for what you say to Dick that you are dropping the intention of coming over this year. But we shall be guided by your decision. We have beautiful weather, and I have just been making one of those rounds of mine in the garden which you so well remember. The blossom is a sight of beauty this year on the fruit trees, and I hope there will be some fruit. Dew[1] and I are diligently following the treatment laid down in the pamphlet Mrs Lushington gave me, and I hope it will answer; certainly the bloom seems finer on the trees to which the treatment is applied than on those to which it is not. In another week the lilac will be out, and a week after that, the broom and the laburnum. It is a heavenly moment of the year in England, certainly. I took the dear dogs the Burwood round yesterday. I got back from London at four, having walked from the station. Both dogs were sitting in the passage with their eyes intent on the hall door, in despair at the day slipping by without their walk, Miss Lu. You may imagine their delight. Max is now no trouble to me whatever; when we enter Burwood at the further lodge Kai is always put in the chain. As we went along that pretty walk under the chestnuts the cuckoo was so loud and so close that Max was fairly puzzled and stood still; at that moment a squirrel seemed to rise out of the ground at our feet, and ran up one of the trees. Kai strained and tugged, but I had him in the chain; Max was so absorbed by the cuckoo that he never perceived the squirrel. I should have liked to have seen your gray squirrels building; I thought them beautiful creatures, and quite as interesting as ours. . . . My love to the Butlers when you see them.—Always, my darling child,   your own loving

Papa

Text. Russell, 2:323–24.

1. The first reference to the factotum, whose name appears in Guthrie's monthly accounts regularly from January 1880, but Arnold mentions the Dews in some detail in Oct.–Nov. 1886.

To [?]Patrick Cumin

May 2, 1885

Noted; but the inconvenience will be great, and I fail to see the need for this haste in beginning.

At any rate I shall leave, as suggested, the marks already entered.

M. A.—

MS. Public Record Office, London.

To Richard Penrose Arnold*

Cobham

My dearest Dick   Sunday, [May 10, 1885]

I hoped to have heard definitely about Chenies before writing to you; I think, however, Lord Tavistock will give me two days in Whitsun week.

I had been having a horrid pain across my chest, and on Friday mamma carried me to Andrew Clark, who has put me on the strictest of diets for one week—no medicine, but soup, sweet things, fruit, and, worst of all, all green vegetables entirely forbidden, and my liquors confined to one small half-glass of brandy with cold water, at dinner. I am to see how this suits me. He thinks the pain is not heart, but indigestion. At present I feel very unlike lawn tennis, as going fast or going up hill gives me the sense of having a mountain on my chest; luckily, in fishing, one goes slow and stands still a great deal.

I have been down at Exeter to inspect the Training School there, and stayed with Lawley at Exminster, where the Exe becomes a tidal river. There are some salmon, but nothing else. The county is pleasant, but not, to me, so pleasant as Surrey. The rains have been very good for the garden, and the new treatment which I have been trying for the fruit trees seems really most successful. I think we are going to have a really great crop of pears and plums; you know, we have not had any to speak of hitherto. It is a great amusement to watch the trees and see the blossom setting. The treatment consists in administering guano while they are flowering; this enables them to resist cold, and gives them strength to set their fruit. I send you rather a nice note I have just had from a young Catholic priest; you may burn it when you have read it. My love to dear Ella.   Your ever loving

Papa

Text. Russell, 2:324–25.

To Charles Myhill

Education Department, Whitehall

Cobham

Dear Mr Myhill   May 10, [?1885]

I have told Mr Helps, who is very hard pressed in July, that you will be able to help him in the first week of that month when I shall be at Peterborough to help Mr Sharpe. We will take our own 3 schools in the latter half of the month.   Truly yours

Matthew Arnold.—

MS. Pierpont Morgan Library.

To Henry Yates Thompson

Education Department, Whitehall

Cobham

My dear Thompson   May 15, [1885]

Before the impression passes, let me say that the leader in Wednesday's P. M. G. is a model of the tone in which your leaders should, in my judgment, be written; as favourable to Russia as you please (my opinions as to our Russian-war party are those of the late lamented Arminius), but not a trace of *influence*, of foreign suggestion, the point of view completely English; sober, also; the editor's name with a *y* added, as it is not added always.[1]

When I shall hear you on France I don't know. I write this at 7 A.M.; a school in Pimlico all the morning, a luncheon in Holland Park at 1½, a sitting to Weigall at 3; down here again to reports and letters at 5.20. Add to this a pain across my chest when I walk, which is probably the beginning of the end. Until I actually quit the world of Gen. Komaroff for that of Gen. Suwaroff,[2] my love to Dolly, and believe me,   Ever truly yours

Matthew Arnold.—

MS. Yale University.

1. "The Defence of the Empire," *Pall Mall Gazette*, May 13, 1885, p. 1. The second article was "A Dutch Editor on English Politics," pp. 1–2. The editor was Charles Boissevain, of the Amsterdam *Handelsblad*, who was highly critical in a way that would have delighted Arnold.

2. Two Russian conquerers with contrasting fates. General Komaroff "had been presented [on May 14] with a golden sword studded with diamonds" for "courage and valor" in the Afghan war (*Annual Register*, p. 261). Marshal Suwarrow, after the infamous victories at Ismail (as in Byron's poem *Don Juan*) and later in Poland and after the death of Catherine the Great, died in disgrace in St Petersburg in 1800.

To Lady Dorothy Nevill

Cobham, Surrey

Dear Lady Dorothy   May 16, [?1885]

Alas, on Wednesday I shall be airing my affectations for the benefit of the Principal of St Mark's Training College, Chelsea, where I have to be all next week.   Most truly yours

Matthew Arnold.—

MS. University of Virginia.

To Patrick Cumin

Mr Cumin.   May 20, 1885

Adverting to your request for Form 8 for quarter ending March 31/85, I find that Mr Sharpe, Mr Stewart, and Mr Fitch have not yet furnished me with their Forms 7. Shall I forward Form 8 without waiting for them?

M. A.—

MS. Public Record Office, London.

To J. B. Pond

London
Dear Major Pond   May 20, 1885

My daughter is coming over here this autumn, so I have given up the thought of re-visiting the States during the present year.

Remember me very kindly to your brother, and also to Mr Beecher when you see him.   Very truly yours

Matthew Arnold.—

MS. Fleming McClelland.

To Thomas Kelly Cheyne[1]

Athenæum, Pall Mall
Dear Mr Cheyne   May 21, 1885

It is a long time since I received your version of the Psalms; but I would not thank you for it until I had read it through, which I have now done. I knew I should be instructed by it, but I confess I did not expect to be so much *pleased* by it as I have been. The diction is almost always satisfactory, and the rhythm more satisfactory than I should have beforehand thought possible for a new version. Some of the alterations—e.g.—"so shall my heart rejoice to fear thy name"—"surely he giveth his beloved sleep"—are delightful.

I wish you had given us more notes, and more clues to your opinion as to the date of the different Psalms. Ewald decides much too confidently; but I should like to know whether you consider it impossible to assign any Psalms to David himself, and to distinguish between those of the Monarchy and those of later periods.

But I sincerely thank you for the help and pleasure you have given me. Most truly yours

Matthew Arnold.—

MS. Bodleian Library.

1. Thomas Kelly Cheyne (1841–1915: *DNB*), Old Testament scholar, formerly a fellow of Balliol, then (1885–1908) Oriel Professor of Scripture. He translated *The Book of Psalms* (1884). He had reviewed Arnold's *Bible Reading for Schools* and *Isaiah of Jerusalem* in the *Academy*, Feb. 19, 1876, and Dec. 22, 1883, and, now one of the "company engaged in preparing the Revised Version of the Old Testament," had "himself published two versions of Isaiah" (Super, 10:486).

To Frederic William Henry Myers

My dear Myers   May 21, 1885
    Would it suit you to give me a day or two in the first fortnight of June to help me in hearing the lessons, reading, and recitation, at the Westminster and Boro. Road Training Colleges?   Most truly yours
                                           Matthew Arnold.—

MS. Texas Tech University.

To Charles Myhill

                                            Cobham
Dear Mr Myhill   May 29, [1885]
    I shall hope to see you at the St Paul's Mission School on the 4th June, and at the Westminster Practising Schools on the 12th; the week following that you had better take for the Practising Schools; the rest of the month you will be free to help Mr Sharpe.
    I send the Forms you wanted, and Mr Sharpe's 7.   Truly yours
                                           Matthew Arnold.—

MS. University of Michigan.

To Lucy Charlotte Arnold Whitridge*

                                            Cobham
My darling   Whitmonday, [May 25, 1885]
    It is a long while since I wrote to you, but you will know how you have been in our minds and on our tongues. Your husband is an angel, but he must come over for the last month, or your visit will not be quite enjoyed by us with a good conscience. I send you a note I have had this morning from Coleridge, which will show you that he is doing honour to your recommendation and entertaining your friends. We will get them down here, too; but, of course, the Coleridge visit is the more important.
    Well, my darling, and now I look at things about the place I say, This must be put right before Lucy comes. It is a beautiful year, the first year that we have had the lilac and laburnum in glory. And such crops of pears! The strawberries are good too, and you will be just in time for them, I hope. We are off this afternoon, mamma and I, for Chenies, where Dick and Ella are to meet us. . . . Mamma will drive Ella over to show her Harrow, and Dick and I shall fish. Lord Tavistock has hitherto given no leave at all this May, so I expect the fishing will be good.[1] The weather is showery, as is right, but I

wish it were warmer. . . . I have got to like Mrs Charles Lawrence very much.[2] I dined there on Friday, and took Lady Hayter in to dinner—beautifully dressed as usual. We dine on the 3rd of June with the Archbishop of Canterbury, which I always think a gratifying marvel, considering what things I have published. I cannot get rid of the ache across my chest when I walk; imagine my having to stop half a dozen times in going up to Pains Hill! What a mortifying change. But so one draws to one's end. My love to your husband, and tell him he is to mind and comply with the injunctions in my letter.— Your own loving and expecting

Papa

Text. Russell, 2 : 325–26.

1. At Chenies, as in the past: George William Francis Sackville Russell (1852–1895), marquis of Tavistock (succ. as tenth duke of Bedford 1895).

2. Catherine Lawrence (*née* Wiggin), wife of Charles Napier Lawrence (1855–1927, cr. Baron Lawrence of Kingsgate 1923), apparently of Arnold's old neighborhood, Chester Square, third son of first Baron Lawrence.

To Frederic William Henry Myers

Athenæum Club

My dear Myers   June 1, 1885

If you can give me the 8th and the forenoon of the 9th at the Boro. Road, it will be a great help. I wrote to you last week, but I now answer your post card which I find at the Athenæum.

On the 16th and 17th I am at Winchester—a light Training College. Ever truly yours

Matthew Arnold.—

MS. Trinity College, Cambridge.

To Bertram Wodehouse Currie

Pains Hill Cottage, Cobham, Surrey

June 2, 1885

We speak and think so much of you and Mrs Currie that I must write you one word of sympathy. We all liked your poor boy—he had so much individuality which pleased—and we have followed the accounts of his illness with a mournful foreboding. He must have been a terrible anxiety, but I did not altogether pity you for having an object of incessant anxiety and devotion. One rebels against the traditionary devotions imposed upon us and one throws them off, and then one discovers that a devotion of some kind is necessary.

All of us here think of you in your loss with affectionate sympathy;[1] of you yourself and of dear Mrs Currie, who will let me come and see her some day later on: meanwhile, believe me, my dear Currie, Faithfully and cordially yours,

Matthew Arnold

Text. Caroline Louisa Currie, ed., Bertram Wodehouse Currie, 1827–1896 *(1901), 2:167–68.*

1. Isaac Edward Currie, the older son, born 1861, died May 31.

To Frederic William Henry Myers

Athenæum Club, Pall Mall, S. W.

My dear Myers   June 3, 1885

Come to Battersea on the 25th and 26th at any rate—and to Boro. Road on Monday & Tuesday next if you can do it without inconvenience; but, if you do not turn up, I shall sigh and conclude this was inevitable.

Can you come to Peterborough for the 1st and 2nd July?   Ever yours truly

M. A.—

write to Cobham, Surrey.

MS. Trinity College, Cambridge.

To Lucy Charlotte Arnold Whitridge

Athenæum Club, Pall Mall

My darling child   June 4, 1885

I did not write on Sunday, and now I am writing for Mamma. she is in London with me; we dined at the Abp of Canterbury's last night and slept at the Bensons'; Mamma sate at dinner between Lord Devon and Lord Norton, and looked very sweet.[1] She was able to speak to Lord Devon about Mademoiselle, who is teaching a little Miss Adderley, a grandchild of his. The weather is glorious, such as one so seldom gets here; perfectly fine and warm, but nothing oppressive; if it would but last to bring you over, and to befriend you while you are here! I sate at dinner at Lambeth last night by Mrs Rate; they are all going away to German baths, and talk of offering us their house in Audley Street for a week; I don't know whether we shall accept. Nelly was at the Combes' ball the night before last and danced everything: three times with Charlie Combe; the Ladies Nevill were there, Lord Abergavenny's daughters,[2] who are the pretty débutantes of the season, and all sorts of smart people: the Combes have made a great success with their ball. But Nelly hesitated about going, and will not go to Mrs Reis's, to which the Sandfords want to take her; tonight we have Mildred Whitmore & Henry to dinner,[3] and that is what she likes. The Cottage is a dream of beauty, it is such a lovely year for bloom and foliage. I am rewarded now for having put in so many laburnums and thorns; you never saw such a sight of bloom. Then the Wistaria covers half the house with its sweet bunches of blossom; and tonight, when we go back, we shall find the irises out, and the great scarlet poppies. I think I told you that the peonies are this year to be counted, not by ones and twos as usual, but by scores. The pleasure of the dear Dicks in their week with us you may imagine: Chenies was a great success (I caught a trout of over 3 lb.) and as for the Cottage, Dick is never tired of it. I have been able, too, thanks to Macmillan having paid me more than I expected for the new edition of my poems, to relieve them of some of their bills; Ella has managed so well for him, that I was particularly glad to be able to give this help: and this summer they will really be out of debt. Did Nelly tell you that John Collier wants to paint me for next year's exhibition, and says he will afterwards give me the picture. I am now bent, if my books go well, on getting Mamma done by Richmond; and then we shall be able to depart in peace, leaving likenesses of ourselves behind to our family. This, however, about Mamma is a secret as it depends on my sales, and besides it is hard to get Richmond to paint any one now. The dear Bensons are pleasant as usual; I think Madge will come down with us today. Lord Coleridge comes on Saturday; the appeal in Bemand's case is decided today.[4] Lord Coleridge has been very civil to the Carys,[5] and liked them. Mr Cary wrote to propose seeing me at the Club, as he is tied in London at present, and I asked him to call here at 3 o'clock the day before yesterday; he did not turn up and there is probably some stupid mistake, but we shall have them down to dine and sleep at Cobham very soon. Your Uncle Walter has got back to Greenhithe, but he mends very slowly. Your Aunt Forster is at Bath trying the waters there for her rheumatism; Francie is with her, Flo is with your Uncle Forster in London. We hope in your next to hear that Fred has made up his mind to follow you in August. My love to him.   Ever, my darling, your loving

Papa—

MS. Frederick Whitridge.

1. Henry Hugh Courtenay (1811–1904), thirteenth earl of Devon, rector of Powderham, prebendary of Exeter; Charles Bowyer Adderley (1814–1905; cr. Baron Norton 1878), whom Arnold had satirized, a little unfairly, nearly twenty years earlier (the grandchild cannot be identified among too many possibilities).

2. Of the five daughters of the marquis of Abergavenny the three unmarried at this date qualify, but Arnold must refer to the twins, Rose and Violet Nevill, age 19.

3. Mildred Whitmore (d. 1925) and her brother Henry Eardley (1855–1909), children of George Whitmore, rector of Stockton Shifnal, Salop, friends and neighbors of the Henry Bunsens (*Landed*). Mrs Reis has not been identified.

4. See above, letter to Mountstuart Elphinstone Grant Duff of Mar. 4, 1885, n. 4.

5. Cary was Frederick Whitridge's law partner, in the firm Cary and Whitridge.

To C. H. B. Elliott

Education Department, Whitehall

Cobham, Surrey

Dear Mr Elliott   June 5, 1885

You have more constant opportunity of observing Miss Gabbitas than I have, but I should doubt (though I like her) whether she is *mature* enough in knowledge, intelligence, and weight of character, to put at the head of your Girls' School at present.   Most truly yours,

Matthew Arnold.—

MS. Wordsworth Trust.

1. C. H. B. Elliott, later an Inspector of Schools.

To Gertrude Frances Talbot Herbert Countess of Pembroke [1]

Athenæum Club, Pall Mall

My dear Lady Pembroke   June 12, [1885]

I wish I could have come—it is always a pleasure to meet Lady Wemyss (with the Flowers I dine on the 17th)—but on the 16th I have to stay all night at Winchester, where I shall be inspecting a Training College.   Most truly yours,

Matthew Arnold.—

P. S. I shall really come to luncheon some day, as you said I might.

MS. University of Virginia.

1. Gertrude Frances Lady Pembroke (d. 1906), daughter of the eighteenth earl of Shrewsbury and wife of the thirteenth earl of Pembroke, of Carlton House Terrace.

To Gordon Graham Wordsworth

Athenæum Club, Pall Mall

My dear Gordon   June 12, 1885

Many thanks to you and Mr Rawnsley for your very kind invitation, but I shall be but one night at Winchester, and so pressed with reporting that

I had better be at the inn. I fear I am expected to lunch at the Training School, but pray look in there and see me for a moment if you can.　　Most truly yours,

Matthew Arnold.—

MS. Wordsworth Trust.

To Goldwin Smith

Athenæum Club, Pall Mall, S. W.

My dear Goldwin Smith　　　　　　　　　　　　　　　　June 19, 1885

I did not write to you at once with my daughter Lucy's address, because her movements were uncertain; now, however, it is settled that she comes to Europe and that we do not go this year to America; I am very well pleased that it is settled so because I am rather tired by my final year of school inspection, and do not wish to have the American fatigue to face again so soon. I think, too, it will be better to let another year elapse before I again try the patience of American audiences. In the autumn of next year, if all goes well, I shall probably come over for a second and last visit. Meanwhile Lucy will be back in New York, at *12, West Tenth Street*, by the beginning of October; and will be delighted and honoured by seeing you and Mrs Goldwin Smith, whenever you are in New York this year after that date.

Today they talk of a hitch in the Ministerial arrangements, but I think Lord Salisbury will come in.[1] I confess to a great feeling of relief in Foreign affairs being taken out of Lord Granville's hands, Colonial Affairs out of Lord Derby's and the supreme direction in both out of Gladstone's. Certainly success has not been attained by the outgoing Government's management in these departments; every one must allow that; and for my part I think Lord Granville worn out, and at the same time his flux of dispatches grows almost as inveterate as Gladstone's flux of speeches. I have, however, no confidence at all in the Tories, though the change may perhaps put an end to some of the fumbling and blundering in our foreign policy. I send you the Lectures, at two of which you so kindly assisted; I wish I could talk to you about Drummond's book which has the utmost success with the religious world over here—they think it at last clears all difficulties, and sets orthodoxy on a firm scientific foundation.[2]

With kindest regards to your wife, I am always　　most sincerely yours,

Matthew Arnold.—

P. S. Lucy's married name is *Whitridge*.

MS. Cornell University.

1. Salisbury's government came in this month.

2. Henry Drummond's *Natural Law in the Spiritual World* (1883), which had stirred up considerable discussion, is mentioned several times later.

To Mr. Holmes

Education Department, Whitehall

Cobham

My dear Holmes   June 20, [?1884]

You are quite welcome to print the "Forsaken Merman." As to the March of Hannibal, I have had great difficulty in finding the right quarter where to direct you. The copyright in that passage has not yet expired, and it had been bought by a firm which no longer exists. I am told that it is now represented by Bickers and Bush, to whom, therefore, you should apply for leave to reprint.

Thank you for your congratulations on Dick's appointment. We are indeed glad to have him back.   Ever truly yours

Matthew Arnold.—

MS. Roger Brooks.

To Charles Myhill

Education Department, Whitehall

Cobham

Dear Mr Myhill   June 20, [1885]

I must be at St Mark's Training School on Friday the 26th, so have changed the Westminster Boys' School to Monday the 29th. It is not absolutely necessary you should meet me there on that day, but come if you can.

I think I have sent notice to the St George's and St Mark's Schools, but I wish you would ascertain.   Truly yours

M. A.

MS. Typescript, University of Virginia (MS. McGill University).

To Andrew Carnegie

Pains Hill Cottage, Cobham, Surrey

My dear Carnegie   June 21, 1885

It is a real disappointment to us not to see you this year, either on our side of the water or yours; and I conclude you are not coming, or you would have mentioned it in your letter. Your kind project of taking us south sounds very tempting indeed. But the Education Department asked me to stay till Lady Day in next year before resigning my office, that I might go round the Training Schools and report on the literary instruction in them; I could not well refuse, and at the same time Lucy decided to come over here for the summer, so the necessity of paying a visit to her in New York disappeared. I think, too, it is as well to let another year elapse before I try the patience of American audiences again. Add to this that I have been having a horrid pain in my chest when I walk fast or go up hill; and as my family is full of heart complaint, my father and grandfather having both of them died of it long before reaching my age, the doctors insist on my taking care of myself; and to go a lecturing tour in the States is not the way quite to take care of oneself. But for the last fortnight I have been better, and I hope that the disablement will pass off entirely and that I shall be able to come out next year sound and well[.] I am glad you liked my comment on Christmas; it gave much offence here, but the set of opinion is slowly tending towards the views set forth in the Comment. Meanwhile a book like Drummond's, with a good deal of haze, is what the public like. Lucy speaks with much pleasure of seeing your mother; all of us send love to her and to you, and I am always, affectionately yours,

Matthew Arnold.—

I send the lines for which you make so flattering a request.

MS. New York Public Library.

To Robert Kirkman Hodgson [1]

Athenæum Club, Pall Mall, S. W.

My dear Hodgson June 26, [1885]
I shall like very much to come down to Gavel Acre next month: I only hope we may have less splendid weather there than last year. Either Friday & Saturday the 17 and 18th July, or Friday and Saturday the 24th and 25, would suit me.   Sincerely yours

Matthew Arnold.—

MS. Bryn Mawr College.

1. Robert Kirkman Hodgson (1850–1924: *Landed*), of Eton and Trinity College, Cambridge, of Eaton Place and Gavelacre, Longparish, Hants.

To Archibald Philip Primrose Earl of Rosebery

Pains Hill Cottage, Cobham, Surrey

My dear Lord Rosebery   June 26, [?1885]

As we had been in America at nearly the same time, and had both of us clasped in friendship the hand of Carnegie the Destroyer, I thought I should like you to see what I had really said to the Americans.[1] I will with pleasure write in the book some day.   Most truly yours

Matthew Arnold.—

MS. National Library of Scotland.

1. *Discourses in America.*

To John Everett Millais

Athenæum

My dear Millais   June 29, [1885]

Nothing could make you more the head of your profession and more admired by the public than you are; but I am very glad that you should shed lustre on the Baronetage—the more so as I remember a conversation at Birnam in which you maintained with a great deal of force that these marks of recognition to artists had their real value and utility. I am glad that the recognition should have been given; and glad too of the opportunity of saying with what cordial admiration, liking, and regard, I am   sincerely yours,

Matthew Arnold.—

I hope and trust you are all right again;—I wonder if Mrs Millais (to whom give my best congratulations) would let me come to luncheon some day in July.

MS. New York Public Library.

To George Frederic Watts

My dear Watts   June 29, [?1885]

To be associated with your noble and high[-]toned art will give a new dignity to the name of Baronet[1]—this is the form which I find my congratulation to you irresistibly takes. But I am sincerely glad that the public should honour itself by offering recognition to what it is so very good for it to be able to recognise—an artist of your worth.

When I get free from my official bonds I shall come and see you—but meanwhile and always you have the kindest thoughts and the most cordial esteem from   yours sincerely

Matthew Arnold.—

MS. Tate Gallery Archives (microfilm).

1. "In 1885 he was offered a baronetcy by Gladstone but declined it" (*DNB*).

To John James Stewart Perowne[1]

The Very Rev. The Dean of Peterborough   St Peters College
Dear Mr Dean   Wednesday, [?July 1, 1885]
    I am here for only one night and have taken my room at the inn, so I will not accept your very kind offer of hospitality; I have a co-inspector with me, too, whom I must not desert. But I hope to come to the Cathedral service at 5.30, and to see you afterwards. I heard you had been ill, and called to enquire how you now are; we never see you at the Athenæum.   Most faithfully yours

Matthew Arnold.—

MS. University of Kansas.

1. John James Stewart Perowne (1823–1904: *DNB*), a biblical scholar, was dean of Peterborough 1878–91, then bishop of Winchester 1891–1901.

To John James Stewart Perowne

My dear Mr Dean   Thursday morning, [?July 2, 1885]
    I find luncheon will be impossible for me: we must take the 1.40 train. I am the more glad of the delightful and instructive stroll I had with you yesterday. What a dream of beauty the place is looking, this morning! Most truly yours,

Matthew Arnold.—

MS. University of Kansas.

To Dudley Wilmot Buxton[1]

Athenæum Club, Pall Mall, S. W.
Dr D. Buxton
Dear Sir   July 13, 1885
    Your invitation did not reach me until after your interesting meeting; I found it on my return home to the country on Friday night.   Your faithful servant,

Matthew Arnold.—

MS. Harvard University.

1. Dudley Wilmot Buxton, M.D., B.S., 82, Mortimer Street, Cavendish Square, W. (*POLD*, 1901).

To Mr Bailey

                                                        Cobham, Surrey
Dear Mr Bailey   July 18, 1885
    It is absurd that in the model sums for my division I should have none from such a mathematician as you; I left you in peace, because you made me understand that you were so very busy. But in looking at what Sharpe has furnished, I feel that it would be an advantage to have a contribution from you also; do you think that by this day week you could let me have 15 cards, ten for Stand. vi and five for Stand vii (Boys in each case)? Send me a line here to say, and pray say "yes" if possible.   Very truly yours
                                                        Matthew Arnold.—

MS. British Library.

To Ernest Fontanès *

                                            Pains Hill Cottage, Cobham, Surrey
My dear M. Fontanès   July 18, 1885
    I have been sending you my *Discourses in America*, and that brings to my mind that I ought to have written to you long since. But I am finishing my business in the Education Department, previous to resigning my office there, and I have been more than usually busy in consequence. But directly I saw the *Life of Gordon* I said to myself that here was the book for you.[1] It is badly edited, but it is full of interesting things, and it has for its subject a man who has struck the imagination of all people. In a superior redaction, and with much omitted, a fascinating book might be made out of the bulky and inconvenient publication which people here are reading, certainly, but are grumbling at while they read it, and asking themselves how it can be that a book about Gordon does not interest them more.
    Have you seen a book by a certain Professor Henry Drummond, called *Natural Law in the Spiritual World*, which has had an astonishing success over here? The best public, perhaps, does not much care for it; but the second best, all the religious world, and even the more serious portion of the aristocratical world, have accepted the book as a godsend, and are saying to themselves that here at last is safety and scientific shelter for the orthodox supernaturalism which seemed menaced with total defeat. I should like much

to know what you think of the book, though I can hardly imagine its suiting any public but that very peculiar and indirect-thinking public which we have in England. What is certain is, that the author of the book has a genuine love of religion and a genuine religious experience; and this gives his book a certain value, though his readers, in general, imagine its value to be quite of another kind. He is a Scotch Presbyterian, quite unknown until the other day, with pleasing manners, and great success in addressing audiences of working men on the subject of religion.

My American daughter is with us, and she, as well as her mother and sister, send you her affectionate remembrances.—I am always   most truly and cordially yours,

Matthew Arnold

Text. Russell, 2:327–28.

1. *The Journals of Major-General C. G. Gordon, C. B. at Khartoum,* ed. A. Egmont Hake (1885), called in the *Annual Register* "the most memorable and saddest book of the year."

To William Gordon McCabe

Athenæum Club, Pall Mall, S. W.

Dear Mr McCabe   Thursday, [*c.* July 20, 1885]

I hoped to find you here today. I shall be here tomorrow at 3; we are out of town, alas, but I should like to arrange for seeing you.   Most truly yours

Matthew Arnold.—

MS. University of Virginia.

To William Gordon McCabe

Athenæum Club, Pall Mall, S. W.

Dear Mr McCabe   July 20, [1885]

I am very glad you can come. Take your ticket at Waterloo on Thursday by 5.20 train to Cobham; at Cobham Station you will find an omnibus which will bring you close to my door. I will have the omnibus met. Most sincerely yours,

Matthew Arnold.—

MS. University of Virginia.

To John Slagg[1]

Athenæum Club, Pall Mall

John Slagg Esq. M. P.

My dear Sir   July 20, 1885

I have to thank you for your kind and flattering invitation; but on the 29th of October, when the Manchester Athenæum celebrates its Jubilee, I shall be quite out of reach of Manchester.   Most faithfully yours

Matthew Arnold.

MS. University of Texas at Austin.

1. Slagg had been the Liberal Member for Manchester since Apr. 1880, was defeated in Nov. 1885 and, as a Gladstonian Liberal, in July 1886 (McCalmont).

To The Secretary, Education Department

Education Department, Whitehall

The Secretary etc. etc. etc.

Inspection.

Sir   July 27, 1885

I have the honour to inform you that I propose commencing my holiday on Wednesday the 29th inst., when my district will be quite clear. I am, Sir,   Your obed[ien]t serv[an]t

Matthew Arnold.—

MS. Public Record Office, London.

To Mountstuart Elphinstone Grant Duff

Pains Hill Cottage, Cobham, Surrey

My dear Grant Duff   August 7, 1885

I have never yet thanked you for your "Comments."[1] Very many of them I remembered; but I am glad to possess them in this handsome Volume. You have a right to feel well satisfied that your remarks on Russia bear re-reading so well at this moment. I have been reading them with very keen interest.

The season has been dry even for Surrey, but I have saved my cypresses by watering them every day with my own hands—and they have now got hold of the ground and are doing well. Cubitt, our member, is a botanist; did you know this? He manages to make his Game-keepers look after plants, and he sent me the other day the Musk Orchis, which one of his keepers has found growing pretty abundantly in one place, and which I had never seen before. He sent me also the Monstrossa Hypossitys, but this I had found myself in the Norbury woods.

I have sent you my American Discourses, and also the Poems to which you have always been so good a friend. I had not read Merope since the year it was published. There is not a stroke of either archæology or botany in it for which I had not authority from reporters such as Pausanias, Leake, Walpole, Sibthorpe; this gives me a tenderness for the production, though the world has never cared for it.[2]

Poor Mark Pattison and poor Mrs Pattison![3] I think John Morley was hard upon him. I did not know him well enough for him to talk freely about *himself* to me; and I was a great gainer thereby, for I hear his talk about himself in conversation did not make one respect him any more than his talk about himself in his Memoirs does. But on the platform on which we met, he was one of the best and raciest companions I have ever known. The report of Dilke's disasters wd have travelled "super Garamantas et Indos."[4] What a shocking training for a man is the English Cockney School (Leigh Hunt & Co.) in one's youth and in adult life a top dressing of French novels and French *moeurs*. I wonder what result it will all take as regards the poor invalid who is staying with you.

I am not going to America this year; Lucy has come over to us. Next year I resign my inspectorship and pay my second and last visit to America; then, if the blind Fury permits me, I will see Italy again and get done one or two long projected things in verse. My affectionate regards to your wife and Clara.—I am always, my dear Grant Duff   most truly & cordially yours
Matthew Arnold.—

Coleridge's intended marriage is a misfortune, but to be made the best of. Unluckily his family seem disposed to make not the best but the worst of it.

MS. British Library Oriental and India House Collections.

1. *Brief Comments on Passing Events, Made between February 4th, 1858, and October 5th, 1881* (pr. pr. Madras, 1884).

2. John Sibthorp, *Flora Græca* (10 vols, 1806–40); Rev. Robert Walpole, *Memoirs Relating to European and Asiatic Turkey* (2 vols, 1817) or *Travels in Various Countries in the East* (1820). Possibly, *The Ansayri or Assassins, with Travels in the Further East in 1850–51, Including a Visit to Nineveh* (3 vols, 1851).

3. These discreet remarks were occasioned by the *Memoirs* of Mark Pattison (d. July 30, 1884), published by his widow, the former Emilia Frances Strong (1840–1904), who on Oct. 3 married Sir Charles Dilke, himself well and truly scarred by a recent divorce exceeded in prurient details only by one involving the Prince of Wales a few years later. ("Dilke, a widower, was named co-respondent in a suit for alleged adultery with his

sister-in-law's sister, whose mother had certainly been his mistress earlier on, and on and off, even before the death of his first wife" [*Album*, p. 97]).

4. "Past Garamant and Indian" (*Aeneid*, 6.794, tr. Fairclough).

To John Earley Cook[1]

[?early August, 1885]

The 7th will do very well, but you do not say your time. I shall conclude it is ½ past 7 unless I hear to the contrary. Excuse this official paper—I write in the midst of school reports.   Ever truly your's

Matthew Arnold.—

MS. University of Texas at Austin (fragment).

1. Guthrie, Aug. 7, 1885: "dine Early Cook." John Earley Cook (b. 1823), a Cobham neighbor whom Arnold perhaps had known at Brasenose in the forties, was a barrister and a governor of Christ's Hospital. His wife, who accompanied them in Oct. to Guildford, was the former Mary Jane Burmester (Kelly).

To Edmund William Gosse

Athenæum Club, Pall Mall, S. W.

My dear Gosse   August 14, 1885

My connexion with the Pall Mall Gazette has for some years past been limited to some very occasional letters about plays and players. I am not likely to write anything for it at present, and I quite agree with you that the harm it has done and is doing exceeds immeasurably what good it may have effected. Stead is a fanatic, and *Das Schreckliche* which may break forth from fanaticism was never more exemplified.[1]

But my relations with George Smith (Yates Thompson's father in law) and his family are such that I could not possibly come forward as a volunteer against the paper; although, had I been in the official position to do so, I would most certainly have seized all the offending numbers under Lord Campbell's Act, without the smallest hesitation, duty constraining me.

I doubt any good being effected by volunteer protesters. Officialdom is ignobly weak both against vice itself and against these corrupting exposures of vice; but even Cross must move at last, one would think, if Stead goes on till Christmas in his present vein.

I am not sure that the circulation of the paper will not be greatly reduced in the end. The meetingers who applaud it will not subscribe to it. Ever truly yours

Matthew Arnold.—

I have to thank you for a too kind but most gratifying letter about my Poems.

MS. British Library.

1. "The Maiden Tribute of Modern Babylon," a series of articles by Stead in the *Pall Mall Gazette*, July 6–10, bolstering the Criminal Law Amendment Bill designed to combat juvenile prostitution and the White Slave Trade. The story is set forth in detail in Frederic Whyte's *Life of W. T. Stead* and briefly in *New Writings by Swinburne*, which includes a poem on the subject, "The Marquis of Stead."

To George Frederic Watts

Fox How, Ambleside

My dear Watts   August 18, 1885

I should not like you to think that I easily forbore from coming to see you before I left home. But the truth is that in these last months of my school-inspectorship I am very busy; and the days on which I had counted for enabling me to pay a visit to Little Holland House were taken up in attending my daughter to Southampton to meet her husband from America.

I am really to be free from school-inspecting after next Easter; then I have to pay another visit to America before I can regard myself as free absolutely: but before I leave England I shall console and fortify myself by coming to shake by the hand the highest and singlest-minded artist of my acquaintance.   Most truly yours

Matthew Arnold.—

MS. Tate Gallery Archives (microfilm).

To John H. Lloyd[1]

John H. Lloyd Esq.   Fox How, Ambleside

Dear Sir   August 23, 1885

My engagements are such that it is impossible for me to accept your flattering invitation to deliver the address at the commencement of the coming season of your Institution.   Your faithful servant

Matthew Arnold.—

P. S. The enclosed envelope will show you by what a stupid mistake at the Post Office this has been delayed. *M. A.* Aug. 30th

MS. Highgate Literary and Scientific Institution.

1. Unidentified.

To Frances Lucy Wightman Arnold *

Duffryn, Mountain Ash, South Wales
August 25, 1885

This must be short because we have been all the morning at the Eisteddfod, and now the girls want me to play lawn tennis before tea, as I am to go out with Lord Aberdare afterwards. I had a very good journey—swarms of people, particularly babies, but all third-class. I had a carriage to myself all the way, except from Carnforth to Preston, and my luggage, portmanteau and all, in with me, the guard saying there was no chance of my being disturbed. I had to change at Crewe and Shrewsbury. There is nothing on the journey more beautiful than the passage at Church Stretton between Caer Caradoc and the Long Mynd, which you have seen; but it is a pleasing country all the way, and the Welsh valleys and rivers, with the high viaducts spanning them, very interesting. There were traces of rain from Abergavenny onwards; they had a little rain yesterday morning, and much the day before; today it is beautiful. This valley is beautiful, and the house and grounds so placed that the mines and houses of miners do it no harm; but the population swarms, it is really one street from here to Aberdare, four miles. . . . Lord Aberdare is a dear, and so is a little French dog, Patou, with whom I have made great friends. This morning we all drove into the Eisteddfod, and heard Sir G. Elliot's address;[1] it was all rather dull, but I got off speaking by saying I would only speak once, and *that* they wished should be on Thursday, the chief day. They want me to stay till Monday, but I shall not. My love to Fan and all, and kisses to the sweet girls. Tell Nelly I am still shocked when I think of the farewell her laziness obliged me to take of her.

Text. Russell, 2:328–29.

1. Sir George Elliot (1814–1893), first bt, had been Conservative M.P. for Durham, his native heath, and would be for Monmouth.

To Frances Lucy Wightman Arnold *

Duffryn, Mountain Ash, South Wales
August 26, 1885

I am ashamed to think of the poor scrap I sent you yesterday, when I look at the charming long letter I have from you today. Lord Aberdare says he cannot quite forgive me for not bringing with me a wife and daughter—*a wife at the very least*, and I am sure this is a place and family you would like. As for Patou, he is angelic; but he must be reserved for our meeting.[1] It is hard to find time to write, one's day is so laid out; and perhaps one of the healthiest things in visiting is that one's day is thus laid out and one has no time for doing more than what one's hosts mean one to do. After I wrote to you yesterday, I had some very good lawn tennis with three of the girls, and then after tea a beautiful walk with Lord Aberdare and another of the girls along the side of the beautiful mountain opposite. Then Miss Napier and two of the girls went to the Eisteddfod concert, and we dined without them. I send Fan the ivy-leaved campanula, which grows in quantities on the mountain where we talked yesterday. All the country has a softness and for-eignness which are not English, and the plants would be very interesting if one had but more time to look for them. On the whole, I did more yester-day, and did it easier, than I have done since I was first visited by this pain. I was a little tired, but the cool champagne at dinner brought me quite round. We have been again at the Eisteddfod this morning; I had to make a little speech to second the vote of thanks to the president, because, it appeared, he wished it. The people here receive me so well that it wonderfully takes off from the difficulty of speaking. The audience is certainly a wonderful sight, and, I shall always think, does credit to the country which can produce it. It was much fuller today than yesterday, and will be much fuller tomorrow than today, because the shops in Aberdare are to be closed early. Lord Aberdare wants me to stay till Monday, in order to go to Llanthony Abbey on Saturday. If he could have gone there on Friday, I think I should have stayed till Sat-urday; but he has to attend the Friday sitting of the Eisteddfod, so I shall come home on Friday, as at first intended.

Text. Russell, 2:329–31.

1. For Patou see the preceding letter. Several possibilities make identification of Miss Napier, below, uncertain. Lady Aberdare was the daughter of Gen. William Napier, and the allusion here and in the next letter suggests one of her two unmarried sisters, Emily Anne (d. 1886) and Caroline Jane (d. 1896).

To Henry Austin Bruce Lord Aberdare

Fox How, Amberside
My dear Lord Aberdare   August 29, [1885]

I have been reading you in the Welsh paper with so much pleasure (and gratitude), that I write to beg you, if your address comes to be printed in a more permanent form, to have the great kindness to send it to me.

What a sight it was! I see one of the papers calculates there were ten thousand people present.

I had a delightful three days, and if we could have finished by doing Llanthony, that would have been perfect. But Llanthony is reserved, I hope, for another year.

My kindest remembrances to Lady Aberdare, Miss Napier, and all your charming circle; and tell Patou my heart goes out to him.

I am always, dear Lord Aberdare,   most sincerely yours,

Matthew Arnold.—

P. S. You can make the journey to Barbon in one day, but you will have to travel, as I did yesterday, very late.

MS. Glamorgan Record Office.

To Archibald Philip Primrose Earl of Rosebery

Fox How, Ambleside
My dear Lord Rosebery   August 31, 1885

I am here this week, next week I am in Scotland, and then I have to go south to see my daughter off for America. Probably you will be gone to Scotland by that time; but if you are at Mentmore again, or at the Durdans, between Michaelmas and Christmas, I should much like to come to you from a Saturday to Monday.   Most truly yours

Matthew Arnold.—

MS. National Library of Scotland.

To Katharine Sarah MacQuoid[1]

Mrs Macquoid   Fox How, Ambleside
Dear Madam   September 4, 1885

Your letter has just reached me here, and no doubt I shall find the book when I return home. The paper you mention was not by me, but I have no doubt that I shall read your new book with the same pleasure with which I have already often read you. Accept my best thanks, and believe me, very truly yours,

Matthew Arnold.—

MS. Princeton University.

1. Katharine Sarah Macquoid (d. 1917: *WWW*), author of novels, stories in magazines and newspapers, and travel books, many of which were illustrated by her husband, Thomas Robert Macquoid (1820–1912: *WWW*), a watercolorist and "draughtsman in black and white." The envelope is addressed to Stanley Place, Chelsea.

To F. H. Hawkins [1]

Education Department, Whitehall

F. H. Hawkins   Fox How, Ambleside

Dear Sir   September 5, 1885

I am refusing all invitations to lecture this coming season, and indeed till I return from my next and last visit to America.

Pray remember me most kindly to Dr Allon when you see him, and believe me,   Truly yours

Matthew Arnold.—

MS. Texas A&M University.

1. Unidentified.

To Charles Myhill

Education Department, Whitehall

Fox How

Dear Mr Myhill   September 5, [1885]

I am just off for Scotland. Report yourself to the Office as being free for work if wanted. I will write about Dalhousie.[1]

Let me have the names of those whose Forms 7 are still wanting. Truly yours

M. A.

I hope you have had a pleasant time.

MS. University of Virginia.

1. Unidentified.

To Sarah Knowles Bolton

Pains Hill Cottage, Cobham, Surrey.

Dear Mrs Bolton   September 18, 1885

I have your kind note here, and yesterday I found your handsome book[1] among a quantity of things which during the holidays have accumulated for me at the Club in London. I shall be interested in reading it, the American lives particularly; mean while I will have the pleasure of sending you, when I go to London, the Discourses of which two had the benefit of your friendly and zealous help at Cleveland.   Most truly yours

Matthew Arnold.—

MS. American Antiquarian Society.

1. *Lives of Poor Boys Who Became Famous* (1885).

To Frederic William Henry Myers

Education Department, Whitehall

Cobham

My Dear Myers   September 24, [1885]
One line by this post to say you can have Myhill till Oct. 20th. Write to him and say you are authorised by Sykes to employ him in your district. I will write to him also. I am very glad to be able to accommodate you. Ever truly yours

Matthew Arnold.—

MS. Trinity College, Cambridge.

To Charles Myhill

Education Department, Whitehall

Dear Mr Myhill   September 25, 1885
The Office have asked me to let you go for as long as I can spare you to the help of Mr Myers, who is without an assistant. I have said that I shall not want you before the 20th of Octr. Mr Myers will write to you and make arrangements. You will find him a very pleasing-mannered man.

I send you the Fitch & Alderson Forms 7.

I also send the list of schools for Westminster, as it may be convenient to you to have it for sending the notices. Write in each case to "*the Correspondent,*" at the school itself—and send all notices through the Office.

I shall fix Oct. 21st for Warwick St. Wes. We have only that & Crown Court for Octr.   Ever truly yours

Matthew Arnold.—

MS. University of Virginia.

To George Washburn Smalley

Pains Hill Cottage, Cobham, Surrey

My dear Smalley   September 26, [1885]
A letter from Philadelphia mentions, as being much read, some kind comments of yours on my Discourses in America. If you would send me the Tribune containing them, it would be very kind of you.[1] I would ask for merely the reference to the date of the paper, but the Athenæum, where we take it, is closed for the present.

I owe you much for kindness in connexion with my American visit and utterances. This time next year, if I live, I shall be starting on a second and last visit there. Before I go, I must have a talk with you on the kinds of subject most suitable for me to take in these last words.

Kindest regards to Mrs Smalley, and believe me,   ever truly yours
Matthew Arnold.—

MS. Yale University.

1. "Mr. Matthew Arnold, His Discourses in America, and the New Edition of His Poems," *New York Daily Tribune*, Sep. 9, 1885, p. 6 (Leichman). The letter was from Florence Earle Coates (Mrs Edward Hornor).

To Lucy Charlotte Arnold Whitridge

United Service Club, Pall Mall, S. W.

My darling child   September 28, 1885

This is your Grandpapa Wightman's birthday—he would have been 101 today! The day is beautiful and we have had nothing yet in the way of weather which makes us uneasy for you; every morning when we wake I say to Mamma—I wonder what sort of a night Lucy has had. We count the days; Mamma thinks you will not be in till Saturday; I hope for Thursday night, or at latest Friday. We shall get a telegram, I feel sure; but how we shall long for letters, and to hear how you have stood this passage, and whether the German line is a success! I have left dear Mamma quite alone but she does not mind that; perhaps she will meet me with two young gentlemen, Miss Lucy, at the Silvermere Gate this afternoon. On Saturday morning Nelly departed to Westgate, and in the afternoon Mamma and I drove to Mrs Cooper's gate with the two boys, sent the carriage home and took the beautiful path over the fields which leads out by the brick-kilns. We came home by Fairmile; it was a long walk, but the autumn afternoon was perfect and Mamma enjoyed it. The boys were in bliss. As we approached the Cottage we met Arthur Wood in a rather terrible check suit; he had a tooth brush with him—that was all his baggage; he had walked over from Walton. We kept him to dine and sleep; yesterday he went back at 6 in the evening, when I took Mamma to church as I did not wish her to have the walk home alone. It has turned cold, but the days are beautiful; I have driven this morning to Walton Station accompanied by dear Kai as of old; no drive could have been more beautiful. Early this morning Mamma and I were awakened by the crying of a dog; Mamma said it was outside the house, but I said I was sure it was Max overhead and that he had had a bad dream; and so it turned out to have been. I am going to the Forsters to luncheon and shall then get the latest accounts: on Saturday he was a little better again. Mrs Maskelyne writes that her daughter is still in bed, not making progress, very weak and very yellow. The accounts of poor Mr Hayes are bad, and of Ella not good, though she writes as cheerfully as she can. Tomorrow and Wednesday I stay with Mamma at Cobham; on Thursday she comes up with me to London and goes to the Forsters till Saturday while I go to Lord Rosebery's; on Saturday and Sunday we have the Teds: on Monday Bessy Whiteman comes; on Thursday we probably go to the Farrars at Abinger till Saturday. I am getting into work at my Ste Beuve,[1] and shall soon be feeling happy and interested; the beginning is what always worries and upsets me. I think with real pleasure of returning to America; the Coateses write me word from Germantown that a very nice letter about me by Smalley has just appeared in the Tribune; it speaks of the line taken in the Discourses and the good done. If you have a chance, you will see Mrs Coates and be amiable to her. But you are always amiable to those with whom you are brought in contact; try therefore and bring yourself in contact with her if she is in New York. My love to Fred— Always, my darling child,   your own dearly loving

Papa.

MS. National Archives of Canada.

1. For the *Encyclopædia Britannica*, ninth edn, 1886.

To John Aitchison

United Service Club, Pall Mall, S. W.

Dear Mr Aitchison   October 3, 1885
I want you to be kind enough to send my *Culture & Anarchy* and *Mixed Essays* to Professor Alfred Ipsen, Kolkbrenderivg, 22, Copenhagen. He is writing a series of articles on my books, and has not these two.

Will you also send to Rt Hon. W. E. Forster, 80, Eccleston Square, the popular editions of *Literature & Dogma* and of *God & the Bible*.

I have not yet had a proof of the corrected *Literature & Dogma*.   Very truly yours

Matthew Arnold.—

MS. University of Virginia.

To Lucy Charlotte Arnold Whitridge*

Cobham

My darling Lucy   Tuesday, October 6, 1885
Yesterday morning while I was dressing, mamma broke in with the telegram announcing your safe arrival at New York. We had very stormy

weather here on Friday and Saturday, and though of course we knew it might be different over there, still the howling wind could not but make us feel anxious. I was at Mentmore on Friday, on the top of a hill, where the raging of the wind was fully felt; I kept constantly thinking of you. And now we are longing to hear of your voyage, and how you are. If you arrived on Saturday *morning*, you took exactly the same time as we took, when we went out in the *Servia*, if later in the day, you took longer. . . . I had a pleasant visit at Mentmore; the house is splendid, and not only splendid but the perfection of comfort. Lord Rosebery is a great man for books and reading, not a mere politician, and this makes him much more interesting. He asked me to go down to Dalmeny, where he is to receive Gladstone in the latter part of this month; but I have promised to do "Sainte Beuve" for the *Encyclopaedia Britannica* by the end of the month, and these visits, though in many ways pleasant and profitable, are fatally distracting. I am not going to Knowsley either, where Lady Derby has asked me. Lord Spencer was at Mentmore— very pleasant.[1] He told me Lady S. had lost by death her beloved Dachs, and he had been in hopes she would never have another dog—her heart got so knit to them; however she has got another. Next week I have to go to Oxford for three days to inspect a training school—that I shall like; and if the Warden of Merton asks us,[2] I shall take mamma and Nelly with me. I think Oxford is still, on the whole, the place in the world to which I am most attached. Take all possible care of your dear self, and so you will best please   your fondly loving

Papa.

Text. Russell, 2:331–32.

1. John Poyntz Spencer (1835–1910: *DNB*; *VF*, 7/2/70), fifth earl, was an important statesman in the Liberal governments; his wife was Charlotte Frances Frederica Seymour (d. 1903), fourth daughter of Sir Horace Seymour.
2. George Charles Brodrick.

To George Washburn Smalley

Pains Hill Cottage, Cobham, Surrey

My dear Smalley   October 8, 1885

Now that I have got home again I must thank you for the Tribune.

It is impossible for a man to be better or more agreeably placed before a public than you have placed me before the Americans.

To be sure I have had so long a stage of what Dr Johnson calls "wholesome neglect" that perhaps notice and kindness, in the end of my days, will not spoil me.

Kindness from *you* I have had always.

The American people is a great deal bigger and stronger than it was, but I cannot agree with those who think it less sensitive to foreign, at any rate to English, opinion. It is natural it should be so, and on the whole, though there are some inconveniences, useful.

Your Tribune letter makes me more than ever desirous to talk to you about the subject for my next and last Discourses in America. But there is plenty of time.

Very kind remembrances to Mrs Smalley and your daughter— Ever most truly yours

Matthew Arnold.—

MS. Claremont College.

To Lucy Charlotte Arnold Whitridge

Pains Hill Cottage, Cobham, Surrey

My darling Lucy   October 13, 1885

I had half a hope that while I was dressing this morning Mamma's door would be thrown hurriedly open, and I should hear her dear agitated voice exclaiming: A letter from Lucy! but the pleasure has not come yet. I only hope it will come before I go to Oxford tomorrow, where I have a training school to inspect. I shall be away till Saturday, staying with the President of Corpus [1]—an interesting college to me, because my father was there. What a week of rain and wind we have had, and what a comfort it has been to think that you were safe on dry land, though on the other side, alas! The cold weather has come, and Mamma has a cough, Nelly a sore throat, and I, a flying neuralgia; but we are none of us very bad. When I go to Oxford tomorrow, Mamma and Nelly go in the Lushington Carriage to Laleham (the Lushingtons are away in Scotland)—and on Thursday they go to the Forsters at Norwood till Saturday. Your uncle Forster is by no means well yet and there is little chance of his being able to go to Bradford for his election; but there is no doubt they will return him. Yesterday Mr Earley Cook sent to propose to drive Mamma and Nelly to Guildford on his dray: Mamma wanted to see Mr Clark, the tailor, about the boy's great coat: Nelly's sore throat made it imprudent for her to go, so I went with Mamma; she in the box, and I, will you believe it, with her hated rival, immediately behind her! The country is beautiful, though in ten days more the colour will be better still: how I should like to take a turn with you through the Central Park, and look at the trees. At Guildford, the rival went to the hospital to see a poor girl there, Mr and Mrs E. C. went to Williamson's, and Mamma and I to the Castle, and then along the Dorking road, and finally to join the E. Cs at

Williamson's. We went all through the rooms and I was much tempted by four Chippendale chairs, the exact thing for our little dining room. I really think I should buy them and have four made to match them; but Mamma says we must then get rid of our side-board—and that makes too expensive a revolution. We saw many interesting things—above all a dinner and dessert service in old Wedgwood china, the forget-me-not pattern—quite charming and very cheap—only 12 guineas. Mr E. C. told Williamson we must go for it was getting dark and "he must not run the risk of breaking Mr M. A.'s neck"; upon which Williamson, to our great surprise, threw himself into my arms and said words could not express what he owed to me! One expects this to happen in an American shop, perhaps, but not in an English one. However, things are moving. The drive was beautiful both ways, the four horses doing their ten miles in the hour as smoothly as possible. Today Mamma and I are going to take the dear men in the Carriage to Byfleet bridge—then we shall send the carriage back and walk home by the Wey meadows and Wisley Common. They will be happy men indeed, Miss Lu. Nelly is to stay at home and nurse her throat. Ask Fred if he has kindly remembered to write to Mrs McKnight, whose letters, I think, he has. At any rate her address is: Silk Willoughby Rectory, Sleaford. Now I must take this to the post, for I have no stamp here for it. My darling Lucy, goodbye. My love to Fred—   ever your own most loving

Papa—

I think our present for young G. Smith will be very successful.

MS. Yale University.

1. Thomas Fowler (1832–1904: *DNB*), professor of logic and author or editor of several philosophical works.

To Anthony John Mundella

Pains Hill Cottage, Cobham, Surrey

My dear Mundella   October 14, 1885

I am just off to Oxford to inspect the Culham Training School. There is indeed a good opening now to speak of middle class education—and nobody takes it.[1]

Look at my Reports in the Minutes for 1878–79, p. 468—and for 1882–83, p. 225.

My Foreign Reports you know. Look also at my *Mixed Essays*, p. 143, and my *Irish Essays*, p. 129. I shall be delighted to give you either or both of these volumes, if I have not given them to you already, as I ought to have done.

To map out the ground, to determine what trust funds are properly available, and to provide buildings, is what we might even now put forward as fitting to be done by the State.

I hope after Easter, when my inspecting ends, to go to France and Belgium for two or three weeks, and to ascertain three points: 1. what the literary instruction in their Training Schools now comes to; 2. whether aid to higher and secondary instruction has increased similarly to that to primary; 3. how gratuitous primary instruction—which is new since I saw the French and Belgian Schools—really works.

Ask Fearon how far it can be said with truth that middle age endowments, now diverted to secondary and higher instruction, were originally designed for *popular instruction*. I don't believe it; I don't believe the medieval founder had any notion of what we call popular instruction. To prepare all promising subjects for the clerical career was his aim.   Ever truly yours

Matthew Arnold.—

Let me have a line here about the volumes of Essays.

MS. Sheffield University.

1. Mundella, now vice-president of the Committee of Council for Education, was preparing an important speech on free education in the Brightside Vestry Hall on Oct. 21 (W. H. G. Armytage, *A. J. Mundella*, p. 230).

To Frances Bunsen Trevenen Whately Arnold*

Education Department, Whitehall

Cobham

My dearest Fan   October 18, 1885

Here we are, all three together again; and we find here a delightful long letter from Lucy—She seems to have been very sea-sick, but the passage was not particularly stormy, and I do not think she was so bad as on the two previous voyages out. On arriving at New York she had done too much, and had had to lie up; but she seemed in good spirits, dear child. Nelly's cold is nearly well; she is going to stay with Flo for a few days this week, while Robin is in Ireland. Flu[1] will have told you her impressions of Robin, they were less dismal than yours. I shall go and see her myself tomorrow, after I have seen the Forsters. Tomorrow I begin inspecting again, but it will be light, as several of my schools are taken by Sharpe. I have been for three nights at Oxford this last week, staying at Corpus in the perfection of comfort; Fowler, the President, is a bachelor. The house is as pleasant and cheerful a one as Oriel is the reverse. I dined at the Oriel Gaudy on Thursday, and met two bishops, Stubbs and Wordsworth; the other two nights there were people to dinner in Corpus. I saw many things I had never seen before; the

Corpus plate which is unique in Oxford, not having been melted down for Charles the 1st; the library which is full of treasures; the long record of Papa's admission as a scholar, in presence, as the fashion then was, of a notary public: the spoons given by Papa when he left the College; these and a mustard pot given by Keble and now put aside as curiosities and not brought into use; finally, Papa's rooms, which had formerly been Bishop Jewell's.[2] The college is a most interesting one; its Founder, Bp Fox, who had accumulated a large sum to found a convent of monks was warned by the King's ministers that monks had had their day and that property left for their benefit would not be safe, so he founded a college for learning instead—at the very beginning of the 16th century. Much was said at Oxford about my coming forward for the Chair of Poetry, and I believe a requisition will be sent to me. But if I find that Palgrave has reason to think he would succeed if I did not stand, I cannot come forward. When he retired in favour of Shairp last time, I said to him that I hoped his turn would come; and he is sure to have remembered this. On Thursday afternoon I paid a long visit to Julia; her house is very nice, far the nicest they have ever had, though not large. She did not give a good account of Tom or of Frank, but was herself on her way to an afternoon tea, and Ethel with her. On Friday I got out to Hinksey and up the hill to within sight of the Cumner firs; I cannot describe the effect which this landscape always has upon me—the hillside with its valleys, and Oxford in the great Thames valley below. The pears are now coming in in good earnest; why are you not here to help eat them? My love to dear old Mary, and to Mr Hayes; I shall see them if they come up to London, but the country in October is the best place. What excellent news of Walter.   Your ever most affectionate

M. A.

MS. Balliol College.

1. These three lines ("Flu . . . than yours"), heavily inked over, were deciphered by Katherine Thomson.
2. John Jewel, the sixteenth-century bishop of Salisbury.

To Richard Penrose Arnold*

Athenæum Club, Pall Mall, S. W.

My dearest Dick   October 19, 1885
    You say you are told nothing from home. I am just back from the Office, where the authorities had sent for me to ask if I would go to Berlin and Paris to get information for them as to Free Schools. I should like it very much, because on one of these official tours one has the opportunity of learning so much. They have to get the consent of the Treasury, but Lord

Cranbrook is certain of obtaining that; and by the beginning of November I shall be off, as they want my report at Christmas, that they may acquaint themselves with the facts before Parliament meets. Won't this be news for mamma and Nelly tonight? I shall go to Berlin, which is an expensive and not delightful place, by myself; and then I hope they will meet me in Paris. I shall not be away more than six weeks. Then at Christmas you and Ella will come to us, which will be delightful. I like to hear of your going out shooting: I think you did very well indeed, though I myself find partridges easier to hit than pheasants. . . . I had a delightful three days at Corpus, staying with the President; it is a college I greatly like. I went alone up the Hinksey hillside towards Cumner Hurst, and enjoyed it more than I can say. I hope your pears will turn out well; they want watching. Ours are delightful. The dear men would send their love, Mr Dick, if they knew I was writing; they took the Redhill round with me yesterday, and were patterns. My love to dear Ella. Your own ever loving

Papa.

Text. Russell, 2:333–34.

To Gordon Graham Wordsworth

Athenæum Club, Pall Mall, S. W.

My dear Gordon   October 19, 1885

From what you told me, I am glad Mr Rawnsley has quitted his partnership with Mr Johns.

I most willingly consent to his using my name on his prospectus.[1]

My kind remembrances to him and his wife; and believe me,   Most truly yours,

Matthew Arnold.—

MS. Wordsworth Trust.

1. The allusions are all opaque.

To Lucy Charlotte Arnold Whitridge

Education Department, Whitehall

Cobham

My dearest Lucy   October 20, 1885

A frosty October morning. I have been going about in the fashion you know, gathering pears, bringing in ripe ones for dessert, picking up walnuts, looking at the flower beds for what is left still blooming in them, and finally cutting a fine Gloire de Dijon rose in the kitchen garden for Mamma. We have been rather disturbed about your state, but I hope that you are now better, and up: if you would but learn that you may be up without running all over the town to every kind of entertainment. I am glad you had a comforting visit from Mrs T. Ward;[1] she was a very pleasant little woman; my kindest remembrances to her. I have had a sweet note from Fannie Coddington; when you see Emily Butler[2] tell her I *did* expect a line from her in acknowledgment of the Discourses; but I suppose she is too busy with single gentlemen calling in the evening. I have just been reading in the P. M. G. a very good account of a Sunday in New York by Haweis;[3] he seems to have been luckier than I was in Ward Beecher's sermon, but all he says of the man is true. Both Mamma and I agreed, as I read out the familiar names, that we should *very much* enjoy finding ourselves in New York again. Nelly is just off to London to stay for a few days with Flo in Robin's absence; I looked in upon her for a short time yesterday and thought her looking fairly well; their drawing room is more "pinchy" than I remembered, but the situation just suits them. Your Uncle Forster was a little better yesterday, having had a good night; but he is by no means out of the wood yet. I and Mamma dine tonight and Friday with Lady Ellesmere; and this day week we dine with the Churchills[4] to meet some Americans; the Combes, too, ask us at least once a week, so we have plenty of dining. I was three nights at Oxford last week, to inspect a training school; I stayed with the President of Corpus, a bachelor, in the perfection of comfort, and met a number of people; they want me to come forward for the Chair of Poetry which is vacant by dear old Shairp's death, and talk of sending me a requisition from Members of Congregation—that is, the body of resident tutors and masters of arts: but I shall not do anything to interfere with Palgrave, who is standing. I was sent for yesterday to the Office to see Harry Holland, the new Vice President:[5] they want me to go abroad to get some information for them about schools and free-schooling; the Treasury has not yet been applied to, but Lord Cranbrook is determined I shall go and there will probably be no difficulty: it is just the sort of mission that interests me, one is enabled to see so many persons and things in the most thorough manner. I had thought of going on my own account after Easter, when I retire, but of course this is infinitely better, except for the cold time of year; all my expenses paid, £50 for my report, government facilities everywhere, and my inspectorship going on all the while. It will be my third errand of the kind, but it will be short, only six or seven weeks, as they want the information by Christmas. I shall probably go alone to Berlin and Saxony and then Mamma and Nelly will join me in Paris; I may have to go to Zurich too. I have not spoken German for 20 years, but now comes in the good of being always reading it; the speaking soon comes. This afternoon Mamma and I are going to drive to Byfleet Bridge with the dear men, Miss Lu; then we send back the carriage and walk home by the Wey meadow and Wisley Common; just what Nelly and I did the other day. My darling child, how I love you!   Your own

Papa—

My love to Fred. What do you hear or see of Farrar?

MS. Frederick Whitridge.

1. Unidentified.
2. Emily Ogden Butler (1840–1927), the eldest daughter of Charles Butler (Leichman).
3. "Sunday in New York and Brooklyn," *Pall Mall Gazette*, Oct. 19, 1885, pp. 1–2.
4. Charles Churchill (b. 1823), of Weybridge Park, Surrey (near Cobham), and his wife, the former Ellen Stooks (*County*, 1904).
5. Henry Thurstan Holland (1825–1914: *DNB*; *VF*, 1/29/87), second bt (later Viscount Knutsford), vice-president Committee of Council for Education in Salisbury's cabinet and Conservative Member for Midhurst, later secretary of state for Colonies.

To Henry Reeve

Athenæum Club, Pall Mall

My dear Reeve   October 23, [?1885]
    I fully hope and intend to return to life and animation this year, and shall probably prove it by coming and dining when the Club first meets in November.   Very truly yours,

Matthew Arnold.

MS. University of Virginia.

To David Binning Monro

Private   Pains Hill Cottage, Cobham, Surrey
The Provost of Oriel—
My dear Provost   October 24, 1885
    I cannot thank you enough for the trouble you have taken: and what a magnificent requisition you have sent me! After such an invitation from a place to which I am so deeply attached, I would face what I should feel extremely disagreeable—the chance of a blowing of trumpets against me in the "Guardian," and a raging of the country clergy. But I cannot forget, nor will Palgrave have forgotten, that I said to him at the last election that I hoped

his turn might come next; and if I find from him that he thinks his promises of support give him a fair chance of success if I abstain, I cannot come forward myself, and shall feel bound to support *him*.

But in any case I shall have to thank you, and Fowler, and Butler, and the signers of the requisition, for one of the most gratifying and pleasant incidents of my life—and I remain, my dear Provost,   Sincerely and gratefully yours,

Matthew Arnold.—

MS. Oriel College.

To Thomas Humphry Ward

Cobham
My dear Humphry   October 24, [1885]
Look at the enclosed: the requisition has since come: 12 Heads, and such a show of Professors Lecturers & Tutors as never was.

I am deeply gratified, because I am so fond of Oxford, and because I know, too, how apt the dear place is to be sniffy, and to think that there is no such thing, in any line whatever, as an "homme nécessaire."

But the point is this. Of course I must write a private note of acknowledgment to Munro, but to whom should my formal answer be addressed? Should it be a collective answer, or addressed to an individual? and in the latter case, to whom.

I told those who first spoke to me about it that I thought myself bound not to interfere with Palgrave, to whom I had said at the last election that I hoped his turn would come. I must now write to him; and if he thinks that his promises of support give him a fair chance of success if I abstain, I cannot stand.

I do not feel quite secure, if I do stand, against a whipping up of the clergy and a blowing of trumpets in the Guardian, against the author of L. & D.;—a thing which would be very unpleasant to me;—still I think I must face that, in case Palgrave tells me he has no chance.

Lang ought to have a turn some day.

I think the Times should mention the requisition—but I will tell you something of great interest to me which it must not yet mention—viz. that the Govt want me to go to Berlin, Zurich, & Paris, to get them trustworthy information about free schooling, &c. The Treasury has not yet consented, but the Office people say its consent is certain, as Lord Cranbrook is bent on my going.

I shall be back by Xmas, and shall take Amiel with me to read on the Journey. Before I go I must do Ste Beuve for the Encyc. Brit.—I have been living in his letters for the last few weeks.

My love to Mary—what an interesting time it is in the garden! Your ever affectionate

M. A.—

MS. Yale University.

To Lucy Charlotte Arnold Whitridge*

Pains Hill Cottage, Cobham, Surrey

My darling Lucy   October 27, [1885]

I have just got Miss Butler's letter; give her my love when you see her and tell her that there was affection in my message to her, and in all my messages to her there will be affection. I was delighted to hear from her; I have had a charming note, too from Fannie Coddington, and another from Bessie Marbury. I constantly find myself thinking with pleasure of once more seeing both the friends I have on the other side the Atlantic and also the country itself. But it seems likely that I shall see the Continent of Europe before I see America, as I think I told you last week. However, I have heard nothing more about it, so I will say nothing more at present except to tell you that I said to Mamma the other morning before I got up: "I have been thinking in the night *how* I shall miss my Lucy in Paris; she is such a perfect companion there." Nelly expects to enjoy it very much; but your knowing French so well and taking so much interest in things gave you a special value as a companion when we were together there. We all agree that Mr Wood-house in *Emma* is rather like *me*; in particular, so far as his sayings to and of his daughters are concerned. Mamma will have told you of the requisition from Oxford about the Poetry Professorship; I send you a charming article by Andrew Lang,[1] which appeared in the Daily News: and I would send you an equally charming one by Escott which appeared in the World, only it seemed to me that the World is the one English paper, besides Punch, which you all see in America. I do not think I shall be Poetry Professor, as I am bound to Palgrave not to stand in his way. We have had a beautiful bright day, like an autumn day in America; and the colours are beautiful too, only we want more of the American reds in addition to our yellows; still the span-ish chestnuts, beeches, birches and hornbeans are lovely pieces of colour. All the morning I was up a ladder gathering the pears, and you should see the baskets of them I brought in. Then I brought in a basket of walnuts; and tomorrow at dessert (we have Admiral Maxse, the Combes and the Helmes at dinner) we shall have grapes, pears and walnuts of our own growing. To-night we dine with the Churchills to meet an American Couple—I don't know who they are; and on Saturday we dine with the Buxtons to meet the Charles Lawrences; she is quite a favourite of mine. Dear Max has been very rheumatic, but is better; this morning while I was gathering the pears he was all the time worrying round the cucumber frame where the yellow cat now establishes himself for want [*sic*: warmth?], uttering a deep "beuglement" and vainly endeavouring to get in; Kai, seated on the path close by, regarding him with astonishment and asking me by his looks: Is he beside himself? The sick members of the family are all of them in a rather poor way, except your Aunt Susy, who has been re-assured as to the state of her nose—one doctor had said the bone was diseased and must be removed—and is cheerful accordingly. But she had shown great and admirable firmness under the bad news.

My love to Fred—Ever my darling girl   your own loving

Papa—

MS. Frederick Whitridge.

1. Andrew Lang's (anonymous) touching tribute and praise in the *Daily News*, Oct. 24, 1885, pp. 5–6, calling Arnold "far the most generally interesting lecturer of the distinguished men who have filled the Chair [of Professor of Poetry]," says his criticism was "the most lively, the most diverting, the most provocative of thought that contemporaries can read or listen to" and hopes that "in the old Chair . . . he will speak . . . not about politics, nor society, nor Isaiah, nor Dissent, nor about any mortal thing but poetry only." (A suggestive parallel between Arnold and Lang is drawn in Richard Le Gallienne's article "Matthew Arnold Escapes the Guillotine," *Literary Digest International Book Review*, 2 [May 1924]: 439.)

To David Binning Monro

Pains Hill Cottage, Cobham, Surrey

The Provost of Oriel—

My dear Provost   October 29, 1885

I have just heard from Mr Palgrave that in his opinion and that of his supporters my retiring in his favour will give him a fair chance of success; I cannot retire in his favour because I have never come forward as a candidate, but I can in his favour decline to be nominated, and this I feel bound, by a former expression of my wish for his success, now to do.

How can I sufficiently express my gratitude to those who have wished again to connect me with Oxford, to which I owe so much and to which I am so unalterably attached? I console myself by remembering that perhaps I am spared the pain of disappointing the kind hopes of my friends there. To re-assume an office at sixty two is not the same thing as to assume it at thirty two; and not even the pleasure of being called to the Chair of Poetry could make up for the distress of not filling it to the complete satisfaction of those who placed me a second time there.

Believe me, my dear Provost,   Truly and gratefully yours,

Matthew Arnold.—

MS. Oriel College.

To Thomas Humphry Ward

Education Department, Whitehall

Cobham

My dear Ward   October 31, [1885]

I sent you Monro's first letter, so I send you this. My position in respect to Palgrave was such that I found I could not let myself be nominated without prickings of conscience.

That extraordinary mortal at first thought, I believe, that I wished in some way to jockey him—and then he sent me a telegram of 137 words which will seriously curtail his profits from the first year's income of the Chair, if he wins it; but he never dreamed of withdrawing, and he is in the hands of Ince, so that perhaps the contest would have been made a religious (!) one—disagreeable for me, and for the University, detestable. But at any rate, if he stood, and thought he had a chance I could not interfere with him.

I should like the Times to say simply that I have gratefully declined the proposal to nominate me for the Chair of Poetry. I will try and send you, for your own reading, a copy of my letter to Monro, when they have printed it.

The Treasury have informally consented to my going abroad, and in a day or two, when the formal consent comes and the Office have settled the terms in which they would like the announcement made, I will send it to you or Buckle.

This last touch of "affairs" before I retire is rather pleasing to me, and I say with Solon: Γηράσκω δ' αἰεὶ πολλὰ διδασκόμενος![1]

My love to Mary: Amiel will cheer or sadden me on my journey. I find there is a letter from Ste Beuve to him—of about the date 1849.   Ever yours affectionately

M. A.

MS. Yale University.

1. Fragment 18.10: "I grow old still learning many things."

To The Secretary, Education Department

The Secretary etc. etc. etc.   Cobham, Surrey
Sir   November 1, 1885

    I have the honour to acknowledge the receipt of your letter informing me that the Treasury has sanctioned my going to certain foreign countries for the purpose suggested by the Department. I propose to call upon you at 12 o'clock on Tuesday, after receiving my instructions, and I will hold myself at the disposition of the Department to start as soon as may be thought desirable. I am, Sir,   Your obedient servant,

                                 Matthew Arnold.

MS. Public Record Office, London.

To Maria Theresa Mundella

            Pains Hill Cottage, Cobham, Surrey
My dear Miss Mundella   November 2, [1885]

    I see your father is moving about: will you kindly tell me whether I could find him on Wednesday either at home or at his Club, and at what time? The Govemt are sending me to enquire as to schools and free schooling at present in Germany, Switzerland and France—and there is no one with whom I so much wish to communicate before setting out as your father. Most sincerely yours

                               Matthew Arnold.—

MS. Sheffield University.

To Archibald Philip Primrose Earl of Rosebery

            Pains Hill Cottage, Cobham, Surrey
My dear Lord Rosebery   November 2, 1885

    The Govt are sending me (like Drummond Wolff, but *haud passibus æquis*)[1] on a mission. I am going to Berlin, Zurich and Paris to enquire about schools and free schooling. Be a good soul and put me in the way of seeing Bismarck, whom I shall of course not come across officially but whom I should much like to set eyes on and speak with. I don't say, Give me a letter to him, but suggest some unofficial means, at Berlin, of getting access to him. You know he has a great interest in English literature, though he stops, cunning old man, at 1800. I am off at the end of the week.

I follow you with interest and quite agree with you about a Second Chamber. A censorship has often been in my mind; but it is just the logical, drastic sort of means which the *tâtonnant* English mind is averse to. At present I doubt whether you will be able to keep your Lord Norton even by the sacrifice of your Lord St Lawrence.

Tell Lady Rosebery I am going to send *her*, and not you who made yourself so unpleasant about it, the new and complete edition of my poetical works, for Dalmeny.   Ever yours truly

Matthew Arnold.—

MS. National Library of Scotland.

1. "But by no means with steps that equal his" (*Aeneid* 2.724).

To Thomas Spencer Baynes

Education Department, Whitehall

Professor T. S. Baynes—   Cobham, Surrey
My dear Professor   November 3, 1885

Here is the Sainte-Beuve; you ought to have had him on the 31st ult., but I am only two days behind. I am going abroad for the Govt, to make inquires about schools and free schooling; with this in immediate prospect, I could not get the uninterrupted days for Sainte Beuve on which I had reckoned. I probably start on Monday next; let me have a line here to say when you will want a proof corrected; I return at Christmas—for ten days or so at any rate.   Ever yours truly

Matthew Arnold.—

MS. Balliol College.

To Maria Theresa Mundella

Athenæum Club, Pall Mall, S. W.

My dear Miss Mundella   November 4, [1885]

I don't think I need telegraph to your father, as he will hear from you this afternoon. I leave England on Monday, and I rely on your kindness to let me know if I shall find him in London before that.   Most sincerely yours

Matthew Arnold.

MS. Transcript, University of Virginia (MS. Sheffield University).

To James Bryce

Athenæum Club, Pall Mall

My dear Bryce   November 5, 1885

Your kindness is delightful and I am deeply grateful for it; and today I have a great memorial from the undergraduates; but I regard myself as under a pledge not to come forward, and though Palgrave has offered me the release from this pledge, I cannot accept it and stand against him. I do really think, besides, that it is for the advantage of the University that new men should have their chance in such a Chair as that of Poetry.   Most truly yours,
Matthew Arnold.—

MS. Bodleian Library.

To Granville George Leveson-Gower Earl Granville

Dear Lord Granville   November 5, 1885

I am going to Berlin to get information for the Office about schools and free schooling; I shall have a formal Foreign Office letter, but, as I have served under you at the Council Office, I should much like to have also a private note of introduction from you to Sir Edward Malet, if you would have the kindness to give me one.   Most truly yours
Matthew Arnold.—

MS. Pennsylvania State University.

To Anthony John Mundella

Education Department, Whitehall

Cobham

My dear Mundella   November 6, 1885

Your letter is most valuable; I assure you I am going with a perfectly open mind. At the present time I am against the abolition of school fees in our country; but this is not for the sake of the voluntary schools at all. I am going to Berlin first—then to Saxony; I had already determined on Chemnitz because of what you have formerly said of its schools. Then I shall go to Lucerne, and of course Zurich. Do you think it really important for me to go to Bavaria, if I am pressed for time? I start on Tuesday, and must get my German and Swiss information by Christmas; to Paris I shall go for a fortnight after the Christmas holidays.

Again let me thank you for your letter, written, too, when you had so much else to occupy you. You are doing the act of a true friend to Forster in going to Bradford.   Most sincerely yours

Matthew Arnold.—

MS. Sheffield University.

To Eleanor Elizabeth Smith

Education Department, Whitehall

Cobham, Surrey

My dear Miss Smith   November 6, [?1885]

A word of thanks for your kind note. I am not coming to Oxford as Poetry Professor but I hope to come there as often as I can in a private capacity, and you may be as sure I shall never come there without trying to see *you*.   Affectionately yours

Matthew Arnold.—

MS. Yale University.

To Charles Myhill

Education Department, Whitehall

Cobham

Dear Mr Myhill   November 6, [?1885]

I forgot when I was writing this morning to enclose Mr Baily's letter and to ask you to attend to it.   Truly yours

Matthew Arnold.—

MS. University of Virginia.

To Thomas Spencer Baynes

Cobham, Surrey

My dear Professor   November 9, 1885

If the proof is ready within the next fortnight, send it to me at the Kaiserhof, Berlin; if it is later than that, send it here to Mrs Arnold who will forward it wherever I am.

How kindly you speak of the Poetry Professorship! but it is better I should not "lag superfluous" on that stage.[1] Dear old Shairp is a loss indeed. Ever truly yours

Matthew Arnold.—

MS. Balliol College.

1. "Superfluous lags the vet'ran on the stage" (Johnson, "Vanity of Human Wishes," l. 306).

To Charles Myhill

Cobham

Dear Mr Myhill   November 9, [1885]

Tomorrow I will send you the parchments and some final things—but I now write to ask you to send me by return 8 cards (not more), two for each of the following Stand[ard]s: ivth, vth, vith, viith. I want to show them, and perhaps try them, in the foreign schools.   Most truly yours

Matthew Arnold.—

MS. Princeton University.

To Zulema A. Ruble[1]

Miss Zulema A. Ruble   Cobham, Surrey

Dear Madam   November 9, 1885

Your request reaches me just as I am starting for the Continent on the mission to enquire into certain matters connected with education abroad. I see no prospect of any leisure for poetry in the next few months; and I should indeed be sorry to send hurried and bad verses to represent me before a Society which I remember with so much interest and pleasure as Smith College.   Most truly yours

Matthew Arnold

MS. Smith College.

1. Unidentified.

To Council Office, Education Department

C. O.   November 10, 1885

In my absence, please forward to Mr Sharpe everything relating to the Westminster District.

M. A.—

MS. Public Record Office, London.

To Charles Myhill

Education Department, Whitehall

Dear Mr Myhill   Cobham, [?*c*. November 10, 1885]

You will be able to give Miss Jones the information she wants.

I send the signed parchments, and the entries.

I have told Mr Sharpe you will furnish him with the P. T. papers as he wants them.

And now really and truly Goodbye, for I am off tomorrow morning. Ever yours truly

M. A.—

MS. Pierpont Morgan Library.

To Lucy Charlotte Arnold Whitridge *

Cobham

My Darling Child—   [November ?10, 1885] [1]

. . . What does Fred say to the astounding attack made by the *New York Times* on Whitelaw Reid? [2] it has been telegraphed over here. The *New York Times* was the paper they told us was their best—the Butlers took it in. Imagine our *Times* writing in this way about the editor of the *Standard*! Say what Carnegie and others will, this is the civilisation of the Australian Colonies and not of Europe—distinctly inferior to that of Europe. It distresses me, because America is so deeply interesting to me, and to its social conditions we must more and more come here; but *these* social conditions! All this for Fred. I have a long and gloomy letter from Milburn, at Buffalo, too. But here things are breaking up, and all the politicians in their multitude of speeches never say one word which shows real insight, one word for the mind to rest upon; so the prospect is not very cheering here, either. I start tomorrow morning. Cardinal Manning has given me letters to the Archbishop of Cologne who is to put me in communication with the Catholics in North Germany, that I may hear other than official accounts of the schools. All this will be very interesting, and I am told that I am going at just the right time for Berlin, and that it has grown into a much finer and most brilliant place in the last six years. We shall see. I did not care for it in 1865. I have a letter for an old country gentleman, Count Canitz, in Silesia, [3] where I hope I shall go for a day or two and see real old German rural life. Then I go to Dresden, then perhaps to Munich, then to Berne, Zurich, Lucerne. . . . From the 22nd of

December to the 4th or 5th January we shall be here, and then mamma, Nelly, and I shall go together to Paris till the end of the month. I daresay the American papers will have told you about the Oxford professorhip, and how 400 undergraduates followed up the memorial of the heads and tutors with a memorial of their own. Every one is very kind as one grows old, but I want my Lucy. How I wish you could eat the Marie Louise pears! they are a perfect success. My love to Fred.   Your ever fondly affectionate

Papa.

Text. Russell, 2:336–38.

1. Davis's *Checklist* dates this letter Nov. 9; Tollers (*Arnoldian*, 3 [Winter 1976]: 6, 12), dates it Nov. 13.

2. Whitelaw Reid (1837–1912: *DAB*) author, journalist, and diplomat, edited the *New York Tribune*, 1872–1905, perhaps its palmiest days. Arnold refers to an editorial in the *New York Times*, Nov. 9 (p. 4), "Secret Foes of the Party," in which Reid was directly involved: "Blaine's friends in New York secretly conspired to defeat a candidate of their party, not because of any flaw in his character or record . . . but to revenge themselves upon the independents who openly opposed Mr. Blaine last year for reasons which they plainly stated."

3. More about Canitz below, letters of Dec. 7, 10, 1885.

To William Henry Rawle[1]

Pains Hill Cottage, Cobham, Surrey

Dear Mr Rawle   November 11, 1885

I have just read your address on my return home after the holidays. You have succeeded in interesting a great many people, me amongst the number. I had no notion that the struggle for existence was so keen in the learned professions with you; I thought everybody with proper equipment could "get along," although these might not be the great prizes which reward the few over here. And now I hear of men making £10,000 a year and upwards at your Bar, so you are coming to have the great prizes too. With all this discipline of pressure and prizes you will at least get the benefits which Aristotle says are so great, of the Education through *difficulties.*   Most truly yours

Matthew Arnold.—

MS. University of Virginia.

1. William Henry Rawle (1823–1889: *WWWA*), lawyer, now vice-president of the Philadelphia Law Academy, and an author. The address may have been his "Oration at

the Unveiling of the Monument Erected by the Bar of the United States to Chief-Justice Marshall," 1884 (Allibone).

To Frances Lucy Wightman Arnold*

Kaiserhof, Berlin
November 14, 1885

I rather hoped to find a letter from you last night, or at least to have had one today, but I have not. I found a letter from Fan waiting for me, but have had no other. I sent you a post-card from Calais, and write [*for* wrote] to you from Cologne; and hope to send a letter regularly every other day. After I wrote to you from Cologne, I had supper and went to bed. The six o'clock *table d'hôte* of Cologne I could not stand, so what do you think of the four o'clock *table d'hôte* here—unless one goes every night to the theatre, what an impossible dinner hour. I went early to bed, was called at seven, had the breakfast you like—good coffee and a roll—and was off at half-past eight. A dull, foggy morning, but Cologne is a beautiful place, and I should like to be a couple of days there with you. The journey to Berlin is long, because the country is thoroughly dull, except a little bit of Westphalia, and of the one or two interesting towns one passes—such as Dusseldorf, Dortmund, Hanover—one sees nothing. I had a carriage to myself, but at Dortmund, two Germans, wealthy merchants I should think, got in. My enjoyment of the day was gone, because when they very civilly asked me if I minded their smoking (there was no absolutely non-smoking carriages except for ladies) I felt bound to say no, and they smoked incessantly, and bad tobacco. However, I kept a bit of window open, and read a great deal; talking enough to them in German (for neither of them spoke any French or English) to convince myself that my German has become, as I told you, shocking. We reached Berlin at half-past eight. It was so dark that when we crossed the Elbe an hour or so before Berlin, I could not see it. At Berlin I had no difficulty, for all is well organised. I got a porter and a *Droschke*, and came to this splendid hotel. I have a very good bedroom on the second floor. The hotel is on the Ziethen Platz, very near the Unter den Linden, and I look out partly on the Mohren Strasse, partly on a church—a very good lookout. Then I unpacked my things and went to bed. I bought *Sapho* at the Calais station, and shall keep it for you. The *data* of the book are, of course, shocking, and deserve all that is said against them; still the book is one of Daudet's very best, perhaps actually his best, and extremely interesting. I have been reading the *Odyssey* today to take the taste out of my mouth, still Daudet imagines his book to be full of *"morality"* (he dedicates it to "My sons at twenty"), and some sort of morality it really has. However, reading it in the train had tired my head, and I was glad to get a good long sleep. I was up at eight, breakfasted in the restaurant on *chocolate* (very good here) and a roll, for coffee does not suit me and the tea is sad stuff. Then I went out and did my Berlin, which has become what is called a very fine city indeed. Exactly what——misses in New York it has in perfection—the finish, care, and neatness; but it is, alack! as new as New York, for the typical houses of old Berlin are gone, or are disappearing.

Text. Russell, 2:338—40.

To Friedrich Max Müller

Kaiserhof, Berlin

My dear Max Müller   November 14, [1885]

I had counted on George Bunsen to enable me to see some of the University professors here, but alas, he is in England! I think you once introduced me to Hofmann in the street, but I do not like to go boring him when he may have forgotten all about it. Mommsen, too, I once came across in Rome; we exchanged words, but I don't think we were even introduced. It would be very kind if you would send me a line of introduction to Hofmann, and also to Mommsen if you know him;[1] and to any other interesting men at the University here; few introductions could have so much weight as yours. I am here for a fortnight, the Government wanting exact information on the matter of school fees, and one or two other points. The Embassy is most obliging, but its relations are rather with Ministers and the "monde" than with the University.

It is 20 years since I was here—I may almost say it is 20 years since I was in Germany at all. I cannot tell you how it all interests me; the worst of it is, my German is shocking; I have been continually reading it and never speaking it; my last reading was Ewald on the prophet Zechariah; and I leave you to imagine how far that helps me to talk to a cabman. However I at least possess an extensive vocabulary—which is something.   Ever most sincerely yours

Matthew Arnold.—

MS. Bodleian Library.

1. August Wilhelm von Hofmann (1818–1892: *Ency. Brit.*), for nearly twenty years director of the Royal College of Chemistry in London, was now professor of

chemistry and director of the laboratory in Berlin University. Theodor Mommsen (1817–1903: *OCGL*), the eminent historian, especially of Roman Law, was also professor at Berlin.

To Louisa Lady de Rothschild *

Kaiserhof, Berlin

My dear Lady de Rothschild   November 14, 1885

I actually started from the Athenæum, before I left London, to call in Grosvenor Place; but I was stopped on the road, and then it was too late; I think I should have persevered had I been sure of finding you, but I knew it was three chances to one you would be at Aston Clinton. But I wished you to know of this impulse, at any rate: it is much too long since I saw you or heard of you. I diligently read the Brecon paper which Miss Morgan sent me; I thought Constance's speech as good as could be. I wish Cyril[1] would not commit himself so unreservedly to disestablishment; they have no idea what they are attempting; but in other respects I thought his speeches good too, all of them; and it is remarkable to see what power his genuine sense of sympathy with others gives him.

I am here because the Government wanted exact information as to school-fees and one or two other points in the German school-system. It is very interesting; but it is 20 years since I was in Germany, and my German is shocking; my latest preparation for calling a *droschke* or ordering my luncheon was reading Ewald on the prophet Zechariah. However, it will come in time; but I think with envy of the beautiful clear German I heard poor Leonard Montefiore talking to Mme Norman Neruda. If you have any friend here whom you would like me to see, send me a line; I shall be here for a fortnight. This town has grown into a very handsome one since I was here last—but interesting it is not, and cannot well be, perhaps. The Embassy, from Sir E. Malet[2] downwards, are most kind; two of the attachés have published poetry, so you may imagine there is a sort of fellow feeling. Lady Ermyntrude (is that right?) is laid up owing to some alarm about her approaching confinement, and I have not seen her.

Ever, dear Lady de Rothschild,   affectionately yours

Matthew Arnold.—

MS. *Evelyn de Rothschild*.

1. Cyril Flower was Liberal Member for Brecon (Brecknock).
2. Edward Baldwin Malet (1837–1908: *DNB*; knt 1881, succ. as fourth bt 1904; *VF*, 1/12/84), a diplomat who deserved the name, had smoothed over difficulties, repaired

damage, or negotiated settlements in Buenos Aires, "Washington, Constantinople, Paris, Pekin, Athens, Rome, Cairo, Brussels, Berlin" (*WWW*), where he was now ambassador. His wife, Lady Ermyntrude (born Sackville Russell), was the daughter of the ninth duke of Bedford.

To Frances Lucy Wightman Arnold*

Berlin
Sunday, [November ?15, 1885]

I said I should not write today, but I shall scratch a line every day if I can; the more so if I have such delightful letters to thank you for as yours of this morning. I will write to my Nelly tomorrow. I don't want you to feel bound to write every day; it is so different when one is in a new place and has always a sort of journal to send; but do not harass your sweet self to write when you are pressed with other things. I shall always understand when I do not hear. I have seen Sir Edward Malet, and like him. Lord Rosebery had written to him about my seeing Bismarck, but Bismarck is not here, and will probably not be here while I am; he does not come even for the meeting of Parliament. I expect tomorrow Sir E. Malet will get his answer from the Foreign Office here, to which he has written for an introduction to the Education Minister for me; and then I shall be able to get to work. You would very much enjoy this place, and I should enjoy it much more if you were here to enjoy it with me. The troops are splendid: Sir E. Malet said it is a constant pleasure to look at them; and so it is. Not the least swagger or ferocity—on the contrary a generally quiet, humane look; but such men and such discipline! I like the looks of the officers too; the Club is full of them, and all in uniform. After I had written to you yesterday evening I went down and dined at the restaurant in discomfort, for a great fête to Rubinstein[1] was coming on and everything was upset. The Berlin Philharmonic gave it. It began with a concert, at which all the best musicians of Berlin helped. This was in the next room to the one where I dined, and ladies were perpetually passing through in full dress, followed by a maid with a bundle; the bundle was to convert them into proper subjects for the *bal costumé*, which was to begin, after supper, at eleven. I suppose you and Dick would have enjoyed the music, of which while I dined I had the full benefit. After dinner I went out into the streets for peace. I was not at all disturbed at night—this house is so large and well built; but indeed the ball ended soon after one.

Text. Russell, 2:340–41.

1. Anton Rubinstein (1830–1894) was, after Franz Liszt (who was nearing death), the most famous pianist in the world!

To Eleanor Mary Caroline Arnold*

Kaiserhof, Berlin

My darling Nelly   November 18, 1885

I have your charming long letter this morning. I wrote to mamma yesterday, so must write again to you today. Again a bright, cold day, without wind; the finest winter weather possible. I like to hear all you tell me about the weather and garden at home. The official people here are slow in moving. I have been to see the Director of the Division for Elementary Schools at the Ministry today; very civil, and happily he speaks French, though bad French. But he can hardly bring himself to understand that one is in a hurry, or that one is not going to give a month to Berlin alone. However, I do hope to see something in the way of schools tomorrow. I am to have documents sent me tonight, and a showman chosen for me. I want, if possible, to get away from here tomorrow week, as I find I must go to Munich; and a week at Dresden, a week at Munich, and ten days at Zurich and Lucerne will take me right up to Christmas. It very much interests me trying to improve myself in speaking German, as I really have a very large vocabulary, which is the great thing. But the usual forms of talk are strange to me, from having known the language by books only. I am now waiting for Rennell Rodd,[1] who is to call for me and take me to Mrs Pendleton's. After that I come home, and take my lesson of my elderly German teacher. Then I get a cup of tea at the café close by, and Rodd and Cartwright call for me to go with them to *The Wild Cats*, a broad, comic piece with songs, at a popular theatre. I am sure this will amuse me more than the opera of *Undine*, or the translation of Shakespeare's *Much Ado about Nothing*, or of the *Duchess of Gerolstein*. We shall have supper at a restaurant after the play, which is over by ten. I find that the young men at the Embassy go to some theatre every night, now that the season has not begun. The season begins about the 18th of January with the Court balls, and goes on till May. The entire absence of late dinners, except under great difficulties, almost obliges the stranger here to go to the theatre; and it is because all the natives have the habit of going there, that the rule of dining early has come to prevail.

Text. Russell, 2:342–44.

1. James Rennell Rodd (1858–1941: *DNB*; cr. baron 1933; *VF*, 1/7/97), of Balliol (with a Newdigate prize) and already the author of two of his nine volumes of poetry and

associated with Wilde, Burne Jones, and Whistler, chose diplomacy as a career and in Berlin was attaché and then third secretary.

William Chauncy Cartwright (1853–1933: *Landed*), also of Balliol, was later knighted (K.C.M.G.) and chief clerk of the financial department of the Foreign Office. Mrs Pendleton was the wife of George Hunt Pendleton (1825–1889: *DAB*), Envoy Extraordinary and Minister Plenipotentiary to Germany 1885–89.

Arnold in Berlin, November 1885

In November Matthew Arnold came to Berlin to stay some weeks and prepare a report on education in Germany. The unmarried secretaries had at that time a little mess for luncheon at Langlet's, an excellent restaurant kept by a Frenchman, at the corner of the Wilhelm Strasse and the Linden, almost next door to the Embassy, and we at once invited the poet to become an honorary member. He lunched with us there nearly every day and we became the greatest friends. We took him to Görlsdorf, the hospitable house of Count Redern, well known in England in the 'seventies. We induced him to accompany us to the plays and the opera, and the great man renewed his youth and entered into all our combinations. Matthew Arnold was fully conscious of his own value and possessed what the Irishman prayed the Lord to give him, "a good conceit of himself" in no small measure, but he was a very lovable man, and I at any rate felt greatly flattered by his friendship. The world had not treated him too kindly, or rather he would never give the world a chance of doing so, for he could not condescend to nonconformist and philistine mentality or "do without contempt." It has always been a pleasure to me to know, as I heard afterwards from his two delightful daughters, that he had greatly enjoyed his stay in Berlin and talked of it with genuine pleasure. One day a slight misadventure befell. We were under the impression that he had gone away for two or three days on a round of inspection. One of our party had invited two extremely smart and amusing French demi-mondaines, who were passing through Berlin, to the mess, parenthetically a quite irregular proceeding, though the mess had no strict rules or precedents. We had just sat down to table when the door of our *Cabinet particulier* opened and Matthew walked smilingly in. Explanations were useless as well as impossible, and a chair was placed between the two ladies for "le cher poète," and as one of them was known for her brilliant wit, the meal was hilarious. His French accent was not by any means equal to his knowledge of French literature, but he struggled manfully and I am quite sure he enjoyed himself. As we strolled away together he put a hand on my shoulder and observed in the grand manner: "Most amusing! But really I cannot imagine that Aspasia and Phryne were quite like that." The episode evidently remained in his memory, for a month or so after his departure I received a letter from the Athenæum, announcing his return to Berlin early in 1886, and adding: "I hope those Sirens, both the silent and the noisy one, have long since departed, and that your luncheons are such as the Bishop and I can approve."

Text. James Rennell Rodd, Social and Diplomatic Memories, *1884–1893, pp. 93–94.*

To Frances Lucy Wightman Arnold*

Carlsdorf Bei Angermünde
November 23, 1885

I begin this here, but I expect to be called away directly to go with Count Redern[1] to see his school—a little village school with not more than fifty children—a specimen of its class which I shall be glad to see, for, of course, the great town schools are what the officials will chiefly take me to. Count Redern is one of the greatest Prussian proprietors; they say he has £70,000 a year. He has been much in England, for he is very fond of racing, and breeds horses; he was at Newmarket last month only. He has fitted up the interior of the house with every modern convenience, and the Khiva carpets, which he brought from Petersburg, would delight you. I write to you from my own salon, a great room with an open fire, but cold, then a large dressing-room, then a larger bedroom, then a bathroom. Fires in bedroom and dressing-room as well as salon. Our party was Count Seckendorff, Cadogan,[2] Rodd, and myself. We started at half-past eight yesterday (Sunday) morning, were met by the Count's carriages at a station about forty-five miles from Berlin, and drove five miles to this place, which we reached for luncheon at eleven. The Count has an English valet, and two English coachmen, and a French cook of great merit. It is a country slightly rolling, with great forests of fir with birch, beech, and oak mixed, and a number of beautiful lakes. We drove out in the afternoon about ten miles to a wooden watch-tower, from which they expected to see red deer. We saw plenty of fallow deer, but no red deer except close to the house, where a few are kept tame; also I saw no wild boar, which I would rather have seen than even red deer; but they keep very close. An admirable dinner, and in the evening they made me repeat some of my poetry, saying it would be an event to remember; I cut it as short as I could. I am very glad to have seen the place, so unlike anything we know; I wish I could have gone to the river Oder, which is only eight miles off. The Count wants me to come back in June, when the woods are in leaf, and the grounds are alive with nightingales. The *soirée* at the Crown Prince's palace was a brilliant affair—about two hundred officers in uniform—very fine men, and I know no uniform which looks better than the Prussian. The Crown Princess came round the circle, and I kissed her hand, as every one here does when she holds it out; she talked to me a long time, and said I must come and see her quietly and comfortably; then the Crown Prince came up and talked for some time; I never saw a man do his duty to his guests better. I was introduced to Count Herbert Bismarck (very natural and pleasant), and to Rudolf Lindau,[3] who is the chief permanent official at the Foreign Office here; the terrible thing is that you have to wait to the end, and having gone punctually at nine, I did not get away till after midnight.

Berlin—6 P. M. I have got back here and found my Nelly's letter; also one from Max Müller sending me introductions to the University people best worth seeing. I dine tonight with the Leveson-Gowers, tomorrow with the Pendletons; Lindau and Seckendorff I am also to dine with this week, and to keep a day for Scott, the first secretary, and also for Sir E. Malet, who returns on Thursday. So I am pretty well filled up. Seckendorff says the Crown Princess will arrange for my seeing, when I go to Dresden, the Saxon royalties, who are very interesting: whether or no she really will, remains to be seen. I wrote to Lucy this morning. I thought she would like to have a letter from a country house in the Mark of Brandenburg. All the Crown Princess's children were there the other day. Prince Henry,[4] in a naval uniform, looked a charming youth. The great Bismarck is not here. Now I must dress. Take great care of yourself, and give a kiss to my Nelly with thanks for her nice long letter. I am sorry the Forsters are not off to Torquay; I must write to Jane soon. The weather has changed to mild and rainy. I am here till Sunday at any rate.

Text. Russell, 2:344–46.

1. "There has just died here, at the age of 84, Count Heinrich Alexander von Redern, one of the high household officers of the late Emperor William. At first he was in the diplomatic service, and represented Prussia in St. Petersburg, but from this career he retired to manage the immense property which he inherited from his brother, who had married a daughter of the Hamburg millionaire, Tenisch" (*The Times*, Oct. 25, 1888, p. 9).

2. Perhaps Arthur von Seckendorff-Gudent (1845–1886), student of forestry (*Ency. Brit.*); George Henry Cadogan (1840–1915: *DNB*), fifth earl, Conservative politician.

3. Herbert von Bismarck (1849–1904: *WWW*) was the son of the "great Bismarck," the chancellor. Rudolf Lindau (1829–1910) was to be also a prolific author (eight columns in the catalogue of the Library of Congress) and a contributor to *Revue des deux mondes* and *Journal des débats*.

4. The second son, Alfred William Henry (1862–1929), grand duke of Hesse.

To Frances Lucy Wightman Arnold*

Berlin
November 25, 1885

I got your long letter last night. I am glad you will now write from Cobham, as I like to get your letters in the morning; they do me good for the whole day. I am still doing very little in the line of visiting schools, though I have plenty of documents to read, but the slowness about doing things is incredible. I told you I had two men named to me as my pilots, one for town, the other for the suburbs; I pass my life in moving from one to the other; neither is at home except for one hour in the day, and one of them, whom I have just visited at great inconveninece and at some distance, has chosen his home hour today for going out to see his doctor. The other I got to at last, and found that he had not yet received his official instructions to take me about; I am to see him again tomorrow. If I can make nothing tomorrow of my inspectors, I shall on Friday go straight to the schools with a letter I have received from the Minister himself, begging all school authorities to admit me. But I should like to have some one to question, like my poor lost Rapet. I was going about so much yesterday that I could not write; after getting this you had better write to the Hotel Bellevue, Dresden, where I go on Monday. Yesterday I wasted my day in trying to see my official guides; but I got my German lesson (very useful) and lunched with my young men at the Embassy. In the evening I dined with the Pendletons—a pleasant dinner. This morning while I was dressing there arrived a tall personage in black to invite me to dine with the "Königlichen Kronprinzlichen Herrshaften"; it was like a play: he mentioned dress and hour and his royal personages, all with the same solemnity. The hour is six and the dress is plain evening dress—which is lucky, as I have no court suit. It is very kind of the Crown Princess to have asked me. I have had a kind letter from Max Müller, with notes for Hofmann, Zeller,[1] and Mommsen; all men of European reputation, whom one ought to see while one is here. I saw Hofmann last evening—a dear, doggy, cheerful old thing, very fond of England, where he lived some years, and married. Then Zeller, the historian—a thin, sweet-faced, refined, elderly man, to him I had to speak German; Hofmann speaks English perfectly. Mommsen, I know, talks French. I am to see him on Saturday probably.

Text. Russell, 2:347–48.

1. Edouard Zeller (1814–1908: *Ency. Brit.*), philosopher and historian, renowned for his *Philosophie der Griechen*, from one part of which Arnold quoted twice in his *Notebooks* (1869).

To Frances Lucy Wightman Arnold*

Kaiserhof
November 27, 1885

I was going to write to Nelly, from whom I had a pleasant letter, but I have such a long and sweet one from you this morning that to you I must write. You need not tell me anything from the *Times*, as I see it regularly. It is the only English paper one sees, but this one is found everywhere—in the hotel, at the club, in the Embassy. The elections are, as you say, profoundly interesting. How I wish we could talk about them together!

Yesterday one of my school guides appeared before I was out of bed, and made an engagement to take me tomorrow to a country school near Potsdam. Then I paid a visit to the director of the Elementary Schools in Berlin, and got the names from him of four Elementary Schools to visit. One of them I have seen today, and another I shall see on Monday. The other two I shall not be able to go to, but two Berlin schools is quite enough. I am also going to the Crown Princess's Kindergarten. I lunched with the Embassy, and then went with Rodd to the Museum to see the Marbles from Pergamos. They are very fine, but, like the Elgin marbles, a little beyond me. It was a black and gloomy day, and while we were in the building on came the snow. I had my German lesson (I am beginning to make a little progress), and then had to dress for the Crown Prince's. None but private carriages are allowed to drive to the door, so I had to stop at the sentry beneath and walk up through the snow. The palace is small, but very cheerful and agreeable. Hofmann, the chemist, who is a favourite with the Crown Prince, was the only other guest. We were shown into a drawing-room, where we were presently joined by the lady-in-waiting. About five minutes afterwards a door was thrown open and the Crown Prince entered in what looked to be a Windsor uniform, but I am told is the evening undress of the Prussian Guards. His two younger daughters were with him, still children. The Princess Victoria followed with her mother, both in high dresses, the young Princesses all white, the mother all black.[1] We went into dinner almost directly, and the Crown Princess put me by her and talked, I may say, all dinner. She is very able and very well informed. . . . After dinner she again made me sit by her on the sofa, and presently the Crown Prince wished Hofmann goodnight and came to the Princess and me. He stood leaning on a chair, so of course I got up, on which he crossed his hands over his breast and said, "I entreat you to stay as you are." They were thoroughly pleasant. We talked much of the English elections, and then they said I must hear the telephone, laid on from the Opera. The Prince showed me how to put it to my ears, and I heard every word of the recitative, which was then going on distinctly, and presently the music also. Then the Princess got up and held out her hand and said, "We must see you again before you go to Dresden."—"Oh yes," said the Prince, "we must certainly see you again." I kissed her hand and shook the Prince's, and then the Princess Victoria came forward and held out her hand, and her two younger sisters followed suit. They then all went out, and the Prince, who went last of them, turned round and shook hands with me again, on the top of the stairs. Then I went down into the snow, rejoicing in my "Arctics."

Text. Russell, 2:348–50.

    1. Princess Victoria (1860–1928), the oldest daughter, and Sophia Dorothea Ulrica Alice (1870–1932) with Margaret Beatrice Feodora (b. 1872), unless Arnold, in a rare lapse, skipped the second daughter, Frederika Wilhelmina Amelia Victoria (1866–1929).

To Eleanor Mary Caroline Arnold*

Berlin

My darling Nelly   Sunday, November 29, [1885]

    I have another letter to thank you for, and I have to thank mamma for one received this morning, which I did not expect. I cannot now write every day, because my days are more and more filled. Yesterday I never got time to look at my newspaper till after twelve at night. I brought my history down to Thursday night. On Friday morning the thaw had come, and it poured with rain. I drove to a great girls' school, and passed the morning there. It was very good, and the slow, distinct speech of the teachers, and the slow, distinct answers which they insist on from the scholars, is a capital lesson in German for me. Yesterday morning I breakfasted in my own room as I got up—a common practice here, where your breakfast is only a cup of coffee and a roll. At nine Dr Tzyska called for me—a sensible, pleasant man who speaks English, who took me to a country school six miles from Berlin— very interesting. I got back in time to lunch with the young men at the Embassy, and to go to the Reichsrath. Sir E. Malet and the Crown Prince had both told me Bismarck would probably speak. I had a very good place in the diplomatic box. One of the French attachés, seeing a stranger enter, politely insisted on my taking his place in the front row; and sure enough there was Bismarck on his legs. He is gigantic, and just the face you know from his photographs; but his expression milder and with more of bonhomie than I had expected. He was in a general's uniform, which surprised me, but I am told he always wears it in the Reichsrath (the word means Imperial Parliament). Just under him, with his hand to his ear to catch what was said, stood Moltke.[1] Bismarck spoke for more than half an hour. He spoke badly,

with short, awkward gestures, and dropping his voice. He had a great portfolio of papers, which he perpetually consulted, and read from. He was answered by Windthorst [*sic*], the Catholic orator, a little old man who is a
firstrate speaker. He got far more applause than Bismarck, who spoke again
when Windthorst sat down. Then Windthorst in his turn spoke again, and
then Bismarck once more rose and was speaking when I had to go away for
my German lesson. Then I dressed in a hurry and out to the Chancery,
where I had a capital cup of tea with two of my young men who went with
me to see *Othello* at the Royal Theatre. Horrid! but I wanted for once to see
Shakespeare in German. I afterwards gave them supper at Uhl's, being glad
of an opportunity to give something to those who had given me so much,
and I think they liked it. . . . This morning I breakfasted with Count Seckendorff at his house close to the Crown Prince's palace. He is kindness itself,
and is managing all sorts of things for me both at Dresden and Munich.

Today it pours with rain; I drove to a great school in the extreme east
of Berlin, and stayed there till one, when the school closed; this school-
seeing interests me here extremely. I walked till I could get a cab, and then
came back here and lunched. Directly after luncheon came a message from
Count Seckendorff to say that the Crown Princess wanted me, if I could, to
call upon her at half-past four, so I went across and put off my German
master, who was coming at that very time, till six. Then I walked in the rain
to the Crown Prince's palace, and was at once taken through a passage filled
with books, to her room. I kissed her hand this time both on coming and
going, and really she is so nice that to kiss her hand is a pleasure. She said she
could not let me go without seeing me again, gave me a chair, and kept me
three-quarters of an hour. She is full of the Eastern question, as all of them
here are; it is of so much importance to them. She talked too about Bismarck,
Lord Ampthill, the Emperor, the Empress, the Queen, the Church, English
politics, the German nation, everything and everybody indeed, except the
Crown Prince and herself. At last I got up, though I suppose I ought to have
waited for her to dismiss me, but I might have been there still; she said I was
of course to come and see them if I returned to Berlin; that she regretted they
could not take me in here, but that if I ever came when they were at Potsdam
they had plenty of room there, and I must stay with them. Then she asked
me where I was going to dine tonight, and I am sure would have asked me
to dinner if I had not been engaged to dine with the Ambassador. I then
went down the beautiful staircase, and allowed my greatcoat to be put on by
a magnificently grown footman, and walked here. I have since had a last
lesson from my excellent old man (born in the same year as myself), have
paid him and taken leave of him. I see William is in;[2] I am very glad (though
I was in no fear about it) and must write to Jane. Now I must really dress; the
last time I dined at the Embassy I was late.

Text. Russell, 2:351–54.

1. Helmuth Moltke (1800–1891), the Prussian field-marshal, the premier military figure in Germany and perhaps the world, was by now a national icon. Ludwig Windhorst (1812–91), below, a lawyer and formerly minister of justice, was a "bitter opponent" of Bismarck (*OCGL*).

"I took him to the Reichstag," wrote Rodd (*Social and Diplomatic Memories*, p. 94). "The Chancellor spoke but that day his voice was almost inaudible. There was a battle royal between him and his bitter antagonist Windhorst, the Catholic and Hanoverian. The latter ended his speech with the words: 'People would say that the late King of Prussia had been pleasanter to live under than the actual government of Prince Bismarck.' These words brought the Chancellor to his feet. They were, he said, a deadly insult to himself and to the Emperor, whose humble and loyal servant he tried to be. He referred to his own increasing years and failing health, and deplored that he should come to the Reichstag only to be affronted."

2. William Forster, elected Member for Bradford, Central, on Nov. 28.

To Frances Bunsen Trevenen Whately Arnold*

Hôtel Bellevue, Dresden

My dearest Fan   December 4, 1885

I have just got your letters; this makes three I have had from you since I came abroad, and I have only written to you once, which is too bad! But my day is very full, and I have more letters to write than I expected. Why did Mary make me clasp hands in friendship with Mr Middleton, who hits ladies in the breast? But I hope that Lord J. Manners will get in for Leicestershire,[1] and the Tory for Westmorland, though I should never myself vote for a Tory; but for the present I wish Lord Salisbury to stay in, the Liberals being so unripe. Ld Salisbury is an able man, and I think he improves, and is capable of learning and growing. When one has seen Bismarck one feels the full absurdity of poor Lord Granville transacting foreign affairs with him; and when one hears him, and perceives how earnestly he is putting his real mind to the subject in hand, one thinks of Gladstone pouring out words as the whim may take him, or party considerations render convenient. I heard a very good debate in the Reichstag, but I do not think there is any chance of my having speech with Bismarck; he arrived in Berlin only just before I left it, and it needs arrangement to get him to see new people unless his duty obliges him. I could not possibly ask Sir E. Malet to help in it; in the first place he would decline, as they are all much afraid of Bismarck. Still, if I go back to Berlin, perhaps it will be managed somehow, but by a private channel. Very good news about Flo, but Fanny Lucy had not seen her. I was sincerely glad W. E. F. got in for Bradford, but I was sure he would; the wiser Liberals, if they have any real political sense, will be very strong in this Parliament. I hope they will not unite with the Tories, and will also resist steadily the temptation of going against their judgment with the Radicals, merely to keep a supposed party together. I am learnng a good deal here, and am at last making some progress in speaking German; but much more time is needed for an enquiry of this kind than I have. It is impossible to see more than one school a day, for they all close for good at one o'clock, and the officials do not like one's hurrying over a thing—and quite right. Then, too, even more important than seeing the schools, is the ascertaining what people think of the system of payment or non-payment in them, and what is likely finally to be done about it. Tell Mary that she had better send Louis[2] to Australia,—or perhaps Cameroon where he will be under the firm hand of Prince Bismarck,—and come out and live here with Mr Hayes. It is a beautiful place, and cheap still; the best places in the best boxes on the grand tier of the opera cost only six shillings. Perhaps that would be no more inducement to her than it is to me; but the picture gallery—that is an attraction indeed! I was two hours there yesterday, and I found that I had not half done it justice before, having come here straight [from] Florence, where the galleries are even better. The city has its public buildings partly in the style of Blenheim, partly in that of Bow Church, if you know those monuments; but the effect is very fine; and the town proper is a real German town of high old houses, not like Berlin, a handsomer Bold[3] Street, all new. Then there is the red-brown Elbe, a perfect beauty, pouring through the bridges, and in the distance hills, real hills, the beginnings of the Saxon Switzerland. Now I must go to the Minister's office, and I have told you nothing; but mind you write to me once more, and here; your letter to reach me not later than Wednesday in next week. I hardly think I shall go on to Munich; I have quite settled not to attempt Switzerland, but to take it, along with Paris, after Christmas. Perhaps from Zurich I may then go on to Bavaria; we shall see. Goodbye, my dearest Fan—   Your ever affectionate

M. A.—

I keep wonderfully well, and here, where we have no Minister and no attachés, I go every night to the theatre—hours from 7 to 9½—to the great improvement of my German.

I was going to write to my precious old Tom this very day, but thought I would answer your letter first.—Down with Cropper! but has he won?[4]

MS. Balliol College.

1. Middleton was probably Richard William Evelyn (1846–1905: *WWW*; *VF*, 4/18/01), chief agent of the Conservative Party, 1885–1903. Manners, a popular candidate, was elected Conservative Member on Dec. 2 and remained in until he succeeded his brother as duke of Rutland in 1888.
2. Louis Hiley, her son by her second husband.

3. *Sic.* Bond?

4. James Cropper (1823–1900), older brother of John Cropper and Liberal Member for Kendal since 1880, was defeated on Dec. 2.

To Robert Burnett David Morier[1]

Dresden

My dear Morier   December 7, 1885

I cannot enough thank you for your two letters, which I have found here, and for the introductions. If I can possibly manage to return by Neu Wied, I will. Munich must wait till after Christmas; I am going home for Christmas, and to make a short report on Prussia and Saxony; then towards the end of January I am going to Paris and from there to Zurich; from Zurich Bavaria and Munich will be very accessible. I find it is vain to think of doing a German country in a week; it takes one that time to deliver one's letters, get them acted upon, and make a start; it is too tantalizing to go away just as one is beginning to see people and learn things. I am going on Thursday for a couple of days to a Count v. Canitz, near Görlitz; I have no doubt you know him, he was in the diplomatic service. To have a glimpse of country life and country schools here, and not merely at the towns, and of the town schools to which the authorities are disposed to send one, is very instructive. I find that except in Berlin itself, and perhaps in one or two other large towns of Prussia, free-schooling does not exist in Prussia and Saxony, though in England it is commonly imagined that it is the rule in both these countries.

The hospitality of the Berlin embassy was unbounded, but outside the court and official circle they know nobody, and I gather that they think it best for them to know nobody. This is inconvenient for me, and the more so, as George Bunsen is away on the Riviera. I am in a fair way of seeing some of the best of the Liberal members of the Reichstag, and Max Müller has sent me introductions to Mommsen and Zeller, but I should like to get at Windthorst; can you help me? I return to Berlin (Kaiserhof) next week for a couple of days. Then back to England, stopping for a day at Cologne to see some Catholic schools. The Crown Princess was charming; I dined with them, and saw her twice besides; in England I thought her shy and constrained, but in Berlin she is quite different. How I wish you and I could dine together one night, or even two, at Uhl's! I look with longing at the Russia going lines, as they stood before me on the map; but it is impossible.   Ever yours, my dear Morier,

Matthew Arnold.—

MS. Balliol College.

1. Morier was ambassador at St. Petersburg.

To Eleanor Mary Caroline Arnold*

Dresden

My darling Nelly December 10, 1885

    This morning I had your letter, so to you I shall write; I wrote to your darling mamma yesterday. Well, I have seen the King! The Prussian minister told me evening dress was *de rigueur*, so after doing a school with my official guide this bitter snowy morning, I came back here at twelve o'clock, and put on evening things and a white tie. I wore also my order, but I was obliged to have in the chambermaid, a red-haired, pleasant-faced girl, to tie it behind for me, which she accomplished with much tittering, and with a lively interest in my making myself *hubsch* (beautiful), because I was going to speak with *der König*, and to speak with him *allein*, too! Then I put on over my evening shoes those comforts of my life, my Arctics, and walked through the snow to the Schloss. I was received by a magnificent creature with a silver-gray greatcoat with immense fur collar and cuffs and a cane. He led me through endless corridors and sentries to a room where the aide-de-camp was, a tall, good-looking man, who was expecting me; he led me through more passages, saying, as we went, that he was glad I spoke German. "But his Majesty speaks English," I said. "Yes," he answered, "but his Majesty is always *genirt* and put out when he is obliged to speak English; he doesn't feel sure about the pronunciation."—"But French?" I suggested. "Oh yes," said my aide-de-camp, in French, "that will do perfectly well," and went on in French himself from that time. He led me into a large bare room, with polished floor, begged me to wait a moment, went through a door, and was seen no more. In a minute or two the King entered, an elderly-looking man in uniform. He bowed and I bowed lower; he at once began in French, saying the Crown Princess had written to him about me. We went on about schools for some time; then we talked about Prince Thomas, whom he did not know to have actually lived with us, though he knew he was at Harrow; then about politics, then about the dependence of people here upon the State and its officials; then about the English language, and about the *masse* of Americans in Dresden, for the English language as spoken by whom his Majesty expressed his cordial dislike. Then he said how glad he was to have seen me, held out his hand, which I shook, and back he went to his own room. I found my magnificent attendant in the furs waiting for me on the landing, to conduct me to the great door out of the palace—I should never have found it without him. I had again to call in my chambermaid to untie her fastening of my order. I assure you it improves my appearance immensely. For the first time since I have been abroad I felt the unspeakable benefit of my French. My Lucy would have liked to hear me talk it. His Majesty and I talked it in much the same manner, neither of us like Frenchmen, but with perfect fluency and perfect solidity of grammar.   Always your most loving

Papa.

Text. Russell, 2:356–58.

To Frances Lucy Wightman Arnold*

Dresden

December 10, 1885

I always reproach myself when I have not written to you or Nelly, but this morning I said to myself: Well, at any rate, *they* had not written either; and now when I come in at one o'clock here is your letter of the 8th. I write at once, that my letter may go by the five-o'clock post; then you will get in on Sunday morning. I was going to Baron v. Canitz's today, but the King has sent through Count Dönhof to ask if I can come to him tomorrow at one; of course I stop for this, and have written to Baron v. Canitz to propose coming on Saturday instead. Then I should stay over Sunday with him and go to the regular Lutheran service in the country place; see his village school on Monday morning, and return here at night. I must return here, as Tuesday was the first day I could fix for being taken to a Saxon country school; the inspector for the district round Dresden is to take me. Then on Wednesday the 16th I shall go to Berlin, and after a few days there shall make my way home by Cologne, where I must stop a day to see schools. But some time on Wednesday the 20th I hope to be at home again, and I feel as if I could never leave you any more. The schools here are so good that I am never tired of seeing them. I am interested to find that Lutheranism is very much more alive than I thought; the hymns and Luther's catechism are a great feature in every school; the hymns are the models on which ours are formed, and are better than ours. The catechism, too, is better than Dean Nowell's which we use;[1] but the remarkable thing is the use which is made of the hymns and catechism, as well as of the Bible; the way the children know them and seem to like them, and the way the inspectors examine them. This morning I have been to a school for a higher grade of boys, those who are going to be engineers, merchants, manufacturers, and so on; but it is all part of a system, so it is well to see it all. It would have surprised you to find how well the boys answered in English history—boys in what would with us be the fifth form. This afternoon I am going to an Elementary school; in the evening I am going to the opera—*La Juive*.[2] We have a Polish lady staying here, short and fat, who is the *prima donna*; she has sung with great success at Warsaw, Milan, and Naples, but the papers here have made unfavourable remarks on her appearance, which greatly distresses her. I have promised to go tonight and applaud her. The librettos in German are so carefully made, and so good, that they are quite another thing from the librettos in English, and are a great help to me in getting through the opera; they interest me, if the music does not. The worst of it is I get out so little, though to be sure the weather is bad for country walks; yesterday we had snow, after a very fine morning, and today there is a slight thaw and slush.

Text. Russell, 2:358–60.

1. Alexander Nowell, seventeenth-century dean of St Paul's, remembered for his three Catechisms, Large, Middle, and Small (*DNB*).
2. *La Juive* (1835), Halévy's opera with Scribe's text.

To Frances Lucy Wightman Arnold *

Mittel Sohra, Görlitz
Sunday, December 13, 1885

I could not write yesterday, so I take a larger sheet today. Yesterday morning I left Dresden at ten, bitterly cold, and the Elbe full of blocks of ice and frozen snow; but the snow had ceased falling. It is always warm in the railway carriages—too warm! and if there is a dispute, the railway officials have orders to decide always in favour of *closing* the window. We went through Saxon Lusatia, a pleasant country, but the windows were so frozen, it was hard to see anything of it; past Bautzen, where was one of Napoleon's great battles; a very interesting place full of old buildings, on the Spree, the river of Berlin. Then to Görlitz, a place of fifty thousand inhabitants, once the capital of Lusatia, but since 1814 given to Prussia, and included in Silesia. In the carriage was an old gentleman in magnificent furs, with his wife; after a few words in German he began to talk English, said he was going back to Dresden, and if I was going back too, he wished I would call on him there; that he was H. M. Consul-General at Leipsic, and a member of the Upper House, now sitting at Dresden. He gave me his card, and it was Baron Tauchnitz, the man who has made his forture by the Tauchnitz editions![1] He seemed really much interested when he found out who I was, and I am going to see him.

Text. Russell, 2:360–61.

1. Christian Bernhard Tauchnitz (1816–1895; cr. baron 1860), German printer and publisher, whose Library of British and American Authors, cheap paper reprints (begun in 1841), was for many years the staple reading fare of English-speaking travelers on the continent (*Men of the Time*, 1884; Simon Nowell-Smith, "Firma Tauchnitz, 1837–1900," *Book Collector*, 15 [Winter 1966]: 423–36—adapted from Tennyson, 2:246n). See below, letter to Tauchnitz of Aug. 10, 1887.

To Charles J. Leaf*

Berlin

My dear Leaf   December 18, 1885

I was very glad to get your letter here, and we will certainly dine with you on Christmas Day. It is delightful to be looking homewards again; and I shall think it an excellent employment for Sunday to spend it in travelling to Cologne. I have the excuse that it is a day on which schools cannot be seen, and I am so pressed for time that I must give to schools every day I can. What I have seen is most interesting and instructive, and the German schools deserve all the praises given to them. I am never tired of attending the lessons in general, but they make me hear too much music. I send you, for Mrs Leaf, the programme of a School-music by which I am to be victimised from ten to twelve tomorrow morning. Walter will be interested in hearing that I had more than half an hour's talk with Mommsen this morning; he is quite white, and older than I expected;—in manner, mode of speech, and intellectual quality something between Voltaire and Newman. I believe I am to see the great Reichs Kanzler tomorrow, but I do not like to say so before the interview really comes off. He is almost inaccessible, but the Crown Princess herself asked him to receive me, and I hear he has consented. I shall hear tonight at the Crown Princess's, where I am going to a "small" tea at nine o'clock. She has been most extremely and markedly kind to me. I very much like the Crown Prince also—and the girls. I am getting to speak German much better than I did at first, but in the "higher circles" almost every one speaks English, so one does not get practice enough; Prince Bismarck transacts all his business with our Ambassador in English. Now I must stop, and go about school business. I have asked all the Americans I meet about Farrar; they had generally been going to hear him. I am glad his visit has been so successful. My love to Mrs Leaf and Walter.   Ever yours affectionately,

Matthew Arnold.

Text. Russell, 2:361–62.

To Frances Bunsen Trevenen Whately Arnold*

Cologne

My dearest Fan   December 21, 1885

Your letter was sent to Munich, where I have not yet been, and was then sent back to Berlin where it reached me just as I was starting on my return to England. I have had a very good time and no ailment except a few hours' face-ache off and on. What I have seen has interested me very much, and makes me wish to see more. Today here I have in the morning seen the Vicar of the Cathedral and the Archbishop, and have passed the afternoon in a free school for poor Catholics. Since that I have dined, and am now really going to start for home, which is delightful. I had meant to sleep at Brussels tomorrow night, but I see no reason for wasting time in doing so, and therefore, though I hate sleeping carriages, I am going to try one once more, and to travel straight through from here to England. I hope to be in London soon after 5 tomorrow afternoon, and at Cobham in time for dinner. This is my last letter, if all goes well, from abroad. I have telegraphed to Fanny Lucy to say I hope to arrive tomorrow evening. My three days in Berlin were very interesting; I saw the Education Minister, Herr von Gossler, who gave me an account of what was going to happen as to free schooling in Prussia quite different from what every one else had given me; I can only suppose that Prince Bismarck has made up his mind that so it shall be, and if he has made up his mind that so it shall be, so it probably will be. He has promised to see me, but his son, Count Herbert de Bismarck, told me he was quite laid up with a varicose vein which has gone wrong, and could not see me till Wednesday or Thursday; I could not wait for that, so I must take Berlin on my way to Munich in February. I was at a small party at the Crown Prince's on Friday, where I met Count Herbert de B. The Crown Princess had herself asked her father to see me. She has been quite charming to me, and the Crown Prince also. But what has touched me most has been the devotion of the smart young men at the Embassy. Two of them came to the station to see me off yesterday; and they have all been sweeter than I can say. The weather is splendid, though cold; it is something to cross, as I did yesterday, in one day, two such rivers as the Elbe and the Rhine. I have just been dining in the very same coffee-room where you and I were together, and I thought of you and of our journey. I am getting on wonderfully with German; I talked it today to the Archbishop, who speaks neither English nor French. What a move is this of Gladstone's in the Irish matter[1] and what apprehensions it gives one! In what in the sphere of high politics, has he ever really succeeded?   Your ever affectionate

M. A.—

MS. Balliol College.

  1. "Proposing to give the Irish a Parliament" (see the next letter).

To Mountstuart Elphinstone Grant Duff

Cobham, Surrey

My dear Grant Duff December 24, 1885

  I have so often in the last few weeks been wishing to write to you, that I must at any rate give effect to the wish now that I am returned home and have a few days' leisure. I was quite unexpectedly asked by Lord Cranbrook at the beginning of November to go abroad and find out what was really the case as to free schooling for the working classes in Germany France and Switzerland. It is twenty years exactly since I went on my last school mission abroad, and I never expected to go on another. However, I accepted the proposal with the greatest pleasure; because I know what opportunities for seeing and learning one has on a journey of this kind. I went straight to Berlin and had a very good time there. The growth of the place in size wealth and splendour in the last twenty years is wonderful. In a cultivated society they are still, surely, very inferior to London and Paris; the professors are specialists, and above them are the officers and the Court, forming "society" strictly so called; but where is there anything like what one finds in London, and what I hope to find still in Paris also, changed as Paris is, when I go there in the latter part of next month? The one person with whom one felt in real sympathy in Berlin was the Crown Princess, your friend; I had never done her justice before, and I still think that in London she is comparatively stiff and uneasy; but in Berlin she is quite charming. I saw a great deal of her, and she was, as I have said, the one person with whom one could talk freely on subjects that interest one. She was kindness itself, and ended by herself asking Bismarck, who now is almost inaccesible, to receive me. He is at present laid up by a varicose vein which has gone wrong, but he has promised to receive me in February, when I shall again be in Berlin. I have returned home for Christmas, because all schools are shut for the Christmas fortnight, so I seized the opportunity to come home. Can all Prussia produce such a golden holly as stands on my lawn here? However they have produced Bismarck instead of producing Gladstone, and that is something in their favour. I was lucky enough to hear Bismarck in the Reichstag on Catholic missions; it was a duel between him and Windthorst; each of them spoke three times; very interesting. Windthorst is as good a debater as I ever heard; Bismarck has all the faults of a bad, untrained speaker; holds himself ill, keeps his head down, does not speak out, makes awkward little pokes with his hands; but the authority of the man, and the weight with which he speaks, make up for every thing. At Munich I shall see Döllinger;[1] at Dresden I saw (by the Crown Princess's good offices) the King; at Cologne (by Manning's) the Archbishop. How dear Arthur Stanley would have enjoyed questioning one about it? And now I have come home to find Gladstone proposing to give the Irish a Parliament: a policy as bad as that of giving them provincial assemblies,—one of them, that in the north, capable of rallying all that is British in Ireland, and of holding the rest in check,—is good. Was there ever so fatal a statesman for a nation arrived at that particular stage of its development to which we are now come? But I must not fill my letter with politics. I look out of my window at a sumach, which I have just put into the ground that I may enjoy the sight of it in summer; it is the one which covers itself with tangles of delicate white-looking hairs; our nurserymen call it, why I know not, the Venice Sumach, but I have been delighted to find that both the Germans and the French call it the Peruked Sumach, and I am determined to call it by that or by the simpler name of the Wigged Sumach for the rest of my life. I hope to be at Lucerne on this school errand of mine in February, and I wonder if I shall see the first frail beginnings of spring in the vegetation—violets for instance? Write me one more letter before you come home, and tell me. Write to me at Cobham—the letter will be forwarded. I saw Mommsen at Berlin, and we agreed that the drama was not Renan's strong point;[2] but I shall be very glad to see something of him and Taine and Scherer in Paris if I can. Admiral Maxse has promised me a letter of introduction to Clemenceau: there is at least this one bond of sympathy between us, that we both of us think Victor Hugo an impostor.[3] Kindest remembrances to Mrs Grant Duff; we shall all be delighted to see you home again; and meanwhile believe me, my dear Grant Duff, yours affectionately

Matthew Arnold.—

MS. British Library Oriental and India House Collections.

1. Johann Döllinger (1799–1890: *Ency. Brit.*), German theologian and scholar, now living (and later dying) in the limbo of excommunication for his refusal to accept the dogma of papal infallibility but honored throughout Protestant christendom for his steadfast, principled stand.

2. Renan's *Drames philosophiques* (1878–86), of which the third, *Le Prêtre de Némi*, appeared in 1885.

3. Victor Hugo's death in May had been seen as an important occasion nationally and internationally: the Panthéon was secularized by decree to receive the body of a freethinker, and the "funeral fête (June 1) was one of the grandest and most important in the annals of Paris, and was described as an apotheosis, not only of Victor Hugo, but of democracy itself" (*Annual Register*, pp. 211–13).

To Alfred and David Nutt

Education Department, Whitehall

Messrs Nutt— Cobham, Surrey

Dear Sirs December 24, 1885

I have only just returned from Germany. With regard to your proposal, I must decline to belong to a Goethe Society, as I have declined also to belong to a Shakespeare Society; I find that engagements of this kind take up some of one's leisure, and I have so very little that I must protect that little as carefully as I can. Your faithful servant,

Matthew Arnold.—

MS. Yale University.

To Reginald Bosworth Smith

Education Department, Whitehall

Cobham, Surrey

Dear Mr Bosworth Smith   December 26, 1885

I am just returned, though for a week or two only. I saw the Times in Germany, and I did not miss one of your letters; you are right in thinking that I found myself, generally, in cordial agreement with them. Many thanks for sending them to me in this pamphlet form.[1]

With every good wish to you and yours, I am always   yours sincerely,

Matthew Arnold.—

MS. *University of Virginia.*

1. He published five letters in *The Times* on disestablishment (Oct. 15, 20, Nov. 4, 20, all on p. 13, and Dec. 15, p. 10) and then collected them in a pamphlet, "Reasons of a Layman and a Liberal for Opposing Disestablishment."

To Frances Bunsen Trevenen Whately Arnold*

Cobham

My dearest Fan   December 27, [1885]

I got your letter from Bristol, and now we have heard from you after your arrival at Torquay. You are excellent in writing: I believe Flu has acknowledged your letter, but I write a hasty note myself to send my love to dearest K and to tell her how full my thoughts are of her and her dear invalid. It looks as if the mischief were really in the liver and this must be a slow business. The Pendletons at Berlin (he is American Minister there) were full of the praises of Dr Huxley at Torquay—of his skill and of his kindness. *She* was a very nice woman indeed; ask him if he remembers her. Ask my K if she got a letter from me from abroad; but of course she did. She must not trouble herself about writing to me now; we shall hear from you. I am greatly tempted to run down myself for a day or two before I go abroad again; but I doubt whether William is not better without me. We have the dear Dicks here, which is very pleasant, and it is uncertain how long they may stay; if it turns cold and there is skating I should not wonder if he takes a fortnight of his leave and they stay till we go to Paris. The Combes have a Fancy Dress Ball on the 19th of January, and Nelly would like to stay for it: between this and that there are four or five other balls, but I shall go to none of them and am ready to start again anytime after the 12th, when the schools will be in operation once more. My work is unusually interesting because it enables me to see and hear so many of the rank and file instead of merely the chiefs, who are all that a foreigner on a mission usually comes in contact with. If I only saw the Minister in Berlin I should report that a system of free schools would certainly be adopted throughout Prussia very shortly; as it is, I very much doubt whether it will be. But the question is being discussed throughout Germany—and this—with the great excellence of the schools—makes it so interesting to be there on an errand like mine. It is odd that while in this extraordinary England no one seems to think of connecting the elementary school question with the question of intermediate schools, though the case is ten thousand times stronger here than there, in Germany the constantly heard argument is: Why is it harder on an artisan with £50 a year to pay 4s/ a year for his son's schooling than on an officer or functionary with £150 or £L200 a year to pay 40s/ a year for his? Lucky country, we might say, where the officer or functionary can get first rate schooling for his son for 40s/ a year, whatever may be done as to relieving other classes! I suppose if they have a Royal Commission that will at any rate give time for the question to be considered, and Chamberlain and his company will not be able to rush free schools in a session.[1] I must stop; we have four turkeys sent us, and how we should like your help in eating them! The Whitridges have sent us a barrel of Blue Point oysters—but those you don't care about.   Your ever affectionate

M. A.—

MS. Balliol College.

1. Joseph Chamberlain (1836–1914: *DNB*), always strong in educational matters and now between Gladstone's second and third cabinets, had been elected Member for West Birmingham on Nov. 24.

To Lucy Charlotte Arnold Whitridge

Cobham

My darling child   December 28, 1885

I had your sweet letter on my birthday: it arrived a day or two before, but Mamma kept it till then. Then as I was dressing on the morning of Christmas Day, your birthday, Mamma brought me your telegram; I wrote the answer at once, and it was pleasant to think that we were thus exchanging greetings within the limits of a few hours. My precious, darling child! And now, today, Nelly has a letter from you, but I am sorry to hear you do not give a very good account of yourself. Keep up your spirits and be careful not to catch cold; these are my two exhortations to you. There are so many difficulties about Mamma's coming over in May and our following her in

October that I think you will very likely see us all in May: at any rate Mamma and Nelly, and I, if I cannot get my foreign report finished in time to come with them, might come a month later, when I hope your affair would be happily over. Then in August we might all return together, to spend in England Fred's holiday. This involves giving up my lecturing, but the notion of a second lecturing tour becomes more and more disagreeable to me, and perhaps, even in the summer months one or two lectures in the very largest towns might be arranged for me, as they were for Huxley, which would pay our expenses without my having the fatigue of a campaign. I should like, too, to see America in summer this time, after having before seen it in winter. Then I should return home to be free from my inspectorship and to try and get one or two literary schemes accomplished—much more to my taste than lecturing. I very much liked Mrs Pendleton in Berlin, and I hope you will make acquaintance with her son in New York. My teacher was a Dr Stadt-hagen;[1] he had never taught Fred, but had met him, and remembered him. I returned to Berlin from Dresden, and had another party at the Crown Prince's; very grand, and the Crown Prince and Princess charming, but the whole thing very dull and formal. Mamma will have told you that the Crown Princess has herself asked Bismarck (who keeps himself very much shut up) to see me, and he has promised that he will; but when I left Berlin he was confined to his room with a bad leg; his son, Count Herbert, told me I must come back in February, on my way to or from Munich, and it should then be managed. At Cologne I saw the Archbishop, a tall sweet-looking old man; his palace was full of Christmas decorations, and so was the square before the Cathedral; fir-trees for Christmas Eve (that is the great time and not the Day itself) were really everywhere. I had a foggy but quite calm passage home; here they have had ten degrees or so of frost but nothing like what we have had in Germany; and when one looks at the evergreens on our lawn here, one feels what the superiority of climate is. Today it is quite mild, with the thermometer at 45. Our Lambart cousin has appeared with an invitation from the Bretts at Esher to meet the new Lord Esher (Balliol Brett); we are asked to a private dinner on Sunday and a public one on Monday; we shall go to the Sunday one, as on Monday there will be speaking.—Tonight we dine with the G. Smiths, all five of us; on Saturday we went all five to the Buxtons to see them give the "Critic"; it was really very amusing—Sydney Buxton, Sybil, and Arthur Butler (the blond man in the Council Office) being particularly good. Tomorrow I am going up to see Cumin and to arrange about my return to the Continent; I expect to have to go on to Vienna from Munich, and to be not less than two months away. On Wednesday Mamma has her Mothers' tea, and we dine afterwards with Lady Ellesmere. Then we have private views at the Grosvenor and the Royal Academy,

a marriage at the house of Millais, and three or four balls in this neighbourhood, ending with a fancy dress one at the Combes'; the Dicks want also to
go to Faust, and I suppose I shall have to ask Irving. I saw capital notices both
of his Olivia and of his Faust in the Indépendance Belge, when I was abroad.
I was at the theatre constantly; the Dresden one is so beautiful that it is a
pleasure to sit in it. I saw one very good comedy, and I was interested in
Siegfried,[2] the story and libretto are so fine. You may imagine how I thought
of you, my darling, in all my theatre going abroad, and how we talk of you
at this season now I am home again. My love to Fred, and do not make things
bad for him by fretting and being nervous; May will soon be here. The dear
men send their love; they have been out with Nelly and me to the stump
where Mike sinned. Always, my precious child,   your own fondly loving,

Papa—

Not good accounts from Torquay—Florence, on the other hand, is doing
very well.[3]

MS. Frederick Whitridge.

1. Unidentified.
2. Wagner's *Siegfried* (1876), an unexpected choice with startling (nonmusical)
reasons.
3. Not clear. Torquay refers to Mrs. Pendleton (see letter preceding); Florence
O'Brien was his niece, formerly Arnold-Forster.

To Edmund William Gosse

Cobham, Surrey

My dear Gosse   December 30, 1885

I have been abroad to make some enquiries for the Government about
School matters; I am going abroad again immediately, and meanwhile I have
had my accumulated letters sent to me here, but not yet books and parcels.
Thank you for what you have sent me; I shall no doubt find it here on my
return at Easter; and meanwhile I am very certain that of nothing said about
me by you shall I have either any right or any disposition to complain.[1]
Most truly yours,

Matthew Arnold.—

MS. Brotherton Collection.

1. Gosse, now Clark lecturer at Cambridge, published his lectures in *From Shake-*
speare to Pope, the book that, about a year later, incited the wrath of John Churton Collins
and blighted Gosse's career.

To Arthur H. Galton

Cobham, Surrey

My dear Galton,   January 1, 1886

I have been abroad for some time on a school-errand from the Government; and on my return I find your letter, verses, and ivy—also the charming photographs of the two dogs. We ourselves have two, and that must suffice us; but if we outlive either of them, his place could not be better filled than by a child of your fascinating Pair.

The merit of the verses is in the firm effort to have and express a definite meaning. I like best the Mercury Sonnet because this effort is there, perhaps, most successful. It would have been more entirely successful still, to my thinking, if you had brought out *on what errands* you conceived Mercury as visitng both the Under-World and this World of ours. Exercise in verse cannot but be valuable to you if you set yourself to be thus distinct; and if you can really succeed in being distinct, with your serious purpose and command of language, you are sure to interest others.

I wish you a happy New Year: I am returning to the Continent almost immediately and shall then have to face a second expedition to America; after that, I hope to have a quiet time, but at present this seems very far off. Ever yours truly,

Matthew Arnold.

Text. Arthur H. Galton, Two Essays upon Matthew Arnold, with Some of His Letters to the Author, *pp. 105–6.*

To Messrs Black

Messrs Black   Cobham, Surrey

Dear Sirs   January 2, 1886

On my return from abroad the other day I found the proof of my *Ste Beuve* here without the manuscript, and wrote to ask for the manuscript. I have not received it, but have received a post-card from you asking for the corrected proof. Be good enough to send me the manuscript; if it has not been kept, I must of course correct the proof without it, but this will be very inconvenient.   Your faithful servant,

Matthew Arnold.—

MS. State Historical Society of Iowa.

To Anthony John Mundella

Pains Hill Cottage, Cobham, Surrey

My dear Mundella   January 3, 1886

One line to say that the Holloway Candidate is not Hastings but Hastings *Crossley*—a brother to the maker of the Otto Gas Engine, at Manchester.[1]

I have had a note today from Goschen which ends with a sentence looking very much as if he were going to take office. We shall know tomorrow, I suppose. I am sure Ld Hartington's taking it would have impaired the majority; perhaps Goschen's will not.[2]   Ever cordially yours

Matthew Arnold.—

MS. Sheffield University.

1. Crossley has not been identified.
2. In the event, Salisbury's government fell and Gladstone's arose.

To Archibald Philip Primrose Earl of Rosebery

Cobham, Surrey

My dear Lord Rosebery   January 3, 1886

How very kind it was of you to take the trouble of writing to Sir Edward Malet about my seeing the great Bismarck! If I had known what I was asking, I should never have troubled you. I find he is, as you say, almost inaccessible. I begged Sir E. Malet, who does not know him well, not to make an attempt which I saw it would embarrass him to make; but meanwhile you had been so good (for so I imagine from what he said to me) as to mention it to Count Herbert Bismarck also; the Crown Princess, without my asking her, had mentioned it to the great man himself; the result of all this being that he has promised to see me when I go back to Berlin in February. He is so interesting a personage that I should go back there if it were only for the sake of this interview. I heard him speak, and he does not speak well—how unlike Gladstone! but then on the other hand how unlike is the sagacious mind, going from success to success, to the fertile tongue, going from failure to failure! And now if there are three unwise things to do in Ireland, they are these: to merge Ulster, to withhold full powers of local government while conceding it in name, and to resort to guarantees from Parnell; and there seems reason to fear that your great leader has all three of them in contemplation. Why did you not teach him better when you had him at Dalmeny?[1]

But this is to be a letter of thanks and not of troublesome questions. I feel very grateful to you indeed; and if I do not at once send the complete edition of Poems, it is because I am not yet perfectly clear as to whether they ought to go to Lady Rosebery or to yourself. But meanwhile will you let me give you Culture & Anarchy?—a slight work, but simple and true. I go abroad again on the 21st.   Ever most sincerely yours,

Matthew Arnold.—

MS. National Library of Scotland.

    1. Dalmeny Park, Edinburgh, the Rosebery seat.

To Frank Preston Stearns

Cobham, Surrey

Dear Sir   January 7, 1886

I have just had, on my return to England, your letter and Mr Wasson's paper, and must thank you for them.

Very much of what Mr Wasson says is true; yet literary style is more than he makes it—the mere dressing up of a material which may be inferior; it is itself in part the material and has an extraordinary value. No great writer is to be disposed of as your friend disposes of Addison and Swift; he says, nothing is to be learned from Swift; why, a sense for the blatant nonsense and clap trap which constitutes three-fourths of our public writing and speaking, and which is a greater curse to your country than even to ours, is to be got from him. Addison has his valuable criticism of life too; I doubt whether to a Taine, a hundred years hence, he will not seem of more importance than Emerson, who was above all things of value in his own day. But I love Emerson.   Truly yours

Matthew Arnold.—

Text. Frank Preston Stearns, Sketches from Concord and Appledore, *pp. 132–33 (facsimile).*

    1. Frank Preston Stearns (1846–1917: *DAB*), American author of books on artists and on literary subjects. He had studied literature with David Atwood Wasson (1823–1887: *Nat. Cyc.*), Unitarian clergyman (somewhat heterodox) associated for a while with Thomas Wentworth Higginson, and poet, whose "paper" ("Arnold on Emerson," reprinted from the *Christian Register*), precedes Arnold's letter in Stearns's book. His *Poems* and *Essays*, both posthumous, appeared in 1888 and 1889.

To Archibald Philip Primrose Earl of Rosebery

Cobham, Surrey

My dear Lord Rosebery   January 8, 1886

"Culture and Anarchy" must come without me, for I am drowned in documents about Prussian Schools, all requiring to be read before I am drowned under a second wave of French ones. But I shall hope to see you between my return from abroad and my start (positively for the last time) for America.   Ever sincerely yours

Matthew Arnold.—

MS. National Library of Scotland.

To Ernest Fontanès *

Pains Hill Cottage, Cobham, Surrey

Cher Monsieur et Ami   9 Janvier, 1886

Votre lettre est venue me trouver au fond de l'Allemagne, à Dresde[n]. Je ne vous ai point écrit en réponse, parce que je ne pouvais vous donner les indications que vous aviez demandées;¹ à présent, j'ai mes instructions, et je puis vous dire que nous partons pour Paris le 21 de ce mois; nous y resterons, j'espère, trois semaines. Nous descendrons à l'Hotel Romain, rue St Roch; nous amenerons nôtre fille, et tous les trois nous serons enchantés de vous serrer la main. Le plus tôt sera le mieux; il est possible que dans les premiers jours de février j'aie à m'absenter de Paris pour voir quelques écoles de campagne.

Tout ce que j'ai vu en Allemagne m'a extrêmement intéressé. Berlin n'a pas ce qu'ont Paris et Londres, une grande société agréable et cultivée. On a une cour, des fonctionnaires, des militaires, des professeurs; les professeurs ont dans leur nombre des hommes très distingués, mais ce sont des savants et des spécialistes, à l'écart du monde proprement dit, lequel reste, je le repète, plus borné, plus sec, et beaucoup moins intéressant que le monde de Londres et de Paris. Mais le très bon côte [*sic*] là-bas, le voici: tout le monde apprend son métier et le practique [*sic*] consciencieusement. Les écoles méritent parfaitement leur haute réputation. Une chose m'a singulièrement frappé dans les écoles populaires—l'instruction religieuse. Elle y occupe une grande place, elle est obligatoire, elle est très bien donnée, bien que trop dogmatique. Or, on vous dit que les deux tiers des parents, dans l'Allemagne du Nord, sont socialistes et athées; pourtant, leurs enfants sont soumis à cette forte instruction religieuse, et, [ce] qui plus est, ils paraissent la goûter. Ils en garderont certainement quelque chose; tout cela aura une action conserva-trice, et je doute fort que la révolution arrive sitôt en Allemagne, même après qu'on aura perdu Bismarck et l'Empereur Guillaume. Le vrai secret pour préparer les révolutions, c'est de former des générations de Gavroches, n'est ce pas?

Adieu, cher Monsieur et Ami; nous causerons de tout cela à Paris. Mille amitiés à Scherer—and believe me—   Affectionately yours,

Matthew Arnold.

Text. Russell, 2:366–67.

1. Arnold ought to have written (and probably did write) "Vous aviez demandées" and, a few lines below, "amènerons notre fille," then, farther along, "côté," "je le répète," "pratique," and "ce qui plus est."

To Frances Bunsen Trevenen Whately Arnold*

Cobham

My dearest Fan   January 11, 1886

It is a long time since I have written to you, but really one had no heart to write a common letter, when one was in such distress of suspense about William. Now things do really look better for the present, though I do not as a matter of presentiment, feel with you that he may go on and on to old age as a creaky invalid; I feel rather that he will either get well, or else have a return of his attacks and sink under them. But this is only a presentiment. Yesterday I skated, and the Pains Hill Lake in snow and ice was as beautiful as ever. I got on very well, and the skating did not bring on the chest pain; smooth motion does not, but laborious motion, making my way uphill or through snow. I did not skate very long, nor attempt going backwards; for Fanny Lucy arrived, and soon wanted to go home again, and as her way took her among some calves of a year old, whom she was pleased to call bisons, and she had the little dog with her, she required an escort. I enjoy my time here very much; I read five pages of Greek Anthology every day, looking out all the words I do not know; this is what I shall always understand by *education*, and it does me good and gives me great pleasure. Then I plunge into my German documents, which I must read more or less, though seeing and hearing is a great deal better. The Dicks are gone to Ted and Minnie but return today and stay till we go; he has got his leave extended. He is, as always, a sweet child in the house. The Leafs have a dance, and the Buxtons, and the Combes; also the Eastwoods whom you do not know; so there is plenty going on. This morning Eliza in calling us told me that the water was coming into my dressing room through the ceiling, the thaw having set in during the night. The water entered at a corner where the books did not matter much, being mainly, as I said to Flu profanely, "a heap of science primers which could be of real use to no mortal soul"; but the room got into a very wet state and I am not sure I have not caught a little cold from pottering about in it removing papers and books. I have been very well till now, however, all through this winter; so much clear gain! I send you a note of Rosebery's with an enquiry for William; he wrote to implore me to come to Mentmore, but I cannot, so I said I would send him "Culture & Anarchy" instead. The preface contains a prophecy which has come quite wonderfully true. If I had time I would write a last political article with the title of "The Nadir of Liberalism";[1] for all I have ever said of the Liberals calling *successes* not things which really succeed, but things which take with their friends, unite their party, embarrass their adversaries and are carried—and how very, very far this is, in politics, from true success, has proved itself to a degree beyond which we shall not, it may be hoped, pass. I send you Goschen, too, to whom the Crown Princess begged me to give a message from her; return him for Nelly wants the letter. I send you one, too, from the old Baron Carl von Canitz, a perfect dear, at whose Schloss I stayed in Silesia; he commissioned me to get him an English flask, so I sent him one as a Christmas present. The missel thrushes are flying in and out of the holly before my window, as they used to in the hollies behind Spring Cottage when Tom and I shot there fifty years ago! The birds are a delight; we have been using your Johns;[2] it is not so good as his Flowers, but still very useful and interesting. So Flo has nearly murdered a bride; it was a thrilling story; it is perhaps quite as well that Flo has taken flight. Love to my K, and the dear sick man; and Francie—how excellent Eds has been!   Your ever affectionate

M. A.—

return Rosebery as well as Goschen.

MS. Balliol College.

1. "The Nadir of Liberalism" (Super, 11:54–77), *Nineteenth Century*, 19 (May 1886): 645–63.
2. Charles Augustus Johns, *Birds of the Wood and Field* (1859–62) or *British Birds in Their Haunts* (1862) and *Flowers of the Field* (2 vols, 1853, 1878).

To The Acting Editor of the *Pall Mall Gazette*

Education Department, Whitehall

The Acting Editor of the P. M. Gazette   Cobham

My dear Sir   January 13, 1886

Lists such as Sir John Lubbock's are interesting things to look at,[1] but I feel no disposition to make one; even if I did, I should have no time, for I am buried in documents about popular education in Germany, and am going abroad again almost immediately.   Truly yours

Matthew Arnold.—

MS. British Library.

1. Lubbock's reading list for the Working Men's College (of which he was principal) prompted the *Gazette* to solicit similar lists from many prominent figures (e.g., Swinburne).

To Goldwin Smith

Pains Hill Cottage, Cobham, Surrey

My dear Goldwin Smith   January 13, 1886

I have often thought of you, but I have never answered your last letter. I have been busy, for this is my last year of inspecting, I resign in May. I shall lose two or three hundred a year, but the pension to which I become entitled in May is my full pension, I have had five and thirty years of inspecting, and I should like to retire from it before I drop. One or two things in verse which all my life I have wished to do I am now probably too old to do well; but on this point I hope the inward monitor will inform me rightly, if I make the attempt to do them. One of them is a Roman play, with Clodius, Milo, Lucretius, Cicero, Caesar in it; Arthur Stanley was always interested, dear soul, in this project: I can hear him now saying to some one: "You know he is going to bring in Cæsar and Cicero." But I am probably too old, as I said. Renan's dramas seem to me a mistake; the personages are mere masks, to utter his own epigrams; and his epigrams are better given when he writes history.

I have had an interesting six weeks in Germany; the government asked me, in this my last official year, to go and find out for them the real truth about free instruction in the schools for the people on the Continent. In a humble mission of this kind one gets a sight of local life and administration which is very interesting; people on grand political missions stay in capitals and see only swells. I heard Bismarck speak three times in one afternoon, and he has promised to receive me when I go back to Berlin in February. He speaks badly, but one contrasts his powerful character with the fertile tongue of our adored William, not to our advantage. With our William everything is possible; still his Home Rule plans I cannot believe in till he produces them. As now attributed to him they have every conceivable vice which a plan for Ireland can have: they merge Ulster in Celtic Ireland, when, in any plan for local government, it should be kept distinct as a centre of natural Englishism and loyalty; they withhold some usual powers of local government, and will thus give occasion for ever renewed complaint and agitation; and they rely on guarantees from Parnell to make them workable. Yours was an excellent little letter in the Times,[1] but you should write a longer one. Fitzjames Stephens is not worth much, though he has a style of vigour. But merely to renew the Crimes Act is poor and barren advice. There was more goodwill to England in Germany than I expected to find; much of the enmity to Gladstone there is because he is really felt to be damaging it, much of the favour to Salisbury because he is really felt to be bringing it out of the mess. I was particularly interested in what you said in your last letter to me about the Church of England: about your wish being at present for Church reform rather than Church abolition; will you let me use those sentences in print if I ever touch the subject again?[2] I have no present intention of doing so, but perhaps I may touch once more on church matters before I hold my tongue about them for ever; and with political matters the same. Do not lose sight of my Lucy on your great Continent; I think the American press, the great danger of the nation, grows worse and worse from all I can see. The Times, Standard, Post, Manchester Guardian, Leeds Mercury, Scotsman, and so on, are real causes for satisfaction here in Great Britain, and forces of conservation. But my paper is ended; my cordial remembrances to Mrs Goldwin Smith;   affectionately yours

Matthew Arnold.—

P. S. We shall probably come over in May, and return in August or September. I cannot face another lecturing tour.

MS. Cornell University.

1. Smith's letter has not been traced; Stephen's long letter ("Sir James Stephen on the Irish Question") was in *The Times*, Jan. 5, 1886, p. 12.
2. He used them in "Disestablishment in Wales" (Super, 11:341), printed in *National Review*, 11 (Mar. 1888): 1–13.

To James Rennell Rodd

Education Department, Whitehall

My dear Rodd   January 14, 1886

If the letter for Paris reaches me by this day week, it will be in time; or you can send it to me, if you like, at the Hôtel Romain, rue St Roch. I hope to be in Berlin again by the end of February or beginning of March. I cannot at all forget you; Cadogan is coming to us for a fancy ball in our neighbourhood on the 19th, and we shall talk much of the Berlin Chancery. How is Cartwright? I hope those Sirens, both the silent and the noisy one, have long since departed, and that your luncheons are such as Bp Titcomb and I can approve.[1] Does Corbett[2] go to bed in proper time? I attach great importance to this.

I shall be very glad to have the book; I had no idea it was so nearly ready.   Ever most sincerely yours

Matthew Arnold.—

P. S. Do not send the letter here, but to *Cobham, Surrey*; if you send it to England at all.

MS. Pennsylvania State University.

1. Jonathan Holt Titcomb (1819–87: *DNB*), formerly bishop of Rangoon, was now coadjutor to the bishop of London "for the supervision of the English chaplains in Northern and Central Europe, extending over ten nations."
2. Unidentified. Perhaps G. Corbett, later vice-consul at Hyères (*POLD*, 1901).

To [?George Morris] Philips[1]

Athenæum Club, Pall Mall, S. W.

Dr Philips—

My dear Sir   January 18, 1886

I hope to be in America in the spring or early summer, but if you like to send the volume here, pray do, and I will write in it.   Truly yours

Matthew Arnold.—

MS. Texas A&M University.

1. Probably George Morris Philips (1851–1920: *DAB*), normal school principal (Ph.D. 1884) Pennsylvania State Normal School, West Chester, and author of several books.

To Charles Myhill

Education Department, Whitehall

Dear Mr Myhill   January 19, 1886

For convenience sake I have told my son, who will open my letters during my absence, to forward everything official to Mr Sharpe; but you will tell Mr S. that you have the Forms 7 for tabulation.

I go to Paris on Thursday, and it is settled that I resign at the end of April; but I hope to see you before that.   Ever truly yours

Matthew Arnold.—

MS. Huntington Library.

To Thomas Humphry Ward

Education Department, Whitehall

Cobham

My dear Humphry   January 19, [1886]

On Sunday I had thought of writing to offer myself to Mary for luncheon yesterday, but the doubt as to when I might be wanted at the office prevented me. I much wished to see you both.

We start for Paris by the 11 o.c. train from Charing Cross on Thursday morning. Shall I go and see Blowitz?[1] From Paris I return to Germany.

I have not yet read my Amiel;[2] I see there is a Mlle Vadier who ought to be read with him. I shall again take him with me; at the end of April I positively resign, and shall regain my liberty—but how late in life, alas, how far, far too late!

I will undertake the Education sketch on two conditions:[3] one, that you never ask me to do anything for any of these infernal compilations again; the other, that I am not expected to begin upon it until I return from America in the autumn. We go there in May, and return, I hope, in September at latest.

I am longing to write a last political article on "The Nadir of Liberalism," which we have now, I think, pretty well reached; but that too, like other things, must wait.

Love to my dear Mary, and believe me,   affectionately yours,

Matthew Arnold.—

MS. Yale University.

1. Henri Georges Stephan Adolphe de Blowitz (1825–1903: *Ency. Brit.*), naturalized Frenchman (born in Bohemia), well-educated and enterprising journalist, was chief Paris correspondent of *The Times*.

2. Mrs Humphry Ward's edition of *Amiel's Journal. The Journal intime of Henri-Frédéric Amiel* (2 vols, 1885) and Berthe Vadier's *Henri Frédéric Amiel, Etude biographique* (Paris, 1886).

3. "Schools in the Reign of Victoria" (Super 11:210–45), in Ward's *The Reign of Victoria* (2 vols, 1887).

To Frederick Maxse

Cobham

My dear Maxse,   January 20, [1886]

A thousand thanks for the letter of introduction to Clemenceau.[1] In Paris we shall be at the Hotel St Romain, rue St Roch, and we hope by all means to see your daughter,—and yourself too, if things go well, as I hope they will, at Effingham,—in the course of our three weeks' stay.

If you could find out from Chamberlain, who I think is a friend of yours, and let me know at Paris, what is the best book on *Orchids* for a florally disposed Secretary of Legation to take with him to Rio Janerio, I should esteem it a great kindness.   Most truly yours,

Matthew Arnold.

MS. Typescript (MS. County Record Office, West Sussex, Chichester).

1. Georges Clemenceau (1841–1929), who, though he became premier only in 1906, was already at the living center of French politics as the deputy for the Var and founder of the newspaper *La Justice*.

To Louisa Lady de Rothschild

Hôtel St Romain, rue St Roch, Paris

My dear Lady de Rothschild   January 24, 1886

One of my sisters is very anxious to get her son a clerkship in the Bank of England, and has written to me here, saying that she sees the name of Rothschild among the directors, and asking if I can help her. I have not a Directory at hand here, and do not know whether it is Alfred or Leopold who is a Director of the Bank of England[1]—I do not think it is Sir Nathaniel. Whichever it is, would you mind asking them if they have, or are likely to have, a clerkship to dispose of? The boy's name is Louis Hiley, and he is 23; I like him, but he has the bad taste, as I think it, to prefer desk-work to being employed to farm and manage some land which his mother possesses. He has been in an architect's office for the last two or three years; but he will make nothing of being an architect, and is very anxious to get a clerkship in the Bank of England. There you have the whole story; I hate troubling you, but there is no one whom I approach, when I am driven to an application of this sort, with such perfect confidence of being forgiven in any case, and helped if possible.

Mrs Arnold and Nelly are with me here; we are just arrived and shall stay about three weeks. The cold is such as one only feels in Paris; but it is interesting to be here, and Nelly is sure to like it. What they have done for popular education since I was here last is wonderful, and though it is not all done in the style and taste one likes, one must be careful to do it justice. Look at an account in the last number of the R. des 2 Mondes, of a Training School for Schoolmistresses at Fontenay; I am going to see it, and wish you were coming with me; I am told the mistress (lay) is a very remarkable woman, and does marvels with those she trains. My love to your daughters when you see them, & kindest remembrances to Cyril Flower.   Ever affectionately yours

Matthew Arnold.—

The accounts of poor W. E. Forster are very unsatisfactory.

MS. Evelyn de Rothschild.

1. Alfred Charles de Rothschild (1842–1918). Hiley got the job, as we learn below on May 4, 1886.

To Henry Edward Cardinal Manning

Education Department, Whitehall

Hôtel St Romain, rue St Roch, Paris

My dear Cardinal Manning   [late January, 1886]

Your letter to the Dom. Vicar at Cologne was most useful; the Archbishop I did not find there at my first visit, but I saw him on my return and was charmed with him. I was unable to get to Oenabrüch, but perhaps I may be in North Germany again in March. Can you recommend me to any representative Catholic *here*, whose view of things I may compare with the official one? [1] I see that in the church of St Roch, close to my hotel, notices are everywhere stuck up of a complete system of *Écoles Libres* in connexion with the parish church; I should like to be enabled to see these schools and to hear from their managers how they prosper.

I think the new Commission is a strong one, and two names on it,— yours and Temple's,—I see with particular pleasure. Believe me,   most truly and gratefully yours,

Matthew Arnold.—

MS. Pierpont Morgan Library.

1. In a note scribbled at the end of the letter Manning recommended the comte de Paris and the marquis de Villeneuve, adding: "They are in opposition."

To Frederick Maxse

Hotel St Romain, rue St Roch, Paris

My dear Maxse,   February 8, 1886

I feared there could be but one end to your anxiety, your mother's age being what it was; [1] but these separations are not the less separations because they are inevitable. We are very sorry indeed not to see you here, and very sorry too, not to see your daughter Olive, with whom we were greatly taken. It was very kind of you to remember my orchid commission. Clemenceau has not come off: I left your letter with my card, and he called, but I was out; since that I have called twice without finding him at home; I daresay he is very busy. We had a very interesting evening with the Renans, and he has sent Nelly his autograph with the sentiment Heureux les jeunes!—which greatly pleases her. Tonight I dine with Lord Lyons, and the ladies go to "Zampa." [2] So John Morley has *arrived*; [3] if you had but come over here how we should have talked politics! We are here till next Sunday: then I go to Berne, and Mrs Arnold and Nelly return to Cobham.   Ever most truly yours

Matthew Arnold.

MS. Typescript (MS. County Record Office, West Sussex, Chichester).

1. Lady Caroline FitzHardinge, daughter of the fifth earl of Berkeley, died on Jan. 20. Olive Hermione was the older of Maxse's two daughters.
2. Opera by Ferdinand Hérold at the Opéra Comique.
3. His first cabinet post, chief secretary for Ireland, in Gladstone's new government.

To Percy William Bunting

The Editor of the Contemporary Review—   Paris
Dear Sir   February 10, 1886
    Your telegram finds me here, where I am conducting an enquiry about schools and school fees for the government; and until that is done and my report made, I can undertake no literary work whatever. With many thanks, I am,   Faithfully yours,

Matthew Arnold.—

MS. University of Chicago.

To John Everett Millais

                                                                  Paris
My dear Millais   February 13, 1886
    At the date you mention I shall be tossing on what the Americans call the Ocean, on my way to the United States. I would almost sooner be speaking at a public dinner, and much sooner be complying with any wish of yours—but it is impossible.
    I was in the Church at the wedding [1] (how well you all looked!) but to my great regret I could not come on to the house—I had to hurry back to

the Athenæum to receive and send telegrams about poor Forster, who at that moment was at his worst.

My kindest remembrances to all your party, and believe me,   most sincerely yours,

Matthew Arnold.—

MS. Pierpont Morgan Library.

1. Millais's third daughter, Alice Sophia Caroline, to Charles Stuart-Wortley.

To Lucy Charlotte Arnold Whitridge

Berne

My darling Lucy   February 18, 1886

Here I am, alone; I arrived yesterday and I told Mamma in my letter, which I then wrote her, that I should write to you today. I saw them off on Sunday morning at 9.40 for England, viâ Boulogne: it was a bright beautiful day, the first really fine day throughout which I have passed in Paris; the crowded state of the streets showed the change; I wished for Nelly. Her gaiety, good-humour, and pleasure in everything she saw were delightful, and acted as a cordial to my spirits, which the cold, and the bad weather, and the change in Paris itself since I used so to enjoy it, somewhat affected. Our rooms were a little gloomy, and the discomfort of Paris life, in serious cold, is intense; also the first week we saw scarcely any one and did not go much to the theatre; but Nelly was always gay. She succeeded with everyone who saw her: Marie, the concierge, came up to me after she was gone, to say how "gentille" she was, and M. Béland, our landlord, was in delight over her pretty pronunciation of French, just as the Duc de Grammont was over yours, my darling. But Nelly's accent is very correct and very pretty; it shows that Mademoiselle did something for your education, at any rate. *Both* Nelly and Mamma get along in conversation quite easily. The last week we had a dinner party at M. Taine's, and then went on to an evening party at M. Renan's; this is the sort of thing a girl of Nelly's age will always remember; she will tell you about it herself, and of our luncheon party on our last day. The last evening we dined at the Café I like best, the Café Voisin; I doubt whether I shall like Delmonico's as well; at any rate, the dinner was excellent, and we kept Nelly's birthday then instead of on Thursday, because on that day she had a bad cold; we wished for you and Fred. Sunday, my last day, was a glorious day for sunshine, as I told you, and Paris was in full beauty: I gave a breakfast at Voisin's to the dear old inspector who has been showing me about, then I let Bonnin, the coiffeur close to the Grand Hotel, cut my hair as he has been longing to do ever since he saw me; he said it was not cut à la mode de Paris; and the result is that the two feathers to which I am liable are so developed that when I see myself in the glass as I stand washing my hands before it I look for all the world like the great horned owl. Then I called on Lord Lyons, M. Victor Duruy the ex-minister, and others; then packed, dined hastily at the Hotel du Louvre, and started for Basle a little before 9 at night. I had not the slightest wish to stay on in Paris after they had left it; in fact, I was very glad to get away. It was a cold night, but I had a coupé-lit; I did not sleep much, however. We got to Basle just as morning was breaking; intensely cold, but clear, and the Jura in exquisite beauty with a powdering of snow; however, as we wound in among them a snow-fog came on, and lasted till we reached Berne about ½ past 10 A.M. Then the sun came out again. I am at the Bernerhof, one of the very best hotels in the world; and oh, the change after Paris. We have about 5 degrees of frost (27 Farenheit), not more, but this is colder than we have had it in Paris; but here we have double-windows and the whole place warmed by hot water. My bed-room, au premier, looks full south towards the Oberland mountains, and running up to the ceiling, in one corner, is a handsome terra cotta column, from which the most sweet and kindly warmth issues; a better system than the American one, with its puffs of sometimes rather stifling air from a grated hole. However, in America one is kept warm, which is the great thing. I lunched, and went to find Mr Adams, the English Minister, but he is in London. However the Chargé d'Affaires, Mr Conway Thornton,[1] turned out a perfect godsend; he went with me to the President of the Bund, and got all my business done in no time; then he took me a most beautiful walk, having first asked me to dinner at ½ past 7; he took me to a pond where the Bernese were skating, with the Great Snow mountains coming out in glory in the distance, under the evening sun. Mrs Thornton is a handsome woman, a relation of Mrs Deacon & Philip Currie; she was Miss Woodhouse. They have one dear little boy and a still dearer Dandie Dinmont whose perfect obedience is very unlike what we see at a certain cottage, Miss Lu. We had a pleasant dinner, and they want me to stay two days more and dine with them each day; but I cannot. They had a ball at 10; dressed in pink, and with an exquisite bouquet from Cannes, she looked very well. I came home to bed, and was in bed by 11, very tired. This morning I lunch with my Thorntons at 12, and start for Lucerne at ½ past 1. From there, in two days from now, I hope to go to Zurich, where I shall have to stop a week, I suppose. Then to Munich. I expect to be at home by Lady Day. Then my report; and then, early in May, I hope to be free. My darling child, how I love you and long to see your pretty face again! I shall be very glad, too, to see the States in spring and summer. My love to Fred, and I am always, always,   your own loving

Papa—

MS. Frederick Whitridge.

1. Sir F. O. Adams, C.B., K.C.M.G., Envoy Extraordinary and Minister Plenipotentiary; Charles Conway Thornton (1851–1902: Kelly, peerage), later secretary of Legation, Lisbon, married Diana Wodehouse, niece of second Baron Wodehouse.

To Frances Bunsen Trevenen Whately Arnold

Zurich

My dearest Fan   February 20, 1886

It is such a pleasure to me to get your letters, that I have every interest to write to you regularly. Write next to the Hôtel des 4 Saisons, Munich, where I hope to go on Wednesday or Thursday. I am here in a not very good hotel for Switzerland, though we should be thankful for it in England; however, their best rooms are shut up for the winter. I have a good room on the first floor, looking out on the mouth of the Limmat and the foot of the Lake of Zurich; one of the most cheerful and charming lakes in the world, studded with pretty villages on its banks; but now all the country is in snow, the thermometer is stationary at about 27, and what is worse a dull fog perpetually reigns. One has no notion of the difference between summer and winter in Switzerland until one sees it with one's eyes; there is no such difference in England. The beautiful hills which guard the town, the Zurich being to the east and the Uetliberg to the west, are quite invisible. The same frost and fog prevailed at Lucerne, perhaps the most beautifully situated place in the world; but one day towards evening the fog lifted for an hour, and one saw the great snowy range at the head of the Lake, and the incomparable outline of Pilatus over-hanging the town. I shall have a busy three days here, the schools are so many and so good. I am rejoiced to find a dear old man still alive whom I saw much of in 1865, a Professor in the University here, George von Wyss; one of the oldest of Swiss families; they trace themselves from father to son from the 14th century, and the first of the family had a grant from the first abbess of Zurich of the fishery of the Lake: she was the daughter of Louis the German, in the 9th century. He is a charming old man, and speaks French perfectly, his wife having come from French Switzerland. I have many other acquaintances here, and have just been dining with one of them, Mr Wunderlig von Muralt, the largest manufacturer on the Continent; he employs 2,700 men. He has a house of his own, not an apartment merely, and his wife is a very nice person also; both of them speak English quite well. They have asked me to dine with them every day while I am here; but the Zurich dinner hour is 12 o'clock. They eat a large meal then, and have tea at about 6 o'clock; I do not make out that they eat much supper, but at 9 they smoke and drink Rhine wine and then they go to bed. I lunch at the 12 o'clock table d'hote, and then have a potage and one thing—mutton cutlet or beef steak—about 8. I have been put down at the Museum, a Reading Room of the very best kind, with all the French and English periodicals and papers, and fine well-warmed rooms to read them in; it is a great consolation in the evening hours, but it closes at ½ past 9; by 10 every one is in bed. The trees are a great pleasure—such lime trees I never saw before, and avenues of them everywhere; then the planes are very fine too, and the ashes, and the walnuts. The hedges are showing their buds, but nothing can come out in this frost; no sign of any flower whatever. I have a letter from Grant Duff, who says that at 10 in the morning he has just sent back an open carriage and ordered a shut one, the sun was so powerful! In Paris, the last day I saw old Victor Duruy, the ex-minister, who has written a good school-history of Rome; he was loud in Papa's praise, and when I went away he took my hand in both of his and said: Dîtes-vous bien que vous tenez la main d'un ami de Monsieur votre père. They have very pretty manners still, whatever may be their faults. At Lucerne Lady Anna Chandos Pole,[1] who was staying there with her daughter, asked to be introduced to me because she had met Papa and Mamma at dinner at Lady Braye's at Stanford, in her first youth, and had never forgotten it. Now I must go and see the School-President of the Canton, then to look at the papers, and then to tea with dear old George de Wyss. He is what they call here an *aristo*, but he is a perfect old dear. I will write you any number of autographs when I come to Fox How; I hope we may come in September if we live to get back from America. Your accounts of W. E. F. make me anxious; but he has weathered many attacks.   Your ever affectionate,

M. A.—

Don't forget to write to Munich. I shall be there ten days, probably.

MS. Formerly, Mrs. Harry Forsyth.

    1. Lady Anna Chandos-Pole (*née* Stanhope, daughter of the fifth earl of Harrington) in 1850 married Edward Sacheverell Chandos-Pole, who died in 1873. In their thirteen years together, she bore six daughters (and five sons). Maria Verney-Cave, Baroness Braye, of Stanford Hall, Rugby, died unmarried in 1879.

To Frances Lucy Wightman Arnold*

Hotel des Quatre Saisons, Munich
February 26, 1886

    I was not entirely comfortable at the Bellevue at Zurich, and never was I thoroughly warm there except once in a café; but the schools were very good, and there are some thoroughly nice people there. After writing to you I went to dine (half-past twelve) with the Wunderlys; an excellent dinner, and he produced real Johannisberg. Then I drove over the slopes of the mountain behind Zurich to Wytikon, a small village; the sun came out, and there were beautiful gleams of the lake, but far too much mist still. I took the school by surprise, and anything more creditable to Canton Zurich you cannot conceive. I had sent back the carriage, and the schoolmaster walked back to Zurich with me, three or four miles, but downhill; his parents live in Zurich, and he was going in to some choir singing. Then I had a long visit from dear old George de Wyss, and then an evening school; then a light supper, packed, and to bed. My bill was very reasonable; at the rate of hardly more than eighteen francs a day. I started by the ten o'clock express yesterday morning for Munich; they call it an express, but it never goes far without stopping, or fast, except for the last thirty miles before Munich. Snow covers the whole face of the land both here and in Switzerland. At Romershorn we took boat, as you and I and darling Tommy did; there was sun, but such fog that we lost sight of the Swiss side directly, and did not see the German side till we were close to it; then, however, we had a fine but dim view of the nearer Von Arlberg mountains, and Lindau, our port, came out well. I lunched on board, the only occupant of the cabin—luncheon cheap. At Lindau I got a beautiful coupé to myself; and indeed from Zurich to Munich I never had any one with me in the carriage. So I read and looked out of [the] window, and was not disturbed by tobacco smoke. I think we went with Tommy to Friedrichshafer for Ulm; but surely you have been with me on the Lindau and Kempten line? As we passed the beautiful little lake (all frozen now and besnowed) of Immerstadt, I fancied I had seen it with you; I have been there myself certainly. It got clearer, but still snow everywhere, and the stiff small pines sticking up out of the snow like Noah's ark trees; I had a day of blessed rest, however, after all my schools.

Text. Russell, 2:369–71.

To Frances Lucy Wightman Arnold*

Munich
Sunday, February 28, 1886

Your announcement of dear Lola's death did indeed give me a pang. I have just been reading your letter again. You tell it beautifully, just all that I should naturally want to know; and all you have done is exactly right, and as I could wish. Perhaps we might have kept a mèche of her hair where it used to come over her forehead, but I should have hated mangling her to take her hoof off, and should not have cared for having it when it was done. You have buried her just in the right place, and I shall often stand by the thorn-tree and think of her. I could indeed say, "Let my last end be like hers!" for her death must have been easy, though I am grieved to hear of her being so wasted and short-breathed. When I was at home at Christmas, I thought she was much as before, and she always liked her apples. I am glad Nelly went to see her. How glad I am, too, that we resisted all proposals to "put her away." How small has been the trouble and expense of keeping her this last year, and how far different is the feeling about her death now from what it would have been if we had put an end to her. There was something in her character which I particularly liked and admired, and I shall never forget her, dear little thing! The tears come into my eyes as I write.

Text. Russell, 2:371–72.

To Frances Bunsen Trevenen Whately Arnold*

Munich

My dearest Fan   March 1, 1886

"It is the first mild day of March" says Wordsworth,[1] and the line has been running in my head for the last fortnight, in the hope that it might come true. But alas, yesterday was grim and cloudy, and snow fell; the snow had disappeared when we entered the Bavarian plain, having accompanied one all through Switzerland; now this morning all the ground is white again and it is piercingly cold. But I have a delightful room in an excellent hotel; a two windowed room, thoroughly well furnished and turned to the south; the stove and the sun together keep it warm all day, though the stove is only lighted for an hour or two in the morning.

These white porcelain stoves, burning wood, are charming things; they look well in a room and throw out heat all round them. I was delighted to get your letter on my arrival here on Thursday night; I left Zurich after a profitable five days as far as schools were concerned, but the fog was provoking, as I knew what a landscape it concealed. However, on my last afternoon I went in a carriage over the spurs of the Zurichberg, to see a village school; and the sun did at last come out and I had fine glimpses of the lake; but not for a moment did I see the high Alps. My great pleasure in Switzerland this time has been from the trees; I had not remembered they were so fine, the planes and limes especially; both of these trees I delight in. On Thursday I travelled in fog and reached Romanshorn in fog, though the sun shone nevertheless, and the morning was thus enlivened; but we lost sight of Romanshorn almost the moment [we] had started on the lake of Constance. I was the sole passenger but one. On the German side things were better; Lindau came out beautifully, and the line of the lower Alps was visible; but when we started in the railroad to Munich snow lay even heavier than in Switzerland, and remained till we had quitted the mountains. I had not been here for thirty five years; it is a beautiful place though I remember I then thought it rather dull, but perhaps I now look tenderly on everything South German I have such a liking for it, and the people are so kindly and seemingly also so happy. There is no English minister here now, only a chargé d'affaires, Mr Victor Drummond, married to a good looking American girl;[2] they are only lately come here and are living at a hotel, so cannot entertain, though they are very hospitable in asking me to lunch and sup with them at their hotel. I find here Lady Blennerhassett, who is a Bavarian; she is staying with her mother, and would be a great resource if I were here longer and not so much occupied with schools. Then I have paid a long visit to Döllinger, whom I was interested in seeing; he is 84 years old, but his hair is still brown and his tall thin figure erect. I have also visited two other professors to whom Morier[3] gave me letters, besides the Ministers and officials who are very civil. The real concern which people in Switzerland and here show about English affairs, and the critical period on which we seem to be entering is remarkable; and is evidently not the affected and mortifying concern of enemies, but the true concern of those who at bottom like England and think her a great and useful force in the world. The schools are interesting from its being here a Catholic country in which the Protestants are treated with absolute fairness; whatever is done for the Catholics is done for them also. I go a great deal to the theatres, the acting is so good; and besides, it is a great help to one's German; to one's understanding it when spoken, which is quite as great a difficulty as speaking it. But my evening has often to be devoted to schools or classes: tonight I am going to a class for young men. I hope to get home by Lady Day at latest; so the beginning of March enables me to say that before the month ends I shall have done. Write to the Kaiserhof at Berlin, where I hope to be on Sunday. Continue to give me accounts of the family and believe me,   your ever affectionate

                                                                              M. A.

MS. Balliol College.

   1. "To My Sister," l. 1.
   2. Victor Arthur Wellington Drummond (1833–1907: *WWW*; K.C.M.G. 1903), chargé d'affaires to the king of Bavaria 1885–90, later minister at Munich and Stuttgart; his wife was the former Elizabeth Lamson of New York (*Landed*).
   3. Russell (unaccountably) prints "Bruce."

To Frances Lucy Wightman Arnold*

Munich
March 4, 1886

I have been kept so late at one of these one o'clock dinners that I must write hurriedly to save the post. I almost hoped for a letter this morning; if not, I shall have to wait till Dresden. After getting this, you will write to the Kaiserhof at Berlin. The day before yesterday, after sending my letter, I walked about a little and then went to the opera to see *Tristram and Iseult*. I may say that I have managed the story better than Wagner. The second act is interminable, and without any action. The hero and the heroine sit on a sofa and sing to one another about light and darkness, and their connexion with love. The theatre was a brilliant sight, and the *prima donna* is a handsome woman with some sweet notes in her voice; but at the end of the second act, at about half-past ten, the piece having begun at half-past six, I was quite worn out and came away. The third act is better, I imagine.[1] But even in that, less is made of the story than might be made. I had a long and interesting visit from dear old Döllinger that afternoon, and am now going to pay him a farewell visit.

Text. Russell, 2:373–74.

1. Arnold's editor is embarrassed to print these comments on *Tristan und Isolde!*

To Eleanor Mary Caroline Arnold

Nuremberg
March 6, 1886

My precious Nelly

Blinding snow and a baddish inn, at least by comparison with the Munich one—but the town is one of the most interesting I have ever seen. I think Carcassone for the Middle Age of Knights and Crusaders, and Nuremberg for that of Burghers and Guilds, are the most perfect things imaginable. The outside decoration of the houses is all preserved, and of the churches likewise; every image seems in its place; and you cannot go a yard without finding a house with a statue or a decorated projecting window that compels you to stand still and get the snow down your neck while you look at it. I got your letter (short) in the afternoon of my last day at Munich; it was bright but very cold. In fear and trembling I dressed (for I have not worn my thin evening clothes since I left Paris) and went to have supper with Lady Blennerhassett; the apartment which her mother has is a very fine one, full of rare things, but in the way of china mostly, which I do not care for. Lady Blennerhassett is very clever, sympathetic, a very pleasant woman to pass an hour with. She tells every one that I am married to a *sehr ausgezeichnete frau*,[1] which I leave you and mamma to translate. Yesterday the morning was fine and cold; I packed and left Munich for this place at twelve. The journeys are long, the trains go so slow; we did not get here till eight in the evening. We crossed the Danube at Ingoldstadt, which I think is a place mentioned by Dugald Dalgetty;[2] Gustavus Adolphus besieged it, and Tilly was mortally wounded in the siege. The Danube was magnificent, of a pale yellow colour, sweeping along. We passed some interesting places, the castles of Pappenheim particularly; and I was in great comfort, having the carriage to myself all day. This hotel has many picturesque bits, but is rather ratty; the cooking not very good, and the beds of the true German kind; a sheet and one coloured blanket over you, not wide enough to tuck in at the sides; and then a great feather bed on the top of you. The cold is so great that use it you must, but I hate it. This morning when I woke the snow was coming down merrily; but when I went out after breakfast I was in amazement, as I told you, at the beauty of the place. I had letters for the Mayor, and for the Director of the Museum; I called on both; the Mayor showed me all over the Town Hall, and I saw a marriage, a civil marriage, they were going to church afterwards; I never saw one before; it was very decorous. Then I drove to the Museum to call on the director, and arranged to go and see the pictures tomorrow morning before I start for Dresden. I walked back, and oh, Miss Nelly, what do you think I saw in one of the open places—the darling himself, the same colour, the same sex, the same age, the same size, the same slow and melancholy way; his eyes were yellower than Max's, that was the only difference. The extraordinary and more than natural crook of one foreleg was the same. He looked at me wistfully, as if to say: "I know you, but we must not speak here." But what makes it almost miraculous is that a minute afterwards Kai ran out from a passage and there they were both together. If you had seen them at Cobham you would not have doubted for an instant that they were our pair. I have seen Max again this afternoon rather pleased with the snow, Miss Nelly; I again had that weird look from him, as if to say that we were in a dream, and must dream on. The Mayor sent his secretary, a charming young man, to show me all over the place; without him I could never have done it in the time. What churches I have seen, what fountains, what painted glass, what statues, what house fronts! I have been over Albert Durer's house, where that great and sad artist worked and died; I have been over the old Burg, the nucleus of the town, the first possession of the Prussian royal family; they were the burgraves of Nuremberg, and the Emperor gave them Brandenburg, the province where Berlin now stands, in the year of the battle of Agincourt. The snow fell endlessly, and the streets are deep; how I shall get through the Saxon hills in the train tomorrow I don't know. But I plunged on up hill and down dale, and have been well repaid; oddly enough, heavy as the walking was, I have not had my pain at all today. It is now between six and seven, and quite dark: I shall not go out again, the snow is so bad. Always your loving

Papa

After getting this (if it penetrates the snow) write to Berlin.

Text. Russell, 2:374–77.

1. A very distinguished lady.
2. In Scott's novel *A Legend of Montrose*, ch. 22 (the sole reference to Ingolstadt!).

To James Rennell Rodd

Dresden

My dear Rodd   March 8, 1886

I hope to be in Berlin tomorrow afternoon, but only for two or three days; however, it will be very pleasant to see you all again, though the time will be short. I go from Berlin straight to Hamburg, and from thence to Paris and home.

We had 11 degrees of frost (Réaumur) here last night; Corbett can calculate it, but I can't.   Ever truly yours,

Matthew Arnold.—

MS. Baring Brothers and Company Limited.

To Richard Garnett[1]

Berlin

Dear Mr Garnett   March 11, 1886

Your kind letter has just reached me here. The day is passed, or I should have been tempted by the proposal to say something about Goethe, of whom I have hardly ever spoken at any length except once, and then less directly and more negatively than I could have wished.

But I must adhere to my resolution to keep aloof from the Goethe Society and from all societies. You hardly know, perhaps, what the feeling of jealous anxiety is with which one is inclined to guard one's freedom, when at last it seems within reach, after one has been thirty five years tied and bound. I have still more promises and engagements to keep than I like to think of—and many of them not to my taste and made because I was too weak to refuse, and, being in bondage already, thought that a little more bondage could not matter—but I am determined to sin in this way no more—for the present at any rate.

Forgive this long story about my sentiments and purposes; and forgive, too, the vile writing to which the worst of steel pens has reduced me. Most truly yours

Matthew Arnold.—

MS. Bryn Mawr College.

1. Richard Garnett (1835–1906: *DNB*; *VF*, 4/11/95) was assistant keeper of printed books and superintendent of the reading room in the British Musuem 1875–90 and then became keeper of printed books, but he was also a poet, and more memorably a scholar (*Relics of Shelley*), and prose writer (*The Twilight of the Gods*).

To Frances Bunsen Trevenen Whately Arnold*

Paris

My dearest Fan   March 20, 1886

I hope this will be the last letter I shall write on the Continent this time, and I am sure you well deserve it should be to you. I have missed none of your letters; the Berlin one I got before I left Berlin, the Hamburg one (short) I got at Hamburg. I rather expected to have had one here, but perhaps it will come tomorrow. The weather changed here the day before yesterday and has become quite beautiful; but I see a storm is predicted for tomorrow, just in time for my crossing. The wind is west, and the new shoots on the euonymus, or fusain as it is called here, of which the public gardens are full, look quite springlike; so do the lilac buds; and on the grass in the Parc Monceau today I noticed a first faint show of green. But the famous horse chestnut in the Tuilleries [*sic*] gardens, which is supposed to be always in leaf on the 20th of May [*sic*], makes no sign yet. The place is quite beautiful, but I do not care to be here without Flu and Nelly who would so greatly enjoy it; if they were here, I could stay a fortnight very well; but I shall really prefer being at Cobham. After I wrote to you from Berlin I had a last and very pleasant dinner at the Crown Princess'; I sate between her and the Crown Prince, with the Princess Victoria opposite to me, whose hand I kissed, as is the Prussian custom, both at coming and going—She is a girl who interests me, though I daresay she is troublesome sometimes; they talk of marrying her to Prince Alexander of Bulgaria.[1] I went from Berlin to Hamburg, and it was almost all new to me; to the Scotch firs were added heather and broom, which I had not remarked in the stretches of pine wood in Brandenburg. Crossing the Elbe was interesting, and I am very glad to have seen Hamburg; but all the streams which pass through it were frozen and the two beautiful sheets of water which give it its character, the Inner and Outer Alster, which are generally alive with little steamers, were fields of snow with the steamers all frozen in. I had very good letters to Hamburg, and the Crown Princess had recommended me to the Ober-Búrgomeister, who has really and truly the title of "Your Magnificence." He is a charming old man; I am really quite glad to have called a man "Your Magnificence" and to have been asked to dinner by him. But I could not go because I had taken a ticket to see Wagner's Tannhauser; his stories interest me so much and his libretto is so poetically written, that I like to see his operas, though of course the music says little to me; but this being so, it is better to pay 5/ in Germany to hear him than a guinea or more (for a similar place) in London. I had a long day from Hamburg to Cologne, but at Münster (where the treaty was made which ended the Thirty Years War) we left the snow; that is, it did not prevail any more over the whole face of the land, but only lay in hollows and hedgerows. It was very cold at Cologne however; I never find myself in the coffee room at the Hotel du Nord there without thinking of you and dearest Mamma. I walked round and round the Cathedral by moonlight for about an hour, for I knew it might be a long time before I saw it again. Next morning I left Cologne for Paris; after Liège it was all knew [*sic*] to me, and the valley of the Meuse to Namur, and that of the Sambre beyond, were interesting, and in parts beautiful; but how much better Wordsworth saw the valley of the Meuse by the sort of travelling in his day! I passed Compiègne, and thought of Walter; but I did not manage to catch sight of the Palace. I came to this admirable hotel, which is as "replete with every convenience" as the poor St Romain is the contrary; but for five weeks, with a party of three, this hotel would be beyond my means. I had a pleasant dinner with Lord Lyons yesterday, and today I have lunched with Lord Edmond Fitzmaurice;[2] we are all against Gladstone's present policy, and I am glad to think it seems threatened with a check; but the mass of middle class Liberalism on which he relies, is so enthusiastically devoted to him and so ignorant, that I am not sure of his being frustrated till I see it happen. I have been all the afternoon at the Senate, where the Minister, M. Goblet,[3] made a good speech for his policy of expelling the Congreganists, and Jules Simon made a poor reply; he spoke very well the other day, however. Now I am going to dine at the table d'hôte, and afterwards go to a last theatre; at 9.40 tomorrow morning I start for Boulogne. Thanks for your enclosure about the sonnets; I wonder if I shall ever get anything more done in poetry.   Your ever affectionate

M. A.—

Write to Cobham—

MS. Balliol College.

1. Her first husband, whom she wed on Nov. 19, 1890, was Prince Adolphe William Victor of Schaumberg-Lippe.

2. Edmond Petty-Fitzmaurice (1846–1935: *DNB*; cr baron 1906), son of the fourth marquis of Lansdowne, and himself an important government figure, M.P. at various times, and on diplomatic commissions, and biographer.

3. René Goblet (1828–1905), politician, currently minister of public instruction. Jules Simon (1814–1896), author, formerly minister of public instruction and then head of the government, now a deputy (*Petit Robert*). The Congreganists are "schools belonging to religious associations" (*The Popular Education of France*, Super, 2:92).

To Clement Mansfield Ingleby[1]

Cobham, Surrey
Dear Dr Ingleby   March 24, 1886
I am at this moment resigning, and take no more part in inspectional functions. I am surprised, however, at what you say of Mr Healing, who was with me for years, and was both trusted and beloved in Westminster. I can not bring myself to the belief that in three years he has so changed as to become the sort of official you describe; however, if I remained in charge of the division, of course it would be my duty to look into a complaint against him just as much as against any other person. But, as I tell you, after five and thirty years service I have had enough of school inspections, and am resigning.   Very faithfully yours

Matthew Arnold.—

P. S. I see your letter is dated in January, but I have only just received it, having been on the Continent to make some enquiries for the government ever since the beginning of the year.

MS. Auckland Central Library.

1. Clement Mansfield Ingleby (1823–1886: *DNB*), LL. D, Cambridge, 1859, but, bored by the practice of law, became a Shakespearean critic and miscellaneous writer, vice-president and foreign secretary of the Royal Society of Literature.

To Henry Arthur Jones

Cobham, Surrey
Dear Mr Jones   March 25, 1886
I have been on the Continent upon business for the Education Department: again and again I have been interested by seeing the Silver King on the boards.[1] Now I have a report to write, and as soon as it is written, to start for a second and last visit to America; I fear I cannot have the pleasure of seeing your play till my return. Many thanks.   Very truly yours

Matthew Arnold.—

MS. Northwestern University.

1. Arnold had seen it in 1882, when it opened.

To Council Office, Education Department

[Education Department]

Inspector

C. O.   March 27, 1886

I have not yet received the Warrant for my salary for this month.

M. A.—

MS. Public Record Office, London.

To William Gordon McCabe

Cobham, Surrey

Dear Mr McCabe   March 27, 1886

Your letter I find here on my return from a tour among German schools which I undertook for the Government. Your book I have no doubt I shall find at the Athenæum; many thanks for it.[1] Come and try the Athenæum again, since you liked it, but do not come this summer, for this summer I am to pay a second and last visit to the States, and I should like to find you there. I shall make one address—about America itself—but I doubt whether at that time of year it will be possible to give it anywhere except in three or four of the great cities. But we shall see. It will go hard with me if I do not manage to set eyes on Virginia somehow—the most attractive of all the States. With kindest regards from us all, I am always   most sincerely yours

Matthew Arnold.—

P. S. I hope to sail in May

MS. University of Virginia.

1. Presumably, *Latin Reader* (1886).

To Andrew Carnegie

Cobham, Surrey

My dear Carnegie   March 29, 1886

Now that they are settled, I must not delay to communicate my American intentions to the first and kindest of my friends over there. Mrs Arnold had promised to go to Lucy for her first confinement; that event is expected in May, and as we do not wish to be separated and I shall be glad to see America in the summer (its winter I know but too well), I shall come in the forepart of this year instead of later on as I had intended. But this will make a difference as to lecturing—a difference, however, which I am not sorry for, as I had great doubts about the expediency of a second campaign. I shall give one address, and one only—"A last word about America," or something of that kind—and in the half dozen chief cities only. I think for one address of that kind, and in those places, even the month of June may be admissible; but I want you to consider the matter—especially with reference to New York—and to give me your advice. I have little doubt about Boston, at any time, and not much about Philadelphia—but I have some about New York. However, your advice will be the best possible.

Mrs Arnold and Nelly sail in the Servia on the 17th of next month. I have been abroad all the winter to get information for the Government about the payment of fees by scholars in foreign schools, and I must get my report done before I can start. I expect to start about the middle of May. I shall come by one of the North German Lloyds, as Southampton is so much more convenient for me here than Liverpool. I hate the passage, but am quite glad at the thought of seeing America and my friends there once more; it will be the last time! the effort and interruption of work and habits are too great. Lucy has a new house and insists on our all coming to her; otherwise I should have come straight to the Windsor. Shall I ever forget your reception of us there? My love to your mother, who I hope is better; indeed love from all three of us both to her and to you.   Ever yours affectionately

Matthew Arnold.—

Your turkey at Christmas was the very best wild turkey ever eaten.

MS. New York Public Library.

To George Washburn Smalley

Education Department, Whitehall

Cobham, Surrey

My dear Smalley   March 29, 1886

You like to have news of my American designs and you always make a kind use of them. Mrs Arnold has settled to go out for my daughter's confinement, so I have determined to go over now instead of in the autumn. I shall then see America in spring and summmer and shall avoid the terrible winter and avoid also the chance of a second lecture tour. We shall return in

August—the end of August; and this will be my last visit to the States; the effort and the interruption to habits and work are too great. I think I shall give one address—"A Last Word about America" in the three or four principal cities; even in June, I should think, this might be managed, but I should like to have your opinion. With such a subject it will be touch and go, but to go out there and give a single lecture on some literary subject—Shakespeare and the Musical glasses—is too devoid of actuality.

But, my dear Smalley, the man for them was and is (I said beforehand that so it would be) not I but Farrar—the man after Cyrus Field's own heart and the heart of the great American nation.[1] Still a few of them may perhaps listen to my whisperings even after his thunder.

Kindest regards to Mrs Smalley and to your daughter. Mrs Arnold sails instantly—I not till I have done my report on foreign schools—about the middle of May.   Most truly yours

Matthew Arnold.—

MS. Hillwood Museum.

1. Cyrus West Field (1819–1892: *WWWA*), merchant and promoter of the first Atlantic cable, had brought suit for libel against the younger James Gordon Bennett (1841–1918), editor of the *New York Herald*. Field was awarded £5,000 damages in the Middlesex Sheriff's court in July.

To A. Wilson

Athenæum Club, Pall Mall

Dear Sir   March 30, 1886

On my return from the Continent I find your letters and a copy of your father's poems, for which I thank you.   Faithfully yours,

Matthew Arnold.—

MS. Roger Brooks.

To Thomas Arnold

My dear Tom   April 2, [1886]

I have told Macmillan to send you the expurgated and annotated edition of my Johnson. If it is what you meant it should be, you might mention the fact to your Catholic friends. I think the Preface—which I have been re-reading—is one of the best things I have done.

I am back from abroad, where I saw very much that was interesting, and now I have my report to write. Fanny Lucy and Nelly are off today for Liverpool, and tomorrow they sail for New York in the America; Lucy got alarmed about herself and telegraphed to her Mother to come as soon as she possibly could. I shall follow them early in May; it is an unquiet life, but as I must go to America once more, I am glad I shall have the variety of spring and summer there.

If it suited you to have quarters within little more than an hour of town any time this next month, you would find them with your affectionate and fastfading brother at Cobham,

M. A.—

I could send you to the train every day. My love to Julia and Ethel. What a nice house you have got!

MS. Balliol College.

To Patrick Cumin

My dear Cumin April 2, 1886

I find on making up my accounts that I am absolutely out of pocket by my foreign journey, owing to the insufficiency of the allowance of one guinea a day for personal expenses to cover the present cost of living at the great hotels in the chief foreign capitals. When I tell you that my bedroom—a small single room on the third floor—cost me twelve francs a day at Paris, and even more—eleven marks or shillings—at Berlin, you will understand that this must be so. The Education Department no doubt proposed the guinea a day because it is the allowance to inspectors away from home here in England; and I accepted it without question for the same reason, and because I had no wish to use my mission for making money. But neither do I wish to lose money by it, and I was told by every body acquainted with these matters, when I got abroad, that the guinea a day for subsistence was too little, and was below the usual rate freely allowed by the Treasury for foreign service. Of course the greater cheapness of country inns in England, and the frequency of private hospitality, make an inspector's expenses away from home in England very much less than they are in places like Paris and Berlin. I must say I think my expenditure has been very moderate; I find that on my two former missions my allowances were much larger. As I said, however, I was very glad to go on my recent mission, and have no wish to make money by it; but if the Treasury allowed me a further half guinea for every day of absence from home, that would only just about cover the expenses which I have actually incurred. I hope you will have no objection to ask the Treasury whether this further payment may not even now, under the circumstances of the case, be allowed.[1]   Most truly yours

Matthew Arnold.—

MS. Public Record Office, London.

1. Guthrie (4:1709) records in May "Addit[iona]l foreign allowance" of £52/10. See below, letter to Cumin of Apr. 21, 1886.

To Joshua Girling Fitch

Cobham

My dear Fitch   April 3, [1886]

You have always been so kind and helpful to me, that I would assist you if I could: but I want to get off to America (whither my wife has already gone, as our daughter there is ill) the moment I can get my foreign report finished, and it will certainly, work as hard at it as I can, not be finished before the 19th of this month, when I cease to be an inspector. The Office promised, when I undertook this foreign mission, to relieve me of my work at home. I have forwarded your letter to Cumin.

My report presses me so that I tried to get off testifying before the Education Commission, but had to compound for two days.   Most truly yours,

Matthew Arnold.—

MS. New York Public Library.

To Joshua Girling Fitch

Education Department, Whitehall

Cobham

My Dear Fitch   April 8, [1886?]

I shall convey to my sister what you say of her husband.

I have telegraphed to Loring[1] to ask him to send you a ticket if he has one left; but I have only just had your letter on my return here, and am afraid the tickets may be exhausted. However you are sure to get a place.   Ever yours truly

Matthew Arnold.—

MS. Acadia University.

1. Forster died on Apr. 5. Loring, his private secretary, "who throughout his illness had been like a son to him in his devoted and thoughtful helpfulness" (Reid, 2:543),

was in charge of the arrangements for the funeral service in Westminster Abbey on Apr. 9.

To Percy William Bunting

Greenholme, Burley-in-Wharfedale, Leeds

Percy Wm Bunting Esq.

My dear Sir   April 10, [1886]

I have no intention of writing anything about Mr Forster; I should have to force myself if I were to do it, and when one forces oneself one does not do things well.   Very truly yours,

Matthew Arnold.—

MS. University of Chicago.

To George Smith

Greenholme, Burley-in-Wharfedale, Leeds

My dear G. S.   April 10, [1886]

In no case shall I write Forster's life: who will write it I do not know, but I should like you to publish it. Everything in regard to it will, however, be settled by my sister, who finds a pleasure in thinking of these things and planning them.   Yours affectionately

Matthew Arnold.—

MS. National Library of Scotland.

To Mrs William Fison

Cobham, Surrey

My dear Mrs Fison   April 12, 1886

I think I left a little oblong black Diary in my room at Greenholme. If so, will you kindly return it to me here, as it is full of Memoranda which I want.

How can I enough thank you and Mr Fison for your kind reception of me on this sad visit to Burley? I hope Mr Fison took no cold on Saturday and that both he and you are pretty well.   Most truly yours

Matthew Arnold.—

MS. Texas A&M University.

To Lady de Rothschild

                                                        Cobham, Surrey
My dear Lady de Rothschild   April 12, 1886
    I am just returned from Yorkshire. My sister is wonderful, but I think
for weeks she had given up hope, so the shock, when the end came, was
perhaps lessened. He showed wonderful patience and was perfectly clear in
mind—but I felt, when I saw him on my return from abroad at the end of
last month, that he could not recover.
    Mrs Arnold and Nelly are gone to America, as Lucy was not well and
made piteous appeals for her mother; they sailed a week ago, in horrid
weather, but I hope they are arrived by this time. I shall follow them as soon
as I can get my report written. I have often thought of you while I was seeing
the foreign schools which are the subject of it. I must not offer myself to stay
at Aston Clinton, I have no time for staying: but do let me come and lunch
with you in London some day that you are there; any day after this week. I
hope to start for New York about the middle of May. My love to the Flowers
if they are with you. Ever, dear Lady de Rothschild,   affectionately yours
                                                        Matthew Arnold.—

MS. Evelyn de Rothschild.

To Frederick James Furnivall

                    Athenæum Club, Pall Mall
Dear Mr Furnivall   April 15, [?1886]
    I am flattered by your proposal, but I leave town at the end of this week
and shall not be here again, except in the middle of the day, till the winter.
    Was there not to be some subscription to the Society? and have I paid
mine?   Faithfully yours

                                                        Matthew Arnold.—

MS. Shakespeare Birthplace Trust.

To Lady Dorothy Nevill

                                                        Cobham, Surrey
My dear Lady Dorothy   April 18, [1886]
    Wednesday is my day down here next week; and even to lunch with
you I must not desert the first swallows and the first nightingale.
    How sad that the rulers of the religious world should not better distin-
guish between their friends and their enemies! [1]

I am going once more to America for a few months, to see where my daughter has established herself in New York; then I hope to creep back into my cottage here to pass the remainder of my days.   Most truly yours,

Matthew Arnold.—

MS. New York Public Library.

1. Leichman (p. 231) calls attention to an article by Harvey Goodwin, bishop of Carlisle, "A Comment on 'A Comment on Christmas,'" *Contemporary Review*, 49 (Feb. 1886): 178–93.

To James Bryce

Athenæum Club, Pall Mall

My dear Bryce   April 19, [1886]
I have been buried in the country all this last week, and have only this moment, on coming here, had your note of the 11th.

I should have been very glad to meet Waddington, as I want to ask him some questions about French schools.   Most truly yours

Matthew Arnold.—

MS. Bodleian Library.

To Michael Field

Athenæum Club, Pall Mall

Michael Field Esq.
Dear Sir   April 19, [1886]
I am overwhelmed with school work in this my last month of service as an inspector, but the glance I have already been able to give at your drama makes me able to promise you that I will read it and expect to get pleasure from it.[1]   Truly yours

Matthew Arnold.—

MS. Bodleian Library.

1. *Brutus Ultor. A Play in Verse* (1886).

To Frances Lucy Wightman Arnold*

Cobham
My sweet Granny   Wednesday, April 21, 1886
How lucky you went when you did, and how you will be repaid. I got the telegram in the middle of dinner on Saturday, the 17th. Mary and Hum-

phry Ward were with me. Of course I am very anxious to hear again of my own darling Lucy, kiss her for me, and kiss the dear little granddaughter too. I shall hear nothing about it in the letter from you which will, I hope, reach me tomorrow, but I shall most resolutely take no news to be good news. I send you a sweet little note from Lady Ellesmere which I found here on my return from London yesterday. I shall go and see her today. I dine with the Leafs. Mrs Leaf is perfectly radiant, and as much pleased as if she had a grandchild herself. I am so very glad it is a girl—and what will it be called?[1] I had a severe week with my article last week,[2] but it is all done now, and Knowles telegraphs to me that it is "magnificent," and that he means to open his number with it. So, at any rate, I continue to give satisfaction to the Editors. I get the strangest letters from people who have read and liked *Literature and Dogma.* One man writes to me to ask if I think he, having read and liked that book, can without hypocrisy serve the office of churchwarden. A mother from a "Norton Hall" in Gloucestershire has read the same book and wants my advice in educating her daughters. . . . The correcting my evidence given before the Commission, and given in the careless manner of conversation, is very hard work, and I wish it were over; it keeps me from my Report. We have nothing but cold and east wind, still we have no frost at night, and the bulb-beds are getting very gay. The greenhouse you would like too. Poor Gina's camellia has been very handsome indeed; the dentrias, too, are beautiful, and the great azalea is splendid. The scented rhododendron has nine blooms on it, and will be out in a day or two.

Text. Russell, 2 : 379–81.

1. Eleanor Whitridge (1886–1936).
2. "The Nadir of Liberalism" (Super 11 : 54–77), *Nineteenth Century,* 19 (May, 1886): 645–63.

To Patrick Cumin

My dear Cumin   April 21, 1886
    I mentioned the half guinea a day because that would come, for the whole time I was out, to something over £50; and £50, a little more or a little less, is what I reckon myself to be out of pocket by my expedition.[1] Truly yours

                                                    Matthew Arnold.—

MS. Public Record Office, London.

1. See above, letter to Cumin of Apr. 2, 1886.

To James Thomas Knowles

Education Department, Whitehall

Cobham

My dear Knowles   April 21, [1886]

The holidays may make it inconvenient to give me a revise of this, and I don't think it will be necessary. It has been quite splendidly printed by Spottiswoode, especially considering how he was pressed for time.

I must not attempt my visit to London and you at present; the article has thrown me back in my report, and in that I must busy myself. But I hope to see you after your Paris [visit], before I go to the States.   Yours ever sincerely

Matthew Arnold.—

MS. *Pierpont Morgan Library.*

To Emma Lady Lingen

Cobham

My dear Lady Lingen   April 22, 1886

I must stick to my hermit's cell here till my report is done, or I shall never get off to America.

When I come back I shall be an old pauper out of work, only too thankful for a dinner and bed.

Lucy had a little girl on Saturday last, and is doing well. That is all I have heard. Her mother had reached New York the Monday before.

My love to your husband.   Ever yours affectionately

Matthew Arnold.—

MS. *Yale University.*

To Frances Lucy Wightman Arnold

Cobham

Saturday, April 24, 1886

At last I have your letter. What a passage! Often and often I have felt miserable for you, and tried to comfort myself by thinking you had got away from the bad weather we were having here, but my heart refused to believe it, and I was never easy till I saw your arrival telegraphed. I had not thought of the pilot. I don't remember our hearing any news by the one that met the

Servia, but I suppose the papers came by it, only they had nothing to interest us. I thought you would be met by Fred and he would tell you. I knew how you would feel it; the tears ran down my cheeks as I read what you write about it. I feel quite sure you will have written to Jane. I have at once forwarded your letter to Dick, though he too will have heard either from you or from Nelly. Dear Nelly, hug her for me. So she has been punished for showing me the green frogs on board the French steamer, long ago, and exulting in my being ill when she was not. And I have got it all to go through still. I am rather glad it is the old *Servia*, for I daresay she rolls about neither less nor more than the others, and at all events I know her and my way about her. I shall strain every nerve to get out by her, for, as you say, "we are too old for these separations," and I cannot bear them. But my Report is troublesome; however, I have now done all the things which at all took me off from it, and hope this next week to make real progress with it. I got on well enough in my examination, but I find I have made, having to answer questions suddenly, mistakes on points of fact which I never should make in writing a report, when I go to my documents for all I say, and even write to my foreign informants if I am in doubt; however, I hope to correct my evidence before it circulates.

Text. Russell, 2:382–83.

To John Duke Lord Coleridge

Cobham

My dear Coleridge   April 24, [1886]

I cannot fix a day, because unless I get on with my report it will be impossible for me to come and stay in town even one night—but I will see you before I go, even if I invade the Courts for that purpose. I hope, however, to be able to come to Sussex Square—but I will write as soon as I can see my way.—How beautiful it must be in Devonshire! even in Surrey it is hard to keep indoors.

Kindest regards to Lady Coleridge.   Affectionately yours

Matthew Arnold.—

MS. Lord Coleridge.

To Charles Eliot Norton *

Cobham, Surrey

My dear Norton   April 24, 1886

I have sent your letter to my sister, because I knew she would be gratified by it. "Integer" is indeed the right word for Forster: to the same effect old Lord Sherbrooke, who did not much like him and felt his want of edge and finish in speaking, said more than once to me in a moved tone the other day: "But he did not think of *himself*, he did not think of *himself*.["]" [1]

It was tragic for a man who so keenly felt the satisfaction of political influence to die just at the moment when the certainty of it presented itself. Whether he who is gone or any of those who remain had or have power to extricate us from our present difficulties and dangers, is another question. I suppose things looked even worse for us at the end of the last century, but to my eye they look extremely bad now.

Mrs Arnold is in New York, having been appealed to by the husband and doctor to come out to Lucy at once. Since her mother's arrival Lucy's baby has been born—a little girl—and all is going well. I cannot follow until I have finished a report on foreign schools—or rather on some points in the system of foreign schools—for the Government; but I shall try my hardest to come out on the 15th of next month by my old friend the Servia. But I wish you could see Surrey in April—and the garden at this cottage, and the trees.

But you mention a country on your side—the Berkshire country, is it not?—which I believe is very beautiful and which I have always wished to see. Most certainly we will if possible come there to you for a week; but of course I should have come to see you wherever you might have been; even the horse cars should not have kept me from Cambridge.

My love to all your party, and believe me ever, affectionately yours
Matthew Arnold.—

MS. Harvard University.

1. Arnold's old opponent, Robert Lowe, ennobled as Viscount Sherbrooke, in May 1880. This is the closest Arnold comes to a criticism of his brother-in-law, whose "want of edge and finish in speaking" (and in other areas as well) was, though notorious, surpassed by that of his son Oakeley, as will appear in later letters.

To Edward Clodd

Athenæum Club

Edward Clodd Esq.
My dear Sir   April 30, 1886

I should like to think that the permanent estimate of the tendencies of my poetry would be that given in your article, even if the praise to the poetry itself should be many times less kind and cordial.   Most truly yours
Matthew Arnold.—

MS. Roger Brooks.

To Louis Davidson [1]

Education Department, Whitehall

Louis Davidson Esqre

Dear Sir   May 4, 1886

When the dinner for which you have so kindly invited me takes place, I shall be in America.   Most faithfully yours

Matthew Arnold.—

MS. Pierpont Morgan Library.

1. Unidentified.

To Louisa Lady de Rothschild

Pains Hill Cottage, Cobham, Surrey

My dear Lady de Rothschild   May 4, 1886

It seems strange to me to turn from the school documents in which I am at present immersed to write out these lines—but I refuse no request of yours.

I shall be in London tomorrow week, the 12th, and had hoped to find you there; I doubt whether I shall be able to spare another day from my report before I sail, or rather steam, on the 22nd. In that case I shall propose myself at Aston Clinton in the autumn when I return—if Cyril Flower's great leader has left me by that time any country to return to. I shall carry out your kind messages: I am curious to set eyes upon the "pretty little midget of a girl," as Mrs Arnold calls Lucy's baby.   Ever affectionately yours

Matthew Arnold.—

How kind you have been, and how successful, about the Bank clerkship! [1]

MS. Evelyn de Rothschild.

1. For Louis Hiley (see above, letter to Lady de Rothschild of Jan. 24, 1886).

To Elizabeth Smith Thompson

Pains Hill Cottage, Cobham, Surrey

My dear Dolly   May 4, 1886

If I went anywhere, it should be to you—but I must go nowhere. I am working against time at my report, to get away by the 22nd; I have put it off for a week already, my going.

Good accounts of Lucy up to the 23rd of April, and of "the pretty little midget of a girl," as Mrs Arnold calls the baby. Ever affectionately yours

Matthew Arnold.—

MS. Yale University.

To John Duke Lord Coleridge

Pains Hill Cottage, Cobham, Surrey

My dear Coleridge   May 8, [1886]

Ld Tavistock has given me Tuesday for what is my chief holiday in the year—fishing at Chenies. I cannot therefore be at the dinner of The Club. I shall be in London next day, Wednesday; and the perfect thing would be if I could come to luncheon in Sussex Square on that day and find both you and Lady Coleridge—but I fear you will be sitting in Court. Let me have a line to say how this is, and where I can see you on Wednesday; in the afternoon I *must* return here to my troublesome report on foreign schools. I have taken my place in the "Umbria" for the 22nd—a week later than I had intended to go, but the report detains me. I have resigned my inspectorship.   Ever affectionately yours,

Matthew Arnold.—

MS. Lord Coleridge.

To Lucy Charlotte Arnold Whitridge

Cobham

My darling Lucy   May 8, 1886

I had a long and tolerably spelt letter from my Nelly yesterday, for which give her a kiss, but this must be to you, to tell you now that I have news of your well doing down to ten days after the dear little baby's birth, how you have been [in] my thoughts and how happy it makes me to think of you now. Poor Laura Lyttelton's death was quite a shock, and as her baby was borne [*sic*] on the same day as yours and we heard of both events on the same evening by telegraph (Alfred Lyttelton telegraphing about Laura to Mary Ward who was with us)[1] the two cases joined themselves together in my mind, although the chances, one might say, were against both of them issuing so unhappily. And I did say this to myself, but still her case rose constantly to my mind when I thought of you, and I was nervously anxious until I got Mamma's report of the 20th. Since that time all the reports have been good, and about the baby as well as yourself: I did not think much about the grand-daughter at first, it was all my Lucy: but I am now getting very curious to see the pretty little thing as Mamma says she is, and I can well believe it, and you know well how fond I shall be of her, pretty or not. My children have been so sweet to me that I cannot but think my grandchildren will follow their example. It is quite touching to see that great big Dick positively "aux petit soins" for me and arranging all his proceedings with a view to me and my goings on; he thinks, as is the case, that I am a good deal pressed by my report, and is anxious to relieve the pressure all he can. Ella seconds his endeavours, and I am getting very fond of her: she is looking so nicely, too, and enjoying her stay here, and the beautiful weather, so much. We went to the high [?]east field yesterday, sending Dick and Kai forward on foot half an hour before; the day was perfect, and never have I heard the nightingales in the wood at the Effingham turning so loud and strong. The cowslips I have seen taller and better; the long winter has pinched them; but still they were an astonishment and a joy to Ella, who had heard so much of cowslips but never gathered them. Max came in the carriage with us, and he and Kai trotted about the field to one of us after the other and were very good. We walked home—Ella walks quite well now. Yesterday your Aunt Fan came down and I drove her to the turning to Martyn's Green, sent the carriage back from there and walked her back by the paths and lanes my Nelly and I followed one day in the winter. She gives a poor account of your Aunt Forster, but to pass day after day in that half-dismantled house must be too dismal. I want her to come here with Francie—I could quite manage—but I don't think they will come. Your Aunt Fan departs today and Ted comes—but tomorrow I go to Froude's to dine and sleep, and on Monday to Chenies with Dick. I have had a cordial affectionate letter from Carnegie; I have quite settled not to "speak" in Boston or New York at all, and to reserve my last thoughts on America for this side after my return; Mamma and Fred were in great apprehension, I could see. I have heard from Buffalo, where they would like the address; both Sawyer[2] and Milburn say June is a beautiful month for Buffalo and answer for my having an audience: I don't know that I shall speak anywhere else, except perhaps in Cincinnati, and in Denver if I go there. But the Milburns want us for as long as we can stay at Buffalo, and Carnegie at Cresson, and Norton in Berkshire—so we are filling up. Newport I shall eschew as far as I can, though I am glad to have seen it. Of course, we must go to Buffalo because of showing Niagara to Nelly; Buffalo could resist any summer with that full and glorious river. Tell my Nelly the tulips are going off, but have been very fine. Her sparaxis, or lilium, continues, and is lovely. The scented rhododendron delights us all. It is a backward year, no May or lilac out yet. I wander how the little one will like the cottage; Max and Kai send their love to their niece, Miss Lu. I have not yet heard what she is to be called—you should bring in *Lucy* somewhere. How pleased Fred must be—as pleased as I was when you arrived, my darling. Kiss that precious Mamma. I hope her cold is long since gone—it is not a time of year for colds. Ever, my own Lucy,   your most loving

Papa—

MS. Frederick Whitridge.

1. Alfred Lyttelton (1857–1913: *DNB*; *VF*, 9/20/84), son of fourth Baron Lyttelton, was a lawyer (and later an important statesman) and the husband of Laura Tennant (older sister of Margot), who had died in childbirth.
2. Sawyer has not been identified.

To Louisa Lady de Rothschild

Pains Hill Cottage, Cobham, Surrey

Dear Lady de Rothschild   May 14, [1886]

My nephew's address is: Louis Hiley, 14, Westmorland Road, Bayswater.

How I wish I could have seen you before my departure! There is so much I should have liked to say to you; I think Mr Gladstone will lose his bill—I wonder if you are sorry.[1]   Ever yours affectionately

Matthew Arnold.—

MS. Evelyn de Rothschild.

1. The defeat of Gladstone's Government of Ireland bill brought down the government and Parliament was dissolved on June 26.

To Edmund Yates

Pains Hill Cottage, Cobham, Surrey

Dear Mr Yates   May 15, 1886

I was grieved to hear of Escott's illness, and will with pleasure sign the Memorial asking for a grant to him from the Royal Bounty Fund. But I start for America next Friday.   Very faithfully yours

Matthew Arnold.—

MS. University of Kentucky.

To Henry Yates Thompson

Pains Hill Cottage, Cobham, Surrey

My dear Yates Thompson   May 17, 1886

I have been away from home—on my return I find your note and book. The book I will convey to the "midget," as Mrs Arnold calls it, with all your good designs for her improvement.

It will be tantalizing to be on the sea during the crisis of the great debate, but probably I shall be too sick to care. What a wind today!

My love to Dolly, and believe me,   ever most truly yours,

Matthew Arnold.—

MS. Yale University.

To The Editor of *The Times*

Sir   [before May 22, 1886]

All next week while the moment for the great vote grows near, I shall be on the sea going to visit our American kinsmen, who abstained from setting up a Southern Parliament themselves, but are so anxious, it seems, that we should set up an Irish one.

Suffer me to say, before I depart, that the mind of the country, which is slowly but surely waking up on this Irish question, will not be satisfied unless the vote is taken on a clear issue and accompanied by a distinct engagement.

The vote is not taken on a clear issue if it is taken on any question but that of a separate national Parliament for Ireland. Mr. Chamberlain and Mr. Trevelyan may be so committed that they prefer to have the vote taken on some other issue than this. They deserve every consideration. They had the merit of opening their eyes when they saw where Mr. Gladstone was going, instead of shutting them tighter and tighter like Mr. Campbell-Bannerman.[1] An indirect issue may suit the convenience of other members also. But a clear, direct issue is what alone will suit the mind of the country.

A separate Parliament for Ireland is Mr. Gladstone's irreducible *minimum*. Ireland is a nation, says Mr. Parnell, menacingly, Mr. Stansfeld gushingly; a nation should have its national Parliament.

Ireland has been a nation, a most unhappy one. Wales too, and Scotland, have been nations. But politically they are now nations no longer, any one of them. This country could not have risen to its present greatness if they had been. Give them separate Parliaments, and you begin, no doubt, to make them again nations politically. But you begin also to undo what has made this country great.

Do not let us be preposterously alarmist. Perhaps, if it suits Mr. Gladstone's purposes, Scotland, Wales, and Ireland may all of them, to Mr. Stansfeld's delight, become politically nations again, and yet this country, such is its force, may still, by new and untried ways, continue great. But it will be a plunge into the unknown, not a thing to be risked without absolute necessity.

In the case of Austria-Hungary, there was such necessity. Hungary was the bigger of the two. But what was done there was a plunge into the un-known and a very grave one. Who will say that the Austria of today is as strong and solid a Power as the Austria of the end of last century, or that by the end of next century Austria's German provinces will not have gravitated to Germany?

But the necessity for making Ireland a separate nation some people find in our ill-treatment of her, and in the failure of coercion. We have let Scotland have her schools and Church to her mind, says Sir Lyon Playfair, we have not let Ireland; therefore we must make Ireland a separate nation! The Northern States could not go on ruling the South by coercion, says Mr. Bryce; therefore we must make Ireland a separate nation! But the North did not give the South a national Parliament; Scotland has not a national Parliament. The course taken has not been to make them separate nations. Scotland had the just and due control of her own affairs left to her; the South was suffered to resume such control. This, then, is what the analogy requires for Ireland, this and this only; the just and due control of her own affairs.

Why should a national Parliament be the only cure for discontent? Read Madame de Sévigné's letters from Brittany in 1675. Four thousand soldiers were quartered on the province, the Parliament had been banished, men were broken on the wheel and hanged by scores; the population was seething with turbulence and hatred. What has changed Britanny—separate institu-tions? No, but a rational and equitable system of government.

Twenty years after Madame de Sévigné wrote, Duke Hamilton was praising Scotland to William III., and the King answered him, "My Lord, I only wish it was a hundred thousand miles off, and that you was King of it!" What has changed Scotland—a separate Parliament? No, but a rational and equitable system of government.

And this is what the awakening mind of the country demands for Ire-land. Not that we should give her a separate Parliament, but that we should seriously engage and set ourselves to give her a rational and equitable system of government. Lord Salisbury's bad and arbitrary temper (I mean, of course, as a politician, a home politician) is as great a misfortune to the country as Lord Randolph Churchill's intriguing. A separate Parliament for Ireland is a dangerous plunge into the unknown, and not necessary; but not necessary on condition only that we do really at last give Ireland a rational and equi-table system of government; and Lord Salisbury can talk of nothing but co-ercion. Let us refuse a separate Parliament with all firmness; but with equal firmness let us insist on the condition which alone justifies our refusal. Lord Hartington[2] has a good temper (I mean, again, as a politician) and is no in-triguer; Mr. Goschen has made local government his special study. They may be trusted, I hope, to make the necessary refusal firmly, and the necessary engagement emphatically. Nothing less will satisfy that which it is indispensable to satisfy, the mind of the country.

The passionate supporters of Mr. Gladstone in his operations are the political Dissenters and the Radical workmen in the great towns. I agree with Mr. Labouchere that aristocracies are not in general the best of guides in politics. But I have too much respect for his undoubted lucidity to believe him capable of really thinking the political Dissenters and the Radical working men to be on a question like that of Ireland any better guides, or even so good. They know little and prize little beyond the one their dissent, the other their union for trade or politics. In the past they would have applauded Cromwell's dealings with Ireland, or William the Third's, as they applaud Mr. Gladstone's now. It is on the country as as whole, and on the mind of the country, that we must rely. I am, Sir, your obedient servant

Matthew Arnold

Text: The Times, *May 22, 1886, p. 15 (rptd Neiman,* Essays, Letters, and Reviews, *pp. 283–85; Super, 11 : 78–81).*

1. Henry Campbell-Bannerman (1836–1908: *DNB; VF,* 8/10/99), Liberal (Gladstonian, Home Rule) M.P., had been chief secretary for Ireland and was now (for a few moments more) secretary for war in Gladstone's cabinet. After many more important government posts he became prime minister, following Balfour, in Dec. 1905.

2. Spencer Compton Cavendish (1833–1908: *DNB;* succ. as duke of Devonshire 1891; *VF,* 3/27/69; 7/21/88; 5/15/02) had also been chief secretary for Ireland when still a Liberal but Home Rule raveled him and he was instrumental in founding the Liberal Unionists and in the course of time became the very model (nearly) of a Conservative.

To Frances Bunsen Trevenen Whately Arnold*

Cunard Royal Mail Steamship "Umbria"

My dearest Fan   May 22, 9¾ P.M. [–May 23, 1886]

One line to tell you I have made a good start in this splendid ship. The sea is quite calm and we are not crowded—180 passengers and they reckon they have room for 400. We left the Mersey at 1 today; dear old Dick saw me on board but had to leave almost immediately, as the Umbria was going to start. I am headachy and bilious, an effect the sea always has on me, but if it remains as calm as this one cannot be seasick. The passengers are not an interesting set—Americans almost all of them. I shall settle down into some regular reading presently, but at present I have done little except walk the decks. The line of Ireland is visible, or was visible an hour ago—it is nearly 10 o'clock now. We ought to be in Queenstown early tomorrow morning, and to leave it between 12 and 1. Then we shall see whether there is any difference between the Atlantic and the Irish Sea. I got your letter at Manchester last night, and was very glad of it: what good news about Mary's accession of means![1] The Dicks have been the dearest care-takers in the world, and have also thoroughly enjoyed themselves. The screw makes such a shaking that I write badly—I will keep this open till tomorrow morning to give you the latest tidings of myself—goodnight, my dear.

May 23rd 10. A.M.—A fine morning and we are anchored off the mouth of Queenstown harbour, waiting for the tender with letters. She will go off with this before her letters are delivered. This ship is comfort itself, but the sea makes me bilious—however by managing myself, and a copious use of lemons and soda-water, I shall do pretty well, I hope. I have had water-cresses for breakfast! that will give you a notion of what life on board these ships is. The low weird hill-coast is very Irish. Good-bye, my dearest Fan— I am so *very* glad about Mary, and about Walter's better case—tell them so. Your ever most affectionate

M. A.—

MS. Formerly, Mrs. Harry Forsyth.

1. Apparently from the death of her husband, Robert S. Bees Hayes, vicar at Wood-house since 1882 (so listed in *Bosworth's Clerical Guide and Ecclesiastical Directory*, 1886).

To Frances Bunsen Trevenen Whately Arnold

Cunard Royal Mail Steamship "Umbria"

At Sea—Friday, May 28, 1886

My dearest Fan   [–New York, May 31, 1886]

My Sunday letter shall be begun here, and I shall hope to post it in New York after seeing my dear trio—or rather my quartett, for the little one must not be forgotten. We have had a good voyage, though yesterday in the Arctic current off the Bank of Newfoundland was a bad day—fog rain and cold with ice all about us and that horrible fog-horn constantly sounding. But today we have made a very good run, and hope to be at the bar, fifteen miles from New York, about sunset tomorrow; probably, however, we shall not be able to cross it till Sunday morning. We have an excellent Captain, his only fault being that he insists on my taking the Chair at the concert tonight for the benefit of the Sailors' Orphanage at Liverpool; the performers will be amateurs among the passengers.

Saturday, May 29th, 2¾ P.M.

At noon today we were 188 miles from New York and shall get to the bar about 8 this evening too late for the tide; we shall anchor there and go up to New York early tomorrow morning. It has been a fine passage and I have only been sick once, for a few minutes, but my head, like poor Mary's, is never comfortable. Yesterday afternoon it became wet and squally and the concert was rather terrible. I was at the end of the saloon where the motion was very much felt, and my head began to swim; many of the performers could hardly get through, they felt the ship's motion so much; one failed absolutely. I stuck to my post, however, and made the necessary little speeches, and we had a very good collection. Then I went up on deck and got a good breath of fresh air though it was blowing so hard I had to hold on by a rope; then down to my cabin where I made myself comfortable on my sofa with a book and iced lemonade, and the faintness passed off. The supply of lemonade is unbounded on board—lemons and oranges ad libitum are included in the provisions given in exchange for the fare you pay—and they make the lemonade very well. It has been the comfort of my life. On board ship I quite lose the taste for wine, even for claret, and like nothing so much as iced soda water, or iced lemonade without sugar. Today it is very bright and fine, but cold; ships are beginning to appear on all sides, and about noon we took on board our pilot. No birds have yet been seen since we left Ireland, but I expect to see them this afternoon. The nautilus was seen yesterday, but not by me, alas. I have not yet been warm, so that the American heat, of which they talk so much, has still to show itself. But the pilot says it is hot in New York. The passengers are all very civil, and the great rich Californian, Mr Mackay, the Silver King, who is on board, has asked me to come out to California to visit him. But a half English family is the family on board I like best; the father is English, married to an American heiress; they are at the same table with me, and the two girls are really nice, what we call nice in England. They all go to Europe every year, and return for the summer, not to the States, but to Canada, where they have a place near Niagara.

New York—May 31st. Here I am safe and sound, in Lucy's very pretty and convenient house. We lay off Sandy Hook Saturday night crossed the bar at daybreak yesterday and reached the dock at 8 A.M., where I was met by Nelly and Mr Whitridge. After a hot and tiresome wait at the Custom House we got up here about ½ past 9, and found Lucy and the dear little grandchild and the precious Granny. They are all well, and it is a sweet little baby, with well cut features and a grave expression. We have come from the cold of the passage to a temperature of 85; I felt the heat yesterday a good deal, but today there are showers and it is very pleasant. We go to Philadelphia this day week; there I give an address before the University of Pennsylvania on "some aspects of Foreign Education,["] and I shall repeat the address at Buffalo and perhaps at one other place—that is all. We shall pay some visits, but I do not think we shall go to the West, though Mr Mackay, the Silver King, has offered to take me with him to California.[1] It is Decoration Day, the day on which they decorate the graves of those killed in the

War, and all New York is keeping holiday and alive with military music. Lucy's love—she is sitting with me while I write this. Direct to me here, in East Eleventh St.   Your ever affectionate

M. A.—

MS. Balliol College.

1. John William Mackay (1831–1902: *WWWA*), Irish-born American capitalist, *one* of the "Silver Kings," a hustler who, having ravaged the Comstock lode in Nevada and become "one of the richest men in the world," then, still hustling, moved on to banking and cable in San Francisco. See Oscar Lewis, *Silver Kings*.

To Andrew Carnegie

⟨12, West 10th Street, New York⟩

17, East 11th Street

My dear Carnegie   June 4, 1886

You may be quite sure that after my visit to Lucy there is no visit in America which I shall have more pleasure in paying than one to you.

I make an address in Philadelphia on "some points in foreign Education," and repeat it at Buffalo.[1] That is all the speaking I shall do; your advice as to lecturing at this season, though hesitatingly given, was of course right, and I am following it. Between Philadelphia and Buffalo we have some visits to pay, but could we not come to you from Buffalo, about the first week in July? From you we should go to Lucy at Stockbridge in the Berkshire Hills, where her husband has taken a house for the summer. Let me have a line here to say whether the time I have mentioned will suit you; if it will you shall hear from us exact particulars as to date and route later on.

At present I am occupied with my address for Philadelphia, but before I see you I shall have read "Triumphant Democracy."[2]

Affectionate remembrances to your mother and Miss Clark and   I am ever yours, my dear Carnegie,

Matthew Arnold.—

MS. New York Public Library.

1. "Common Schools Abroad" (Super, 11:88–105), *Century*, 32 (Oct. 1886): 893–900 (first republished in Neiman, *Essays, Letters, and Reviews by Matthew Arnold*).
2. Carnegie's *Triumphant Democracy; or, Fifty Years' March of the Republic*, just published and obviously an embarrassment to Arnold, who in public played the artful dodger, adroitly finessing his criticism both in "Amiel" and in "Civilization in the United States" (Super, 11:179, 365), though in private he was more candid (see below, letter to Mountstuart Elphinstone Grant Duff of July 29, 1886).

To Frances Bunsen Trevenen Whately Arnold*

Germantown
My dearest Fan   June 9, 1886

I had your letter of the 25th May before I left New York—I have no doubt another letter is on its way. The cable is the only quick correpondent; owing to the difference of time they were able to cry the H. of Commons division in the New York streets on Monday night. And the papers have long accounts of what passed—all coloured by favour to the Irish, but still very interesting. They had made up their minds here that Gladstone was going to win—from the first I had thought he would lose, but I was not prepared for so good a majority. A load is taken off my spirit—but unless Ld Hartington and Goschen bestir themselves and seize the occasion, it will pass from them and the Home Rulers, pure and simple, will win. Of course I have not seen the comments of the English papers on my letter to the Times, but on this side the water it has done good by drawing the distinction between giving to the Irish legislative control over their own local affairs, and giving to them a *single national legislative body* to exercise such control. They all here go off saying—Of course Ireland ought to have Home Rule just as all our States have, and till the thing is pressed on their attention they do not see the difference between what their States have and what Gladstone proposes to do. But this would lead me too far.

How one thinks of the position in which this division, and the important speech he would certainly have made, would have placed dear William Forster! It was a tragic cutting short indeed—although life is full of such things. I was talking of him last night to one of the best men in the United States, Wayne M[a]cVeagh, who was Attorney General of Garfield's government. Ellis Yarnall was there too—a man of sweet nature, who is bent on coming to see Jane when he is [in] England, for which country he starts in a week. A group of men I met yesterday were the first men I have seen in this country who were serious and cultivated enough to understand the Irish question. The President of the Pennsylvania University [1] had got up at some unheard of hour in the morning to get the newspaper as soon as it was published—so anxious was he (on the right side) about the division. All this is pleasant. Today we have a drive in the Philadelphia Park, one of the noblest in the world—3000 acres of beautiful undulating country with a fine river. Then we have a dinner party in Philadelphia. On Thursday we have a reception at the Music Hall—one of the receiving ladies is Mrs Reid, widow of Wordsworth's friends. On Friday I breakfast at the University and we go on to Washington in the afternoon. We return to New York on Monday, but start visiting again immediately. The weather is superb, not too hot for me as yet, with rain occasionally at night, and the sun of Naples to stimulate the vegetation, which is magnificent. The great feature at present in this [city] is the tulip tree, or tulip poplar as they call it; it flowers badly in England but here it is covered with its green and orange tulips from top to bottom. And the leafage and growth of the tree are enchanting. The plane is the great tree—I believe the tulip tree is a plane, certainly the American maple is. The trees and the green are brilliant—a great contrast to what I saw on my last visit, when I never beheld the colour of green at all. We drove out to MacVeagh's to dinner after my lecture at the University (quite a success)[2] yesterday; it might have been England, the country was so green, so fenced and so cultivated; the distances were like Hertfordshire distances, only one missed the being able to say that here or there was such and such an interesting place. The clover both red and white are [*sic*] everywhere—else the flowers are somewhat different, composites and spiky uninteresting specimens so far as I have yet seen. But I have seen little yet. The house [is] a delightful stone house, bigger than Fox How with a great verandah; a well kept garden and splendid roses. Nelly is enjoying it greatly; I think my dearest Flu enjoys it also. But she feels the heat more than I do and the gnats. My Lucy's baby is a real pleasure to me and I nurse it a great deal. It is such a refined calm looking little thing; "we count her quite English" her nurse says to me. Now I must stop for we are going on our drive—Tell Mary I have had her letter and Louis's; I hope they may find that their change of purpose has a prosperous issue. I shall write to dearest K tomorrow—I wonder whether she is at Fox Ghyll— Your ever affectionate

M. A.—

MS. Balliol College.

1. William Pepper (1843–98: *WWWA*), physician and author, was provost and professor at the University of Pennsylvania.

2. Leonard (pp. 265–66) quotes a student publication, *The Pennsylvanian:* "His presence is most commanding, with a large, brawny frame, and bold, striking features, a dark sunburnt face and large side whiskers, the hair but slightly tinged with gray—a typical Englishman—Mr. Arnold makes a remarkable showing for a man of 64 years. His style of delivery is poor, but his clear and powerful voice, with marked accent and intonation, gave force to a lecture which was full of plain, striking truths. . . . The lecture was listened to closely by the six hundred persons present, who appeared sympathetic and appreciative."

Leonard also quotes from Pepper's manuscript diary: "Introduced Matthew Arnold for his lecture on Foreign Education.

"Vigorous and well-preserved. Bad enunciation. Terrible pronunciation of some words—girls *geeeerls.*— Quiet, clear, caustic, appreciative. . . . He held his MS in his left hand and read from it, very often bringing it close up to his face. The room holds 600 and was crowded. I sat just behind him on the little platform and called 'louder' at short intervals."

To Richard Watson Gilder

Hancock Street, Germantown

My dear Mr Gilder   June 10, 1886

I refused to give the reporters my manuscript and appealed to all their better feelings to cut me as short as possible; I think they have responded fairly enough to appeal. The address is promised at Buffalo for some day between the 24th and 30th of this month; and immediately afterwards you shall have it.[1] It is in the form of an address to the University of Philadelphia, and don't you think it will have more character if that form is preserved? or would you like it to be altered so as to give it the form of a Magazine article? Let me find one line at my daughter's in New York to say this.

You and Knowles are so liberal that you spoil one for other editors. Ever truly yours

Matthew Arnold.—

P. S. I have refused to give the address anywhere in future except at Buffalo, where it was long ago promised.

MS. *University of Virginia*.

1. Published in Gilder's journal, the *Century Magazine*.

To William Pepper

Hancock Street, Germantown

Dr Pepper—
My dear Sir   June 10, 1886

Very many thanks for your kind note and handsome cheque. Lecturing would indeed be a pleasant trade if it could always be exercised under such auspices as those of you and your University.[1]   Most truly yours

Matthew Arnold.—

MS. *University of Pennsylvania*.

1. Pepper wrote on the back of the letter: "Preserve permanently. / Matthew Arnold's acknowledgement of cheque for $500 June 9/86." (Leonard transcribes this endorsement as $100. His reading may be correct, but see Arnold's version below, June 13).

"On June 11th, Mr. Pepper had a breakfast at the Social Art Club for Matthew Arnold. . . . [and] jotted in his diary the following hasty notes on Arnold's conversation:

"'At breakfast we talked of Clubs—Ours he finds expensive: the University Club, N. Y. $300 entrance and $100 per annum—when Athenaeum in London is only £8 per annum. But everything with us—except rent—is higher. And of the late hours which are becoming the rule at many Clubs—The Cosmopolitan—Garrick—so that men must drop out of them as they get on in years.

"'Of the notable positions now occupied by several newspaper correspondents—(Smalley, e.g.) etc. Spoke of a breakfast carré with Chamberlain, himself, some fellow with a title, and Smalley.

"'Of Farrar whom he described as embittered because he gets no Church preferment.

"'He said he liked Boston and Philadelphia so much better than New York—and that Chestnut Street was the most attractive street in America because it was just like a comfortable English street.

"'One turns to what Arnold [wrote] with more liking after having seen and talked with him'" (Leonard, pp. 269–70).

To Mrs Wister

Hancock Street, Germantown

My dear Mrs Wister   June 10, 1886

I have been talking to Mrs Arnold about Butler Place, and I wish we were going over to see you there today: it is provoking your being at Stockbridge just when we are not, and not here when we are. I can only hope you may be reachable from Stockbridge when we go there; we shall be there for the chief part of July. Lucy was so anxious to have her mother with her that we changed our plans; I cannot regret it, because it is now impossible for me to make a lecturing tour, and also, if I had not come in June, I should never have given America credit for the splendid verdure and vegetation which I now find all round me. The tulip tree and all the family of plane are a perpetual delight. And grass, real grass, as lush and sweet as in England! after the brown wastes I saw all through October and November when I was last here, and the endless snowfields of the months following.

I shall look out for the Kalmia—it is a favourite garden shrub with us at home; to see it wild will be delightful.

I hope Dr Wister and your son are quite well, and that you are cherishing a kind feeling for poor distracted England in all her present troubles.

Kindest remembrances from Mrs Arnold, who is here with me.   Ever most sincerely yours

Matthew Arnold.—

MS. Duke University.

To Jane Martha Arnold Forster*

Metropolitan Club, Washington, D. C.

My dearest K   June 13, 1886

How often have I thought of you in the closing days of the great debate, and how you must have been thinking of the part which dear William would have taken in it, and of the important position which he would at this moment have been occupying! For my part, I think constantly of what, after all his experience, he would have considered really expedient and feasible in the way of Home Rule. I regretted his expression of general objection to Home Rule, but I know that by this he meant only Home Rule as understood by Parnell. In this country it is supposed that England refuses every kind of Home Rule, and as this is eminently the country of local government, almost every one goes for Gladstone as the only propounder of a scheme of local government. The moment any politician produces a counter-scheme, free from the great danger of Gladstone's, the separate national Parliament, but giving real powers of local government, opinion here, which is extremely important if for no other reason that [*sic*] that most of Parnell's friends come from America, will undergo a change. The Americans are not really indisposed to England, I believe, but they are not closely informed on Irish matters, and they see no Home Rule proposed but Gladstone's measure. I doubt if Salisbury is disposed, or Hartington laborious enough, to make one; William and Goschen together would have been invaluable for this purpose.

How are you, my dearest? I shall send this to Wharfeside, but I have hopes you are at Fox Ghyll. I have met with two Americans who have spoken to me of William with real knowledge and real feeling; one was Ellis Yarnall, the other was Wayne McVeagh, the man whose company I prefer to that of any other American. Ellis Yarnall goes to Europe immediately, and is bent on coming to see you wherever you may be. I am sure a visit from him—I do not mean that he should stay with you, but that he should come and talk to you for an hour—would give you pleasure.

We have the sun of Naples here with the vegetation of Virginia, and that vegetation heightened by a wet spring. The heat is great, but there are as yet hardly any mosquitoes, and in a town of trees, like this, I can bear almost any amount of heat. We had it at 85 in the shade yesterday. Flu and I drove up to Arlington, a beautiful place on the wooded bluff above the Potomac, which belonged to General Lee and was bought by the government from his heirs to make it a national cemetery for the soldiers who fell in the war. About 12,000 are buried there and the place, in addition to its natural beauty and admirable situation, is exquisitely kept—the only well kept public thing I have seen in America. Nelly was taken by Archibald Forbes,—

who has turned up here and is going to be married to an American,—to the Capitol, to a garden party and to make a round of visits. We dined in the evening with General Meigs, the United States Quartermaster General,[1] and had a pleasant party of diplomatic people and others in the evening. Tell Fan that I have found here much more interesting wild flowers than hitherto; and merely to see the kalmia and the magnolia growing wild everywhere in the woods, is worth making the journey to see. I must not begin about the trees, or I shall fill my letter with them. We return tomorrow to dearest Lucy and little Eleanor at New York. The following day we go to the Butlers'; then back to Lucy again, then to Boston, Buffalo, and Canada. I hope by the 10th of July we shall be settled with Lucy at Stockbridge. My lecture did very well at Philadelphia; I send you the letter with which the President of the University enclosed a cheque for 500 dollars—£100.[2] The Century gives me £100 more for the right of printing it, and I daresay the Buffalo people will give nearly as much more for hearing it; I have refused to give it anywhere else, as wherever I give it there is an attending ceremony of receptions and social business which in this hot weather is very tiring. But £300 will amply pay the expenses of our journey as except this visit to Washington we shall have little or no living at hotels. I do not yet know what my pension will be, nor indeed whether I will have got one at all; but it will all come right, I have no doubt. However, I am glad to have covered, being in this doubt as to my means of subsistence, the expenses of this journey. Love to dear Francie; Nelly enjoys herself greatly, but I do not think she will marry an American— Dearest Fanny Lucy enjoys herself too, and every one is charmed with her; but she feels the heat more than I do, and what mosquitoes there are torment her singularly. It *is* hot in the trains. Ever, my dearest,   your most loving brother

M. A.—

MS. Frederick Whitridge.

1. Maj. Gen. Montgomery Cunningham Meigs (1816–1892: *WWWA*).
2. See above, p. 158, letter to William Pepper of June 10, 1886.

To Charles Eliot Norton

148 Charles Street, Boston

My dear Norton   June 19, [1886]

Why, oh why, did Harvard dissemble its love so long? on the 30th I am doubly and triply bound in Canada. Most certainly I would have made my engagements fit in, had I known of the honour proposed for me.[1]

As for our meeting, that is quite secure, I hope. At Stockbridge we shall

be in your neighbourhood for a month at least—and we are all looking forward to it.   Affectionately yours

Matthew Arnold.—

MS. Harvard University.

1. "Had Matthew Arnold and President Cleveland . . . . been present today, as it
was at one time expected, they would have received the customary courtesy of the LL. D."
(*New York Times*, July 1, 1886, p. 2, quoted from Leichman, p. 260).

To Frances Bunsen Trevenen Whately Arnold

The Buffalo Club, 200 Delaware Avenue

My dearest Fan   June 26, 1886

This morning has brought us a letter from you with a bad account of
almost every one about you. To balance it, we have a note from dearest Lucy,
whose household has been ill, announcing their improvement. The baby is
thriving, and Lucy says "she misses her Grandpapa dreadfully." They are all
in a conspiracy to make out that the child takes to me, but it does not need
that to make me very fond of her, she is such a sweet little thing. I wrote to
you from Boston on Sunday, I think; the next day we went to Beverly Shore
to lunch—a most beautiful sea indeed, with walnuts and sycamores coming
close down to the beach; a landscape I did not think Massachusetts capable
of. The weather was glorious, the rocks are granite and the sea quite clear.
Nelly and I had a charming half hour on the beach by ourselves. We returned
to Boston in the afternoon and drove straight to the Old Colony Station for
Newport. It was hot, but the drawing rooms [*sic*] cars are pleasant in hot
weather, and we did very well. We drove out seven miles to the place of
Mr Whitridge, Fred's father[1]—fine sea views but an uninteresting road at
first, until we came to lanes thick with bird-cherry and bay-berries, a sort of
magnified bog myrtle—and purple irises and a sort of osmunda. Mr Whitridge's place is a wooden box on a grassy bank above an arm of the sea. It is
solitary, but I could get along there for a summer. We were comfortably put
up—he is a goodlooking man and we liked both him and his married daughter and her children—the husband was not there. Next day Mr Whitridge
drove us in an open carriage into Newport and all through the best lines of
villas and along the ocean drive. The villas are beautiful, but the place has no
remarkable natural beauty; the Americans talk so much of it because it is their
own place where wealth and luxury are in full possession, and where the
scrambling ugly half finished scale of American life is not visible. We drove

home, lunched and walked on the shore; at six we dined and at 8 started again for Newport where we embarked at 9 on board a great night-steamer, a really floating palace, for New York. It came on wet, but the coast and the lighthouses interested me very much. We were none of us ill—and reached New York in pouring rain at 7 in the morning. We drove up to Lucy's and passed the day in packing and making preparations. We are taking our berths on the Aurania, which sails the first Saturday in September. Lucy does so long to feel that she has us for the whole of August. She is a greater darling than ever. On Thursday morning we started by the Chicago express for this place; splendid travelling, 440 miles in less than eleven hours, and a first rate dining room car. I got all the proof of my report corrected and have now done with it. We were met at the station by Milburn, and are hospitably entertained by him as before. Yesterday we went in a private steamer to lunch at a Club-house on an island in the Niagara river; that river and Lake Erie are something to see. In the evening the Milburns had a dinner party. Nelly enjoys it all and makes herself pleasant; Flu is troubled from time to time by tooth-ache, but enjoys America pretty well on the whole. Tonight I lecture; we dine tomorrow with some pleasant people here, and on Monday go to Niagara; on Tuesday to Galt in Canada. But write still to New York. I say nothing of Home Politics, no one takes quite the line I want to see taken. My love to dearest K and to Francie— Your ever affectionate

M. A.—

MS. Balliol College.

1. John Whitridge.

To Lucy Charlotte Arnold Whitridge

The Buffalo Club, 240 Delaware Avenue

My darling Lucy   June 28, 1886

The photographs have just come; I am delighted with *you*, quite delighted, and with one of Nelly's. I am passable, but hardly so good as in Sarony's.

June 29th So far I wrote yesterday, then I was fetched for Niagara. We had a glorious day—unclouded sun but a cool breeze; the summer climate of this place deserves all the praise they give to it. We had the old party— the Sawyers and the Judge—Judge Lewis [1]—and everything arranged, as before—no tickets to take—all on velvet. A great many of the fragments are swept away, and the New York side is greatly improved though not yet perfect. The vegetation on Goat Island was wonderful—but in general the blue of the water and the green of the woods surpassed everything I had expected. We began with Goat Island and did that until luncheon; luncheon where we lunched before; Mlle Lehmann the singer was there and I was introduced to her—very handsome and pleasant.[2] A good luncheon—then came the really new feature, the voyage on the Maid of the Mist up to the edge of the Falls. We were enveloped in sailors' waterproofs, and they say that Mamma and I sitting side by side on the hurricane deck were a sight. The pitching is as of the sea, and the spray of the American Fall is as torrents of rain. From the Canada Fall you keep a more respectful distance but there is plenty of spray there too, and the green sheet of river coming over the rock, as you see it through the mist near at hand, is awful. Twice we went up and came down; I must make the voyage with the Midget some day. Then we did the Rapids, with which last time we began; then the Whirlpool—the most beautiful river-view of all—which we did not do last time. Then back to those horrid franchises and to the trains. Delicious cool evening air as we drove up here to the Milburn's house from the Ferry Station, at 8 o'clock. Supper, one or two callers, and bed. Today we have glorious weather again: Mr Wilks[3] meets us at Galt which place we reach at 5 p.m. I am curious to see this Canada country life, but we do not like to hear of your cold this morning from Fred; you cannot surely catch a serious cold this weather. Nothing is said of the sweet Midget, so I conclude she is well and virtuous. Everyone here is delighted with your photograph; we talk much of you; Mamma has just said to me, talking of Nelly's helplessness at packing, "how beautifully Lucy used to pack, and how quick." You are a dear, sweet child. Nelly amuses every one, and likes the whole circle here; but this house is not nearly so nice as the Rogers', where we were before. I am longing to be quietly with you at Stockbridge; I hear it is just what I shall enjoy. The lecture did very well, and I expect I shall get about 250 dollars. The hall where I spoke before is burnt down, and they thought the Music Hall, which holds over 1500, would be too large; so they fell back on a poor little hall which holds only 200 or so. But they were quite right—the big hall half empty would have been depressing. Now I must stop and see to the luggage—all the arrangements Fred had made for us on Thursday were excellent. My love to him.   Your ever fondly loving,

Papa—

MS. *Frederick Whitridge.*

    1. Neither the Sawyers nor Lewis has been identified.

    2. Lilli Lehmann (1848–1929), German soprano, now (1885–92) at the Metropolitan Opera, New York (*Oxford Dictionary of Opera*).

    3. Unidentified.

To J. C. O'Connor Jr[1]

The Buffalo Club, Buffalo, N. Y.

To J. C. O'Connor, Esq. Jun.:

My dear Sir,—   June 28, 1886

I cannot possibly attend your meeting tomorrow, but I am glad you are going to hold it. I hope you will make clear one point in especial. Mr Gladstone says that he insists on the "principle of giving Ireland an effective government by Irishmen," and would gladly have the world believe that all his opponents are hostile to this principle. On the contrary, all the best of them are favourable to it. But they think his proposed mode of giving effect to it a bad and dangerous one. Mr Bright is as favourable as Mr Gladstone to "the principle of permitting Ireland, with proper limitations, to govern herself."[2] But the question is what those proper limitations are. Mr Bright believes, and the best of the Liberal party believe, that a national Irish Parliament would be a sure source of trouble in the future, and that some plan for Irish self-government must be found which does not involve the establishment of such a Parliament. If Mr Gladstone were twenty, or perhaps only ten, years younger, he would think and say the same. But he is in a hurry; he wants to settle the Irish question at once, and he thinks he sees his way to settling it for the moment by securing the Parnellite vote, which can be secured only by conceding a national Irish Parliament. The trouble in the future he will not live to see.

Let Americans ask themselves what they would have thought of a statesman who assumed that the only way of giving the Southern States an effective government by Southerners was to create a general Southern Congress at Richmond. With the talents which the Southern men have for politics and oratory, such a Congress would inevitably have grown into a power confronting a Washington Congress and embarrassing it, however sincerely the Southern men might have professed, in first asking for it, that into this it should never grow. So as to Ireland. The very talents of the Irish for politics and oratory will inevitably make an Irish Parliament grow into a power confronting the Imperial Parliament and embarrassing it, however sincerely the Irish may now profess that they do not mean their Parliament to grow into anything of the kind. I by no means blame them for asking for such a Parliament. But I say that an English Minister who concedes it may be a dexterous politician and parliamentary manager, but is no statesman.

Let, however, "the principle of giving Ireland an effective Government by Irishmen" be your principle as firmly as it is Mr Gladstone's.   Very faithfully yours,

Matthew Arnold.

Text. The Complete Prose Works of Matthew Arnold, *ed. Super, xi:373–74 (rptd from* Pall Mall Gazette, *July 19, 1886, p. 4.)*[3]

1. Unidentified by the present editor, by Super, and by Leichman (p. 262), who, without conviction, suggests Joseph O'Connor (1841–1908: *WWWA*), a Rochester teacher, attorney, writer, poet, and journalist, editor formerly of the *Buffalo Courier* (1879–85), now of the Rochester *Post-Express*.

2. Super (11:496–97), noting that Arnold's letter originally appeared in the New York *Evening Post*, quotes a long comment by E. L. Godkin demolishing Arnold's argument as a misrepresentation of Gladstone's.

3. From Gladstone's speech in Manchester, June 25, as reported on the front page of the *New York Daily Times* on June 26.

To Andrew Carnegie

Buffalo

My dear Carnegie   June 29, 1886

At the end of this week we must go back to Lucy, who is longing to have us, and our first duty is to her; but I will write to you from Stockbridge next week. We are just off for Galt in Canada; I had meant to come to Cresson[1] from there, but Lucy has a troublesome cold, and we think that instead of taking the train on Saturday from here to Pittsburgh, as we had intended, we ought to take it to Albany and Stockbridge. Love to your mother—ever affectionately yours

Matthew Arnold.—

We had really a capital audience in Philadelphia; I wish you could have been there. We had good audiences here too. Now I have no more lecturing, thank God.

Tell your mother I am become much less "ministerial."

MS. New York Public Library.

1. Carnegie's summer home, in the Alleghenies, where Arnold spent three days in mid July.

To Frances Bunsen Trevenen Whately Arnold

Barrytown P. O., Dutchess Co., Steen Valetje[1]

My dearest Fan   July 4, 1886

I was beginning to think no more letters were coming to us from England, when last night, as I was going to bed, Mr Delano put into my hand an envelope directed to me by Lucy, full of letters, yours among them, and one from Ella also. She tells me that the first edition of Dick's song is already sold out, which pleases us very much. You tell me of Oakeley's standing for Darlington[2]—of which I had not heard either, and of there having been a notion of his leaving Cassell's. Has he money for Parliament? But Durham is a Gladstonian county, so perhaps he will not have to determine that question. I should have been more hopeful of Edward's candidature for Bradford—but really one is too far off for these things. The daily cablegram given by the American papers is wonderful, but of course it deals with results merely, and yet the details are so full of interest to us English people. The case of Leith is the only election about which the American papers have given details; they are delighted with whatever success befalls Gladstone. Today they are in the dumps, and are beginning to say that sooner or later his home rule will win, even if it does not win just yet. And so it will, to be sure, if the others do not produce something better, and this is what I am anxious about. The difficulty about Bright's plan is that in a Grand Committee settling Irish matters the northern members would constantly be out-voted; they would not like this and would be for ever appealing to the English and Scotch members to up-hold them—and difficulty of this kind might be very serious. I see no hope of the Irish getting a due control of their own local affairs unless the provinces are separated and the North controls its own while the Celts and Catho-lics control theirs in the other provinces. We are here staying with a sort of Rothschild—it is the first place where I have found an anti-Gladstonian atmosphere. I suppose he alarms the *classes* in both hemispheres. This is a beautiful place and a most comfortable house; at the foot of a wooded slope flows the Hudson, like a Windermere a hundred miles long; on the other side rise the Catskill mountains, 4000 feet high. It is very beautiful but very hot, however I suffer from heat less than most English people. We left Buffalo at ¼ to 9 yesterday morning and got here at 6; the parlour car is a comfort, for there is a movement of air, one is not cramped for room and everything is in brown Holland; still, Nelly and Flu felt the heat a great deal. I enclose a note which will interest you from the head of the Delafields over here; he is quite a rich man; Flu has a similar letter from his wife.[3] We shall not be able to go to them, however. Tomorrow or next day we go to Lucy at Stock-bridge, and I long to be at peace with that dear child; but there are still one or two visits we must pay, and the distances are immense here. We had a pleasant visit in Canada to the Wilkses; Mrs Wilks is aunt to that pretty Miss Langdon[4] who is in London and who they said was to marry the Duke of Portland. Mr Wilks was in bed with rheumatic fever, but would not let us be put off or told of it; his children, two sons and two daughters, *ran* the house as they say here. The house is a real country house as in England, with a park prettily laid out, the old forest trees, great sugar-maples, towering up in it nobly, and the Grand river, as wide as the Thames but shallow, flowing through the wide valley. Galt is a prosperous town peopled by Scotch chiefly. Who do you think turned up as a Bank manager there? George Greenhill;[5] he came out to call on us and every one was very civil to him; he is said to be doing well there. He has not preposesssing manners, but they are those of a man who is prospering not failing; his wife is said to be a nice little woman. We had a glorious visit to Niagara; the green of the woods, the splendid vegetation, and the blue of the great river, made a wonderful contrast to the Niagara we had seen before. Everything was arranged for us as before and we went through the whole excursion without trouble and without expense. The interesting part of all was the going up close to the falls in a steamer, the Maid of the Mist; you are dressed in sailors' waterproofs; you should have seen Flu and me! You are in blinding torrents of spray, the boat rocks like a ship in a storm, and through the spray you see the pale green sheets of water, the depth of a great ship they say, pouring over the semi-circular rock for ever. I wish you could see the wild grape vine; also the milkweed or wild cotton, also the wild lilies, also the chrysanthemums with their rich dark centres—black-eyed Susan the country people here call them. Write to me at Laurel Cottage, Stockbridge, Massachusetts. We have taken our places on the Aurania for the 4th of September. My love to dearest K; I was going to write to her from Canada, when I found Flu had actually begun a letter to her; my love to Francie too.   Your ever most affectionate

M. A.—

I cannot find Maturin Delafield's letter to me, so I send his wife's to Flu.

MS. Balliol College.

1. The letter is written on Delano stationery, showing an engraving of the palatial home, Steen Valetje.

2. Oakeley Arnold-Forster, a Liberal Unionist standing for Darlington, was defeated in the election on July 3 by Theodore Fry, a Gladstonian Liberal. Edward, his older brother, did not in fact stand.

3. Maturin Livingston Delafield (1836–1917: *NCAB*), son of Maj. Joseph Delafield and grandson of John (older brother of William, Arnold's cousin and benefactor), who had moved to the United States and become very rich indeed (see 1:380 n. 3). Maturin wrote an article, "William Smith—Historian," *Magazine of American History*, 6 (1881): 418–39. See also *The Livingston Family in America and Its Scottish Origins*, compiled by Florence Van Rensslaer, arranged by William Latimer (New York, 1949).

4. The Wilkses and Miss Langdon have not been identified.

5. Presumably, the older brother of William Alexander Greenhill, husband of Arnold's cousin, Laura Ward.

To Andrew Carnegie

⟨12 West 10th Street, New York⟩

Laurel Cottage, Stockbridge, Mass.

My dear Carnegie   July 7, 1886

I am afraid one of us must stay with Lucy, but my daughter Nelly and I propose to come to you at the beginning of the week after next—July the 19th or 20th—if that suits you. You may be sure I have no intention of letting my time in America end without a visit to my first friend and host in this country. I think we go on the 17th to G. W. Childs at Elberon,[1] and spend Sunday there; then on Monday or Tuesday we might come by Philadelphia to Cresson. Let me hear if this will suit you. I am rejoiced we are in agreement about Gladstone's present line; we are agreed, too, in having no great opinion of Lord Salisbury and the Tories; but I have hopes of Lord Hartington[.] His Liberalism is limited, but sound; and he has no political tricks.

Love from all of us to you and your mother.   ever affectionately yours

Matthew Arnold.—

I am here for the next ten days.

MS. *New York Public Library.*

1. George William Childs (1829–1924: *WWWA*), publisher and philanthropist, donor of a fountain at Stratford-upon-Avon and of memorial windows in Westminster Abbey and St Margaret's Church. See below, letter to Frederic William Farrar of Jan. 4, 1888. Arnold's address (Super, 11: 328–33) was partly quoted in Childs's *Recollections* (1890), and, without naming him, Arnold quotes Childs in "General Grant" (Super, 11: 144–79), in a rare poignant and personal passage (pp. 178–79).

To Jane Martha Arnold Forster*

Laurel Cottage, Stockbridge, Mass.

My dearest K   July 8, 1886

I should have written to you last week, but Flu told me she was writing; I am very, very often thinking of you. I have just got the Springfield Republican, a prominent Massachusetts local paper, and my eyes are gladdened by the heading "The Liberal Defeat becomes a Rout." The newspapers here are so sensational that they always exaggerate even when, as at present, all their wishes are against the side which is winning; still the counties do seem to have begun well. We get no details except as to very interesting elections, such as Sexton's for West Belfast, or Whitmore's for Chelsea;[1] I suppose Oak-eley did not get in, as I see Theodore Fry's name in a list of successful Glad-stonians, and I think he sate for Darlington which is the place Fan told us Oakeley was contesting. What induced him to stand, and would it have suited his means? Till I know what you wished, I do not know whether to be glad or sorry at his not succeeding. Edward for Bradford is what I should have liked—for one Parliament at any rate; but I see Shaw Lefevre is re-turned.[2] The Americans are fairly puzzled; they thought Parnell was going to win. You cannot make them understand that his cause is not that of the local self government which is universal here and works well. The truth is we have not their local self government in England or Scotland any more than in Ireland; Parliament has been at the same time local and national legislature for those countries, as well as for Ireland. But as government in England and Scotland has been in accordance with the wishes of the majority in the respective countries, the system has worked well enough hitherto, though public business is now getting too great for it. But in Ireland, where gov-ernment has been conducted in accordance with the wishes of the minority and of the British Philistine, the defects of the system have come into full view. Therefore I am most anxious that the question of local government should be in every one's mind; if it comes to be fairly discussed, the Ameri-cans will be capable of seeing that there is no more need for merging Ulster in Southern Ireland than for merging Massachusetts in New York State.

This is a pretty place, with many hills of 2000 feet and one of 3,500. But the heat of an American summer is great, and makes itself felt even here, where we are 1200 feet above the sea. We came here on Monday from the Hudson, expecting to find this much cooler; but a spell, as they call it, of hot weather arrived with us, and we found the thermometer at 85 and the mos-quitoes active. Yesterday was a terribly warm day, the thermometer above 90 in the afternoon and not below 80 at night; but today the wind is changed and it is about 75 which I like well enough. But between 10 A.M. and 5 P.M. you cannot go out comfortably, except along the village street beautifully shaded with American elms and maples. It suits the baby to be here, and her nurse a thin and nice looking woman, likes the heat, but the baby has to be enveloped in a net when she goes out because of the mosquitoes. At 5 I have a carriage and we drive out; there are a great many people in the neighbour-hood, some of them nice. The country is pleasing but not to be compared to Westmorland; it is wider and opener, and neither hills nor lakes are so effective. The villas are very pretty; the American wooden villa, with its great piazza where the family live in hot weather, is the prettiest villa in the world.

And the trees are everywhere; indeed they cover the hills too much, to the exclusion of the truly mountainous effects which we get from the not higher mountains of Langdale. Lucy is well, and in spirits at the well-doing of her dear baby; I very often carry it about, and this morning I saw the little thing in its bath which it greatly enjoys. It is a pretty, well-covered little thing, with a grave countenance;[3] I shall like to see it at Fox How. Fred is in New York, but returns from Saturday till Monday. At the end of next week Nelly and I go for a few days to the Alleghanies, on a visit to Mr Carnegie; we then return here for another ten days, when we go to the Adirondacks, a wild mountain region between northern New York and Canada. Flu will stay with Lucy while we go to the Alleghanies, but will come with us to the Adirondacks. But it is hard to leave Lucy. We have taken our berths on board the Aurania for the 4th of September. I long for Europe, though it delights me to be with Lucy. Tell Francie I have just read a good address by Moody to his young men at Mt Hermon.[4] My love to the dear child, and to Delafield; it seems so odd to be writing to Delafields in this country; they are quite prominent people. Tell Fan I wish she could see the flowers; the great lilies would delight her. The Housatonic (Indian name) flows at the bottom of our garden; it is as big as the river at Newby Bridge, but not nearly so nice, being injured by paper mills.

Now, my dearest, I must stop; write to me here; we had delightful letters yesterday from Emily Buxton and Mrs Deacon.   Your ever most affectionate

M. A.

I thought the photograph made the hill and grave wear quite another aspect.[5]

MS. Frederick Whitridge.

1. Thomas Sexton (1848–1932: *DNB*), Irish politician, journalist, and a Parnellite at present (but later an anti-Parnellite), said to be "an eloquent speaker and a skilful obstructionist," and Charles Algernon Whitmore (1851–1908: *WWW*), out of Eton and Balliol, a Conservative from Cadogan Square, was returned for Chelsea.

2. George John Shaw-Lefevre (1831–1928: Baron Eversley 1906; *DNB*), a Gladstonian Liberal, occupied William Forster's old seat for the next ten years, called "a statesman and administrator of extraordinary industry and public spirit."

3. Fat, already, as a new-born infant, and described by someone who knew her as an adult as "the fattest person I ever saw."

4. Dwight Lyman Moody (1837–1899: *WWWA*), the evangelist, who, with Ira David Sankey (1840–1908: *WWWA*), was as well-known in Great Britain as in the United States. He was from Northfield, Mass., and his school at Mt Hermon was fifty-odd miles from Stockbridge.

5. Forster's grave in the hillside burial ground at Burley.

To Charles Eliot Norton

Stockbridge, Mass.

My dear Norton   July 9, [1886]

I have your letter this morning. One of us must stay to take care of Lucy, so Mrs Arnold and I will come along to you. We will be at Shelburne Falls at 10.42 A.M. on Tuesday next, the 13th inst., if that suits you; stay Wednesday with you, and return here on Thursday. On Saturday Nelly and I have to start for Cresson.

It will be delightful to see you, and I expect your country is better than this which is a pretty country, too, but the guide books overpraise it. My ancient trout rod always travels with me, tell Richard,[1] so we will fish together if we fish at all—but in this country I am always fearful of hearing the sad report: *River fished out!*

I felt sure of *you* on the insane project of an Irish Parliament. The elections take a load off my heart—but how much is yet to be done before we are clear of danger!

Our love to all your party—   Ever affectionately yours

Matthew Arnold.—

MS. *Harvard University.*

1. Richard Norton (1872–1918: *WWWA*), his youngest child, later an archaeologist.

To William Gordon McCabe

Stockbridge, Mass.

My dear Mr McCabe   July 10, 1886

I knew I should hear from you. But alas, Virginia is out of the question this time; all our plans were changed by my daughter's urgent summons to us to come at a time different from that which we had intended. At the end of August we must return to England; till that time we shall be at Stockbridge for the most part, though we have a visit or two to pay in the adjoining State of New York.

How delightful to find at last an American who is sound on the subject of Gladstone's desperate Irish policy! Lord Salisbury has now a great opportunity;—if he lets things drift, he will lose it, but I hope for the best. What is wanted is a sound plan of Home Rule instead of a vicious and dangerous one.

I like to hear of your boy going to England, but you must not drop the habit of coming there yourself.   affectionately yours

Matthew Arnold.—

Mrs Arnold and my daughters wish to be most kindly remembered to you.

MS. University of Virginia.

To Frances Bunsen Trevenen Whately Arnold*

Stockbridge, Mass.

My dearest Fan   July 11, 1886

Fred brought us your letter from New York last night, with Mary's and Walter's enclosed. Both are [?doleful]. Write here in future; we gain a day or two by not having to wait for Fred's coming. The letters from home seem terribly old news when they arrive and so do the papers; our latest is the Pall Mall Budget of June 24th, before the elections began. On the other hand, the column of cable-gram in the American papers every day is something wonderful; and Smalley's despatches to the Tribune are our only indication of their being any other opinion expressed in the world except a pro-Gladstone one. Of course the elections tell their own tale, but not in speech. Today we hear of Trevelyan's defeat and Ld Hartington's return, both of which you yourself, at Fox How, did not hear of till this morning, if this morning. The Pall Mall splashes about more wildly than ever, but I suppose it represents a certain phase of Liberalism. I shall perhaps write another letter to the Times, as now comes the critical moment. Ld Salisbury and Ld Hartington have an opportunity offered to them, and if they miss it now, it will never return, and the worst of it is that the English do not know how much more than other people—than the French, the Germans, the Swiss, the Americans—they are without any system of local government of an effective kind themselves, and what they lose by being without it, so they can the less understand the necessity of granting something of the kind to the Irish, though they see in a dim way that a necessity there is.

But to turn to more pleasant subjects. The great flora of this country begins to shew itself to me; I send you three things I have gathered within a quarter of a mile of this house today; two Pyrolas (I think) and a meadow rue. Nelly and I had an expedition yesterday to find a stream with the un-promising title of Muddy Brook; it is not a muddy brook at all but a brook flowing through marshy ground; we must have walked and scrambled ten miles at least; we found our brook, and there were no trout in it, but we were consoled by the new and inexhaustible flowers; I wish you could see the milkweed; but I like nothing better than the great Meadow Rue (they have several kinds) waving its blooms everywhere at this season. I wonder what the *hard-hack* is, a bush covered with a golden flower like the cistus; then the lilies are superb, three splendid varieties quite common; then there is an arbutus and a kind of Lysimachia; but it is rather guess-work as there are generally some differences between the American flower and ours. This is a beautiful country, and one of the townships five or six miles from the railway—Washington township, or Otis township, or Savoy township would suit me perfectly. Here we are too civilised, have two [*sic*] many callers, and the trout is extinct. But it is a beautiful country, and the climate has its great merits though it is too hot. We have had it above 90 all day and at 80 all night, and the mosquitoes active. But today it is about 73, with a fresh breeze, and this glorious sun. We are going to a ½ past 7 o'clock tea (an institution here) with some people called Ward;[1] he is Baring's agent and was a friend of Emerson's. They have a place 5 miles off at Lenox (you remember how Harriet Martineau used to talk of Lenox and of the Sedgwicks)[2] with a perfect view over Stockbridge Bowl a lake larger than Grasmere with mountains of 2000 feet round it. We shall drive back by moonlight. Lucy has not been well; she is a good nurse, but the baby is rather a drain upon her and she has her bad headaches. To see Flu with the baby—the most sweet serious-looking little thing in the world—is very pretty. The baby sleeps perfectly all night, and is out all day long in the garden or in the piazza. Flu and I go to the Nortons at Ashfield on Tuesday— 40 miles of beautiful hill country like this—we return on Thursday. Then on Saturday Nelly and I go to the Childses, very rich people, at Long Branch, on the Atlantic coast, and then to Cresson Springs on the ridge of the Alleghanies, where we stay for a week with the Carnegies—Mr Carnegie and his mother, I mean. When we return here we shall go some excursions; Greylock, the highest mountain, is 3,500 feet high, the height of Snowdon; then the "Dome of the Taconics" has a wonderful view from it and the falls of Bish-bash (Indian name to describe the sound of the water when low) are worth seeing. Love to my dearest K—I wrote to her the other day. I wish you were here with me—you would like this place and the people.   Ever your affectionate

M. A.—

MS. Frederick Whitridge.

1. Samuel Gray Ward (1817–1907), Baring Brothers' agent from about 1850 to the end of 1885, poet, essayist, and translator, introduced by Margaret Fuller to Emerson, some of whose letters to him, edited by Charles Eliot Norton, are in *Letters from Ralph Waldo Emerson to a Friend 1838–1853*, 1899 (Leichman).

2. In 1836 Harriet Martineau had been the guest in Lenox of Catherine Maria Sedgwick (1789–1867: *WWWA*), well known as a writer.

To Mrs Dickinson[1]

Mrs Dickinson—   Stockbridge, Mass.
Dear Madam   July 15, 1886
    The best photograph of me is, I think, that of Savony in New York. Your faithful servant,

Matthew Arnold.—

MS. *Yale University.*

    1. Possibly, Susan Huntington Gilbert Dickinson (1830–1913), wife of William Austin Dickinson, the brother of the poet (Leichman).

To John Osborne Sargent[1]

John O. Sargent Esq.   Stockbridge
My dear Sir   July 17, [1886]
    I shall be most happy to dine with you on the 27th.
    I am just starting for Elberon and Cresson Springs. I hope Miss Sargent is getting rid of her hay fever, and I remain,   most truly yours,

Matthew Arnold.—

MS. *New York University.*

    1. John Osborne Sargent (1811–1891: *WWWA*), lawyer, journalist, translator, and "a Lenox summer resident at his estate, Twin Elms" (Leichman). Georgiana Wells Sargent (1858–1946) was presumably his daughter (Leichman).

To The Editor of *The Times*

[Stockbridge]

Sir   July 24, [1886]
    When I was leaving England two months ago you printed a letter from me on the Irish question. In my letter I expressed the conviction that the country was minded to reject Mr. Gladstone's Irish policy, but also to give the Irish the due control of their own affairs.
    I write now from the United States, where the conviction that Mr. Gladstone would be victorious has been universal. Everything favourable to

him has been current here; nothing unfavourable. However, my faith in the country which, with all its shortcomings, has yet more of solid political sense than any other country has been justified. Mr. Gladstone is defeated. The American newspapers are now crying out that the defeat is but momentary; that his speedy and complete success is certain. Mr. T. P. Gill[1] writes to them that "the situation looks first-rate"; Mr. John Morley[2] predicts that "within a year Mr. Gladstone's Irish proposals will carry with them Parliament and the country"; Mr. Gladstone exults that he has "the civilized world" with him.[3]

All this confidence would be more impressive if its entertainers had not been equally confident of Mr. Gladstone's success in his late appeal to the country. They were wrong in their confidence then; why should they be right in their confidence now? But in a matter of this gravity one cannot be too prudent. Let us see, then, how the case really stands now that the elections are over.

And, first, as to the unanimity of the civilized world in Mr. Gladstone's favour. This would be important if true. I suppose in no country is the unanimity in his favour stronger than in the United States. And yet, even here, if you weigh opinions instead of counting them, the balance of opinion is against Mr. Gladstone's Irish policy. High intelligence and wide knowledge are rare everywhere; they are rare in America. Moreover, it is notorious that in no country do the newspapers so little represent the best mind of the country as they do here. But yet, even here, whenever you meet with a man of high intelligence and wide knowledge, you will almost certainly find him a disbeliever in the wisdom of Mr. Gladstone's Irish policy. "I admire Mr. Gladstone," he will probably say, "but I think he is making a mistake in Ireland." I have myself found but one stanch supporter of Mr. Gladstone's Irish policy whom I should call a man of high intelligence and wide knowledge—Mr. Godkin, the well-known editor of the *Evening Post* and the *Nation*.[4] And Mr. Godkin is an Irishman.

The general American public knows that over here the several States have the control of their own affairs, and that Ireland has been badly governed. It hears that Mr. Gladstone proposes to give to Ireland Home Rule. It inquires no further, but says,—"Mr. Gladstone is right; by all means let Ireland have Home Rule." The Americans are glad to be able safely to do a pleasure to the Irish, who live among them in large numbers and have great influence on elections and journalism. This is the main motive. Some ill will there may be in the masses, some pleasure in abetting embarrassments to a country which unaccountably goes on attracting more of the world's attention and interest than "the greatest nation on earth." But the main motive is the temptation to do the Irish a pleasure safely. The weighty opinion is not that of the general public who yield to this temptation; it is that of men who resist it and who look deeper into the matter. Of these serious people in America the opinion is, I repeat, against Mr. Gladstone, and I strongly suspect that the same thing is true of the rest of "the civilized world" also.

Nevertheless, the Americans do sincerely think, one and all, that the Irish ought to have the control of their own local affairs. They cannot understand its being disputed. The same feeling prevails on the Continent of Europe. And, therefore, I return to the second point of my former letter—that the English nation is now minded, at the same time that it rejects Mr. Gladstone's policy, to give the Irish the due control of their own affairs.

The newspapers here keep repeating Mr. Gladstone's declaration that his principle is "to give Ireland an effective government by Irishmen." But this is, I believe, as much the principle of the English nation as of Mr. Gladstone. The question is, how can it be properly done? Mr. Gladstone says, "By establishing a legislative body in Ireland for the management of exclusively Irish affairs."[5] Change one word in this, for "body" read "machinery," and you pass from what is supremely dangerous to what is supremely expedient. A legislative body in Ireland means a national Irish Parliament. With the history of Ireland, and the character and bent of Irishmen before our eyes, any prudent man can see the dangers from such a Parliament. Place what restrictions upon it you will, it will, by the law of its nature, be forever striving to pose as an independent Parliament; to make Ireland count as an independent nation. The case is precisely parallel with that of the South over here. If a Southern Congress had been conceded, you might have guarded your concessions by what restrictions you pleased, but it would still have been a perpetual source of danger. The remembrance of past enmity, the traditions of the political talents and weight of men like Clay and Calhoun,[6] would inevitably have made a Southern congress always seek to pose as an independent Parliament, to erect the South into an independent nation.

What the Americans did, therefore, was not to establish in the South a legislative body for the management of local affairs, but a legislative machinery. They let the localities manage their own affairs. In this there was great advantage and no danger. And this is what we have to do in Ireland.

A legislative machinery by which the localities can manage their own affairs is as much wanting in Great Britain as in Ireland. Even that basis of all local government, a municipal machinery, is wanting. We have isolated municipalities in towns, but the country as a whole in regard to municipal government is in the condition of France before the Revolution. This is because our people, being conservative, and both they and our aristocracy moderate in temper, the existing state of things has worked on without our feeling its defects to be intolerable. Local government culminates in local Legislatures. But our Parliament in Westminster has had to act both for the localities and

for the nation; it is, to use the American terms, Congress and State Legislatures in one. On the whole, Parliament has done, both in England and in
Scotland, what the majority wanted. Its size is now unwieldy, its work is
unwieldy; moreover, we are without a safeguard and an education which
organized local government affords to those who possess it; there is great
need to organize it for us also.

But the need to organize it in Ireland is most urgent of all. For undoubtedly the Parliament at Westminster has not been that tolerable though
imperfect substitute to Ireland for local Legislatures which it has been to
England and Scotland. It has not done what the majority in Ireland wanted,
it has done what either the minority in Ireland wanted, or the British Philistine. The situation is only made hopeless by denying this or by shutting out
eyes to it. Ireland is treated, say many, precisely like England and Scotland.
And they say this with the Established Churches of England and Scotland
before their eyes; with the Universities of Oxford and Cambridge before
their eyes, Edinburgh and Glasgow. Of all details of local government, where
what takes place in Ireland differs widely from what takes place in Great
Britain, they may be ignorant; but what is done in Church and education
cannot surely be invisible to them. The allegation that Ireland is treated just
like England and Scotland must to Irishmen be almost maddening. And
therefore I have never inveighed against Mr. Parnell and his followers, irritating as much in their language and proceedings is, bad for Ireland as I think
their policy, firmly as I would resist it, rigorously as I would suppress, if necessary, their seditious and incendiary newspapers. What they do is often most
evil and dangerous, but I consider the provocation they have received. To
have Parliament treating the local affairs of Ireland as the Irish minority or
the British Philistine desire, and then to be told that Ireland is on the same
footing as England and Scotland! It needs an Irishman of Burke's calibre to
be a reasonable politician under such circumstances.

The dangers of this state of things are nearly as great as those of Mr.
Gladstone's proposed plan of dealing with it. Of this the country is becoming
conscious. It rejects Mr. Gladstone's plan, but it would give the Irish the
control of their own local affairs. If the Conservatives cannot see this, if they
think they have only to keep order in Ireland, if they let things drift, then the
present great opportunity is lost and we are given over to Cleon and his
democracy.

If, on the contrary, the Conservatives do as the country wishes and
produce a suitable plan of local self-government, for Ireland first, then for
Great Britain also, the situation, to borrow Mr. T. P. Gill's phrase, "looks
first-rate." To establish such a plan the Unionists can work in perfect concert
with Lord Salisbury. It matters little whether their leaders enter the Government or not, though the leaders of one contingent of them should certainly

not enter it without the leaders of the other. What is important is that the Unionists should certainly not allow themselves to be divided, that they should determine resolutely to postpone all other questions to those of procedure and local government, and that on these, and till these are settled, they should act with Lord Salisbury. The future will shape itself, will take care of itself. Sufficient for the day are the needs thereof.[7]

Lord Salisbury may perfectly well frame a plan of local self-government. But he must weigh his words as well as his measures. He complains of those that say that he has nothing to propose but coercion.[8] He ought, on the contrary, to be grateful to them. When he said that what Ireland requires is governing, he did not mean, he tells us, that all she required was a firm hand over her; he meant that she needed good government of all kinds. Be it so. But his mode of expressing himself was unfortunate, and he ought to thank those who by seizing on his expression, call attention to what is his side of weakness and danger. Perhaps all public men have such a side, and we critics, were we in public life, should show ours fast enough. Lord Hartington's is some want of flexibility and fertility. Mr. Goschen's some want of sympathy with man's instinct of expansion. Mr. Chamberlain's some want of respect for the past. Lord Salisbury's is an imperious and scornful treatment of popular wishes. *Beati mansueti.* There never was a moment which tried tempers more than the present moment, or where more was to be gained by controlling them.[9] What is the use of being irritated by the exaggeration, violence, and hatred of Irish members, or by the lively nonsense of Mr. Labouchere? To good temper, good sense, and honesty all things are possible—to negotiate with the Irish members without intriguing with them or surrendering to them, and to make Mr. Labouchere laugh at his own nonsense. Do not let us assume that the Liberals of the nadir must of necessity find a lower nadir still, or that Mr. Gladstone must become more and more of a Cleon. Of Mr. Gladstone's recent performances it is indeed difficult to speak without grave and stern reprobation. The desperado burning his ship, the gambler doubling and trebling his stakes and mortgaging the future as luck goes against him, are the images which come irresistibly to one's mind. This Prime Minister's passionate tirades against a social fabric intrusted to his charge and against a union which it is his duty to maintain, have centupled the difficulties of mending either the one or the other. But wisdom, we are told, is justified of her children, and I suppose that unwisdom must needs be justified of hers also. Yet of one with such gifts and graces as Mr. Gladstone I, for my part, will never despair. If Lord Salisbury produces a good scheme of local government for Ireland I should not be surprised if Mr. Gladstone supported it. The important thing is that Lord Salisbury should do as the country wishes and produce it. I am, Sir, your obedient servant,

Matthew Arnold

Text. Super 11:82–87 (from The Times, *Aug. 6, 1886, p. 12); also pbd in Neiman, pp. 285–89, and Leichman, pp. 277–84.*

1. Thomas Patrick Gill (1858–1931), formerly associate editor of the *North American Review*, now Member for South Louth, Tipperary. He had written in the *New York Daily Tribune* on Dec. 15 of the Irish elections: "The situation looks first rate. The Tories will not have a majority, and no coalition will hold together" (Leichman).

2. *New York Daily Tribune*, July 11: "Mr. Morley, Chief Secretary for Ireland . . . said that within a year Mr. Gladstone's Irish proposals would carry Parliament and the country" (Leichman). In point of fact, Salisbury's government stayed in office five years.

3. Gladstone said it in a letter to a defeated candidate quoted in the *Manchester Guardian*, July 14, 1886 (Leichman).

4. Godkin replied in "American Opinion on the Irish Question," *Nineteenth Century*, 22 (Aug. 1887): 285–92 (Leichman), and Arnold wrote to Godkin on the subject on Oct. 3, 1887.

5. Arnold quotes Gladstone from the *Pall Mall Budget*, June 24 (Leichman).

6. Two southern senators, a unionist and a secessionist, Henry Clay (1777–1852), a Virginian, known as the Great Pacificator or the Great Compromiser, John C. Calhoun (1781–1850), a South Carolinian, identified with states' rights.

7. Adapted from Matthew 6:34. Below, *Beati mansueti*, blessed are the meek, is from Matthew 5:5, and near the end "wisdom is justified of her children" comes from Matthew 11:19.

8. Leichman, citing the *Manchester Guardian*, June 19, quotes Salisbury's forked tongue on the subject: "No one has proposed to govern Ireland by coercion . . . we have not recommended political coercion," etc.

9. The implication of dictatorial demagoguery is a palpable hit.

To Frances Bunsen Trevenen Whately Arnold *

Stockbridge

My dearest Fan   July 26, 1886

I hear on all sides of your being written to, but I must not get out of the habit of writing myself. Nelly and I have been away for a week, first at Long Branch on the New Jersey Coast with Mr & Mrs G. W. Childs; he owns the Philadelphia Ledger and has entertained all the English who come over here. From thence we went to Cresson on the Alleghanies—a journey of 12 hours. Mr Childs saw to our luggage, brought us our tickets for which there was nothing to pay, and as the express dropped us 15 miles from Cresson and we should have had to wait three hours for a local train the Pennsylvania Company ran us on to Cresson in a special without charge, immediately after the express. The ascent of the Alleghanies by the famous "horse-shoe curve" is interesting, but all the mountains lose by being rounded in form and wooded to the summit. One longs for bare ridges. The endless brooks of northern Europe are also wanting, and the streams in the bottoms run over such good

soil that they are seldom perfectly clear. Cresson is 2000 feet above the sea
and was beautifully cool and free from mosquitoes. The railway company
put the hotel there because of a beautiful and unfailing spring of water; it is a
kind of toy hotel to look at, in wood and quite pretty; it holds 1000 people.
It is common for the richer people to live in wooden cottages in the grounds
and only to take their meals at the hotel. Carnegie does this and we were at
his Cottage. We stayed three days; the first day we went down to see his
works at Pittsburg, 100 miles by rail; the country round Pittsburg is full of
natural gas, which you see here and there towering into the air in a clear
flame through an orifice in the ground; this gas they have lately conducted
to the works and made to do the work of coal; no more coal is used, and
there is no smoke. As a consequence, Pittsburg, from having been like a town
in the Black Country, has become a seemly place. Its situation is beautiful; it
lies between two rivers, the Monongahela and the Alleghany at a tongue of
land where the old fort, called after the first Pitt, was built; Pittsburg is now
a city of 250,000 people. The two rivers after joining become the Ohio,
which we saw, with its islands and a width like that of Windermere, disappearing under the setting sun. The next day we had a long drive through the
Alleghanies to Holidaysburg, a country town in the plain; we drove through
woods and gorges, chiefly interesting to me from two new flowers which
were everywhere, the great Veronica Virginiana, from 3 to 5 feet high with
great spikes of white flowers, and the pokeweed, a great herb yet taller, with
tassels of pink flowers from the berries of which red ink is made. Once I got
Carnegie to stop near the stream and got out that I might look at the water;
to my joy I found edging the stream and running back over swampy ground
into the forest great rhododendrons still in flower; the blossom is white, the
plants as big as the big ones at Fox How, and the trusses of splendid size. We
gathered a good many; the kalmia, too, was everywhere, but going out of
flower. We lunched at Holidaysburg, and returned through the mountains
by another route, over awful roads; but the horses here can go anywhere. We
did not get home till after 8 o'clock. Carnegie, who is immensely rich, has
bought 500 acres on the crest of the mountains and will build a Scotch ba-
ronial house there. I would sooner build it in Scotland. Next day we drove
to Loretto, a Catholic settlement founded by Prince Gallitzin[1] at the beginning of this century; the beauitful culitvated side of Pennsylania could not be
better seen. The wild cherries are wonderful; we pulled up under a row of
them and might have filled the carriage with cherries perfectly black and
ripe; they are too numerous for the birds, who prefer the bird or choke-
cherry. Next day we returned to New York, a long day—slept at the Windsor where I was received with open arms, and returned here in the evening.
I wish I could take you into the wood behind this house. I would shew you

magnificent Osmunda, but you would especially like the Monotropa uniflora, called here Indian Pipe or Corpse plant (excellent names both) and the Pyrola rotundiflora, which are all over the place. I shall not rest till I have got the great scented Lady's Tresses and the Pitcher Plant, which grow in the swamp near here; I have found the Impatiens to my great delight. Covering waste ground, like gorse with us, is the Shrubby Cinque-foil—Potentilla fruticosa. I have Asa Gray's American Botany lent me—a most useful book. I have had a long and sweet letter from K—my love to her. I will write to her before long. I rather hope no Unionists will go into Ld Salisbury's ministry; there will be divisions if one wing enters without the other, and I suppose Chamberlain's wing cannot enter. All well here—though America does not suit me so well as Europe. Your letter to Flu has come today—all very interesting. That poor Taylor boy![2]   Ever your most affectionate

M. A.—

I send you Maturin Delafield's promised letter.

MS. Frederick Whitridge.

1. Demetrius Augustine Gallitzin (1770–1840: *WWWA*), a naturalized American of a princely Russian family and an ordained priest, was a frontier missionary.

2. The "poor Taylor boy": according to the *Ambleside Herald, Lake News and Visitors' List*, July 9, p. 5, a coroner's inquest found no explanation of the death of two girls or the illness of their brother, children of "a man of means" (Leichman).

To Mountstuart Elphinstone Grant Duff*

Stockbridge, Massachusetts
My dear Grant Duff   July 29, 1886
    I had a letter from you before I left England in May; I like to think that you will have been in general agreement with what I said about the Irish question and Gladstone in the Nineteenth Century. There was a rumour you were coming home, but I suppose you will stay out your time. The elections are a great relief; what a power of solid political sense there is in the English nation still! And now, unless the Conservatives let things drift and miss their opportunity, we have a really interesting and fruitful political work before us: the establishment of a thorough system of local government. How different from the Wife's Sister, Church-Rate and Disestablishment business familiar to modern liberalism! I thought (and said in the Times six weeks before the election) that Gladstone would be beaten; but the majority against him exceeds my best hopes. Then I came here, where the newspapers are all Par-

nellite & Gladstonian, suffering nothing to appear but what favours the side they are on. They now console themselves (like John Morley) by saying that in six months Gladstone will be in again and carrying his measure triumphantly.

Gladstone is and always has been *unwise*—was there ever such proof as he has lately given how far-reaching and all-devouring a disease that is in a politician—and the greater his gifts, the worse!

But I am not going on about English politics. You should read Carnegie's book "Triumphant Democracy"; the facts he has collected as to the material progress of this country are valuable, and I am told the book is having a great sale, being translated into French and German, &c. He and most Americans are simply unaware that nothing in the book touches the capital defect of life over here: namely that compared with life in England it is so uninteresting, so without savour and without depth. Do they think to prove that it must have savour and depth by pointing to the number of public libraries, schools, and places of worship. But I must not go on about the politics and sociology of America any more than about those of England.

Nature—I must give the rest of my letter to that, in memory of our walk at Eden when you showed me the difference between Hawkbit and Cats Ear, took me to where the Linnoea and the Goodye[a]ra repens grew, and founded my botanical education. In beauty and form the landscape of the eastern and middle States (I have seen no more) is deficient: this Berkshire County in Massachusetts, where I now am, which the Americans extol, is not to be compared to the Lakes or Scotland. The streams, too, are poor; not the great rivers, but the streams and mountain brooks. The heat is great in summer, and in winter the cold excessive[;] the mosquito is everywhere. But the flowers and trees are delightfully interesting. On a woody knoll behind this Cottage the undergrowth is Kalmia, which was all in flower when we came; the Monotropa uniflora (Indian Pipe or Corpse Plant as they call it here—excellent names) is under every tree, the Pyrola rotundifolia in masses. Then we drive out through boggy ground, and towering up everywhere are the great Meadow Rue, beautifully elegant, the Helianthus giganteus and the Milk-weed—this last (Asclepias) in several varieties and very effective. I believe it is an American plant only, and so I think is the shrubby Cinquefoil which covers waste ground as the whin does with us. The pokeweed (phytolacca) is I think American too, and quite a feature by the woodborders in Pennsylvania. But the great feature in Pennsylvania was the rhododendron by the stream sides and shining in the damp thickets: bushes thirty feet high, covered with white trusses. I was too late for the azalea and for the dogwood, both of them, I am told, most beautiful here. The Cardinal flower I shall see—it is not out yet. A curious thing is our garden golden rod of North England and Scotland, which grows everywhere like the wild golden rod with us; they have more than 30 kinds of Solidago. What would I give to go in your company for even one mile on any of the roads out of Stockbridge. The trees, too, delight me; I had no notion what maples really were, thinking only of our pretty hedge-row shrub at home; but they are, as of course you know, trees of the family of our sycamore, but more imposing than our sycamore or more delicate. The sugar maple is more imposing, the silver maple more delicate. The American elm I cannot prefer to the English, but still I admire it extremely. And the fringe-tree! and the wigged sumach— this latter growing with a strength of shoot and an exuberance of wig which one never sees in England. Still I shall be very glad to be back in England; the more so as I have a slight heart trouble which this climate and its habits do not suit. Write to me at Cobham and tell me all about yourself and your wife—my love to her, and to Clara. We have taken our passage for the 4th of September. Between this and then I am going to the Adirondacks. The fishing is, as the Americans say, "a fraud"; the rivers all fished out. "Where every man may take liberties, no man can enjoy any" (Coleridge).[1]   Ever yours affectionately

Matthew Arnold.—

MS. British Library Oriental and India House Collections.

1. In Coleridge's *On the Constitution of the Church and State, According to the Idea of Each*, ch. 11 (Leichman).

To Arthur Howard Galton

Stockbridge, Mass.

My dear Galton   July 30, 1886

The best thing I can do here for the Magazine[1] (in which I am inter- ested for Image's sake as well as yours) is to get my son in law to lay it on the table of the University Club in New York, the best centre that I know of for the kind of people likely to be interested in such a publication.

What you have written on Assisi is full of interest, but for the general public it should have perhaps had more about Assisi itself, although the ques- tions of criticism treated in the middle and latter part of the paper are in themselves highly important, and you have treated them with judgement and insight.

This climate does not suit me, though my daughter and grand-daughter are a great consolation; but, as far as health and efficiency are concerned, I shall be very glad to be back in England again.   Ever truly yours

Matthew Arnold.—

I hope to find the state of Nabr [*sic*] Scar less afflicting than you say.[2]

MS. *The College of Wooster.*

1. *Century Guild Hobby Horse,* 1886.
2. "In the summer of that year, the Manchester water works were being carried through the Rydal valley, at the back of Wordsworth's house and above his favourite walk" (Galton, *Two Essays upon Matthew Arnold,* p. 107).

To Jane Martha Arnold Forster

Elizabethtown, N. Y.

My dearest K   August 1, 1886

It is your birthday, my darling and I must write to you upon it—a sad birthday, but let us fix our thoughts upon what we retain and enjoy rather than upon that which we lose and regret. You retain of dear William, in what you told me in your most interesting letter, what must make you follow the present course of things in Ireland with double attention; he could not of course have joined this government, and if the Conservatives have the term which their present situation seems to me to promise, his age would hardly have left him time to be of the Liberal government of the future; his talent for administration was such, and I should have so much liked to see him at the Colonial Office, that it would have added to my sorrow if his death had deprived him of the chance of being now Colonial Minister. I confess I watch the present course of things with good hope—and so I think would he too have watched it; while his public spirit and unselfishness would have made him particularly useful in aiding Lord Hartington to keep the great end steadily in view and to prevent divisions and complications. I think very highly indeed of Ld Salisbury's intelligence, and surely he will now see the need of being conciliatory and discreet in speech. These silly newspapers over here are all agog as to the certain and speedy ruin presaged by Ld Londonderry's appointment and Ld Randolph Churchill's; but Ld Londonderry's appointment is, I suspect, a positively good one, and the reminiscence of Ld Castlereagh is too remote now to work harm. Few people like Ld Randolph Churchill less than I do, but I can see the need for having a vigorous and spirited personage to speak for the government in the H. of Commons, and one not likely to be overborne by Gladstone, Morley, Labouchere and the Irish; and this need the appointment of Ld Randolph will meet. I also think the appointment of Matthews a good one.[1] Altogether I am, as I say, in good hope about public affairs; I wish Shaw Lefevre had been beaten at Bradford, and I cannot think the candidate who opposed him a good choice; dear Edward or James Cropper would have been a thousand times better! Oakeley would not have suited because he is now a political young man in his promotion, and a candidate was needed whom the constituency might have returned not to serve *his* purposes but simply to express their own respect for W. E. F. But Oakeley seems to have made a good fight at Darlington. All you tell me about him interests me, and the change in his position at Cassell's seems to involve but a very light loss in money.

What will be my position as regards money I do not in the least know; I suppose I have got a pension but I have heard nothing about it and have no notion what it will be; however I shall know in time and meantime I am drawing no money from home and indeed shall bring home some of the money earned by my one lecture here.

I write from the Coddingtons in the Adirondacks; you remember that nice Marie Coddington, stout and with fair hair, rather lame, whom you met at the Buxtons' at Lucy's wedding; she wishes me particularly to remember her to you and dear Francie. She and her sister lost their father this spring; we greatly liked all three, and they have been Lucy's best friends here; the girls are quite rich [and] have a good house in Fifth Avenue and a villa at this beautiful place in the Adirondacks. I am writing in the sage-green-coloured wooden piazza, while a thunderstorm dies away; in front of me, on the horizon, is the peak and ridge of Wodo-nayo, "the Mountain of hurricane," over 3700 feet high, 200 higher than Snowdon; in the foreground the village of Elizabethtown, looking like a village in Bavaria or Austrian Tyrol, with its metal cupolas to the Churches and red roofs to the houses. For the first time in America I find real, exquisitely beautiful mountain outlines and abundant streams. Elizabeth-town is not bigger than Ambleside, though it is the capital of Essex County and has the Court House and prison. This mountain district of the Adirondacks covers 2000 square miles; this gives you a notion of the scale of things here. We are going tomorrow to Keene Valley at the foot of Mt Marcy, the highest mountain of the region, 5450 feet high, 1000 feet higher than Ben Nevis. We left Lucy yesterday morning, Nelly remaining to keep her company; both of them, and also the sweet midget, quite well. Nelly will probably go with me to Mount Desert, a beautiful sea place on the Maine Coast, and that will be our last visit. The days are hot here, but the thunder-storm has brought the temperature down to 70; the nights are always cool. At Stockbridge it is too hot; even at night we too often have it up to 70 and more. I long to be back in England, though I can never regret that we have had this time with my Lucy. Her husband is getting on in his profession quite remarkably well. The baby is beginning to smile at its friends. My love to Fan; it seems to me ages since I heard from any of you, but that is because of the uncertainty with which the steamers arrive. Tell my dear Edward I cannot lecture at Bradford this year—nor at all, if they continue to return Shaw Lefevre. Love to Francie. Ever my own dearest K, your most tenderly affectionate brother

M. A.—

MS. Frederick Whitridge.

1. Charles Stewart Vane-Tempest-Stewart (1852–1915: *DNB*; *VF*, 2/6/96), sixth marquis of Londonderry (a descendant of the notorious viscount Castlereagh immortalized by Shelley and Byron), was Lord Lieutenant (or viceroy) of Ireland; Randolph Churchill was chancellor of the Exchequer; Henry Matthews (1826–1913: *DNB*; *VF*, 9/10/87), later Viscount Llandaff, was home secretary.

To Constance Cary Harrison

Elizabethtown, N. Y.

Dear Mrs Burton Harrison   August 4, 1886

Your kind letter has reached me here. Far from forgetting you, I had several times asked Lucy about you; had seen with pleasure in the Berkshire Guide-book that you had a house at Lenox, and learned with disappointment that you had it no longer. We return to England at the very beginning of September, and to leave Lucy again now is not easy; we go back to her at Stockbridge tomorrow. Her mother will certainly not leave her; but if I might bring my daughter Nelly with me in her place, and if the beginning of the week after next suited you, I should be much tempted to pay you a flying visit of two days. Let me have a line at Stockbridge to say whether Nelly and the 14th or 16th of August would be convenient to you; and believe me,   most sincerely yours,

Matthew Arnold.—

MS. Library of Congress.

1. Constance Cary Harrison (1843–1920: *WWWA*), a southern novelist and author transplanted to New York, Massachusetts, and Bar Harbor, Maine, by her marriage to Burton Harrison, a New York lawyer.

To Constance Cary Harrison

Stockbridge

Dear Mrs Burton Harrison   August 8, 1886

I have just had your note. We cannot come until the 16th, Monday: that night we propose to sleep at Boston, and to come on by the day train on Tuesday, reaching Mount Desert Ferry about ½ past 9 in the evening. Nelly is afraid of the sea, but I hope to persuade her to return by way of sea as far as Rockland at least. We shall really only be able to stay with you Wednesday and Thursday, but to those two days I am looking forward with great pleasure.   Most truly yours

Matthew Arnold.—

MS. Library of Congress.

To Frances Bunsen Trevenen Whately Arnold*

Stockbridge

My dearest Fan   August 10, [1886]

Fanny Lucy complains that she never gets a chance of writing to you, because I am always writing: but at the end of this week I go with Nelly to Mount Desert and Fanny Lucy shall write instead of me, as I shall be travelling. I had your letter yesterday; I did not know the Thalictrum majus grew on Windermere; I knew the Comarum palustre did. It is hard not to talk flowers to you, you are so interested in them, and there are so many here to interest you. A dear girl called Emily Tuckerman[1] took Nelly and me to a river meadow yesterday where we could find the Cardinal flower (red lobelia); I send you a specimen, though I don't know whether it will reach you in a recognisable shape; never, since I turned aside from the hill-road from Mentone to Gorbio and entered a little enclosure where the double scarlet anemone was in flower, have I had such a sensation as when I pushed yesterday through a thicket of milk-weed, blue vervain, meadow rue and yellow loosestrife, and saw a plot of scarlet lobelias by the stream side, nodding in the breeze.[2] They are from 1½ to 3 ft high. Lucy and Fanny Lucy are to be taken to the place on Sunday, as it is within easy reach. We found all sorts of other things, the wild smilax or greenbrier, and the wistaria of the north (our garden wistaria is wild in the southern states) the Glycine Apios of Linnaeus, with its beautiful leaves and fragrant brown-purple flowers. Also the plants of the great Cypripedium, Lady's Slipper, very interesting in leaf and stem, though the flower is over. But I must not go on about the flowers, or my letter will contain nothing else.

We came from the Adirondacks with one of our hostesses, Fanny Coddington, to Lake George, as her guest. She did everything for us, down to checking the luggage and ordering my bath in the morning. I am getting so used to the devoted way in which my friends attend to me here that I begin to take it as a matter of course; but it is really wonderful. It is as if one lived with a succession of young people with the sentiments towards me of Arthur

Galton and the opportunity of carrying them out in practice.[3] But I thirst for England, and this climate has not entirely suited me. Here we have it very warm again, and the voice of the mosquito, alas, is again heard in the land;[4] in the Adirondacks there were none, and it was quite cool. But it is not so bad by any means as when we first came; the thermometer does not reach 90 by day nor keep above 70 by night. It suits the dear baby perfectly, who gets prettier and more flourishing every day; really one of my pleasantest moments in the day is my first visit to her when I am on my way to the bathroom; at that time she is lying awake in her little crib, enchanted to see visitors, and always receives me with a smile or two. The other day she snatched a five dollar note out of my hand, and waved it in triumph like a true little Yankee; today for the first time she has clutched my eye-glass and played with it. Lucy looks a little pulled down by all the nursing, but she makes a capital nurse, and it is best she should go on through this hot American summer, which is very trying to infants. Fred is down here this week. This afternoon, a Mr Choate,[5] a great New York lawyer, takes us out driving over Bear Mountain; tomorrow Miss Tuckerman takes us driving to Mohawk Lake, and in the evening we dine at Lenox with another New York lawyer, Mr Parsons.[6] On Thursday Flu and I go for two days to Ashfield in the next county, on a visit to the Nortons. Next week Nelly and I make a long journey to Bar Harbor, in the north of Maine, a watering place which is now the rival of Newport; sea and mountains meet there and it is cool; but we shall have too much social business. We stay with a Mrs Burton Harrison. Lucy begs me to send you her particular love, and Fanny Lucy and Nelly to tell you with what delight they think of seeing you and being at Fox How; it will be far best to come from Liverpool. We ought to be able to reach you from thence either on Monday the 13th or Tuesday the 14th. Tom's letter was interesting, and of course the value to a people of having such an object of "admiration, hope and love" as a great religion, cannot be over-estimated. Still, Irish Catholicism cannot last as it is. On the whole I am in good hope about politics; the two great points are to keep the Unionists together, and to produce a local government plan.   Your ever affectionate

M. A.—

MS. Frederick Whitridge.

1. Emily Tuckerman (1853–1924), resident, with her parents, of Stockbridge, sister of Bayard (*WWWA*), the writer and teacher.

2. An almost Wordsworthian "spot of time."

3. Leichman cites Galton's poem "To Apollo Belvedere" and his article "Assisi," both in the *Century Guild Hobby Horse* and both reverent in praise of Arnold.

4. Song of Songs 2:12.

5. Joseph Hodges Choate (1832–1917: *WWWA*), a very prominent lawyer and

diplomat (who had introduced Arnold at his last New York lecture in Chickering Hall, N.Y., Mar. 1, 1884) and a Stockbridge summer resident.

6. Possibly, John Edward Parsons (1829–1915: *WWWWA*), New York lawyer.

To Frances Bunsen Trevenen Whately Arnold

Stockbridge

My dearest Fan   August 16, 1886

I have not gone to Bar Harbor, as I was not feeling well enough to face the long journey for a visit of two days to be probably filled with parties and gaieties: perhaps I shall go at the end of the week if I feel better, but very likely I shall not move from here again until we go to New York just before our departure. I have been a good deal troubled with the ache in my chest for the last two or three weeks, and I think the doctor here, who was attending Lucy and extended his attentions to me, gave me too much digitalis, or continued it too long, for a being with such a slow circulation as mine is, so that I have been reduced beyond what is expedient. One good result of staying at home is that I see more of Lucy and her dear baby, which is now called "the belle of Stockbridge" and is pointed out to everybody, the nurse says, as "Matthew Arnold's little granddaughter.["] Another good result is that I am able to write my weekly letter to you; I am sure you deserve it you are so good, not only in writing to me but in sending me whatever you think may interest me. I am glad the Times (Humphry I suppose) is taking up the Report[1] as it may lead to its being of use; to be of use is more and more my aim in what I write; my name is quite as much "up" as I can expect or wish it to be, and I no longer want any place or preferment. Perhaps one's writing, when one is in this case, actually gains something which it had not before. But my former reports had little or no attention paid to them by the press when they appeared, and this was certainly a disadvantage to them, from whatever cause it proceeded. I have not read the Times comments through, but I have seen enough of them to judge that they will carry the report into many hands. It will not be quite acceptable to the Office.

I have had a sweet but sad letter from dearest K. How good of her to have Fan Taylor![2] I have always liked Fan, and in these last years all I have heard and seen of her has made me admire her qualities greatly. You girls do all the duties of attention and hospitality to all branches of the family; my occupations and the small size of the cottage partly excuse me for doing so little, but not entirely. How good you have been to Ella, and what pleasure it gives us to find you and dearest K thinking and speaking of her so affectionately. She has an excellent nature indeed.

Flu and I returned on Saturday from a visit of two days to the Nortons about forty miles north of this. The Norton children adore her in a way which is pretty to behold—George W. Curtis,[3] one of the men I like best in America, has his country place close to the Nortons; he took us a long drive through a country very pretty and very prosperous, but wanting in *something* as all America is—all America, that is, outside of the vegetable kingdom. We go on botanizing, and Nelly has become quite bitten with it, and has begun, quite of her own accord, a list of the plants we have found. The Monardia [*for* Monarda] is our latest treasure. Asa Gray's book on American botany is excellent, I only wish you were here to handle it with us. The quite common things here, which are yet strangers to us, are what interest me particularly; such as the Roman wormwood or as the Collinsonia—so called from a London citizen, a friend of Linnaeus, who busied himself much in having the plants of N. America searched for and sent to him. Fred is gone off to New York and will have to go on to the State of Michigan probably, for a law case in which he is concerned. I like him increasingly, and there can be no doubt of Lucy's strong attachment to him. Nevertheless she will feel the parting from us very much; to judge from the baby's demonstrations, when I visit her you would think that she would do the same—but she will not—Dear old Walter will be with you when you get this; love from all of us to him and his. Keep K at Fox Ghyll till we come if possible. Ever, dearest Fan,   your most affectionate

M. A.—

MS. Frederick Whitridge.

1. *Education Department. Special Report on Certain Points Connected with Elementary Education in Germany, Switzerland, and France,* 1886 (Super, 11:1–53), noticed as "Mr. Matthew Arnold's Report," *The Times,* July 30, 1886, p. 9; a "thorough outline and substantial portions" of it appeared on Aug. 4, p. 13 (Leichman).

2. Possibly, one of the "Misses Taylor, High Side, Bassenthwaite" listed in Martineau among her eighteen entries under this name.

3. George William Curtis (1824–1892: *WWWA, OCAL*), a widely traveled author, reformer, journalist, editor of *Harper's Weekly* from 1863, close friend of Norton's, easily qualified as a parfit, gentil Arnoldian. He had introduced Arnold in New York at his Emerson lecture on Jan. 4, 1884; Henry James wrote to Norton Dec. 6, 1886: "I saw Matt Arnold the other night, and he spoke very genially of you and of his visit to Ashfield—very affectionately, too, of George Curtis—which I loudly echoed" (Leichman).

To Constance Cary Harrison

Stockbridge, Mass.

Dear Mrs Burton Harrison   August 20, 1886

I have deferred writing because I was really anxious to propose coming to you next week, but last night I had again one of the attacks of pain across the chest which your too stimulating climate has given to me; and as I read in the papers that at Bar Harbor a man liable to sea-sickness is thought intolerable, what would be thought there of a man liable to spasms of the chest?

I have therefore unwillingly made up my mind to remain quietly here, and to deny myself the very great pleasure of a visit to you.[1] We sail for England on the 4th of September, and I shall need all my solidity for the passage. But I assure you that to fail in my engagement to you is a grievous disappointment to me; I only console myself by the hope of seeing you before very long on the other side of the Atlantic. Believe me, dear Mrs Burton Harrison,   most regretfully and sincerely yours,

Matthew Arnold.—

MS. Library of Congress.

1. "A few days before this Mrs. Arnold had written to announce her husband's disposition: 'Instead of writing to tell you the train by which Mr. Arnold and N[elly] hoped to reach Bar Harbor on Tuesday, I am sorry to say I must ask you *not* to expect them at all on that day. Mr. Arnold has not been well lately, and though he was better the beginning of this week, he has gone back the last day or two, and I am afraid he is not equal to the long journey. He is very much disappointed at being obliged to give up a pleasure he had been so looking forward to, and he still hopes, if it is convenient to you, to merely postpone his visit for a few days. . . . He has been suffering a good deal from pain across his chest and the doctor forbids all exertion; but with a few days' entire rest and quiet, we hope he may be better again, though he will have to keep strict rules as to exercise, such as walking uphill, or doing as much as he has hitherto done'" (Mrs. Burton Harrison, "Mr. Arnold's Health in America," *Critic*, new series, 9 [May 26, 1888]: 259.)

To Frances Bunsen Trevenen Whately Arnold*

Stockbridge

My dearest Fan   August 24, 1886

We had our English letters yesterday—how faithful you are in sending me what you think will interest me. But for you I should not have seen my letter in the Times. The state of things here is curious: no part of the letter which spoke of the best American opinion being adverse to Gladstone's proceedings was given but a telegraphic summary of part of the letter appeared with this heading: *Mr M. A. favourable to Home Rule.* And so they go on; not a word from any one except the Irish, or Englishmen who take part with them. And a constant assertion of the embarrassment of the Government, and of the estrangement, rapidly growing, of the Unionists. The situation is in truth so critical, that it is easy to become alarmed when one is at a distance, and I shall be sincerely glad to have done with the American newspapers.

The enclosed will shew you what was in store for us at Bar Harbour.[1] I could not go last week, I was not sure enough of being free from pain, and this week we found that it would be a comfort to dearest Lucy if we gave it up, so give it up we did. It would have been a hot two days journey, then two days in a whirl, and then a hot two days journey back—so we are well out of it. This place has become very enjoyable; I see at last what the American autumn which they so praise is, and it deserves the praise given it. Day after day perfectly fine, the thermometer going up from 60 to 75 but not higher, in the course of the day, and averaging 60 at night. Fred is away in Michigan, uncomfortable enough, on some law business; he cannot get back till the end of the week. Next week we shall all probably go to New York together, and I hope to write you a last line by the North German Lloyd on Wednesday the 1st of September. The baby is a little darling—she paid me a visit in bed this morning; now she is gone off to Lu to be photographed. Her nurse is excellent, and so indeed are all Lucy's servants. We live just as we should at the Cottage at home, except that we get more fruit—peaches bananas and pears sent from New York. We breakfast at 9, lunch at ½ past 1 and dine at ½ past 7. Lucy looks a little pulled down by the nursing, but it will cease at the end of September, I think. I wish you could have been with us yesterday—that is, if you are not nervous in a carriage, for the roads look impossible in places and the hills are awful. But the horses are the best tempered and cleverest in the world, the drivers understand them perfectly, and the carriages are so light that they re-bound from all shocks. We went to a lake called Long Lake, and at last I found a solitary spot for a house—a clearing which looked upon the lake, a wooded range behind, and to the south a wide valley with the Dome and the other high Taconic Mountains in the sunset at the end of it. We were perpetually stopping the carriage in the woods through which we drove, the flowers were so attractive; we settled that you would be particularly struck with the Gherardia [*for* Gerardia] flava (False Foxglove) and the Desmodium (Tick Trefoil). But I think myself you would be so plunged in the varieties of the Golden Rod and the Aster that you would go mad over them and be left in an Asylum. I steadily refuse to concern myself with their varieties; I will only say that you have no notion how beautiful the Asters are till you see them. I remember the great purple one (A. patens, I think) grows wild about Yarmouth in the Isle of Wight. There is a nice youth here, a German called Hoffmann,[2] who is an enthusiastic botanist. Did I tell you we had a grand specimen of the Osmunda in the field below the house? The orchards are getting splendid; the apples scent the air as you drive along. The feeling against drink is such that the people are even ceasing to make cider, and quantities of the apples are really left to waste. My love to the Walters,[3] and to Lake if he is still within reach. Your ever affectionate

M. A.—

MS. *Frederick Whitridge*.

1. Probably described in Mrs. Harrison's *Recollections, Grave and Gay*, p. 352: "I had arranged for Mr. Arnold's pleasure . . . a water-pageant of Indian birch-bark canoes, one of the prettiest and most characteristic spectacles imaginable, as seen from the rock-bastion of our lawn over the sea. The canoe club duly made its appearance from behind Bar Island, went through its manoeuvres, and came in for tea upon the lawn. There was some confusion in the anouncement that our guest of honor was after all not present, and most canoeists went home firmly believing they had been seen and admired by the famous apostle of sweetness and light, our local newspapers duly announcing the great man's presence."

2. Ralph Hoffman (1870–1932: *WWWA*), of German *extraction*, born in Stockbridge and educated at Harvard, became a teacher and headmaster and, finally, director of the Museum of Natural History, Santa Barbara, Calif.

3. Arnold's brother and (in a rare reference) his wife.

To Susanna Elizabeth Lydia Arnold Cropper

[*c*. August 25, 1886][1]

to be back in England again, though I am glad to have had this time with my Lucy; but I shall never return to America. Meanwhile I acquaint myself with the country and flowers as well as I can; after luncheon today I go by train to Great Barrington and am there met by a Mr Mackie who will drive me to a point of view for seeing the Dome, the principal mountain of the neighbourhood, and a very grand one: back to tea at his house, and then I return here for an 8 o'clock dinner. Tomorrow a young lady, called Laura Sedgwick, drives me in her gig round a mountain called Tom Ball.[2] Saturday I take out my grand-daughter for a drive to Hagar's Pond and Echo Lake. So we go on—it never rains, so the drives are never interfered with.

My love to John and may he keep you for thirty more birthdays! How well you look, considering you must be close upon fifty! Or is it only forty? All here send their love to both of you, and I am always, my dearest Susy, your most affectionate brother,

Matthew Arnold.—

MS. *Frederick Whitridge (incomplete)*.

1. Susy's birthday.

2. Mackie has not been identified. Laura Brevoort Sedgwick (1859–1907), daughter of William Ellery Sedgwick, married Henry A. James, a New York lawyer, and became

one of the first settlers of East Hampden, Long Island (family information from Alexander Sedgwick).

To [?]Marie Coddington

Stockbridge

My dear Miss Coddington   August 25, [1886]
    This will show you (what you did not, I hope, doubt) that I instantly comply with any request of yours.   Ever your affectionate,

Matthew Arnold.—

MS. *University of Virginia (photocopy).*

To Mr Whittemore[1]

Mr Whittemore   Stockbridge
Dear Sir   August 25, 1886
    I am not sure whether the poem you mean is that "To a Gipsy Child by the Sea Shore, Douglas, Isle of Man," or "The Scholar-Gipsy."   Faithfully yours

Matthew Arnold.—

MS. *Bryn Mawr College.*

    1. Unidentified. Possibly, Benjamin Franklin Whittemore (1824–1994: *WWWA*), Methodist minister and former congressman, now a publisher in Woburn, Mass.

To Charles Eliot Norton *

Stockbridge

My dear Norton   August 27, [1886]
    I am better, but this climate makes me feel too sensibly my mortality, and I shall return to it no more. I am the more glad to have had those two glimpses of you at Ashfield—I read the account of your meeting; the speeches were good, but I am doubtful about your petty academies, just as I am more than doubtful about your pullulating college and universities. *Das Gemeine*[1] is the American danger; and a few and good secondary schools and universities, setting a high standard, are what you seem to me to want, rather than a multitude of institutions which their promoters delude themselves by taking seriously, but which no serious person can so take.
    But I suspect your opinion on this matter is much the same as mine, though you sacrificed to the local deities at Ashfield.[2]

I like Berkshire more and more, and having given up Bar Harbor I have seen more of this neighbourhood than I expected to see. The Dome is a really imposing and beautiful mass; I have seen it now from many points and in many lights, and with ever increasing admiration. But your Ashfield country has more variety of outline than Berkshire. How strange it will seem to be looking at Coniston Old Man and Helvellyn in a week or two's time! I was shown the Green River yesterday, the river "immortalised by the American Wordsworth"—i. e. Bryant.[3] But the Dome, at any rate, will live in my admiring memory.

I hope we shall see Sally; tell Richard with my love that I have made out the third flower—Gerardia flava, the False Foxglove.

Love from both of us to all your party, and let us see you in England before long.   Your ever affectionate

Matthew Arnold.—

MS. Harvard University.

1. "The common and average thing," from Goethe's "Epilog zu Schiller's Glocke." As Leichman points out, a recurrent attack in Arnold's writings, early and late (see Super, 11:410), most recently in his lecture "Common Schools Abroad."

2. A fund-raising dinner for Sanderson Academy held at the town hall in Ashfield (Leichman).

3. William Cullen Bryant's poem "Green River."

To Frances Bunsen Trevenen Whately Arnold*

Stockbridge

My dearest Fan   August 30, 1886

Your letter to me reached me before Flu got your letter to her, though mine was written two days later; I am sorry for Susy's anxiety about the poor little twin boy. I am sorry, too, for Lucy Ada's recall, poor thing; I know what that is, to be recalled by a child's illness. I hope we shall get a letter from you in New York before we sail, but we cannot be sure of it. It is, however, delightful to think that we are really to make our start for England, if all goes well, next Saturday, and that this will be my last letter home. I think I told you we had given up Bar Harbor, but there is a good deal going on here and if we had stayed for September, which is the great month for this region, we should have had more visiting than I like. On Saturday we had a garden party at Lenox at Mr Whitney's, the Secretary to the Navy;[1] tonight we have to go to an evening party here, tomorrow some people dine with us (the Sedgwicks among them, Harriet Martineau's friends, very nice people),[2] the night after Lucy Fred and I dine dine [*sic*] out here; Fanny Lucy and Nelly will have gone in the afternoon to New York and the change in the evening will be better for my darling Lucy than the diminished party here. I stay over Thursday with her, and then on Friday morning I follow to New York; the Aurania sails at ½ past 9 on Saturday morning. There was a talk of Lucy's coming to New York with us, but the doctor is against it on the baby's account; the dear little thing is doing splendidly and it is a pity to run any risks. New York is a very bad place for children in summer; we have had another hot wave, 85 to 90 in the day and up to 70 all night; of course in New York it is yet hotter than it is here. I could not have got about among the hills here to fish the brooks, even if we had had rain; as it is, they are so low that to fish would be quite useless. Much is to be said for the certainty of fine weather in this climate, but I greatly prefer the English climate on the whole. The great relief will be to cease seeing the American newspapers; here one must read them, for through them only can one get the European news; but their badness and ignobleness are beyond belief. They are the worst feature in the life of the United States, and make me feel kindly even to the Pall Mall Gazette by comparison with them. The P. M. G. remark on my possible drowning was touchingly friendly. The accident was nothing; a wave carried me heavily against a taut rope under water, put there for the safety of bathers; but the shock exhausted me rather, and was followed by a week or so of troublesome attacks of pain across the chest. I am slowly getting back my power of walking, which is what I most care about.[3] The heat is beginning to tell on the flowers, but we shall bring you a list of found plants which will make you envious. I must make an effort to get at the Pitcher plant before I go, but it is in bad swamps. I am glad to hear that my Walter has done his duty at his business; and I am glad you have had the Frank Penroses. If we reach Liverpool on Sunday the 12th we shall of course sleep that night at Liverpool: I make out that the Croppers will be at Buxton. We will telegraph to you when we arrive: I hope we shall be with you either the 13th or 14th. How delightful it will be! Ever, dearest Fan,   your most affectionate

M. A.—

Ted's letter will shew you how amusingly keen he is on his new Magazine.[4] He will get on.

MS. Frederick Whitridge.

1. Williams Collins Whitney (1841–1904: *WWWA*), Yale College and Harvard Law School and admitted to the New York bar in 1865, was active in reform, especially of the Boss Tweed ring, had even been a school inspector, and was now (1885–89) secretary of the navy under Cleveland.

2. Henry Dwight Sedgwick (1824–1903: *WWWA*), lawyer and author, and his wife (and cousin), the former Henrietta Ellery Sedgwick, both cousins of Charles Eliot Norton, had resumed Stockbridge residency since his retirement in 1880. Leichman cites his article "Reminiscences of Literary Berkshire," *Century*, 50, n.s. 28 (Aug. 1895): 552–68, with drawings of Laurel Cottage and a revelation unmentioned by Arnold: "Mr. Arnold had here one of the seizures to which he was subject, and which he then said would some day carry him off—a prediction which was fulfilled within two years. He lived in a cottage rented by his son-in-law, Mr. Whitridge, . . . where he was the center of a home life as scholarship had been abolished. What a delight it was for those who chanced to be his neighbors, after looking somewhat apprehensively at the classic poet and relentless critic who had dropped from Oxford into their New England nook, the tender husband, the fond father, the kind friend, and appreciative and grateful and grateful guest."

3. "Mr. Matthew Arnold was nearly drowned the other day while bathing with Mr. Lawrence Barrett, and was only fished out by a boat-hook in the hands of the laughter-provoking Mr. Crane. 'His mind,' says the veracious American reporter, 'was a blank verse for some time afterwards, and his nose was blue' " (*Pall Mall Gazette*, Aug. 13, p. 3, quoted from Leichman). Neither Lawrence Barrett (1838–1891: *WWWA*), noted American actor who was beginning this year his partnership with Edwin Booth, nor William Crane (1845–1928), a comedian, appears to be mentioned elsewhere in an Arnoldian connection.

4. *Murray's Magazine*, which began publication in 1887 with the new year.

To Robert Charles Winthrop[1]

Hon. R. C. Winthrop—   Stockbridge
My dear Sir   September 2, [1886]

If I had known that you were keeping at home on Monday morning, I should certainly have come to see you. I am very glad to have the final Washington address, which I have been reading with the same pleasure as that with which I read its predecessor. With kind regards to Mrs Winthrop, I remain, most sincerely yours,

Matthew Arnold.—

MS. University of Virginia.

1. Robert Charles Winthrop (1809–1894: *WWWA*), former congressman and then senator from Massachusetts, Bostonian but presumably a summer resident in Lenox or Stockbridge.

To Lucy Charlotte Arnold Whitridge

Cunard Royal Mail Steamship "Aurania"
My darling child   Sunday, September 5, 1886

We had your sweet letter when we came on board yesterday; its affectionateness sharpened the hunger Mamma and I were feeling for you, so that

I should have really liked, as I said to her, to put the vessel about land, and rush back to you at Stockbridge. These pangs of longing pass off, but the intense love and fondness do not relax for a moment. I see your dear little figure, your quick firm step and set face as you went back to the station from the train—I go over all we did together on that last delicious day—and I talk to dear Mamma about it, whose Lucy fills her thoughts as incessantly as she fills mine. Nelly loves to talk of you too, and we do not forget the darling midget, or Fred, who has been so excellent to us all the time, and who inspires a confidence which would reduce our pangs in leaving you, if anything could do that. Mamma will have told you of our coming on board; the first day is always rather miserable, and to us it was very miserable, except that your dear letter caused us some pleasant tears. We are at the Captain's table; he asks much for you and Fred. We are on his right; on his left is a large American family of which I will give you the name tomorrow; they are pleasant. We had a fine day for the start, and there was but little roll, enough, however, to make my head ache. We were all of us a little so-so, but we took our places at lunch and dinner, and so far have none of us been ill, though my night was nearly sleepless. Today is fine with a light breeze from the east, and the soft warmth of the gulf stream. We had made 372 miles from Sandy Hook by noon today. We have had lunch, and I am beginning this letter in the saloon; we did not at first find Fred's stores, but they have turned up this afternoon; the grapes are splendid, and so, no doubt, the other things too will prove. I wanted to begin this to my darling, but I must not write more today—it makes my head ache. God bless you, my precious child.

Monday, Sept[em]ber 6th, 3 P.M. I write again today, my darling, because the weather is fine and I can write without difficulty; it may possibly change and writing be impossible. We are getting on; our run announced at 12 today was 390 miles, but I have lost a pound over it. Bertram Buxton bought the highest number, 399, for £5 and offered to sell me a fifth share in it; Nelly was very keen for me to buy and to make her a sharer in the profits, so I bought, expecting, I own, that we should make at least 410 miles—and we have only made 390! There is no chance, I suppose of our being in before Sunday, but the comfort of this smooth start is immense. It is smoother than on my passage out, and Mamma is on deck nearly all day—which she has never done before. Our party at dinner is pleasant: the American family at the Captain's table is called Van Schaick;[1] they are all nice, and abound in fruit, as, thanks to Fred and to Mr Butler, we do also. The Captain is very pleasant; he and Mamma drank one of Fred's pints of Champagne yesterday; Nelly and I did not feel up to anything with the sweetness of Champagne. After I had written to you yesterday a headache came on, and I thought

I was going to be ill, but I picked up after dinner and had a good night. It is very warm but the moonlight is delicious; I sit on deck till after 10, and Mamma and Nelly till after 9. It is very warm below; I want Mamma to sleep in my bed while I lie on the sofa; I lie outside the bed, so I should lose nothing by taking to the sofa—but she will not consent.[2] Nelly is very happy, and consumes a great deal of fruit. It is getting colder as we approach the banks, and the clear sunshine is a little dimmed, but it is still calm. My bath of sea water each morning is delicious. You are getting ready for your drive, and the sweet midget is probably already out on her perambulations. Mind you take Fred to Hagar's Pond. What an afternoon that was! And all the day following,—the swamp expedition, the Lenox drive! God bless you, my precious child.—

Tuesday, Sept[em]ber 7th 1886. My own Lucy—still fine weather, though it is clouded over; but there has been no fog to stop us, and at 12 today we were off the banks—off in the sense of away from them. But I have that horrid pain in the back of my head which you know so well at sea and this hinders my being comfortable though I am not sick. Mamma is quite wonderful, and Nelly is flourishing also, though both of them complain that they do not sleep well. Our run at 12 today was exactly the same as that of the day before—390 miles. But we are able at this season when there is no ice, to keep our direct course, and have not to lose time by going ever so far to the south of it, as we did on the Umbria. We have made acquaintance with Capt. Lowley and the other young men; and the Van Schaick family turn out very well. There is a Charterhouse Master on board who of course knows Leonard Huxley and his wife quite well; he says they are much liked.[3] The Captain insists on having the concert tomorrow, because the weather may be bad on Friday; for that matter it may be bad tomorrow. But it is a horrid bore to be called out to take the chair and make a speech when one is weighted with headache. How far sooner I would be visiting the sweet and gay midget in her little bed at that hour! Goodbye for today, my darling.

Friday, Sept. 10th. 2.10 P.M. My darling—I wrote last on Tuesday. On Wednesday morning we woke up to a rocking sea and rolling boat, and so it has continued ever since; today, however, the wind has changed to south west, with heavy rain; there is more sea but less rolling, as the sails are effectual to drive the ship straight through the water. Just before lunch the mainsail burst in two with a sudden squall, and to see its flying ends and the men climbing the rigging in the furious rain to get the fragments in was exciting. A good many people are ill, but we three have stood it all, to our own great satisfaction; we have not missed a single meal and I have taken my bath every morning. This comes of beginning with a calm sea; all Sunday I was headachy and miserable, and if there had been any rolling on that day I should have certainly succumbed; as it is, though my head is never comfortable, I had got over the smell and movement of the vessel before the rolling began, and though breakfast has sometimes been a difficulty, I have got along. Mamma and Nelly have been wonderful—on deck all day until today, when it rains, and they betake themselves to the music-room. We do not sleep well, but some sleep we manage to get. The Captain has been most pleasant and he [?]feeds me himself with the most comical solicitude. I have unluckily to take the chair at the concert tonight; when that is over I shall be able to look forward to the delight of seeing land. The Ship report gives our distance at noon today from Fastnet at 435, but it is whispered we are even nearer than that. By ten on Sunday morning the Captain hopes to land us in Liverpool. This day week I left you—my darling, precious child! How I love you, how I love to think of you! Goodbye for today.

Saturday, Sept. 11th, 1886. Still blowing from the south west and raining; it is doubtful whether we shall stop at Queenstown in such bad weather, but we are told to have our letters ready. It is ½ past 2 P.M.; we passed Fastnet and Browhead about a quarter of an hour ago, and may expect to be off Queenstown soon after 5. Not one of our trio has been once sick or missed a single meal; yet the last three days have been days of quite bad weather, and there are numbers of invalids. Fred's fruit was excellent while it lasted, and since it was finished we have been constantly supplied by Mr Maitland, to whom [?]Cuffe introduced us.[4] Mamma has been wonderful—finds out the suffering steerage passengers and gives them grapes and pears. We hope to be at Liverpool by 9 or 10 tomorrow morning, and to be met by the Dicks there. How we shall think of our Lulu, our precious Lulu whom the last few months have made dearer to us than ever, if possible! Fred, too, has his place in our hearts, and that sweet midget! I wake early and lie thinking of her, and of her morning smile and wriggle of her little body in welcoming me. God bless you, my own darling, and bring you safely to us next spring.   Your own fondly and tenderly loving,

Papa.

MS. Frederick Whitridge.

1. Unidentified.

2. "It is very warm below . . . will not consent" lined through by another hand.

3. Lowley has not been identified. Leonard Huxley (1860–1933: *DNB*), an old Balliol man, was an assistant master at Charterhouse 1884–1901, and, though less illustrious than his father, whose life he wrote, made a name for himself as assistant (from 1901) and then sole editor of *Cornhill Magazine* (1916–33).

4. Maitland and Cuffe have not been identified.

To Hardwicke Drummond Rawnsley

Fox How, Ambleside

Dear Mr Rawnsley   September 10, 1886
    I do not find myself attracted by the Library project.   Truly yours
                                                        Matthew Arnold.—

MS. Texas A&M University.

To John Duke Lord Coleridge

Education Department, Whitehall

                                                    Fox How, Ambleside
My dear Coleridge   September 14, [1886]
    I have come straight here from Liverpool and find your letter. You have
done all that was kind and helpful. No doubt Dick was at one time slack in
his work—but what is inexplicable is that he should have been passed over
at this stage without a word of warning and without a word of communication with his chiefs in Manchester. I hear from his and [?]Meade King's chief,
the Superintending Inspector in Manchester, a Mr Coles, that he is "thun-
derstruck" at what has been done, and can recall no instance of a like proceeding; that he, if he had been applied to, should have said that Dick was
entirely fit to take a district now, though in the past he had not been as
diligent as he ought to have been.
    But if Matthews applies to Dick's Manchester superiors for their report
on him,[1] that is all I ask, and that, I understand, he has promised to do.
Meanwhile the step has been given to another, but for this I do not so much
care; the lesson will do Dick no harm, but the stigma of unfitness to take a
district will have been removed from him by his superiors' report.
    You remember G. W. Childs? The enclosed letter will shew you that I
had not been neglectful of Gilbert's wishes, of which I was informed by his
letter to Lucy. My American son in law has likewise applied to the proprietor
of the New York Times—I have not heard again from Childs: if Gilbert
seriously wants employment of the kind, he should go over there himself for
a few weeks, with a view to seeing the newspaper men and bringing them
to the point.
    I must not write more now, I am overwhelmed with accumlated letters.
Once more, my dear Coleridge, let me most warmly thank you—tell me
whether I had better write to Matthews or leave the thing in his hands at
present.
    Kindest regards to Lady Coleridge. I wish I could say we will come

straight to Ottery! but from here we must go to my poor sister in Yorkshire, and then we have to settle things at home after a six months' absence. Most affectionately yours,

Matthew Arnold.—

MS. Lord Coleridge.

1. Meade King and Coles (see below, letter of Lucy Charlotte Arnold Whitridge of Sept. 24, 1886) have not been identified. Henry Matthews was home secretary.

To William Thomas Stead

Fox How, Ambleside
My dear Sir   September 19, 1886
I am much obliged to you for sending the newspaper, and much obliged to the newspaper for the fulness, levelness and general freedom from political bias with which it treats the subject of public education.[1] As to myself, I shall not be in London at present; but if I were, I should have nothing to say at the end of my thirty-five years as school inspector beyond the speech made by the man who lived through the French Revolution: "J'ai vécu!"[2]   Very truly yours

Matthew Arnold

P. S. If you would kindly mention in the P. M. G. that I have only this last week returned from America, having been absent since the middle of May, you would save me from many reproaches of those who have been writing to me and wondering at receiving no answer.

Text. Joseph O. Baylen, "Matthew Arnold and the Pall Mall Gazette," South Atlantic Quarterly, *68 (1969): 533; rptd from facsimile in* Pall Mall Gazette, *April 19, 1888, p. 12.*

1. Leichman suggests that the newspaper may be the *Pall Mall Gazette*, Aug. 3, 1886, with the article "Free Schools and Their Supporters. A Report by Mr. Matthew Arnold."
2. Emmanuel Joseph Sieyès said it.

To Charles Waldstein

Professor Waldstein—   Fox How, Ambleside
My dear Sir   September 21, 1886
I am sure to read your testimonial with attention, but I write a line in answer to your letter because I met both your brother and your mother while I was in America. I had the pleasure of seeing your mother the other day at

Stockbridge, and we spoke of you. I am afraid she finds the climate of America trying, in which I entirely sympathise with her. The summer and autumn weather over there is beautiful, but we Europeans pine for the air and scenes of Europe.[1]   Most truly yours

Matthew Arnold.—

MS. William Walston.

1. See 5:243.

To Lucy Charlotte Arnold Whitridge

Fox How

My darling Lucy   September 24, 1886

This morning we have had your charming letter to your Aunt Fan, with the photograph of yourself with the midget. You look as if it had been a cold morning and you were a little nipped, but it is my own Lulu, and I like it very much. The sweet midget's picture I do not so much care for. I prefer the one with Annie as Gorgon, it is more the midget herself—but no photographs at that age please me much. Your Aunt Fan and your Mamma like it, however. The sweet midget is constantly in my recollection; I hear her talk, and see her throwing back her eyes to see her visitor as he leaves the room. You have never told us that you received our telegram on landing; mention this. I wonder on what day you got my letter written on board ship; it could not be posted till we reached Liverpool. This is the last letter I shall write to you at Stockbridge, I suppose; there will always be a corner in my heart for that place, and I am glad that we settled down in it and got to know it instead of rushing here there and everywhere. It is very sweet of you to keep up your observation of the flowers; the supply here seems very poor after America. For instance where there is one plant of the grass of Parnassus in a Loughrigg bog, there are fifty in your field. Send me a bit of the "little white flower like an orchis" which you mention; it will travel perfectly well; I send you a bit of golden rod (our only English sort!) which I gathered in going round the path here at Fox How this morning. Tell the Butlers that we have here now, beautifully preserved, the lovely specimen of fringed Gentian they gave me, and which I put in a book I was reading and brought home; I brought the Sedgwicks' pitcher plant in like manner, and I sent in a letter to your Aunt Fan one of the Cardinal flowers you and I gathered—it is in very good condition. Mind you take Fred to see Hagar's Pond; it is one of the most complete things I saw near Stockbridge; the landscape drawn well and closely together. Remember me to the woman who offered us the sweet apples. Tell me if you really get any good apples, and what the "September stripes" are like. We were much interested in your account of the picnic; remember us to Charley. Mamma and I took a drive by the Ferry yesterday, over Sawrey hill down upon Esthwaite and Hawkshead and so home; the turn out would not compare in appearance with Charley's[1] but the carriage was comfortable and we drove fast; such roads, too! one feels what audacity it is in the Americans to call even their Berkshire roads good, though to be sure they are the best they know. We brought American weather with us here, except that the sun-warmth and brightness cannot equal yours; but we have actually had not one minute's rain since we arrived here last Monday week; you will know what a stupendous phenomenon such a spell of fine weather here is. But it is too cold, and the wind is northeast; thermometer goes down to 40 at night and does not get above 55 in the day. Every day I have been walking, getting on better and better; it is odd what a difference the change of air makes of me; tell Dr Holcombe so, with my kind regards.[2] Mamma and Nelly try to keep me in leading-strings too much; but yesterday morning I stole out alone (Mr Foss! as Nelly says) at ½ past 11, walked to Clappergate, thence up to the Brathay tarn and home over Loughrigg, you know the route. I had not a minute's pain all the way; I took the ascent very easy of course. I have no attacks of pain at night, either. But the cold drive yesterday gave me a touch of lumbago, which is disagreeable. We had the dear Dicks here for last Sunday; they brought Nelly with them, whom I miss greatly when she leaves us. Except an occasional visit from Aubrey de Vere we have been very quiet here; one night the James Croppers came over to dinner, and today Lawrence Oliphant, whom I met by chance in the road, comes to luncheon; he is a very pleasant fellow indeed, though quite mad. I told him you Mamma and Nelly had been over to see the Lebanon Shakers thinking to interest him; he replied very shortly that he had no more to do with the Shakers than with Mrs Girling, who has just died at the Shaker settlement in the New Forest. Ask Fred who Ephraim Harris was; Oliphant had to do with *him*. But his latest craze is the land of Gilead in the Holy Land. Your Aunt asked the Dicks to return here tomorrow, but today Ella writes to say Dick has early work on Monday and they cannot come. I think Dick is not working well. I found a kind letter from Coleridge saying he had seen Mr Matthews, the Home Secretary, who had promised to do as I wished and write to Mr Coles for a report on Dick; as we heard nothing I have now written to Mr Matthews myself but have not got his answer yet. Parliament is just ending, and I daresay he puts off attending to Office matters till its ends. I saw Mr Coles at Manchester, and he told me Dick was now working well, and quite fit to take a district; but he said he had been very slack once, and had not improved sufficiently after he was first spoken to; a first speaking to of which Dick had told us nothing. We go to Wharfeside on Tuesday, and on the Saturday (Oct. 2nd) to dear Cobham. We all of us got quite fond of Bertram Buxton on the passage; have they told you that his mother has bought Fox Warren of him? He said that he wished the Aurania's head was turned the other way, and that he liked hearing American talked all round him rather than English. Nelly wants you to ask Mora, when you go to New York, what he means by charging 7 dollars for six copies of her photographs: Savony only charged me 1½. There must surely be some mistake. She wants you to pay Mora, and then she will pay to me, for your account, what you pay for her. And now I must end this trivial letter. How I love you, my darling child, and how I love to think of all we did said and saw in our time together! What nice people you have in Stockbridge! I like to think of that too. Remember us kindly and specially to the Coates, Butlers, Tuckermans, Sedgwicks, & Mr Laurence[3]—I think I told you in my ship letter how good Fred's fruit was; my love to him. I shall not forget his cheese. Kiss the midget ten times for me—remember me kindly to Annie and your servants—always your own

Papa

MS. Formerly, Mrs. Harry Forsyth.

1. Like Annie above (presumably, a nurse or housekeeper), Charley was clearly part of the household staff.

2. Possibly, William Frederic Holcombe (1827–1904: *WWWA*), a doctor from Sterling, Mass.

3. The Arnold ladies went to the Shaker community in Mount Lebanon, New York. In the rest of the letter, Ephraim Harris, Mora (presumably a New York photographer), and Mr Lawrence have not been identified. Of Dick and Mr Coles at Manchester (see above, letter to John Duke Lord Coleridge of Sept. 14, 1886) the most appropriate comment would seem to be "Plus ça change, plus c'est la même chose."

To Aubrey Thomas De Vere

Fox How, Ambleside

My dear Aubrey De Vere   September 25, 1886

I have read the enclosed, and agree with a great deal of it. I have less hope from "the educated and independent classes" in Ireland than you have, but I should be glad to see the more solvent half of them retained, as you propose, and another chance given to them. As to "the strong and steady hand" I agree with you entirely; but the real question is, how is society in Ireland to be re-organised; for it has now come to that.   Your letter is of a kind better fitted for a monthy review, I think, than for a newspaper, and might be fashioned into a short article quite suitable for "Macmillan" or for the "Nineteenth Century." It was very pleasant seeing you here.   Ever yours sincerely

                                              Matthew Arnold.—

MS. National Library of Ireland.

To Mr Barnett[1]

                              Wharfside, Burley-in-Wharfedale, Leeds
My dear Mr Barnett   September 30, 1886
      I have just had your letter: I shall not be in London by Saturday, and even if I were I should not like to speak on the subject you propose without more thought and preparation than I could at present well give.   Most truly yours

                                              Matthew Arnold.—

MS. Geoffrey Tillotson (who made the transcript).

      1. Unidentified.

To Arthur Howard Galton

                        Education Department, Whitehall
Arthur Galton Esq.   Cobham, Surrey
My dear Mr Galton   October 4, 1886
      The picture has much imaginative feeling—many thanks to you, and thanks to Mr Image also.[1]
      If I am in Oxford this autumn I shall hope to see you.   Most truly yours,

                                              Matthew Arnold.—

MS. The College of Wooster.

      1. Identifiable with nothing in *Century Guild Hobby Horse*.

To Lucy Charlotte Arnold Whitridge

                                                       Cobham
My darling Lucy   October 5, 1886
      I could not write on Saturday because we were travelling, and besides I felt sure I should find a letter from you here; I did not, but it came on Mon-

day—one of your long, natural, delightful letters, and all to myself. That dear little dirty thing, the midget; how I should like to see her spitting! When I had read your letter I went out to look at the thermometer: it was 72 in the shade, and had not been below 55 all night. We have the perfect Indian summer you ought to be having. I have carried the great rocker out on the lawn and sit there with Kai at my side. Jane had brought them to meet us on Saturday: it was a lovely afternoon and I was looking out of the window as we approached the Lushington's hill, and saw Kai; we got out and the dear boys devoured us. They both look very well, with beautiful coats. When we drove on Max looked at us, but stuck to his Jane; Kai passed all his time running backwards and forwards between our carriage and Jane. We are rather burnt up, it has been such a hot September, but the greenhouse has never looked so well. Your smilax is beautiful and we have more grapes than usual. We found a note from Mrs Buxton asking us to dine; on Sunday the George Smiths came over and we have promised to dine with them; last night, Monday, we dined with the Deacons. So we have three dinners in our first week. It is dreadful not having Mamma; the best thing I can do is to send you her letter which has just reached me; you will know in what distress she will be lest she should leave your Aunt Fan too soon. We had three wet days at Wharfeside, but I am very glad to have been there; I found your dear Aunt Forster able to take much more pleasure in her garden, her trees, and the country, than I been led to expect. They have the carriage and horses still, and Morris looks very smart; they have James too, and dine at ¼ to 8 every night. We were very comfortable but Francie is haunted with the notion that they will be poor, and they will not be, certainly, so well off as I expected. Edward is very happy in his independence, and the mill is doing better, Mr Fison told me, than it has done for the last six years. He has gone out of business, and he says his son and Edward will make more money in their first year than he and your uncle Forster made in the last six years. Edward says it is not so good as that, but there is decided improvement and he is in spirits. The children are dear little things; Iris gets more and more nice-looking. Nelly has heard from her Doltie [?Dottie] to say that her engagement is broken off;[1] no particulars, but the Leafs, with whom we lunched on Sunday and who are very sweet, say that he was carrying it on with some married lady.—I feel sure you never had our telegram or you would have mentioned it; we were distressed at missing the Umbria, but knew you would conclude what had happened. They seem to be having good passages; only half of ours was good, but our sailor qualities were wonderful. I said to Nelly I could not help wishing myself on board the Aurania as she entered the river on her return journey to New York: the force of fondness for my Lucy could no further go. My love to Fred; I continue to improve, and fished all day in the Wharfe last week in heavy rain without being the worse. I also got up to Rydal Head, also in the rain, and fished there, on my last day at Fox How. A box has just come from Stockbridge: the Indian baskets no doubt: 10/8 to pay; do not send many boxes.   Your own,

Papa—

MS. Frederick Whitridge.

1. Iris Mary Arnold-Forster, the third child of Edward Penrose Arnold-Forster; Doltie (?Dottie) has not been identified.

To Percy William Bunting

United Service Club, Pall Mall, S. W.

My dear Sir   October 11, 1886

I think I mentioned it at the time I contributed the paper, but I should like to have a line from you to tell me that I am at liberty to reprint "A Comment on Christmas" in a volume of Collected Essays which I am about to publish.

Please address me at *Cobham, Surrey*, and believe me,   most truly yours,

Matthew Arnold—

MS. University of Chicago.

To Miss Churchill [1]

Cobham

My dear Miss Churchill   Thursday, [?October 14, 1886]

I hoped to have gone by the early train today which your father meets, but I am kept later. So I write one line to say how sorry we were that the weather made our lawn-tennis impossible yesterday; the carriage was ordered, and we sate looking and hoping for the rain to stop and the clouds to disperse, but in vain. I am afraid there will not now be much more lawn-tennis this year; nevertheless, if there comes a spell of fine weather, we will try and get one game, late as it may be. Believe me,   most truly yours,

Matthew Arnold—

MS. University of Rochester.

1. Probably the daughter of the Arnolds' neighbor, Charles Churchill, Weybridge Park (Kelly).

To Lucy Charlotte Arnold Whitridge

Cobham
My darling Lucy   Saturday, October 16, 1886

Your letters are one of them nicer than another. I *should* like to see the Stockbridge hills & woods in their autumn glory; I have before me that high bank by the Housatonic and an active little Lucy scrabbling up it for the yellow fox-glove. Here we have no change of colour yet to speak of, and no frost at night; of course if you have frost at night and the flowers are all killed, the place loses much of its charm. Still, I could not easily bring myself to go to New York, if I had Laurel Cottage, before the end of October. Here, after a dry summer, we have deluges of rain; two days this week have been regular Fox How weather. Mr T. Bennett,[1] whom I met riding in the rain yesterday, told me it was much wanted and would do great good. But I have caught a troublesome cold; and when I cough at breakfast I say to Nelly: Can't you see ⟨Nelly⟩ Lucy looking in your face and Mamma's when I cough and shrugging her shoulders, half annoyed at the coughing, have [*for* half] amused at her own annoyance? That will shew you how you are one of the party still. I am meaning to go to London twice a week until I have been round and taken leave of my teachers; but this week I have been up only once, the weather was so bad and my cold troubled me; what a thing it is not to be obliged to go up unless I choose! The Westminster teachers have raised £60 to make me a present on leaving, and have written to Mamma to consult her as to what it shall be; it is sweet of them, but I think I can only accept a salver or a bowl or something of that sort as a remembrance, and the rest must be spent on the district. A bowl like yours, eh, which we all admired? The worst of it is I shall have to make a speech to them on receiving it. I am very busy and it is hard to set to work writing anything after the idle time I had in America; but my own family will not suffer me to be idle. Mary Ward claims her Amiel article, Humphry an education one, and Ted has been down here in person to look after his interests; I think I shall try and give him an article on Gen. Grant's memoirs which have been little read or noticed over here,[2] which are very interesting, and on which I can write sympathetically. We have just had a visit, early in the day as it is, from poor Mrs Conybeare; her daughter Grace is in such bad health that George Macaulay is trying for the Sydney professorhip of literature in hopes of giving her a change of climate which may set her up again; I am one of the eight electors; he will not get it, poor fellow, and Mrs Conybeare cannot altogether wish he should, but she is in a great flutter about it, poor woman. Grace has five children under six, and bleeding from the lungs.[3] Such is life.[4] Tonight we have Admiral Maxse and Violet to dinner; he has sold 400 acres at Effingham Hill, the house included, and kept 400, on which he is going to build. Walter

Leaf is coming to meet them and brings Andrew Lang, which I am glad of as he has done me many a good turn in print; he says the two authors he really knows are Montaigne and myself, which is pretty well. The Leafs are away with Hubert [?Herbert]. Your Aunt Fan is all right again, we have heard this morning. Dr Hamilton has taken his leave, says both places have healed perfectly and there is nothing bad to follow, recommends care and quiet, but that is all. Minnie not confined yet. You see I give you all the family news. Your Aunt Forster is gone back to Wharfeside, with a cold and cough; Dr Hamilton[5] says she looks "wrecked," which is true, but I found her spirits better than I had expected. Nelly is nailed to help Miss Blunt one evening a week at her boys' recreation; Nelly will be very good but we do not like losing her. We dine out three times next week—the A. Butlers', Lady Grey, and the Moons;[6] the Combes have asked us twice but we were engaged for both days. The Combe girls lunch here tomorrow: they have had a heavenly excursion to the Hartz Mountains with Miss Cazenove.[7] This is just about the time we were starting three years ago, and the Aurania's passage will be a bad one, I expect, as ours in the Servia was; the glass is low and the wind high. Nevertheless I am wonderfully cured of my dread of the passage. The Aurania arrived at Queenstown last Saturday at precisely the same time as we had got there—5½ P.M.; she had a rough but a fast passage. Mamma asks me to send the enclosed pattern of the stuff for the midget's pelisse—kiss the little darling for me—she thinks you will like to see it, to match with the fur. My love to Fred; I was disappointed to find that a bulky letter addressed by him contained not a word of his, but a tiresome request for a preface. Beecher is going back; he has had good audiences, but not the best people, who do not care about him. I shall try and see him before he goes. Major Pond has been giving very large accounts of what I made in America by lecturing.[8] Now I must stop—Nelly has been arranging flowers and will not wait till we come and admire them. My darling child I am always your own

Papa—

MS. *National Archives of Canada.*

    1. Probably, Thomas Bennett, of Cobham, but perhaps his son, Thomas Henry Bennett (b. 1846), J.P., Surrey, Master of Foxhounds, Boodles, of Cobham Court (Kelly).

    2. "Amiel" (Super 11:265–81), *Macmillan's Magazine,* 56 (Sept. 1887): 321–29, rptd *Essays in Criticism, Second Series,* 1888; "Schools in the Reign of Queen Victoria" (Super 11:210–45), *The Reign of Queen Victoria,* ed. T. H. Ward (2 vols, 1887); "General Grant" (Super, 11:144–79), *Murray's Magazine,* 1 (Jan. 1887): 130–44, (Feb. 1887): 150–66.

    3. George Campbell Macaulay (1852–1915: *WWW*), from Eton and Trinity College, Cambridge, now an assistant master, Rugby School, later professor at University College of Wales, Aberystwyth, and then lecturer in English, Cambridge, and editor of *Modern Language Review,* also author or editor of many works, including *Selections from the*

Poems of Matthew Arnold, 1896. In 1878 he married Grace Mary Conybeare, daughter of the Rev. W. J. Conybeare.

4. Possibly, Mrs Gamp in Dickens's *Martin Chuzzlewit*, ch. 29.

5. Dr Hamilton has not been identified.

6. Lady Grey, the former Dorothy Widdrington (d. 1906), was the first wife of Sir Edward Grey (1862–1933: *DNB*, later Viscount Grey of Fallodon; *VF*, 2/5/03, 3/26/13), of Winchester and Balliol ("sent down for incorrigible idleness," 1884), now Liberal M.P. for Berwick-on-Tweed and later an extremely important statesman but always a fly-fisher and birdwatcher ("front rank of English nature writers").

The Rev. Sir Edward Graham Moon, second bt, rector of Fetcham, Leatherhead, a few miles from Cobham, and his wife the former Ellen Sidney (d. 1906).

7. Miss Cazenove remains unidentified but was perhaps the daughter of one of the several Cazenoves listed in *POLD* as residents of Chester Square, Seymour Street, Portman Square, and Cadogan Square.

8. "Notwithstanding all his eccentricities, the best people of America paid $2 a ticket to see and hear the great poet and critic, and he returned to England with a very handsome sum of money, which he must have needed or he would never have allowed himself to be subjected to so ridiculous a spectacle as he made of his performance" (Maj. J. B. Pond, *Eccentricities of Genius*, p. 324).

To George Lillie Craik

Cobham, Surrey

My dear Craik   October 20, [1886]

By all means send the cheap Essays to the Colonists, and the £25 to me.[1]

I will come to luncheon on *Friday*, if that suits you—but let me have a line to say your hour.   Ever truly yours,

Matthew Arnold.—

MS. Texas A&M University.

1. Craik had written on Oct. 19: "Few of our books at the large prices reach the colonies & we are trying if we can induce purchasers by making special & cheaper editions for Colonial and Indian circulation. It is something like Tauchnitz series which never sells in England & I do not think our series can affect the English sale. It is an experiment, but we should like to include your Essays if you will allow it & take £25 for your permission." He added, in a postscript, on Oct. 21: "I enclose £25 for the Essays in the Colonial Library series—" (Buckler, p. 74).

To John Churton Collins

J. C. Collins Esq.   Cobham, Surrey
My dear Sir   October 21, 1886

I have received your letter, and I have to thank you and Mr Murray for sending me the Review, which no doubt I shall find in London. I have however already read your article.[1]

I was, as you rightly suppose, in America till very lately, and did not receive the previous communication from you which you mention. But I received yesterday from the Editor of the Pall Mall Gazette some extracts which are probably to the same effect as the communication which failed to reach me.

Of course much may with great truth be said of the unsatisfactory condition of literature at the present time. Nor have the attempts of the Universities to improve been, in my opinion, judicious. What you seem to propose is to join English authors with the Latin and Greek authors taken up at Moderations. I do not think this would accomplish what you wish; the Moderations' Examination is not of sufficient importance, and the men who undergo it are not sufficiently ripe. I have always much regretted the loss of the old examination in honours, with philosophy, history and belles lettres all included in it; Bishop Butler was one of the authors taken up, and there is no reason why other English authors should not have, as you wish, been taken up too, so as to make the examination one in the best literature (in the large sense of the word *literature*) of Greece, Rome and our own country. Honours I would have reserved for this examination, while giving simply degrees in the several "Fächer." But this is vain speculation; to do these things one needs position and power, and I, in spite of what you kindly say, have neither:—have no longer even the wish to have either.

The real good which we who have not position or power can do to literature, is by producing literature which is not rubbish; and I have long regarded the author of the Essay on Bolingbroke as one of our benefactors in this way.[2] Believe me, my dear Sir,   Very truly yours,

Matthew Arnold.

Text. Typescript, Texas Technological College.

1. Collins's notorious demolition of Edmund Gosse's book *From Shakespeare to Pope*, "English Literature at the Universities," *Quarterly Review*, 163 (Oct. 1886): 289–329 (which later elicited some of Swinburne's vintage vituperation).

2. Collins's *Bolingbroke. A Historical Study* (1886), following his three articles on Bolingbroke in the *Quarterly Review*, 1880–81.

To Jane Martha Arnold Forster*

Cobham

My dearest K   October 21, 1886

I was going any way to write to you this week. First, let me answer about the P. M. G. I had written to them to ask them to send the paper to Cobham—but I wrote from Wharfeside, on Wharfeside paper, and they took that address. I could not conceive why the paper did not come, and had ordered it from my newsagent. I have now written to the P. M. G., and the paper will cease troubling you. The marble candle-sticks have arrived and stand on the little side table where I write in the dining-room; they hold a delightful candle, double dwarf sixes, which I get myself at Turner and Brecknell's—every one agrees how well the candle-sticks look there, and how useful they are. I remember them well in William's room in Eccleston Square.

I am afraid I do not watch South Africa very attentively just now, but it is very necessary that South Africa should be watched attentively by some one. I think Stanhope[1] is a good man, though a little defective in health, and therefore also, perhaps, in energy. On the whole, I think there is hope. Ld Randolph has *freshness*—a great thing. The fatal thing at this moment, as I have so often said, is drifting—and the stale old hacks always love to talk plausibly and to drift. I do not wish to have anarchy in Ireland, or to disestablish the Church of England. But Lord Clanricarde as an Irish landlord, and Lord Lonsdale as the patron of forty livings, have become impossible; they must be seriously dealt with; the old hacks want still to leave them as they are, to talk plausibly about them, and to drift; the same as to Winans in Scotland. Lord Randolph, as I say, is *fresh*; he perceives that something serious must be done. Lord Salisbury's intellect is such that he perceives the same thing, perhaps with clearer and deeper view than Ld Randolph; but I doubt whether without Ld R.'s freshness and go to stimulate him, he will act. I shall probably write one political article for Knowles at Christmas, simply to try to be of use by keeping people's eyes fixed on main issues, and preventing their going off on side ones.[2] I should like to write one political article a year—only one—and an article of this nature. My leisure is delightful, but I can as yet hardly turn round, I have so many letters to answer and promises to fulfil. An editor has offered me £250 a year for four articles on subjects of my own choice; this would make up the income I lose by resigning my professorship, but I have refused, because I want to keep myself free and not to make writing a trade. Little things take much time: you remember the Claudes: I promised, for the sake of old times, to give Louis Claude a few lines of preface for an edition of his sister's "Twilight Thoughts" they are publishing in America; I have had to read the little book carefully through, and now to write two pages of preface gives me more trouble than you would imagine. Then there is that poor Morell who was dismissed; I have promised him four or five pages about a so-called work of Tauler which he has translated; this, if I do not take care, will be "the sea to drink." Then Ted is at me for his magazine; I think I shall do Genl Grant's Memoirs for him; the Americans will like it, the book has hardly been noticed in England, and Grant is shewn by this book to be one of the most solid men they have had;

I prefer him to Lincoln; except Franklin, I know hardly any one so *selbst-ständig*, so broad and strong sighted, as well as firm-charactered, that they have had. But with all this I cannot get to my own work, to things I had myself purposed to do, at all.

Horrid weather, not like October in Surrey at all; but the farmers say the water was failing with the August and September drought, and we want all the rain we can get. There is no colour in the trees. I go about the garden, and arrange little matters of planting; however bad the weather may be; it is good weather for planting. We have five or six dozen pears of the prime sort; we had many more last year, but these are something. I like gathering them and looking at them. They will not be eatable for ten days yet. We dine out too much—four days in this week! people hurry to ask us because we have been so long away. Has your beech hedge turned yellow? Love to Francie, and take great care of your precious self. Ever my K,   your most loving,

M. A.

When you see Mr Wemyss Reid, thank him from me for the book of Stevenson he has sent me. It is not to be compared with "Kidnapped," however.[3]

MS. Frederick Whitridge.

1. Edward Stanhope (1840–1893: *DNB*; *VF*, 4/12/79), son of the fifth Earl Stanhope, and in his brief life a statesman of substance, was colonial secretary in Salisbury's second cabinet (from Aug. 1886) but from Jan. 1887 secretary for war. (In Salisbury's first cabinet he had been vice-president of the Committee of Council on Education, with a cabinet seat.)

2. Arnold wrote much more than he had reckoned on. He refers in the following sentences to "The Zenith of Conservatism" (Super, 11 : 122–43), *Nineteenth Century*, 21 (Jan. 1887): 148–64 (collected in Neiman's *Essays, Letters, and Reviews by Matthew Arnold*, 1960); Preface to Mary S. Claude's *Twilight Thoughts: Stories for Children and Child-Lovers* (Super, 11 : 120–21); "A 'Friend of God,'" (Super' 11 : 180–89), *Nineteenth Century*, 21 (Apr. 1887): 499–506, a review of J. R. Morell's translation of Johannes Tauler's *The Following of Christ*. "The sea to drink" has not been traced; "selbständig," rendered severally by Arnold in this sentence, could be translated as "independent-minded."

3. Probably, *The Strange Case of Dr Jekyll and Mr. Hyde* (1886).

To John Churton Collins

J. C. Collins Esqre   Cobham, Surrey
My dear Sir   October 24, 1886
     I have no difficulty in saying that I should be glad to see at the Universities, not a new School established for Modern Literature or Modern Languages, but the great works of English Literature taken in conjunction with

those of Greek and Latin Literature in the final Examination for honours in *Literae Humaniores*. I return your enclosures, and remain,   Truly yours,

Matthew Arnold.—

MS. University of London.

To Emily Meymott Shand

Pains Hill Cottage, Cobham, Surrey

My dear Mrs Shand   October 26, [?1886]

I am here till Christmas, very busy; and though I would go to London to see *you*, I cannot go there to hear lectures, however instructive. Pray let me know when you come up: it is far too long since I saw you. Your foreign wintering probably explains it, for I daresay when you return from abroad you go straight to Scotland. I wish I too could winter abroad, but I cannot work anywhere except at home, and now that I have retired from my inspectorship of Schools I must do some work for editors to maintain my poor family in decent comfort. The Grant Duffs are going to winter on Mount Carmel, where Laurence Oliphant has lent them his house; that is even better than Algiers.

Remember me affectionately to Lord Shand; if Mrs Arnold and Nelly were with me they would send many messages—   ever yours most sincerely

Matthew Arnold.—

MS. Yale University.

To Lucy Charlotte Arnold Whitridge

Cobham

My darling child   October 27, 1886

We have heard of you today in a letter of Aunt Fan's from Fox How. She quoted actual sentences of yours, sentences that were like bits of your dear self—so we feel to have heard from you today. She was delighted with your letter, and with your thought of her in her illness. I don't think she writes in good spirits, but for some time she will be nervous about a return of her ailment. You reported yourself to her as having a hard cough, which I hate to hear of, and all the maids had colds. I cannot but wish you had stayed at Stockbridge, as I advised you, to the 15th or 20th of Octr—you would have then got back to New York at a better time; I well remember what fine days we had in 1883 quite up to the beginning of November. However, you are gone back to New York and there is an end of it, but when we had a rapturous letter from Emily Tuckerman about the beauty and colour and fresh air of Stockbridge, I could not but wish you and the midget were bene-fiting by it. How I should like to leave my letter, and go upstairs, and try and get a smile out of that sweet little woman! We have horrid weather here nothing but rain—and though the leaves are colouring at last, there is no sun to show the colours off. But we have had no frost or anything like it and Dick's magnolia is really coming into bloom—its first bloom. The garden makes me very busy, and Dick, who was here for one night when he came up for Mrs Knight's funeral,[1] was delighted with the place. The pears are splendid, I think Fred would own that they are finer and better than the California ones; unluckily there are not enough of them, but they will take us through the month of November. I am delighted with my new existence, and when I have done making my adieux to my schools I shall go up but once a week. I have just finished writing a short preface, which gave me an infinity of trouble, to Mary Claude's stories; I don't think you know them, but I wanted to do her brother a good turn, and about her I have a sentiment and her looks as I remember them forty years ago and more. Now I have another preface to write for a distressed Roman Catholic, and then some-thing for Ted's magazine—Nelly and I have been walking to the old man's gate with the dogs; Kai is quite recovered, having had a nasty operation to extract a dew claw which had grown into his foot. Mamma was busy in our absence pottering about the World's End and selling copies of the Parish Magazine. Since then we have had Mr Gay to tea, who complains greatly of the damp and dismalness of Cobham; but Mamma is finding him plenty of work to do. Poor Mrs Dew is quite off her head, and Dew, instead of let-ting her go to the asylum at Caterham has brought her home here because she wished it; he is beautifully patient and good and sits stroking her hair and saying—Come now, Anne dear! It shows how moral qualities impress people that Mr Gay says Dew is universally beloved in Cobham; it is not for his "esprit," certainly. He is better, but cannot walk much; I think he could use his arms to saw wood, and I wanted to give him some work of that kind to do, to prevent the dreadful tedium of his unoccupied day; but I find that so long as he is on his Club he must do no work, not even dig his own garden! Mr Gay thinks Mrs Dew cannot live many weeks, but about this I do not feel sure at all.[2] We had rather a pleasant dinner at the Moons, Lady Egmont looking wonderfully well, but over dressed; Lady Butt very pretty, but does not like the change from London to Ockshott.[3] I took in Lady Lawrence, Sir Trevor's wife, whom I always find pleasant company; on my other side was Miss Moon, very nice-looking, I think, and pleasant. At Lady Ellesmere's on Monday we had only Dr Kingsley, but he is good com-

pany; he passed months in the west with Lord Dunraven, hunting, when elk and great game were still abundant; he knew Mountain Jim, Miss Bird's friend, and knew Buffalo Bill, Nelly's dream; he does not give a favourable account of either. Mamma goes up with me tomorrow to see nurses with Lady Ellesmere, and to be introduced to Mary Oakeley's baby, the little William Edward; we have asked the Hayeses for Sunday. Tomorrow I lunch on oysters with G. Smith and young George who is delighted with his baby. Then I have to assist in the election of a Professor of Literature for the Sydney University; nearly £1000 a year, so candidates are plentiful. The day after tomorrow we dine with the Helmes; I have never yet been able to dine there. Next week we dine with the Gartons and the Wilford Bretts. The week after my teachers give me something or other of silver and I shall have to make a speech, alas! Tell Fred that Oakeley has written to me for particulars about the firm of Cary & Whitridge, with a view to Cassell's employing them in American business. I hope it will come off. Now I must stop; I have written you a letter of nothings, but my love for you is not a nothing.   Your own
                                                                    Papa

I hope Mr Whitridge is better. What has been the matter with Mr Carnegie?

MS. Frederick Whitridge.

1. Unidentified.

2. Dew, apparently a journeyman, is listed invariably in Guthrie's accounts (often several times a month) from Jan. 1880 to Jan. 1886, Mr Gay never.

3. Lady Egmont (formerly Lucy King of Eaton Square) married in 1869 to the seventh earl of Egmont (d. 1897), the very type of suburban Surrey (D.L., J.P., Bucks. Yeoman Cavalry).

Lady Butt (formerly Anna G. Rodewald), of Prince's Gate, was the wife of Sir Charles Parker Butt (1830–1892: *DNB*; *VF*, 2/12/87), P. C., president of the probate division of the high court of justice.

Lady Lawrence (formerly Bessie Matthew of Park Lane), also of Prince's Gate, was the wife of Sir Trevor Lawrence (Kelly; *VF*, 1/26/99), serjeant-surgeon to the queen, who, after serving in India as a medical officer, became president of the Royal Horticultural Society and treasurer of St Bartholomew's Hospital, and represented Surrey constituencies in Parliament as a Conservative 1875–92.

George Henry Kingsley (1827–1892: *DNB*), M. D., brother of Charles and Henry, traveler ("most of the countries of the world") and author (*South Sea Bubbles by the Earl and the Doctor*, 1872, and other works), and medical adviser to the earl of Ellesmere's family. In 1874 he traveled in the American West, especially the Yellowstone region with Windham Thomas Wyndham Quin (1841–1920: *DNB*; *VF*, fourth earl of Dunraven and Mount-Earl).

Isabelle Lucy Bishop (1831–1904: *DNB*), born Bird, a world-class traveler who spent most of her life on the wing but who during intervals of rest and recuperation recorded her adventures and observations in some half-dozen books. Here, Arnold refers to *A Lady's Life in the Rocky Mountains* (1879). "Buffalo Bill" was of course William Frederick Cody (1846–1917: *WWWA*), the frontier scout, Indian fighter, actor, and, by now,

"Wild West" showman who, as we see, captured the imagination of even proper young English ladies. "Mountain Jim" Nugent (dates unknown), who could have been a Byronic hero of "one virtue and a thousand crimes" ("idolised by women," "chivalrous," "dark mood," "superbly handsome," "golden curls," *A Lady's Life*, p. 241), was the son of a British officer, and a government scout, trapper, squatter, desperado, about 45 years old when he served as "Miss Bird's" guide in the Rocky Mountains a few months before he was shot to death.

Oakeley Arnold-Forster, married in 1885 (not 1884, as in *DNB*) and had four sons, William Edward, Mervyn, John, and Christopher, named in the half-title dedication of his wife's memoir, *Hugh Oakeley Arnold-Forster*, and apparently nowhere else.

The Hayeses, if not the family of his sister Mary's husband, remain unidentified.

The Gartons have not been identified. Col. Sir Wilford Brett (1824–1901), K.C.M.G., of Moore Park, Esher, younger brother of first Baron (later, first Viscount) Esher, Arnold's old friend and London neighbor Baliol Brett.

To Frances Bunsen Trevenen Whately Whitridge *

Cobham

My dearest Fan   Friday, October 29, 1886

You did not write in very good spirits and I want to be sure your trouble is not coming back again. I am in tearing spirits, simply from the weather; the east wind is gone, the south west wind is come and the thermometer is now (noon) 62 in shade to the north. The colour has come at last and the horse chestnuts and poplars are a sight. Yellows we can manage to perfection—it is the reds in which the States beat us. I send you some maple leaves I received from Stockbridge last night, and I send the note which came with them. I go about the garden and cannot come in to work; examine the acorns on the Turkey oak with their curly-haired cups, which I had never noticed before—they are very effective. Then I give Flu, who is driving to Lady Ellesmere's, a Duchess pear to take to Lady Ellesmere, who says she shall carry it to her gardener to show him how much finer pears are grown at the Cottage than at Burwood. Then I go to pick up some Spanish chestnuts— At last I come in to work.

Oct. 30th. So far I wrote yesterday. Today is again beautifully mild, but we have little sun to bring out the colours. Nelly and I have been cutting grapes, and then picking up acorns and giving them to the pigs. I have also been seeing some irises transplanted. I have a long and delightful letter from Jane this morning. I hope to write regularly to her once a fortnight. We had Mrs Deacon and Lady Enfield to lunch yesterday, Lord Enfield was called away in the morning to his father, but had wished Lady Enfield to come all the same; the first thing she told us was that all was over. The old Lord Strafford was a gambler, and anything but a worthy character; Ld Enfield, his son,[1] was excellent. Flu and Nelly drove with Mrs Deacon to Ockshott to call on the Butts who have just settled there; he is the Judge of that name and she is a very pretty and pleasing woman, an American, a Southerner. I drove out with the dogs and walked home, enjoying the country and the views and the air extremely; the lane I took is one where the spindle tree grows abundantly, the berries on which are just reddening. I send you a flower I put in a book I was reading in America: is it not a kind of sorrel? how well flowers dry by being merely laid in a book! We had tea up at the Leafs, and dined with the Helmes—a pleasant dinner; I was between Lady Butt and another pretty woman, a Mrs Hume. We have three dinner parties for next week which is too much, but the dining will abate presently. Now I must wash my hands for luncheon.—

Sunday Morning. Again a soft south wind, thermometer at 60, the leaves falling fast, and everything full of colour, but unspeakably soft and lovely. I had never noticed till this year the exquisite light yellow which the Abele turns. We have a row of them in the Mole island opposite to us. I walked yesterday afternoon, after a tiresome hour at accounts, with Fanny Lucy along the Walton road and wished for you; the plantations are mainly Spanish Chestnut, and that and the fern did indeed make a feast of brown and yellow. We had four pheasants, three partridges and a hare sent us, and must have somebody to dinner. We had a successful sitting on the Sydney business on Thursday, and reserved three candidates; George Macaulay not among them, his standing and claims are not sufficient. I must write a line to Mrs Conybeare, who I fear thought his chance better than it was. It must be a relief to her to keep her daughter, but I daresay she looked to the change of climate, too, and to the improvement in income, as objects of desire. I think we shall make a good choice. I am glad that Ld Salisbury has given Trinity to Butler; I am not particularly fond of him, but Flu is, and I think he will make a good Master. He was quite uncomfortably ill off at Gloucester. Poor dear old Tom—how well by his nature he was fitted for academical preferments of this kind, and how impossible they have become for him! I saw Humphry the other day and learned from him that they are all come or coming up—so you will have no one at Fox Ghyll. When are you coming south? I am wonderfully better, can read in bed and lie in cramped positions, neither of which I could do in America without pain, and my pace in walking has nearly doubled since I came home, so that I outwalk Fanny Lucy and Nelly instead of begging them to stop for me. I have written and sent off the preface for Mary Claude's stories. Now I have my poor Popish friend to assist, and then Master Ted.   Your ever affectionate

M. A.—

Are my Homer Lectures at Fox How?

MS. *Frederick Whitridge.*

1. George Stevens Byng, second earl of Strafford (1806–1886), died the day before, and viscount Enfield, his eldest son by his first wife, succeeded. Mrs Hume, a few lines later, has not been identified.

To Lucy Charlotte Arnold Whitridge *

Cobham

My darling Lucy November 13, 1886

I meant to have written on Wednesday, but I have had a horrid week with my speech to the Westminster teachers—you know how a thing of that kind worries me.[1] However, last night it came off and very well. You can imagine Mamma and Nelly on the platform, and Mamma's face when I mentioned her. There was a whole line of reporters and there is sure to be a full account somewhere; you shall have it. The things they have given me are very beautiful; I was afraid of a tea-service. Plate in general, and China, I do not care for so much as many people do; I could get through life with a wooden spoon and platter, but the jug and salver they have given me will look well on the sideboard. When Mr Carrick Moore[2] asked me, "But what would you really like, if you don't care about plate?" I answered, "A carriage, a pair of horses, and to have them kept for me! Not that I should use them much myself, but I should like to have them." The affection and responsiveness of the teachers was touching.

Noon.—I wrote the foregoing before breakfast; now the Times has come with a report of the meeting and a leading article. You shall have whichever of the papers is best. You can imagine the relief with which I have been going about the garden this morning and planting. It is a beautiful moment, a clear morning after days of rain, and the last colour on the trees showing charmingly. We have had no frost yet, and Dick's magnolia is still trying to come into bloom. Numbers of summer flowers—the red salvia, for instance—are blooming. The birds are happy in the open weather, and the sweet robins keep following Collis[3] and me about as we open the ground to plant rhododendrons. Kai sits in the sun at the door of the greenhouse and watches us. The thermometer is 50, and in the night does not fall below 40. I so often think how fond the Midget will get of this cottage. I cannot forgive you for not staying quietly on at Stockbridge with a friend or two to visit you till the very end of October, and weaning the Midget very gradually. She was doing so beautifully at Stockbridge on the food and nursing combined. However, the thing is done now, and all one can hope is that the trouble and expense of the wet nurse may be repaid by the Midget's thriving. A strange thing happened last night, talking of wet nurse. A note was put into my hand before the meeting, with a message that the writer was waiting in the porch. The note was from Dean[e],[4] whom I had not seen for twenty years, at least. I had her fetched in—she looks wonderfully well still, was nicely dressed in black and seems prospering: she has married again. Just the same manner as formerly: I always rather admired her liveliness and spirit, though she was so far from satisfactory. We saw her again for a moment after the lecture, but we have now her address and shall not lose sight of her. We shall be in peace here for some time now, I hope; I am asked to stay with the Webbs (Barbara Lyall) at Milford,[5] and with Butler at Cambridge for the Trinity Gaudy; but I shall do neither. Possibly I may go to Aston Clinton for a day, as I want to see dear Lady de Rothschild; but if possible I shall see her in London. The storm of dining out must now abate here a little, because we have dined everywhere. We have George de Bunsen coming tonight: do you remember him at Bonn when we were at Rolandseck: he is very pleasant, and your Mamma likes him; that nice Mrs Travers (the Bp of Gloucester's[6] daughter) and her husband, who have now a house at Weybridge, are coming to meet him; also Mildred & Henry Whitmore, who were neighbours and friends of dear Henry Bunsen in Shropshire: I think it will be pleasant. You may imagine how busy Nelly is with her flowers and the coloured leaves of the Ampelopsis (small Virginia Creeper): the latter are worthy of America. You cannot think how often Stockbridge and its landscape come into my mind. None of the cities could attach me, not even Boston; but I could get fond of Stockbridge. Do you remember our drive to Mohawk Lake and the glorious briskness and brightness of it all—and Annie carrying the sweet Midget along the dyke and pulling everlastings as she went? What Virginian creepers trailed over the trees there! I cannot write a long letter today, things have accumulated on me so while I was worrying about my speech; but I send you a charming letter I have had from Henry Cochin, as my mind always turns to you when I am in relations with France and French things and people. Give me news of Mr Whitridge père. My love to Fred and ten kisses to the Midget: always your own

Papa.

MS. Frederick Whitridge.

    1. ["Thirty-five Years of School Inspecting: Mr. Matthew Arnold's Farewell"] (Super 11:373–79), *The Times*. Nov. 13, 1886, p. 5, in which he paid generous tribute to fellow-workers in the Education department (Lingen, Sandford, Cumin, Chester, Bowstead, Clough, Healing, Myhill, Sharpe, Fleming) and to his wife: "Though I am a schoolmaster's son, I confess that school teaching or school inspecting is not the line of life I should naturally have chosen. I adopted it in order to marry a lady who is here to-night, and who feels the kindness as warmly and gratefully as I do. (Cheers.) My wife and I had a wandering life of it at first. We had no home; one of our children was born in a lodging at Derby, with a workhouse, if I recollect right, behind and a penitentiary in front."

2. John Carrick-Moore (b. 1805: Kelly), F.R.S., F.R.G.S., a neighbor, from Eaton Square and Brook Farm, Cobham.

3. Collis is named in Guthrie's monthly accounts only in Dec. 1882, Sept. 1887, in 1888 eight times from Jan. to April.

4. Nursemaid in the early fifties.

5. Robert William Webb (b. 1831), of Milford House, Godalming, Surrey, J.P. Surrey; his wife was the daughter of the Rev. A. Lyall, rector of Harbledown, Kent (Kelly).

6. Bishop Charles John Ellicott (1819–1904: *DNB*; *VF*, 7/18/85).

To Frederic William Farrar

⟨Education Department, Whitehall⟩

To Frederic William Farrar

Cobham

My dear Farrar   Saturday Morning, [?November 13, 1886]

Many thanks for your "neat end" and for your encouragement, too, beforehand. When I opened my mouth and heard my own voice I felt all right instead of, as I had feared, all wrong. I hope you are well through your sermon cares for the Festival: You will have a fine opportunity. Kindest remembrances to Mrs Farrar—   Most truly yours

Matthew Arnold.—

MS. Bodleian.

To George David Boyle

Cobham, Surrey

My dear Boyle   November 17, 1886

Of course I shall be extremely interested in seeing your volume, when it reaches me. I am touched with what you tell me of dear old Shairp; he had come to look upon me as a very lost sheep, so his fidelity to my verse is the more sweet in him.[1]

Some day I must see you under the shadow of your cathedral. Yours ever sincerely

Matthew Arnold.—

A thousand thanks for your kind words on my retirement.

MS. Pierpont Morgan Library.

1. Boyle, now dean of Salisbury, wrote a notice on Shairp in the *Guardian*, Sept. 30, 1885, which William Knight drew on in his book *Principal Shairp and His Friends* (1888).

To William Knight

Professor Knight　　　　　　　　　　　　　　　Cobham, Surrey
My dear Professor　　　　　　　　　　　　　November 17, 1886

　　I shall be much interested in seeing your selection, but I am not inclined to return to the Criticism of our dear Poet, and I am sure it is better that in the Volume now in question I should not.[1]

　　My daughter in law felt the death of her Aunt—one of her few relations in this country—very deeply, as you supposed she would.　　Most truly yours,

　　　　　　　　　　　　　　　　　　　　　　Matthew Arnold.—

MS. Pierpont Morgan Library.

　　1. *Selections from Wordsworth by William Knight and Other Members of the Wordsworth Society* (1888).

To William Knight

　　　　　　　　　　　　　　　　　　　　　　November 19, 1886

I am touched by what you tell me of dear old Shairp. He had come to look upon me as a very lost sheep, so his fidelity to my verse is the more sweet in him.

Text. William Knight, Retrospects, *p. 200.*

To Mr Hugh [1]

Mr Hugh　　　　　　　　　　　　　　　　　Cobham, Surrey
My dear Sir　　　　　　　　　　　　　　　November 21, 1886

　　I have read your enclosures with interest, and have had pleasure in writing on the photograph.　　Truly yours

　　　　　　　　　　　　　　　　　　　　　　Matthew Arnold.—

MS. Pierpont Morgan Library.

　　1. Hugh has not been identified.

To William Sharp [1]

　　　　　　　　Athenæum Club, Pall Mall

William Sharp Esq.
Dear Sir　　　　　　　　　　　　　　　　November 22, 1886

　　You are quite welcome to use the passages about and of Maurice de Guerin which you mention.　　Very truly yours,

　　　　　　　　　　　　　　　　　　　　　　Matthew Arnold.—

MS. National Library of Scotland.

1. William Sharp (1855–1905: *DNB*), ultraromantic writer (poetry, prose, translations—much of it as "Fiona Macleod"), traveler, and biographer. His use of the Guérin passages has not been identified.

To George Macmillan

George Macmillan Esq.   Cobham
My dear George   November 23, 1886
    Miss Woods's is rather a large order, but if the Firm have no objection, I have none.[1]   Ever yours truly

                                          Matthew Arnold.—

MS. University of Virginia.

1. Mary A. Woods, *A Second School Poetry Book* (1887).

To Lady Dorothy Nevill

Pains Hill Cottage, Cobham, Surrey
Dear Lady Dorothy   November 24, [1886]
    On Sunday I am engaged to pay a visit near Dorking.[1] I wish I could come and see you, but I am really and truly "out of London" now. Sincerely yours

                                          Matthew Arnold.—

MS. University of Virginia.

1. To the Trevor Lawrences (see above, letter to Lucy Charlotte Arnold Whitridge of Oct. 27, 1886).

To Anthony John Mundella

Athenæum Club, Pall Mall
My dear Mundella   November 26, 1886
    One line to say that the *Minister* before my mind, who knew nothing about my work, was not you, but the man who gives preferment and opportunity—the *Minister* in the Continental sense.[1]
    Ld Ripon and Ld Aberdare both of them tried, in their time, to get opportunity given to me—but in their case, too, the politics and ignorance of the *Minister* stopped the way.

However, no one made so strenuous an effort as you did, and I must some day make public acknowledgment of it.

You are right, the permanent officials know I cared little about my performances; but all I meant to say of them was that in the routine work I had to do for them they were entirely friendly.

The pension was expressly for literary and poetic performances, not educational. It is as a functionary of public education that I say I owe nothing to Governments. The recognition and opportunity which would have been useful to me they never gave me. It does not matter now; the work will be done by others, and I rejoice to hear that you, for your part, mean to take it in hand. Literature is henceforth my business, if at sixty three it is not presumptuous to speak of having still a business.   Ever most sincerely and cordially yours,

Matthew Arnold.

Text. MS. University of Sheffield; typescript (after "cared little about my") University of Virginia.

1. That is, Cabinet minister: Arnold is alluding to the second paragraph of his farewell to inspecting (see above, Letter to Lucy Charlotte Arnold Whitridge of Nov. 13, 1886, n. 1).

To Ernest Fontanès *

Cobham, Surrey

My dear M. Fontanès   November 27, 1886

I was very glad to see your handwriting again. First, let me answer your literary question: the passage quoted in the discourse on Numbers is from a very good history of Greece by Dr Ernst Curtius, a German professor. It has probably been translated into French.

I am sorry you cannot give a better account of the health of Madame Fontanès. I do indeed wish that we were all going to meet in Paris this winter, but that is impossible. I had four or five months of idleness in America this summer visiting my married daughter, and on my return home I find myself confronted by half a dozen editors, who allege promises made by me to give them an article when I became free; and, as I have at last resigned my inspectorship, they summon me to fulfil my promises. Something I must do to satisfy them, and this will keep me busy up to Easter; then I shall be able to look round me and decide upon my future course. Perhaps we shall go to Italy for April and May, and then we should have a chance of seeing you on our passage through Paris. Politics occupied me much during the first half of this year. The chief work I have done was a political article for the *Nineteenth Century*. The title of the article will give you a notion of the line I took; the title was "The Nadir of Liberalism." In the last months of Mr Gladstone's

Government the Liberal party did indeed reach its lowest, its *nadir*. The result of the elections gave me indescribable relief. The political prospect, however, is still very anxious. I confess I do not look forward to any close alliance of this country with France, the character and aspirations of the two nations have become so different, and are daily becoming more so. But that is no reason why they should not live peaceably side by side. You mention M. Pécaut; if you see him, pray ascertain whether he received a copy of my *Report on Foreign Schools*. Much as I dislike the *jacobinisme autoritaire* of your Ministry of Education, I like and admire M. Pécaut,[1] and have endeavoured to do justice to him in my Report. You do not mention Renan's *Abbesse*; he has been on the *pente* tending towards such a production some time. I suspect that outside of France he has almost annulled, by that production, his influence as a serious writer, which is a pity. I am republishing *St Paul and Protestantism*—that old friend of yours—with a new preface and some additional matter. I shall send you the volume.

　　We all send affectionate remembrances to you and yours.—Most cordially I am,　　your affectionate friend,

Matthew Arnold.

Text. *Russell, 2:413–15.*

　　1. Félix Pécaut (1828–1898), formerly an inspector of schools, had been director of the normal school for women at Fontenay aux Roses since its foundation in 1879. See the letter to him below, Dec. 22, 1886.

To Lucy Charlotte Arnold Whitridge

Cobham

My darling child　　　　　　　　　　　　　　November 27, 1886
　　Of Mamma's tumble you have heard—her hand is still weak, and she ought not to use it, so I said I would write today instead of Wednesday. This is the last time a Cunarder takes the letters; every one talks of the letters and of the loss as to time for posting letters if the Queenstown route is given up; but I think of passengers and the blessing to them of going on without break when once started, and I hope and trust the Cunard Company will *not* come to an agreement with the Post Office. As I was getting up this morning I actually heard your dear voice; our expeditions to the muddy promontory for snow-drop bulbs came into my head, I don't know why, and I saw you raise up your head from the oozy ground and half-dug-up bulbs, and laugh merrily and call out to Nelly. These are the glimpses which give me delight. We have dark, foggy weather, but not thick fog any longer, and no cold— the thermometer does not drop below 40. The strawberry plant and borage

are in bloom in the kitchen garden, and I have just brought in to mamma a beautiful rose off Lady Charles Russell's tree. Collis has been digging the border, and there is a soft smell of earth, which a pair of sweet robins—the inimitable red robin, no American thrush—sit on the rails to enjoy. Poor Mrs Dew is very bad again; Dew somewhat better, but in low spirits, as is natural. After Christmas when he is on quarter pay from his Club, I shall try to give him or find him a little light work; at present, while he is on half-pay, he may not take any work. Mr Leaf's nurse, whom she had just set up in the house next D. R. Smith, has collapsed; the cook from Pains Hill went to tea with her and stayed out till ½ past 10, the Leafs being in London; on her return here, Mrs Leaf heard of it and complained to the nurse, who insolently gave warning. She has twice bandaged your Mamma's hand beautifully, so I have a friendly feeling to her; however, I daresay Nurse Rooke, the new Parish Nurse, will be capable of that too; but Mamma says Mrs Leaf's nurse is a very superior person, though Mrs Leaf has spoilt her. Last night we dined at Fox-Warren; I took in Lady Butt and had a Mrs Mary Coutts on the other side, an ex-Churchill. Lady Butt is a very pretty woman, but has rather forgotten the American art of dressing; we had asked them to dinner for next Wednesday but they were engaged; the Cornish Moores have accepted, we have no one else and Nelly is in despair. I say, try the Macaulays; and she rolls her eyes horribly. This evening Mamma and I, with Eliza (for Mamma cannot well dress herself just now) go to the Lawrences at Burford Bridge; I shall be glad to see that country again, and I believe the house is very comfortable. The Evelyns had asked us for the same Sunday. Nelly goes to Fox Warren, with many sighs at not going to Rogates instead. This day fortnight we all go to the Stewart Hodgsons; that too is a country which always gives me pleasure. We are asked to dine at the Hendersons, for the first time since my John Henderson, says Nelly, threw me over; her successful rival is a tall handsome woman whom I rather like;—but we have decided it is too far off to drive in winter. Next Thursday I dine at the Oxford & Cambridge Club with Cumin (who always asks for you) to meet Lord Lingen and an old office party. I am much pressed with work, but in good spirits, as it is work which is more or less congenial, and not school-inspecting. I have written a preface for the American edition of Mary Claude's stories which you will like; a short preliminary notice for an edition of Wordsworth—a preface for the popular edition of St Paul & Protestantism; and now I have to write, rather against time, an article for Ted on Gen. Grant's Life, of which not 300 copies have been sold in England. That makes it an all the better subject, as there are really materials in the book for a most interesting article, and no one has used them. Then I have promised Knowles a political article for the beginning of the session, and half a dozen pages on Tauler (whom I was reading at Stockbridge) to help a poor ex-colleague who has translated him. There is also Amiel to be done, to fulfil a promise to Mary; so you see I have my hands full. Amiel has not taken here at all in Mary's translation; I did not much think it would; it is not a book for the general English public, and the few can read it in French. If you have access to the Encyclop. Britannica, read my article on Ste Beuve in the last volume. He would have been pleased by it himself, poor dear man, I think. Now you have had enough about my writings. Nelly is quite right that the photograph you sent of the Midget will not give a good impression of her to strangers: but somehow it reminds me of the darling, and I like it. How I wish I could go into her room of a morning and hold her little feet while she stares in my face! I pity Fred going to Indianapolis; it was a beast of a place; I should like, however, to see Stockbridge today: I wonder if the snow has come. I became attached to that place and landscape, somehow. I hope Fred's cold is well, and that you do not cough. The accounts of your poor Aunt Susy are wretched, and of your Aunt Forster anxious, though she is easier. Poor little Vernon cannot shake off his fever.[1] I am quite my old self again; walked about London all yesterday in the fog without choke and pain. My darling, how good you were when I was suffering!   Your own always loving

Papa.

MS. Frederick Whitridge.

1. In this chatty letter, obviously designed to appeal to Lucy, most of the names, however familiar to her, cannot be identified. Fox Warren was the home of the Buxton neighbors, and the reasons for Nelly's attraction to [?]Rogate ["with many sighs . . . instead" lined through] elude the editor.

Robert Henderson (1851–1895: *Landed*), out of Harrow and Christ Church, of Sedgwick Park, Horsham, Sussex, and of Randalls Park, Leatherhead, Surrey; at some point he became a director of the Bank of England and was married to Emma Caroline Hargreaves. His younger brother, John (b. 1852), who in 1881 apparently threw Nelly over for Eveleen Mary Smith, of Mickleham Hall, Surrey, and had produced a son (b. 1883) and probably twin daughters by now, attended Harrow and Trinity College, Cambridge, and was now high sheriff of Surrey.

Vernon was the second child of Edward Penrose Arnold-Forster.

To Frances Bunsen Trevenen Whately Arnold*

Burford Lodge, Dorking

My dearest Fan   Sunday, November 28, 1886

Here we are at this pretty place under Box Hill, which looks really precipitous as it rises straight from the river at the back of the garden. The house has been rebuilt since we were here twenty years ago, and the Trevor

Lawrences, who live here are very rich—everything is the perfection of comfort. We have here the American Minister (Mr Phelps) and his wife, a Mr Reed (a philanthropist who gives away his fortune) and his wife,[1] Sir Edmund & Lady Henderson, and Norman Lockyer. Sir Trevor Lawrence is one of the chief growers of orchids, and we have been through his houses with him and learnt something—though orchids are to me more curious than attractive. The fog hangs about, but is not so bad as it was; however it makes breathing a little more difficult to me when I walk; so this morning, instead of going with the walking party to Mickleham I went with the carriage party—Flu and Lady Henderson—to Dorking. Dorking church is a fine one, and of a kind that I like; I had not seen it since it was rebuilt. We had our reward—a sallow man in tumbled episcopal robes got into the pulpit—I did not know him but was struck with him at once; he preached a wonderfully good sermon on the text "Take heed that ye despise not." One oratorical movement about the drunkard—not even the drunkard might be an object of contempt—was very fine indeed. A good deal of the actor, I thought, but the good actor—and plenty of thought, observation and feeling. When we got out we met Mrs Rate (Tait's great friend), and found that it was the Bishop of Ripon (Boyd Carpenter)[2] we had been hearing and that he was staying with her. She wanted us to come with her to luncheon, and to be introduced to him—but we had Lady Henderson on our hands and the Lawrences' carriage and horses, and could not. But I am glad to have heard him; I did not know that I had such a good preacher still to hear. After luncheon Flu and I went to see Mrs Risbridge at the farm at West Humble where we stayed two successive years;[3] the lawn there is full of memories of Tom and Basil. Then on to Camilla Lacy to see the Wylies who were very hospitable to us; poor Mrs Wylie has just had a terrible operation, the removal of an eye, but they liked our going to enquire. Then on to Fridley, Mrs Drummond's; she is a charming old lady, and the walk to Fridley was in view of Norbury and its woods all the way. Tomorrow after breakfast we go back to Cobham, and I shall have plenty of work to get my article for Ted written. Sir Edmund Henderson tells me Ted has applied to him for his experience with the police; the little man, as Dick calls him, will make an editor. I hope your next will give us better accounts of poor dear Eddy; as to dearest K, I was afraid at first we were going to have something of the same kind; the real mischief (supposing we have got it rightly named) does not seem to me so very alarming. What a pity you are all of you in those northern parts and so out of reach! but are [?]we [1½ *lines inked over and illeg.*] and the sweet little Vernon? I do not like the persistence of the fever. You yourself are not all right yet, I am sure, and need taking care of. Nelly is staying at Fox Warren, and will meet the Humphry Wards there. I am rather in dismay at parliament's meeting in January, for Knowles will now want for that month an article I had promised for February. but I find that I can still get work done, when I must. My love to dearest K and to Francie—ever, my dearest Fan,   your most affectionate

M. A.—

MS. Frederick Whitridge.

1. Edward John Phelps (1822–1900: *DAB*), lawyer, professor of law at Yale, and then (1885–89) minister to Great Britain; his wife (m. 1845) was the former Mary L. Haight. (Mr Reed and his wife remain unidentified.)

This discreet allusion to Col. Edmund Yeamans Walcott Henderson (1821–1896: *DNB*; K.C.B. 1878; *VF*, 3/6/75) would not have been lost on Fan. Henderson, who had in a sense spent most of his professional life in prisons, had been chief commissioner of metropolitan police since 1869 and was of course accountable for the "Black Monday" riot of Feb. 8, 1886, and its aftermath (to which Arnold, in the United States, makes no allusion in these letters). Henderson was allowed to resign on Feb. 20 (*Annual Register*).

Norman Lockyer (1836–1920: *DNB*; knt 1897), astronomer, currently of the science and art department, South Kensington Museum, and from 1890 director of the observatory and professor at the Royal College of Science.

2. William Boyd Carpenter (1841–1918: *DNB*; *VF*, 3/8/06), had been bishop of Ripon since 1884. Mrs Rate has not been identified.

3. In 1866 and 1867; Mrs Risbridge and, below, Camilla Lacey and the Wylies have not been identified.

To Thomas Arnold

Cobham

My dear Tom—   November 30, 1886

How I wish we had you here today, you dear old boy! What a long way back it is to the School Field at this season, and the withered elm leaves, and the footballs kicking about, and the November dimness over everything! I wish the accounts of Julia were better, but her pluck does actually make her suffering lighter, I have no doubt. I was glad to hear that Ethel had given up the stage. A brilliant success there is no doubt a delightful thing, but beforehand one would rather that none of one's belongings went in for that career. Mary was at Fox-Warren with Humphry yesterday and Nelly met them; I am sorry to say they passed the Sunday morning in that making of "many books" which the Preacher truly tells us has no End.[1] Now that I have retired the Editors begin to claim half promises to give them something, and till Easter I shall hardly be free; I call it being free when one writes only what one is self-moved to write, not plagued into writing. However I am interested in writing an account of Gen. Grant's Memoirs, which I promised Ted for his new magazine. It is curious how little the book has penetrated in England; Mrs Grant has made 300,000 dollars by it in America and is comfortable for life; here not three hundred copies have been sold. Grant interests me just because he is so free from the American faults: the ever-restless self-consciousness and itch for praise, the insincere puffery of everything American, the "buncombe." When I met him I thought him a dullish Philistine; but his "morale," when you come to read his Memoirs, proves to be of a really high order. We passed the day before yesterday, Sunday, at Burford, the place of Sir Trevor Lawrence one of the members for Surrey; the Phelpses were there, and they also are Americans to be respected and liked. The Lawrence's house is in a meadow by the Mole with Box Hill coming sheer down to the water's edge: a broken chalk side wooded with beech, yew and box, and more precipitous and effective than anything of Loughrigg. That whole Dorking country is delightful, but the only real mountain effect is that one effect at Burford. We are going to Lord Coleridge in London, and to the Stewart Hodgsons at Haslemere—two nights at each place; but for these visits, we shall be at home till the end of January, I hope, and always glad to see you. I so liked having you here in the spring. What you say of Ireland gives me pleasure; I think we agree about that country, and I trust what you say. Quite right of the Government to stop seditious meetings and newspapers like United Ireland: on the other hand, with the spread of reading and information, a Lord Clanricarde becomes almost intolerable and *must* be remedied.

You are three and sixty today—just my age. May you get into port at last and enjoy yourself there, after all the travail and tossing you have had! Flu and Nelly send love and good wishes—   your affectionate brother

M. A.

I was delighted to have your letter. You must come and drink out of the Teachers' claret jug.

MS. Balliol College.

1. Ecclesiastes 12 : 12.

To Percy William Bunting

Percy Bunting Esq.   Cobham, Surrey
My dear Sir   November 30, 1886
I have promised Shelley elsewhere, if I do him at all in connexion with Dowden's book; but my doing him at all is doubtful.[1]   Ever truly yours
Matthew Arnold.—

MS. University of Chicago.

1. A review of Edward Dowden's *Life*, 1886, Arnold's essay "Shelley" (Super 11 : 305–27) appeared in *Nineteenth Century*, 23 (Jan. 1888): 23–39 (rptd *Essays in Criticism, Second Series*, 1888).

To Constance Flower, later Lady Battersea

Cobham

My dear Mrs Flower   November 30, [1886]

The earlier meeting of Parliament obliges me to be a month earlier with an article I have promised Mr Knowles, and I must accept no fresh engagement between the 10th and 20th but reserve every hour I can for work. Such is life, even when one has got free of schools! My love to your mother and Cyril.   Ever your affectionate

Matthew Arnold.—

MS. Texas A&M University.

To David Masson

Athenæum Club, Pall Mall, S. W.

My dear Mr Masson   December 3, 1886

I am sending you a notice I have written of my dear friend and master, Ste Beuve, for the Encyclop. Britannica, because I have always felt in such perfect sympathy with you about him, and I have said, in this notice, how very high I estimate him.[1]   Most truly yours

Matthew Arnold.—

MS. Liverpool Record Office.

1. "Sainte-Beuve" (Super 11 : 106 – 19), *Encyclopædia Britannica*, ninth edn, 162 – 65.

To [?] John Churton Collins

Cobham, Surrey

My dear Sir   December 4, 1886

I was sorry not to meet you in London. I am in the same difficulty as Mr Browning; I am unwilling to appear in a question which is mixed up with the question of the merits of Mr Gosse, with whom I am acquainted, though but slightly. The wider question, however, is so important, that I would not forbear to speak altogether; but I studiously expressed myself somewhat formally and briefly.

I must tell you frankly that I have small confidence in the Board of Studies at Oxford. If it is possible to intervene with any good effect later, and when the question is cleared of Mr Gosse, pray communicate with me.— Of course your interest in my work gives me great pleasure. But it is the support of the few, such as you are, which has been with me to enable me to do it. Most truly yours

Matthew Arnold.—

P. S.[*sic*]

P. S. You are a critic, so let me send you a copy of a notice which I have written of the father and master of us all, Ste Beuve. It is buried in an Encyclopaedia, but I have a few copies to send to those likely to care for the subject.

MS. University of Texas at Austin.

To William Thomas Stead

Private   Cobham, Surrey
Dear Mr. Stead   December 9, 1886

Many thanks for the judicious correction in your last night's paper. I was disturbed at seeing how Lord C. quoted me, and I am glad to have what I *did* say recalled. Ste Beuve thought Greek and Latin a lost cause absolutely, and perhaps in France they may be, but here I do not think they are.[1] Very truly yours

Matthew Arnold

Text. Joseph O. Baylen, "Matthew Arnold and the Pall Mall Gazette," South Atlantic Quarterly, 8 (1969): 553–54.

1. Coleridge "seemed to imply that Arnold had concurred with Sainte-Beuve's view of the decline of Greek and Latin in the schools" (Baylen, p. 553 n).

To Lucy Charlotte Arnold Whitridge

Cobham
My darling Lucy   December 10, 1886

We have your cheerful letter this morning. When the midget is mentioned I sniff up the air and I almost feel that I perceive her sweet, fresh, midgetty smell. She is a darling indeed. How she will like this place! it is beautiful in winter, and this morning I longed for you as I stood on what I call the terrace by the little iron gate into the Paddock, looking at the yellow holly and the cork-tree shining in the sun, and the banks of Pains Hill, red with fallen leaves, through the stripped trees. We have had a tremendous gale—the barometer fell to 27.75, lower than I have ever seen it and we had rain like the rain of Stockbridge, and a great flood. But there is no snow and no cold—and with this beautiful sunshine we have [?]fine weather and the thermometer between 40 and 50. We had asked Mr Cary[1] to dine and sleep tonight; he says he cannot come because he has to work in the evenings as well as in the day time—An American never treats his dinner with proper respect, and that is why their digestions are bad; he must dine and he had better dine comfortably, and he might get up two hours earlier in the morning to do his work. We particularly wanted him to come, that we might hear of you from him, and we had got the Butts—he is Divorce Judge and she a very pretty and pleasant woman—whom he would have liked to meet. He proposes to come when he is less busy, but when will that be? Tomorrow we go to the Stewart Hodgsons at Haslemere, and from there we go on Monday to the Coleridges, not returning here till the middle of next week. On Wednesday the 15th Mamma and I are going to a function at Sion College, to meet the Prince of Wales.[2] Last night we dined at Horsley; a day or two after Mamma's call there Lady Margaret and one of the brothers in law rode over with an invitation to dinner;[3] they over took me in the Cobham Court-lane and I said we dined with the Deacons; next morning two of the brothers in law rode over with an invitation for another day; Nelly was included and wanted to go, so we went though it was my day for finishing my article for Ted. However I got through in time with the article. There was a large party—the ladies all very much dressed, which interested Mamma and Nelly. Lady Margaret looking very well, and it amuses me to see and hear her laugh. There were Lord & Lady Kintore—she a daughter of the Duchess of Manchester and very handsome. Lady Mayo and her daughter Lady Florence Bourke. Lord Douglas Compton, St John Brodrick and Lady Hilda—all staying in the house. I went in with Lady Florence Bourke, but as Lady Lovelace made me come and sit by her, I talked to her more than to Lady Florence, whom I liked, however—Lord Lovelace is, as you know, always disposed to talk to me. Nelly had young King Noel, the son, who is now in the lancers—he is shy but a very nice youth. Lord Kintore devoted himself to Nelly after dinner, finding her good company, no doubt. Mamma went in with Bycott Jenkins—she says he was always listening nervously to Lady Margaret. Now I must tell you that I have sent a Stilton to Fred, but as the man said he did not [know] how to get the carriage paid without a good deal of delay, I told him to send the cheese at once; but you must tell me without fail what the carriage comes to, as I want to pay the whole thing; we will put the charge into the accounts that pass between you and Mamma. I think Fred had better not send us oysters: Nelly does not eat them, and Mamma eats so few that we do not get through them. Newtown pippins would be better. I say this though I like oysters myself but they won't keep for ever and I don't see how we should get through them. We have heard today from Lily Norton and Blossom Sedgwick,[4] besides a delightful letter from Fred to Mamma. The Nortons are properly admiring of the Midget. Blossom Sedgwick tells us of Stockbridge; the Dorres [Dornes, Dowes?] are still there, but every one else is gone! She says there is snow covering the pond, but not deep yet; bright sunshine of course. She writes cheerfully—Nelly's Theodore has become a railway clerk in Chicago. You see I like to tell you American news. I have been much interested in reading General Grant, and shall make him the subject of two consecutive articles, à la Ste Beuve, for Ted. I have sent you my Ste Beuve, because I always liked your pleasure in that charming writer; in England people learn little about him, but he would have been pleased with the record I have borne of him in our great English cyclopaedia. I did not tell you of the meeting because I thought Mamma or Nelly would; I could not describe my own appearance. I spoke better than usual because I held in my hand what I meant to say and felt that I could turn to it if I needed. Mademoiselle's pleasure was a thing to see. I am sure I told you of Dean[e]'s appearing. This letter will go by our old friend the Wyoming, which is not a fast boat. I confess that a day or two gained or lost with letters does not move me much: what I like to think of is the gain of time for *passengers* by the fast Cunards going straight; now we have only to find better ports than Liverpool and New York, with their stupid bars, and it will be seen how long the passage, from start to finish, does really take. The Umbria will have had a rough time, if she caught this gale. It is expected that she will beat the German boat which left on the Thursday night—but we shall see. But are not *you*, my darling, who are likely to make more passages than I, glad that that abominable halt at Queenstown is given up? Now I must stop; Mamma's wrist is mending, but a torn ligament takes time. She likes the notion of going to London for a day or two. The Wolseleys have got the Haslemere manor house, so we shall probably meet them at the Stewart Hodgsons, and Nelly will rejoice. My love to Fred, and kindest regards to Mr Whitridge if he is still with you. We are all of us so glad he is better. Kiss the midget, and do not let her be *too* fond of musical boxes; I was often tempted to throw her first one out of the window. This will reach you very near your birthday— *our* birthdays. How I wish we could hug one another, my darling! The dear boys send their love; they are happy and good. Mamma and Kai are a pretty sight.   Always your own

Papa—

MS. National Archives of Canada.

1. Frederick Whitridge's law partner.

2. The new Sion College, on the Embankment, was opened on Dec. 15 by the Prince and Princess of Wales.

3. Presumably, Margaret Harriet Bourke (1825-Dec. 29, 1886), daughter of the fifth earl of Mayo; Algernon Hawkins Thomond Keith-Falconer (1852–1930), fifth earl

of Kintore, and his wife, Lady Sydney Charlotte Montagu (d. 1932); Blanche Julia Bourke (d. 1918) (daughter of Baron Leconfield), countess of Mayo, and her daughter Florence Blanche Madeline Bourke (b. 1861); Lord Douglas Compton (b. 1865) was the fourth son of the fourth marquis of Northampton; the Lovelaces were of course neighbors, at Ockham Park, and Lionel Fortescue King Noel (1865–1929), Nelly's dinner companion, succeeded as third earl of Lovelace, in 1906, on the death of his half brother; Bycott Jenkins was Lady Lovelace's son by her first husband.

4. Unidentified, but perhaps Jane Minot Sedgwick (1859–1914), classicist and water colorist (courtesy Alexander Sedgwick).

To Arthur Howard Galton

Cobham, Surrey

My dear Mr Galton   December 16, 1886

I like the sonnet, and the man who inspires it is indeed excellent reading.[1] I have a political article to write which I would fain write in his sense as much as possible: but I know, if I begin to re-read him, I shall go on and on and leave the promised political article unbegun.

We all send sympathy to Port—affectionate sympathy.   Ever yours sincerely

Matthew Arnold.—

MS. The College of Wooster.

1. "Sonnet on Marcus Aurelius, published in the *Hobby Horse* for Apr. 1887" (Galton, *Two Essays upon Matthew Arnold*).

To Elizabeth Smith Thompson

Pains Hill Cottage, Cobham, Surrey

My dear Dolly   Friday, [?December 17, 1886][1]

That giddy Dick does not return till Monday, but I think of hobbling over on my crutches about 4 tomorrow if it is fine, to try and replace him at lawn tennis. I must go away at 6 as we dine out. Do not change your plans if you were meaning to be out between four and six; the walk will do me no harm, and I shall hear how your Mamma is. It is an age since I saw any of you.   Affectionately yours

M. A.

MS. Yale University.

1. The date is a guess.

To Charles Eliot Norton*

Pains Hill Cottage, Cobham, Surrey

My dear Norton   December 22, 1886

I was very glad to get your long and kind letter, but when I got it I was hard pressed; a little nephew of mine, who is starting a magazine for Murray, appealed to me for help in his first number, and I had also promised Knowles a political article before the meeting of Parliament. Mrs Arnold would have written in my stead to tell you how much better I am, but she fell down one fine morning in her bedroom and sprained her wrist—tore a ligament, they say; it was the wrist of her right hand and she has been much disabled; she is now at last getting much better, but has to spare her hand still. As for me, I could not have believed that what they talk of "native air" and its benefits could have come so true; but indeed I began to mend directly I got on board ship, and now am much as I was this time last year; if I go too quick, I am stopped by a warning in my chest, but I can go about as much as I like if I go leisurely, and I have no attacks of sharp pain. There were some nights in America when I thought that my "grand climacteric"[1]—an epoch in life which I used to hear a great deal of from my dear Mother—would see the end of me; and I think, by the way you looked at me once or twice at Ashfield, you thought so too. However, here I still am, and what is more I found myself able to answer to the spur and to produce my two articles under pressure, without any bad effects—and I think the stuff produced is of about the same quality as usual—not worse. Opinion here is entirely with you in the Carlyle case, and Froude's fretful letter to the Times[2] did him great harm; unluckily, he has begotten a distaste for Carlyle which indisposes the public mind now to give him the attention which they eagerly gave him not long ago. The account of your Harvard celebration in the Times was too brief, but well done so far as it went; only a few sentences were given to Lowell's address,[3] but we shall get that entire in a volume which Macmillan is to publish. The solemnity seems to have had a thorough public importance, and it is just one of those to which it is so good for America to give public importance, and to be proud of giving it. I suppose you are now besnowed and beiced for the winter; we have had a characteristic week of an English December; three days ago, after open weather, a powdering of snow and a hard frost, the thermometer falling to 16; three days of this, the ice becoming strong enough to bear and we all getting our skates out; this morning at breakfast Nelly looks up and cries—"Why, it's thawing!" and when we went to the window, so it was; dripping everywhere, and the wind southwest and the thermometer 42. I have been out a long walk, and it is like a cold stormy day in April. But I do enjoy this Surrey country and climate, and even this small old cottage which Mrs Arnold despises; we hope to show it to you some day, and do not let it be too long hence. Love from all of us and best wishes for Christmas and the New Year, to all your party.   Ever affectionately yours

Matthew Arnold.—

I am going to send you a new edition of my St Paul, for the sake of a word of new preface.[4]

MS. Harvard University.

1. Often associated with the 63d year (*OED*).
2. Froude's letter was in *The Times*, Nov. 2, 1886, p. 8.
3. [Harvard . . . Times . . . Lowell] On the 250th Anniversary of the founding of Harvard College—in *The Times*, Oct. 14, 1886, p. 12.
4. *St. Paul and Protestantism with Other Essays* (1887); Preface, Super 6 : 3–4.

To Félix Pécaut[1]

Pains Hill Cottage, Cobham, Surrey

Mon cher Monsieur   22 décembre, 1886

J'ai voulu vous communiquer mon rapport, et pourtant j'ai prévu que vous ne seriez pas content de ma critique de la politique anti-religieuse— dites plutôt, si vous voulez, anti-cléricale—suivie dans les écoles publiques de Paris. J'ai remarqué la même chose en causant avec Monsieur Buisson;[2] vous croyez, vous et lui, qu'un étranger ne se rend pas bien compte des motifs qui vous poussent à suivre votre ligne actuelle, et qu'il court risque, par con-séquent, de tomber dans l'injustice et dans l'erreur en vous jugeant. Je ne juge pas votre différend avec le parti clérical; je dirai seulement qu'il n'y pas de guerre sans accommodement possible; tout dépend des hommes et des procédés. Mais je m'empare de l'enseignement religieux et moral que j'ai entendu a Fontenay; cet enseignement est parfaitement liberal à coup sur,[3] mais il a ses bases dans un esprit religieux Protestant, dans une tradition, un sentiment Protestants. Il est si large et si judicieux qu'il s'adapte aux élèves Catholiques; eh bien, si vous faites école, vous avez, pour les écoles normales, une instruction religieuse et morale heureusement trouvée. Il ne s'agit de faire quelque chose de pareil pour les écoles élémentaires. Je suis persuadé que vous, mon cher Monsieur, vous seriez capable de le faire, et très bien; mais, dans votre qualité d'ancien pasteur protestant, vous seriez suspect; cependant, tôt ou tard, l'homme se présentera. Il trouvera un enseignement religieux et moral pour les enfants catholiques, qui ne les déconcertera pas en leur faisant rompre violemment et absolument avec le passé, qui leur parlera l'ancien langage tout en en élargissant l'esprit; et en faisant cela, mon cher

Monsieur, cet homme ne fera que bâtir sur les fondements que vous jetez à Fontenay.

Je vous prie de me rappeler au souvenir amical de Madame Feldberg et de vos bonnes et intéressantes élèves, et de me croire toujours, mon cher Monsieur, votre bien dévoué ami et serviteur,

Matthew Arnold.—

Recevez, en avance, tous mes souhaits pour la nouvelle année!

Je me permettrai de vous envoyer une édition populaire qui va paraître, de mon écrit sur St Paul.

Text. Xerox of holograph formerly belonging to Lucien Carrive.

1. See Lucien Carrive, "Lettre inédite de Matthew Arnold à Félix Pécaut," *Etudes anglaises*, 29, no. 4 (1976): 583–92.

2. Ferdinand Edouard Buisson (1841–1932), director of Primary Education, instrumental in "formulating the laws that made elementary instruction free, lay, and compulsory" (Super 11:388). Below, "the superintendent, a widow lady, Madame Feldberg, excellently chosen" (Super 11:40).

3. In the fourth sentence Arnold omits the accents in "entendu à," "libéral," and "sûr."

To Henry Frieze[1]

Professor Frieze   Cobham, Surrey
My dear Sir: December 23, 1886

I have been travelling either in Europe or America all the year nearly, and have only quite lately had your letter and volume. Your volume I have just read; it is charming. I am sorry it did not come out in America, for it is the sort of book to do America good. But it is the sort of book to do every body good; at any rate, it has done good to *me*, and I thank you for it cordially.   Most truly yours,

Matthew Arnold

MS. Typescript, University of Virginia (MS. University of Michigan).

1. Henry Simmons Frieze (1817–1889: Allibone), professor of Latin, University of Michigan, author of *Giovanni Dupré: the Story of a Florentine Sculptor* (1886).

To Claude Joseph Goldsmit Montefiore

Education Department, Whitehall

Cobham, Surrey
My dear Mr Montefiore   December 23, 1886

I have been in Germany on a school errand from the Government; I am just come home for a fortnight or three weeks, and then (certainly before the 28th January) I am going back again.

I am not easily brought to make a speech: but it is curious that on my way home I should have been reading the enclosed, which you need not return. It pleased me much.

With kind regards to your mother, believe me,   very truly yours
Matthew Arnold.—

MS. Texas A&M University.

To Lucy Charlotte Arnold Whitridge

Cobham

My dearest child   December 24, 1886

Today is my birthday and tomorrow is yours—how we all long to have you with us! I said to Mama [*sic*] when I woke between 6 & 7 this morning: Don't you wish we had the midget in here between us? She owned she didn't, but then she had not had the experience I had of the midget when you popped her into my bed that last morning at Stockbridge. I find myself continually thinking of that sweet little thing, and do not agree with Mme de Sévigné who says: "Vous savez combien je suis loin de la radoterie qui fait passer violemment l'amour paternel ou maternel—aux petits enfan[t]s; le mien est démeuré tout court au premier étage, et je n'aime ce petit peuple que pour l'amour de vous." [1] I love the sweet midget "pour l'amour" of herself—but nevertheless I can truly say to the midget's darling Mother in Mme de S.'s words: "Ma très belle et très aimable, je suis à vous par-dessus tout!" Your cake, or my cake as Dick calls it, has not yet appeared; I suppose it will come at dessert tonight. We have in the house four pheasants two hares, two turkeys and two rabbits which have been sent us—and now [?]Sydney [?]Buxton, who is just back from Russia has sent us some fresh caviare. Lady Ellesmere has a Christmas tree, and we have all of us just returned from it; we all had presents. The Dicks gave me this morning a really beautiful barometer—with a label which I send you; you remember Nelly's name for me of *Mr Fox*. The Alfred Egertons [2] want Nelly to go and stay with them in Grosvenor St but she will not leave the Dicks. Tomorrow we all five dine at the Leafs; they came down today; he has been very unwell again; he has sent me three dozen of various wines from the Park Hill cellar. Mrs Leaf has given me what looks like a white brilliant ball with matches coming out from it like rays; just the sort of thing I like for my writing table. The dear Dicks are perfectly enchanted to be here, and it is delightful having them. They came the day before yesterday and will stay about a fortnight, I think. Mr Cary came down on Sunday; we have had four days of hard frost and he came in the middle of it; we met him on the Walton road, his fly could hardly get along. Ted was here and it was pleasant; we wanted Mr Cary to stay the night but he could not. Pains Hill lake is frozen over, good ice and it had just begun to bear the day before yesterday when the thaw came. However there was a powdering of snow which I detest, and I am glad the thaw has come to sweep it all away; today we have a green world, a west wind and thermometer at 42. I am to give you the fondest love of Dick, who has just come in; he says he is going to write to you very soon. I have had a letter this morning from Mrs G. W. Childs—rather a copperplate letter; but Nelly has had one from Sarah Jewett which is quite charming. All the family invalids are somewhat better; but I have not had today a single letter from any member of my family, and all three posts are now in. Mamma's wrist is very much better; dear little Mrs Helme tumbled down on the ice on Monday, and hurt her wrist just as Mamma did—but worse; the pain and swelling are very great and she has to wear her arm in a sling. Poor Mrs Barnard Hawley [?Hanley],[3] that pretty woman at Fetcham, has just died in her confinement; she had gone on quite well for a fortnight, and then died from a *clot*, quite suddenly; people are greatly shocked, and the meets of the hounds are put off, because Mr B. Hawley [?Hanley] used to be master of hounds and every body knew him and her. We are all astounded at Lord Randolph Churchill's resignation; but this is the sort of thing of which the American papers tell you plenty. I had just finished a political article for Knowles, but luckily it had not gone to press and I am able to alter it so as to meet this new turn of affairs. I think Lord Randolph has done himself much harm; he is thought *personnel*[4] to a ruinous degree. Little Ted is full of his magazine, as you may imagine. I doubt whether he has quite the [?]talent[5] or Murray quite the liberality required for making a new Magazine a brilliant success nowadays, but the first two or three numbers will do well. Bain tells me everyone is buying this first number. Dick Wood[6] is to be married on the 4th of January, and we were asked to Barrington for it; we are not going but have sent him a present. The Learmonth's are quite [?]ruined; when the bailiffs came into the house near Windsor, the girls telegraphed to their mother who was in London to ask what they were to do; she telegraphed back: "Do as you like, dears; we are dining out and going to the play." You remember enough of Mrs Learmonth to be amused at this. She says she thinks she will go out as a companion. Mr Cary says he will come down again before he returns to America; we have been very attentive to him, and so has Dick. Poor Emma Lazarus![7] I am truly sorry for her. My love to Fred—we all send kisses to you and the darling midget; I wonder when this letter will reach you; I am posting it on the Friday. Ever, my darling child,   your own loving

Papa

Maude White is setting my "Too Late."

MS. National Archives of Canada.

1. Letter, August 16, 1675 (Madame de Sévigné, *Lettres*, 1:829, Pléiade edn). The second quotation seems to be an inexact recollection of perhaps the most familiar phrase in all her letters.

2. Probably, Alfred John Francis Egerton (1854–1890), younger brother of the third earl of Ellesmere, and his wife, the former Isabella Corisande Gertrude (born Meath).

3. Unidentified.

4. Egotistic.

5. The entire sentence is inked over, this word more heavily than the others

6. Richard Somerville Wood, one of the ten children of Flu's sister Caroline, married Frances Moodie, daughter of a barrister.

7. Emma Lazarus (1849–1887: *WWWA*) was among the crowd of well-wishers on the departure of the *Servia* from New York in Mar. 1884. In the last sentence, Maude Valérie White (1855–1937: *OCM*) was a noted composer of songs.

To Percy William Bunting

Cobham, Surrey

My dear Sir   December 26, 1886

My engagements are such that I see no prospect of my being able to contribute to the *Contemporary* in the coming year, but some day or other I hope to comply with your kind request and to give you another article.

With all good wishes of the Season, I remain,   most truly yours

Matthew Arnold.—

MS. University of Chicago.

To Elizabeth Smith Thompson

Pains Hill Cottage, Cobham, Surrey

My dear Dolly   Sunday, December 26, [1886]

I had been passing Christmas eve in the dejection in which we may suppose poor old Methuselah to have passed the latter birthdays of his life, when your pretty present and sweet little note arrived to light up the gloom. Thank you a thousand times: your last present has never yet left the back of my chair except to be washed—now it will take turns with this one. Ever yours affectionately

Matthew Arnold.—

A happy Christmas to you and to your husband.

MS. Yale University.

To Frances Bunsen Trevenen Whately Arnold*

Cobham

My dearest Fan   December 27, 1886

It was no use writing yesterday, for my letter would have stayed all day in London. I got yesterday, the 26th, your letter, and John's, and Jane's, written on the 23rd. Thank John for me, and give a kiss to my precious Susy. My love to Walter also, and tell him to cheer up. Today we have no post at all, the mail cart has been waiting all day at Weybridge for the mail from the South; to London the line is open, and letters will be sent there tonight. How much farther they will get I know not, but Knowles will get the corrected proof of my article at his house in St James's, and take it to the printer. I send you his note; that is being a good editor to do everything to facilitate your contributor's task instead of worrying him. Of course it was an awkward circumstance, Lord Randolph's sudden resignation coming when my article was already in type; then came Chamberlain's speech also, to change the posture of things still further; but I have made everything right, and think the article will do very well, and, I hope, be of use. I am told the pantomime people are in despair: all their jokes and allusions have gone wrong; they were full of Ld Randolph, as the rising and powerful minister. On Christmas Day we skated at Pains Hill—beautiful ice. Yesterday the weather changed to thaw; Dick and I walked through Burwood in the rain and I called on the Leafs, where we had dined the night before; then I came in to work, and when Eliza brought my hot water for dressing she told me there was a deep snow; the wind rose too. After supper we heard a heavy fall; it was the second part of the double beech tree in the clump of the field; the first part fell when you were here, and the line of rending from the second tree was visible, but the second tree was a fine one for all that, and is a loss. But, my dear Fan, the havoc! the cork tree is a wreck, it has lost great limbs at the top and at the side; the ivied firs in the shrubbery have snapped off in the middle, half a dozen of them, and lie all over the evergreens. We have had a busy day; Dick has been sawing off the shattered branches of the cork tree, I have been getting rid of the snow which was breaking down the evergreens. The hollies are terribly split and twisted; the yews and laurels have resisted better. Pains Hill lawn is a desolation, with the great limbs of cedars lying upon it. Even the oaks in the park have suffered, besides a number of trees that are down altogether. Tonight it is a hard frost, with snow on the ground six or eight inches deep. It being that goose Lubbock's holiday, the British workman was passing his day at the public house, and no help could be got; but Dick has been a tower of strength. We dined with the Leafs on Christmas day, and it was pleasant; we were to have dined with the George Smiths at Walton tonight, but can neither go nor telegraph; the roads are impassable and the telegraph wires broken. The Buxtons have theatricals tomorrow night, and how we are to get there I don't know. We dine out Wednesday and Thursday; a nice time for such pleasures! I wish we had you here and could take care of you, for I am sure you are not right yet: of course Dr Hamilton says what is perfectly true when he says that your sick relatives prevent your getting well. Perhaps you would be worrying about them if you were here; but still I wish that here you were. Susy ought to be at Cannes, but in the north of England their ideas of change do not go much beyond Blackpool. I send you a pretty note from Morley which you must return. I thought Jane's letter written in fair spirits: the baby is evidently a great pleasure to her. We telegraphed to Lucy on her birthday and had a long message in reply: the midget sent "special love to Grand'pa." Good bye, my dearest; I wish we were all at the top of Loughrigg in the snow, and had to get home as we could. Your ever loving

M. A.—

You have sent me a very pretty little book: Burroughs is a good writer.[1]

MS. Frederick Whitridge.

1. Perhaps John Burroughs's most recent book, *Signs and Seasons* (1886), 16mo. His *Fresh Fields* (12mo) is listed in *Note-books*, pp. 619, 622 (1885, 1887).

To John Churton Collins

Pains Hill Cottage, Cobham, Surrey

J. C. Collins, Esqre
My dear Sir,   December 29, 1886
I have no difficulty in saying that I should like to see standard English Authors joined to the standard Authors of Greek and Latin literature, who have to be taken up for a pass, or for honours, at the universities.

I should be sorry to see a separate School, with degrees and honours, for the modern languages as such, although it is desirable that the professors and teachers of those languages should give certificates of fitness to teach them.

I would add no literature except that of our own country to the classical literature taken up for the degree, whether with or without honours, in Arts.

These seem to me to be elementary propositions, when one is laying down what is desirable in respect to the University degree in Arts. The omission of the mother tongue and its literature in school and University instruction is peculiar, so far as I know, to England. You do a good work in urging us to repair that omission.

But I will not conceal from you that I have no confidence in those who at the Universities regulate studies, degrees, and honours. To regulate these matters great experience of the world, steadiness, simplicity, breadth of view, are desirable. I do not see how those who actually regulate them can well have these qualifications; I am sure that in what they have done in the last forty years they have not shown them. Restlessness, a disposition to try experiments and to multiply studies and schools, are what they have shown, and what they will probably continue to show—and this though personally many of them may be very able and distinguished men. I fear, therefore, that while you are seeking an object altogether good—the completing of the old and great degree in Arts—you may obtain something which will not only not be that, but will be a positive hindrance to it. I am, my dear Sir,   Your faithful servant,

Matthew Arnold.—

MS. British Library.

To George Smith

Cobham

My dear G. S.   December 30, [?1886]

A thousand thanks for your elegant present, which will enable me, when I have young people to dinner, even now in my extreme old age to assume the airs of the rake and the man of pleasure.   Yours affectionately

Matthew Arnold.—

MS. National Library of Scotland.

Anthony John Mundella to Matthew Arnold

16, Elvaston Place, Queen's Gate, S. W.

My dear Arnold   December 30, 1886

Your recommendation of Mr Hastings shall secure for his claims the fullest consideration when we come to consider the staff of the Holloway College.

Pray accept my best greetings and wishes for the New Year. Health Peace and Prosperity to you! Continue to do something for the promotion of Educational work, and *don't neglect the Muse* and I shall ever remain Cordially and gratefully yours

A J Mundella

I heard a leading publisher, who *is in earnest*, praise your report enthusiastically today. Do you see that everybody wants to turn the Schools into Workshops!

MS. British Library.

To Miss Bevan[1]

Athenæum Club, Pall Mall

Dear Miss Bevan   Thursday, [?1887]

The lines are from a poem of mine called "The [*sic*] Modern Sappho."
I think it is in the first volume of my poems.   Very truly yours

Matthew Arnold.—

MS. Pierpont Morgan Library.

1. Miss Bevan was probably one of the four daughters of William Latham Bevan
(1821–1908: *DNB*), vicar of Hay, whom Arnold probably knew at Rugby and Balliol.
(The date, a guess, is based on handwriting alone.)

To Louisa Lady Rothschild

Pains Hill Cottage, Cobham, Surrey

Dear Lady de Rothschild   Sunday [?1887]

For fear of inflicting upon you an unpleasant surprise, I write one line
to say that it has been agreed between your daughters and me that I am to
come to lunch with you tomorrow at 2, in Grosvenor Place.   Affectionately yours,

Matthew Arnold.—

MS. Evelyn de Rothschild.

To James Bain

Pains Hill Cottage, Cobham, Surrey

Dear Mr Bain   January 2, 1887

Will you be so kind as to bind the Essays in *2* vols., calf extra, and to
send them, before the 10th inst., to Miss Knowles, Queen Anne's Lodge,
St James's Park.[1]

And will you also kindly send the new number of the XIXth Century
to my daughter,

Mrs Whitridge
16, East Eleventh Street,
New York City
U. S. A.

I wish you a happy New Year, and am   truly yours

Matthew Arnold.—

MS. Bryn Mawr College.

1. Beatrice Knowles (b. 1866), James T. Knowles's eldest daughter, who married W. W. Skilbeck in 1894.

To Frances Bunsen Trevenen Whately Arnold*

Cobham

My dearest Fan   January 3, 1887

A fresh disaster—a thaw came on in the night, with wind; I suppose the frost had made the stems brittle; and on going out this morning I find the great head of the Souvenir de Malmaison rose-tree, of which I am particularly fond, blown right off and lying on the lawn. The cork-tree has suffered much, but can be trimmed into shape, and will still be an interesting object on the lawn. The Pains Hill cork tree has not lost a branch, but a great cedar near it, which probably you do not remember, has suffered more than any cedar in the place, and the ruin is really a grand sight to see, the trunk and boughs of big cedars are so vast and impressive. We have had very hard frost—I fancy you seldom have it so cold in Westmorland—it was at 12 on the lawn yesterday; both that day and the day before the trees were more beautiful with rime than I have ever seen them: the Pains Hill lake and woods were a sight; I wished for you. The skating was good, and I still skate, though with a good deal of reluctance to try figures or skating backwards. Now we have a thaw, and I only hope it may continue and not turn to snow. Travelling has been horrible, and I rejoice daily that I have not to go up and down to London. The Dicks leave us today; it has been very pleasant having them, but a district is likely to be vacant soon and he had better be at work when the vacancy comes. The skating has been a great delight to him, and he is, and always has been, very fond of his home and its goings on. I send you the telegram we had from Lucy on Christmas Day; we had telegraphed to her in the early morning. I also send you one or two other letters as you like to see these things; Flint[1] is a Scotch journalist. All may burn, unless you like to keep Goschen as an autograph. I declined the speech, and today have another letter from him urging me again. His last sentence makes me think he is going to take office—we shall know tomorrow.[2] I am sure Ld Hartington's taking it would have led to intrigues and to a wearing down of the majority; I am inclined to think Goschen may join without inconvenience. He is isolated; and then on local government he will be a tower of strength to them. I am very much afraid of a weak bill there, if Goschen does not intervene. Ld Hartington will exercise a very greater influence on Chamberlain's section of Unionists by remaining as he is; Chamberlain himself is "remuant" and dangerous, but his followers will feel Ld Hartington's influence whether

Chamberlain does or no—that is, they will feel it so long as he holds his present independent position. I think we shall go to London early in February. Nelly goes today to the Rates near Dorking for a ball; the Money Couttses have another this week, at Weybridge,[3] but to that Nelly will not go. I hope Ted has been bestirring himself about his second number; now would be the time to get Ld Randolph Churchill. Ted has hardly literary instinct enough for his new line, though he has all possible wish to succeed and to make money. I have heard from dear old Tom; I wish I could get him you and Susy here together. But the place I want to get Susy to is the Alhambra.[4] Love to Walter and his two companions.[5] I hope Sarah's cold is better. From Burley we hear nothing. I read your Burroughs through yesterday; he is a naturalist of great merit, and a good critic of men too. What a pity he has the American disease of always bringing into comparison his country and its things! They all do it, however, except you get a man like Emerson. He much overpraises the song of the American (so-called) robin. Ever, my dearest Fan, with all New Year's wishes, your most affectionate

M. A.—

MS. Frederick Whitridge.

1. Unidentified.
2. Goschen succeeded Randolph Churchill as chancellor of the Exchequer.
3. Francis Burdett Thomas Money Coutts-Nevill (1852–1923), later fifth Lord Latymer, a poet and prose writer, married (1875) Edith Ellen Churchill, Weybridge Park, Surrey (Kelly, *CBEL*)
4. The theater in Leicester Square.
5. Probably, his wife and her daughter, Sarah and Nelly. (The nine manuscript lines "Ted has . . . cold is better" are heavily inked over, but the transcription is probably accurate.)

To Henry Charles Howard Earl of Suffolk and Berkshire

Pains Hill Cottage, Cobham, Surrey
My dear Lord Suffolk January 4, 1887
It is ages since I have gone about in rural France. The "verderbende Elemente"[1] which Goethe warned them against have made great progress; still I believe that if you and I were to go about today in Berry or Anjou we should find ourselves more at home with the people, more able to talk freely and naturally with them, than in England. I am sure, too, that we should find their dinner one which we would rather share than an English cottage dinner. Do you think Lady Verney substantial and natural enough to be trusted in these matters? I do not. You have only to look at her.[2]

Of Paris and the great towns I have long thought badly, and am now disposed to think worse than ever.

Neither party will like what I have said in the Nineteenth Century, but, as I have just been telling Goschen it is not at present party which is keeping the Government in or which will compel them to go out; their strength is in the goodwill towards them of the great majority of quiet reasonable people throughout the country and this goodwill they must cultivate and retain.

I ought to go and see Mrs Cooper;[3] I have sometimes a vision of a woman, bowed and wrapped, passing me in a close carriage; but I ought to go and see her, and will. It would be pleasanter if I were to meet you and Lady Suffolk there, as on former occasions; but then my visit would be of less positive benefit to Mrs Cooper. I hope we shall go to town for February and March; I wonder if you will be there; in my opinion they are the two best London Months.

With kindest regards from both of us to you and Lady Suffolk, I am most sincerely yours

Matthew Arnold.—

MS. Balliol College.

1. The "destructive element," as in Conrad's *Lord Jim*, ch. 20 (untraced in Goethe).
2. Frances Parthenope Verney (d. 1890), sister of Florence Nightingale, and wife of Sir Harry Verney (1801–1894: *DNB*; *VF*, 7/15/82), second bt, was the author of several books, including *Peasant Properties* and *Cottier Owners*, both 1885.
3. Mrs Cooper has not been identified.

To Lucy Charlotte Arnold Whitridge

Cobham

My darling child   January 10, 1887

I have been very busy writing my second article for Ted, but I finished it just before luncheon today, so I told Mamma I would write to you. My liberty will be very short for Humphry Ward has already written to me to claim an article on Schools which I promised him for a Jubilee publication. I must keep this promise but I mean to make no more promises of the kind. It seems a long time since I wrote to you, but you are often in my mind; we have heard today from your Aunt Forster that Clifford Allbrett, of Leeds, a very good physician had seen poor little Vernon, and says he cannot possible [*sic*] recover; he has now the disease of which Budge died, meningitis, an inflamation of the brain: he has suffered much distressing pain, but the doctor thinks the pain is over now. Till now Edith would not have a nurse but attended herself to him entirely; now the doctors have insisted on a nurse, and they have one from Bradford whom this dear little patient likes. He is a sweet little boy; he has got to like his doctor, Dr Rab something, an Italian name; when they told him Dr Allbrett was coming he said, Oh yes! and then added—but will Dr Rab mind it? Your Aunt Forster seems better and stronger—I daresay Mamma will go to her for a week when Flo comes up to London. Your Aunt Fan is rather suffering again, but she has had a house full of invalids and no rest all Christmas time; now she will be quiet; I want her to come here but she will not. The good news is that your Aunt Susy is better—really much better. Mamma wishes me to tell you that Dolly Thompson is coming over to America sooner than she expected—probably in February, and will bring anything for you. You will like seeing her, but you will be thinking of coming soon yourself, my darling, when you see her. That sweet midget—I should like to see her dear little teeth. But I hate to hear of all her squeaking presents; you will over-excite the poor little thing, and spoil her nerves and her brain; I wish she had a single wooden doll to play with and nothing more. I am annoyed about the cheese; I am going up to town tomorrow and will enquire at Craft's.[1] The oysters have been a great success; every one likes them, and we have given away a great many; I myself like them extremely and have got to prefer them to natives; I eat them daily, and they still go on. The Leafs are delighted with theirs; but Mr Leaf has written to you. It is long since he has enjoyed any *nourriture* so much, or taken so much of it. The turkey we had was excellent too. I am anxious that part of your cake should be taken to you by Mr Carey,[2] it is so good, and you will like to have part of what has day after day stood on the table at home. We have just heard from Mr Carey, whom we thought to be in Paris; his business has been prospering but keeps him very much engaged. We have had snow on the ground for about a fortnight but really the house is delightfully comfortable; Mamma and I found a stove at Barron and Wilson's[3] which burns Joyce's Patent Fuel, a preparation of charcoal; it has bad effects but gives a very different heat indeed from the gas stove, which has been banished; we have a temperature of about 55 in the passages, and 65 in the rooms, which suits us all well enough. Every day the thermometer out of doors is about two above freezing and every night about two below; so we go on. I have been very busy clearing the place from the wreck caused by the snow and wind together; Pains Hill is a sight[;] you should see it. Today I have been round the park with the two dogs, Miss Lu; Max likes snow and is always in spirits at it; you know how he hates rain and mud. Chain is never mentioned, Miss Lu, but he has freer range in [the] park this weather, because the snow makes it easy to see him. He crossed the ice on the lake at one place and it broke with him and let his hind-quarters in—he struggled out without any help however. I like to think of him and Kai with the midget. Dear Mamma is almost well again in her wrist; Nelly has gone off today to stay with Mrs Egerton; Alf is to chaperon her to a children's ball at

Bridgewater House which will be a gay and pretty affair; poor Mrs Egerton is delighted to have Nelly, and I like them for liking the dear child so much. The Combe girls came to see her yesterday afternoon, Sunday[,] and stayed two hours.[4] Mrs Leaf came in, and turned her back on them without speaking. Herbert seems happy in his engagement, and the young lady is pretty and lively, her mother is as despairing over the loss of her daughter as Mrs Leaf over that of her son so they make a doleful pair. At the Shakespeare reading at the Helmes the other night Nelly seems to have had signal success—and next after her, Walter Leaf. We have had a letter from Mademoiselle who goes daily to Miss Webster and gets on with her capitally. We are all much relieved, as she had no pupils at all. I wonder how the Americans will like my articles on General Grant; you will tell me if you hear anything of importance. We had little Ted here on Sunday, he departed this morning, and Minnie[5] rejoins him from Sedgwick tomorrow; I hope his Magazine will do well; Murray seems quite satisfied with him, which is the great thing. But he has certain deficiencies as an editor. My love to Fred and a kiss to my precious midget—   always your own

Papa—

MS. National Archives of Canada.

    1. John Craft, cheesemonger, St George's Place, Hyde Park corner (*POLD*).
    2. Arnold had spelled his name correctly exactly a month earlier.
    3. Later, Wilson and Smith, 7–8. King William Street, Strand (*POLD*).
    4. Daughters of Charles Combe of Cobham Park (m. 1861, father of nine sons and six daughters), snubbed by Mrs Charles John Leaf for reasons not known to the editor but obviously familiar to Lucy, "for a bird of the air shall carry the voice, and that which hath wings shall tell the matter." (Below, Miss Webster has not been identified.)
    5. Ted's wife.

To Arthur Howard Galton

Pains Hill Cottage, Cobham, Surrey

My dear Mr Galton   January 13, 1887
    When I take up the "Hobby Horse" to look at it, I find myself going right through it; it has so much merit that its title and its restricted publicity are really to be lamented. Could not something be done?
    I think my sister, as owning Fox How, best represents the family in the Memorial project.
    What you say of Symonds is true and good.[1]   Ever yours,

Matthew Arnold.—

I am very sorry Port is amiss.

MS. The College of Wooster.

1. "The Italian Renaissance," *Century Guild Hobby Horse*, 2 (Jan. 1887): 20–28. (Below, "Port" was an ailing dog.)

To George William Erskine Russell

Pains Hill Cottage, Cobham, Surrey

My dear George   January 13, 1887

I telegraphed to say I would come. If you can give me a bed, as you kindly propose, that will be extremely convenient; I was going to my sister in Portman Street, but the distance is a great objection this horrid weather. Affectionately yours

Matthew Arnold.—

MS. Yale University.

To Edward Tyas Cook

Cobham, Surrey

My dear Mr Cook   January 19, 1887

I could not well speak of Renan without speaking of his repulsive "Abbesse," and as I know him personally, I should not like to speak of this as I feel about it. But indeed I am so busy for the next 6 weeks with a horrid paper on Schools which I have promised to Humphry Ward's Jubilee Volume that I can undertake nothing whatever at present besides.   Very faithfully yours

Matthew Arnold

MS. Joseph O. Baylen, "Matthew Arnold and the Pall Mall Gazette," South Atlantic Quarterly, 8 (1969): 534–35.

To Edward Tyas Cook

Cobham, Surrey

Dear Mr Cook   January 21, 1887

I will not send the book back—indeed I think you are well rid of such a version of the Fourth Gospel—Paley—though a man of some learning, has no common sense.[1] But there is, believe me, no chance of my reviewing this or any other new book. My promises are more than I can well discharge, and what I now pine for is a little liberty.   Truly yours

Matthew Arnold

MS. *Joseph O. Baylen, "Matthew Arnold and the Pall Mall Gazette,"* South Atlantic Quarterly, *8 (1969): 555.*

1. Frederick Apthorp Paley, *The Gospel of St John: A Verbatim Translation from the Vatican MS* (1887).

To Lucy Charlotte Arnold Whitridge

Cobham

My darling Lucy   January 26, 1887

Today we have your long letter from Chicago. All about the poor little baby was so sad that I could not bear to have Nelly read it to me, and must wait for Mamma and her dear voice which makes things less painful and overwhelming. We were indeed amazed at your date; your letter was to Mamma, but we should have opened it instantly had we known it was from you; as it was, we saw the Chicago post-mark and never seriously thought the letter was from you, but Nelly said: The writing is rather like Lucy's. I then opened it; the accounts of the dear Midget are good, and that is a consolation. Poor Grace, I am sorry about her, but not altogether surprised. Of course you will take the opportunity of coming to England to part with her. It seems the madness your going to Chicago, but I say no more about that as I can understand your longing for some change after the misery and distress you had seen and shared. I hope you will see Mrs McClurg and dear little Ogden;[1] he has something attractive and touching. How well I remember Chicago in winter and that grand lake—not *Erie*, but Michigan. How well I remember Madison too, and my long journey there through that monstrous country: but Madison itself I liked better than most American towns, and my entertainers there were very nice people.[2] Dear little Vernon died last week; he had gone on so long that I thought he would pull through, but he is gone: he was a sweet little fellow, both face and voice full of interest. Mamma goes to Wharfeside today: your Aunt Forster seems to me better, and of course, though the death of little Vernon moves her, no sorrow can make much impression compared with the great sorrow she had already weighing on her. In having Mamma she will have what she will like better than almost anything I can think of; Mamma will never be tired of hearing and talking about your uncle Forster and I will never fail in sympathy. The stone for the monument too, has come at last and will probably be put up while Mamma is there; your Aunt was very anxious she should see it. Mamma has liked being with the Dicks—but of this visit she will have told you. Nelly and I are having that sort of interlude which redeems our winters: a week of beautiful open weather, all the snow gone, the sun shining, and the thermometer from 40 to 50; the bulbs are coming up everywhere and the garden is as green as in April. I never look at the lawn without thinking of the Midget and the pleasure I hope the garden will be to her. Your account of Annie is very satisfactory. We have got a house in Wilton Street, Lady Maud Seymour's,[3] we looked at it once before, with you, I think. We have it from the day after tomorrow, Friday the 28th and you must direct to us there—*No. 3*. Lady Maud leaves a housemaid, which troubles Mamma's mind greatly, but I have sent Eliza up to see the accommodations, I have no doubt they will all manage very well. Nelly and I walk daily in the park at Pains Hill, the havoc of the storm making every part worth a visit. The Leafs are here, and dined with Nelly and me on Monday: I think they liked it, but poor Mrs Leaf is constantly crying when she is alone at the thought of losing Herbert. I don't see why she should lose him any more than she has lost him now; except perhaps that she will lose the *management* of him; somebody will always manage him, and perhaps it will be his wife, but I myself should not much wonder if it was still his mother. We dined last night at the Deacons; very pleasant; tonight we dine with Lady Ellesmere; both Nelly and I wish we were going to stay at home. On Saturday we dine with the Deacons again, and then, Nelly, at any rate, will not wish to stop at home. The bliss of the dear men at their daily walks in the park you may imagine, Miss Lu. Discipline had to be administered to Max the day before yesterday for slipping away in a very deceitful manner; for a day or two after discipline he is always quite angelic; a hint for the Midget's education. This is a shabby letter, but I am fairly overdone with work. I have a horrid paper on schools to write—then I will have nothing more to do with that subject. At present I am as much pressed and hampered as when I was an official, and so it will be till I can get this horrid paper on schools done. I shall send you a letter from your Aunt Fan to give you some news—but it is not a very lively letter. I like to think of your having the prospect of seeing Mr Carey who has actually been here with us—but we saw him only on that one hurried visit though we really tried all we could to see more of him. I am glad business is prospering; in a country where they build 11,000 miles of new railroad in a year lawyers *must* prosper. My love to Fred—and I am always, my darling, though over-driven,   your fondly loving

Papa—

Aunt Fan makes the letter too heavy.

MS. Frederick Whitridge.

1. The McClurgs were Arnold's hosts in Chicago; see 5:372–84.
2. At Madison on Jan. 25, 1884, his host was the former governor, Lucius Fairchild, a teetotaler whom Arnold liked for other reasons.
3. Unidentified.

To Florence Earle Coates*

Pains Hill Cottage, Cobham, Surrey

My dear Mrs Coates   January 29, 1887

I had been thinking of you and your husband this Christmas, and had sent off to you a republication of one of my books, which contains some new matter, and would, I thought, interest you. Now comes your letter, which I am glad to receive, though it tells me of your grandmother's death. I remember her perfectly. She was a woman of great vigour of mind, and it was a pleasure to me to make her acquaintance. One should try to bring oneself to regard death as a quite natural event, and surely in the case of the old it is not difficult to do this. For my part, since I was sixty I have regarded each year, as it ended, as something to the good beyond what I could naturally have expected. This summer in America I began to think that my time was really coming to an end, I had so much pain in my chest, the sign of a malady which had suddenly struck down in middle life, long before they came to my present age, both my father and grandfather. I feel sure that the Philadelphia lecture had nothing to do with it. I do not think I enjoyed any days in America more than those I spent with you at Germantown; the heat did not oppress me and the beauty of your vegetation was a perpetual pleasure. Shall I ever forget your Pennsylvania tulip-trees? But the American summer I found trying, and I cannot resist the conviction that the climate does not suit the heart-trouble which I undoubtedly have; the tendency to pain in the chest diminished as soon as I went on board ship to return home; and now, in the friendly air of this dear, stupid old country, it has almost entirely disappeared. I am not likely, therefore, to attempt America again, though I should like to have seen the South and West. Philadelphia and Germantown have already a secure place in my affections, and cannot lose it.   Always affectionately yours,

Matthew Arnold.

Text. Russell, 2:422–24.

To Henry Arthur Jones

Pains Hill Cottage, Cobham, Surrey

My dear Mr Jones   January 31, 1887

Your kind note reaches me just as we are starting for London. I could very well go on Friday in this week to the theatre, if you could send me a box for that night.[1] We shall be at 3, Wilton Street, Belgrave Square. If I see you on Friday, we can arrange for your coming some day to have the talk you propose.   Most truly yours

Matthew Arnold.—

MS. *State University of New York, Buffalo.*

1. Jones's *Hard Hit*, which had opened Jan. 1 at the Royal Opera House, Haymarket.

To Louisa Lady de Rothschild

Athenæum Club, Pall Mall, S. W.

My dear Lady de Rothschild   February 1, 1887

I arrived in London last night; this morning I went past your house, and found it, as I expected, blank and shut up. But we are close by, at 3, Wilton Street; and how delightful if when you come up you will lunch with us, and if you will come *soon* and give us this very great pleasure. I was delighted to hear from you but shall not be satisfied until I have again seen you. I am very busy just now with a stupid article on Schools for a Jubilee volume (just imagine) but I hope and believe that this will be my last contribution to School literature.

My love to the Flowers and believe me always   affectionately yours
Matthew Arnold.—

MS. *Evelyn de Rothschild.*

To William Gordon McCabe

Athenæum Club, London

My dear Mr McCabe   February 3, 1887

I am unable to speak as to your special studies in Latin; but I know, in general, that your love of culture and your interest in letters are such as to fit you eminently, in my opinion, to hold a literary Chair in a University or College. And a yet higher value is given to your love of culture, inasmuch as you have proved your desire and power to make this love live and work in others also; what I have heard of your labours and success at Petersburg has interested me warmly, and all the more because I have understood that it was the reading, during the War, of my father's Life which set you upon the design of teaching—a design which you have prosecuted with such excellent results.

With every wish for your success at Columbia College, I am always, my dear Mr McCabe,   Truly and cordially yours,

Matthew Arnold.—

MS. University of Virginia.

To W. Stanley Withers

Pains Hill Cottage, Cobham, Surrey

W. Stanley Withers Esq.

My dear Sir   February 5, 1887

As you rightly suppose, the publishers have a voice as to cheap editions, and Messrs Macmillan are not at present favourable to cheap editions of the Poems and the Essays in Criticism—"Friendship's Garland" is quite out of print, and I do not find Messrs Smith and Elder forward to reprint it at all— certainly not as a cheap book.   Most truly yours

Matthew Arnold.—

MS. Manchester Public Library.

To Edward Frederick Smyth Pigott

3, Wilton Crescent
Belgrave Square

My dear Pigott   February 18, [1887]

We hope you are disengaged on Thursday next, the 24th, and that we may persuade you to come and dine here on that day at ¼ before 8.   Most truly yours

Matthew Arnold.—

MS. Roger Brooks.

To Henry Arthur Jones

⟨Athenæum Club, Pall Mall⟩

(3, Wilton Street S. W.)

Dear Mr Jones   February 24, [1887]

We expected you on Ash Wednesday, but you did not appear; I hope you were not ill. We must try and fix another day. Mrs Arnold has not yet

availed herself of your kindness, as she is still afraid of the draughts at a theatre; but we will talk of this when you come.   Most truly yours,

Matthew Arnold.—

MS. Pierpont Morgan Library.

To ?

Athenæum Club, Pall Mall, S. W.

Dear Sir   February 25, [?1887]
    You are quite welcome to print the pieces you mention. I remain
Yours faithfully

Matthew Arnold.—

MS. Pierpont Morgan Library.

To Alexander G. Ross

Athenæum Club

Alex. G. Ross
Dear Sir   February 28, 1887
    When I paid my subscription at the beginning of this year it was with
the intention of not any longer continuing to belong to the Incorporated
Society of Authors, and this intention I now write to announce to you.
Having resigned my official post, I am likely to live a good deal abroad, and
must be a member of as few societies at home as possible.   Most faithfully
yours,

Matthew Arnold.—

MS. Roger Brooks.

To [?Edwin Beaumont] Johnson[1]

3, Wilton Street, Belgrave Square
My dear General Johnson   March 2, [1887]
    I cannot enough thank you for the photographs of the grave. Lord Na-
pier of Magdala told me it was in a bad condition and he was going to have
it cleaned and repaired: but the aspect of it now, and of all the place where it
stands, is far more pleasing than I expected, even after his restoration, to find

it. I shall have the photograph framed, to hang in my own room along with poor dear Willy's likeness. How often I wrote his name once and how seldom I write it now!

I am sure my sister Mrs Forster would greatly like to have the photograph. She is now at Wharfeside.

We are hopelessly engaged to dinner while we are here, but we should be so glad if you could come to luncheon this next Sunday, at half past one.   Ever truly yours

Matthew Arnold.—

MS. *Pierpont Morgan Library*.

1. Edwin Beaumont Johnson (1825–1893: *DNB*; K.C.B. 1875, G.C.B. 1887), whose whole adult life had been in the Indian service, either at home or in India; promoted general 1877.

To Henry Arthur Jones

Athenæum Club, Pall Mall

Dear Mr Jones   March 2, 1887

We are now so much engaged that the theatre is almost impossible; however, if I have a chance, I shall profit by your kindness and see "The Noble Vagabond"; "Sophia" I must not attempt.[1] Do write and offer yourself to luncheon some day after your return.   Most truly yours,

Matthew Arnold.—

MS. *State University of New York, Buffalo*.

1. Jones's *Noble Vagabond* was at the Princess's, Robert Buchanan's *Sophia* at the Vaudeville.

To Lucy Charlotte Arnold Whitridge

London

My darling Lucy   March 3, 1887

At last I have done my paper on Schools for Humphry Ward, both first and second part, and can write to you before I turn to anything else. Your Aunt Fan was delighted with your letter to her. I have a letter from your Aunt Forster this morning who says: "I *long* to see the midget." Her licking my picture is delicious. I even see her eyes as she does it. How often I comforted myself by leaning over her and watching her while one of those horrid pains in my chest passed off! They have quite ceased in that horrid form of

spasms now; sometimes they give me a little warning, just to say—you must
not expect to play lawn-tennis or go up Sea Fell any more. I hope you will
come by the Aurania or Umbria, as I know and like both boats so much.
Your Aunt Forster wants us to come to Fox How in June this year, because
she and Francie will then be at Fox Ghyll—in the summer they must let it,
she says; I fancy she finds the two houses rather a strain upon her present
income. But we shall be guided entirely by what you and Fred do; I think
the 7th of May a quite perfect time for your start, but oh, how I sometimes
wish for you here with us now. It is just the weather you Nelly and Mamma
like—invariably dry and clear; we have had not a drop of rain or snow since
we came to London. For my part I hate as you know the dry hard north west
or north east winds which we have been having with just three or four degrees of frost each night; but it is pleasant weather enough for walking—and
above all, your dear sex can get about in it without dirtying their petticoats.
Nelly enjoys herself greatly, though she says she is worn out; you know how
popular she is, and if we stayed longer, I tremble to think of what the house
would be at 5 o'clock tea time. Tonight we have the Teds, the Stephen Coleridges, and Bernard Holland dining with us at home; afterwards we go to
Mrs Jeune's, who has the [?]Christies.[1] Last night we were at Lady Salisbury's,
a great crush. Before that, Mamma and I dined with Lady Stanley of Alder-
ley; young Lord Airlie was there, but not his pretty wife, who has just had a
little girl.[2] I was by Lady Revelstoke[3]—her brother in law is your Mr Tom
Baring in New York and her son was over there too. Her husband is rather a
heavy man, but a good sort: Lady R. is a sister to Lady Ponsonby, and I used
to know her mother, Lady Eliz[abe]th Bult[e]ell; we talked of you and New
York, I need not say. We received in the course of yesterday no less than six
invitations to dinner, only one of which we could accept; we are full for the
next three weeks. The big parties are beginning, so Nelly, who enjoys them,
will have the benefit: I never go to Cobham without longing to stay there,
and the 1st of April, when we return, will be a joyful day indeed. I think the
pressure of engagements tires your sweet little Mamma somewhat; she looks
more than usually pale and sad in a morning: but she enjoys her London for
all that. We have broughams from a protégé of George Russell, close by, and
get very good carriages and horses; you know how Mamma and Nelly delight in a carriage. Last night at Lady Salisbury's we sent the carriage away
and walked into St James's Street and got a cab; this abridges the getting away
wonderfully, and when it is quite dry and fine, as it was last night, a great
many people do it.—I have just been interrupted by a dinner invitation from
Sir Fowell & Lady Victoria Buxton, which I have answered as Mamma is
out; and being in the passage and hearing the voice of Max I called him up,
and he is now lying on the rug by me and sends his love to Miss Lu and his

blessing to her midget. He gets along better than he did, for like the rest of it, he forms his habits with time; but he is never properly happy either in the streets or the parks; when I take him down to Cobham he is another dog. Jane went down there yesterday and took him with her; she says Kai is made much of by a nice little girl belonging to the woman who takes care of the house; but he never left Jane for a single moment, nor does he leave me when I am down there. Max was delighted to see Kai; Kai more cool about seeing Max. Jane brought up quantities of snowdrops out of the garden, and five or six camellias; we shall have a great many camellias presently—they have never done so well. Mamma has just come in and bids me say she will send one or two of the frocks, which are not yet ready, by Mrs Chadwick the wife of the Naval Attaché.[4] You will like to see Dolly; tell her to put on the gown for you which she wore at Lady Hayter's the other night; I never saw her look so well. I have told her, when she has embraced you for herself, to give you a regular hug for me. Yates Thompson has had a great deal of cold-shouldering to bear because of the rowdy and sensational line taken by the P. M. G., to say nothing of the "revelations";[5] Dolly is all that is calm and sensible about it, but of course she must feel it. Unluckily her Yates T. is not liked personally, let alone the style of his newspaper. You will have been amused with the "Forty English Academicians" and my place amongst them, if the account of that absurd competition came to America.[6] My love to Fred, and tell me how his father is, and his sister, and those dear children. Ever, my own precious Lucy,   your fondly loving

Papa—

MS. National Archives of Canada.

1. Bernard Henry Holland (b. 1856), barrister-at-law, grandson of Sir Henry Holland. The Christies cannot be certainly identified.

2. David William Stanley Ogilvy (1856–1900), eighth earl of Airlie, whose wife (m. 1886; d. 1900), the former Mabell Frances Elizabeth Gore, was the eldest daughter of the fifth earl of Arran; their daughter, Kitty Edith Blanche Ogilvy, was born Feb. 5.

3. Lady Revelstoke (m. 1861, d. 1892), the former Louisa Emily Charlotte Bulteel (1892), was the wife of Edward Charles Baring (1828–1897: *WWW*; cr. Baron Revelstoke 1885; *VF*, 9/15/88), distinctly abdominally ovoid, of Baring Bros; sister of Lady Mary Elizabeth Ponsonby (d. 1916), wife of Rt Hon. Gen. Sir Henry Frederick Cavendish (1825–1895: *DNB*; *VF*, 3/17/83); and daughter of John Crocker Bulteel, M.P. Devonshire, and Lady Elizabeth (d. 1880), second daughter of second Earl Grey.

4. The Chadwicks have not been identified (unless, improbably, he was the Lt Charles Chadwick, listed in Whitaker).

5. The usual Irish broth, with articles for example on "Constitutional Home Rule," the Coercion Bill, attacks on Salisbury, Hartington, etc.

6. After more than a century this is still of interest as a document in the history of culture, taste, and ideas. The first ten names were: Gladstone, Tennyson, Arnold, Huxley,

Herbert Spenser, Ruskin, Froude, Browning, Morley, and Tyndall. The second ten: E. A. Freeman, Swinburne, Farrar, Max Mueller, Sir John Lubbock, William Morris, Cardinal Newman, Leslie Stephen, and Jowett (*Pall Mall Gazette*, Feb. 24, 1887, pp. 1–4).

To Lady de Rothschild

Athenæum Club

My dear Lady de Rothschild   Saturday, [?March 5, 1887]
    Mr Hutton, of the Spectator, has fixed Monday afternoon next for a long proposed visit to Cobham. It is too provoking—but I do not like to ask him to change the day, as he has difficulty in getting away from his newspaper, and one or two projects of visit have come to nothing already—so that he will think me an impostor if I put him off now that he has fairly found a day that suits him.
    But nothing, except a prohibition from *you*, shall hinder my appearing at luncheon on Monday week.   Affectionately yours
                                                          Matthew Arnold.—

MS. Evelyn de Rothschild

To Henry Thompson[1]

Sir Henry Thompson   3, Wilton Street, Belgrave Square
Dear Sir Henry   March 7, [1887]
    I shall be happy to dine with you on the 22nd; it is very kind of you to ask me.   Most faithfully yours,
                                                          Matthew Arnold.—

MS. University of Virginia.

    1. Henry Thompson (1820–1904: *DNB*; knt 1867, bt 1899; *VF*, 8/1/74), prominent and fashionable surgeon and author.

To Wilfrid Ward

Athenæum, Pall Mall

My dear Mr Ward   March 10, [1887]
    Many thanks for your volume which I have found here today. I am probably more in sympathy with you than with the other parties to the "quadrangular duel"—at all events I shall read you with interest.   Very truly yours
                                                          Matthew Arnold

Text. James C. Livingston, "A Note from Matthew Arnold to Wilfred Ward," The Arnoldian, 6. no. 2 (Winter 1979): 15–19 (MS. University of St Andrews).

To Edmund Hay Currie[1]

Pains Hill Cottage, Cobham, Surrey

Sir Edmund Hay Currie—

Dear Sir   March 12, 1887

I am flattered by your invitation, but I am likely to be so much absent from England in the next year or two, that I am declining all engagements of the kind, and must also decline, therefore, that which you kindly propose to me.   Your faithful servant,

Matthew Arnold.—

MS. Bryn Mawr College.

1. Edmund Hay Currie (1834–1913: *WWW*; knt 1876), chairman London Hospital and vice-chairman of the London School Board 1873–76, 1882–85.

To Lady Dorothy Nevill

3, Wilton Street

Dear Lady Dorothy   March 14, [1887]

Any day next week would suit me, except Sunday the 20th or Saturday the 26th. I seldom go out to luncheon, and shall accept no invitation for luncheon in next week until I hear from you.

I hope your Roosevelts will do as well as your Mrs Potter—better they could not do.[1]   Most truly yours

Matthew Arnold.—

MS. University of Virginia.

1. Theodore Roosevelt, married in December in St George's church, Hanover Square, and, recently returned to London from honeymooning on the Continent, sailed for the United States in a few days. (For Mrs Potter, see next letter.)

To Lucy Charlotte Arnold Whitridge

London

My darling Lucy   March 14, 1887

I have this week to perform my last of the promises made before I retired—to write a short notice of Tauler, a German mystic before the Reformation, to help a poor man who has translated one of his works. I did not mean to write to you this week, but whenever one of your letters arrives it makes we wish to write to you and we have had two from you lately, both delightful; and I have had a letter from Fred too which I was very glad indeed to get and for which you must thank him. We are all much excited to hear of the possibility of your coming in April and we have changed our plans in consequence. On the 1st of April, when we leave London Nelly goes to Shropshire and Mamma and I had talked of paying a visit to Newent and Barrington; but now we shall go at once to Cobham, Mamma and I, which I shall infinitely prefer. However I write because I yesterday met Mrs Potter[1] who talked to me quite affectionately about you; and whom I liked very much. She was different from what I expected—people always are—and perhaps hardly so attractive, but more likable and respectable—more *steady*. Her manners were quiet and good, and I think she will keep her footing well, in the trying career on which she has entered. I met her at luncheon at Lady Dorothy Nevill's; we had the Prince of Wales, Lord Lytton, Sir Henry Thompson, Mr Matthews the Home Secretary, Mr Jeune, and Cecil the actor; luncheon was at 2, and afterwards Mrs Potter recited; I did not care for any of her pieces, the interesting ones were not pleasing, and the inoffensive ones were not interesting; but she recites well, and her manner and bearing were thoroughly good. We did not separate till ½ past 5 when the Prince departed; he was very civil to me and laughed immensely at the Chicago description "He has harsh features," &c.[2] I had meant to go on to tea at Mrs Jeune's to meet the Roosevelts, but it was too late; however Lady Dorothy is getting up another luncheon at which I am to meet them. It is rather a storm but it all ends on the 1st of April; we dine out every night but one till we go and that one we are keeping for Dandy Dick at the Court Theatre; I liked Cecil. Tomorrow I lunch with Lady Airlie, and on Wednesday with Lord Lytton, on Thursday with George Russell. Mamma is much better, having been quite ill one day last week, with face-ache, chill and liver all together. Nelly is in great force; she looks extremely well and animated when she is out, her clothes suit her and her manners are a real blessing. She went alone with me to Lady Hayter's on Wednesday and to Lady Stanhope's on Saturday. Today Mamma has gone out driving; I had promised to dine at Grillion's, but I have given it up, as Mamma has been left so much alone lately, and we shall dine quietly together and go to bed in good time. Tomorrow I hope Mamma will be able to begin going out again, but she will not be easy in her mind until she has done with Freeman.[3] On Thursday we dine with the Charles Lawrences—you know how I like her—and they have an evening party afterwards. We have nothing but east wind, but no snow or rain, so the streets are dry and clear, a great comfort in getting away from parties. Nelly and I walked a whole side of Grosvenor Square the other night to the carriage, without her dress getting the least dirty. We have had an alarm that Mr Leaf sold all Pains Hill to the [name obliterated], but it has blown over.[4] I was down at Cobham on Saturday: the camelias have never been so good— ten fine blooms on the "Alba plena." I long to see the six teeth in the dear little mouth of the midget. I do not care in the least about the deficiency of hair—it will come in time. We have had Nelly Radcliffe[5] and Geraldine Coleridge at luncheon each with her eldest boy: Johnnie is a darling. Now I must write my article—love to Fred and the Coddingtons—ever my darling Lucy,   your own

Papa—

MS. Formerly, Mrs. Harry Forsyth.

1. Cora Urquhart Potter (d. 1936: *WWWA*), American actress now making her professional debut, at the Haymarket Theatre in London; below, Arthur Cecil Blunt (1843–1896: *DNB*), the actor, now playing at the Court Theater in Pinero's *Dandy Dick*.
2. See 5:383.
3. Freeman has not been identified.
4. "We have had . . . has blown over," lined through (one name indecipherable).
5. Nelly Radcliffe has not been identified. Geraldine Coleridge (born Lushington, d. 1910) was the first wife of Stephen and the mother of John Duke (1879–1934).

To Constance De Rothschild Flower, later Lady Battersea

3, Wilton Street, S. W.

Dear Mrs Flower   March 15, 1887

I am indeed shocked: I thought Mrs Arnold, who answers invitations generally, had answered yours. We have been engaged some time to dine with Lord and Lady Coleridge on the 30th. We had a most instructive and pleasant afternoon last Friday; I wish I could have finished it at your tea table.   Most truly yours

Matthew Arnold.—

MS. University of Kentucky.

To Norman Lockyer

Athenæum Club, Pall Mall

Dear Mr Lockyer   March 16, 1887

I have to go out of London at the end of this month, and shall not be back in town again till after Easter.   Most truly yours,

Matthew Arnold.—

MS. University of Virginia.

To Margaret Dyne Symons Jeune

3, Wilton Street

Dear Mrs Jeune   Monday [?March 21, 1887]

I am engaged to luncheon tomorrow with that important personage to an author, my publisher;[1] but I must manage to see you before I leave London.   Most truly yours

Matthew Arnold.—

MS. Texas Tech College.

1. The George Smiths (Guthrie 4:1730).

To George Butler[1]

3, Wilton Street, S. W.

My dear Butler   March 22, 1887

It had crossed my mind to come to Winchester for the celebration, and now your kind letter revives the thought; but I had dismissed it, and have engaged myself here for both the 25th and 26th. Many thanks to you and to Mrs Butler for your kind invitation; I should have much liked coming to you had it been possible. I am sorry to hear of your having been ill; but the good time of year is coming.   Most sincerely yours

Matthew Arnold.—

My Cobham is in Surrey, not Kent.

MS. St. Andrews University.

1. George Butler (1819–1890: *DNB*), canon of Winchester, son of George Butler, an earlier headmaster of Harrow and older brother of Henry Montagu, headmaster during Matthew Arnold's residence there.

To Bram Stoker

Athenæum Club, Pall Mall

The Secretary etc. etc. etc.

Dear Sir   March 22, 1887

I regret that absence from London will prevent my taking any part in the Committee formed to raise a Testimonial Fund for Dr Westland Marston.[1]   Your faithful servant,

Matthew Arnold.—

MS. Brotherton Collection.

1. John Westland Marston (1819–1890: *DNB*), poet, dramatist, critic, and contributor to *DNB*.

To Sydney Buxton *

3, Wilton Street

My dear Sydney   March 25, 1887

I am refusing every invitation to lecture and to make addresses this year, or I shall never establish my freedom. It is the duty of a public man to appear in public, and he has many compensations; but I am not a public man, and the "saying a few words," which to a public man seems the most natural thing in the world, is to me an artificial and unnatural performance, quite out of my line.   Ever yours affectionately,

Matthew Arnold.

Text. Russell, 2:424.

To Frances Bunsen Trevenen Whately Arnold

Athenæum Club, Pall Mall, S. W.

My dearest Fan   March 27, [1887]

I shall have time to begin this before I start to walk home. The weather has much improved—the wind is west, though a little north of west, and we have had some showers which might almost be called April showers; things are coming on fast. I heard this morning a really admirable sermon from Walsham How, the Bishop of Bedford; [1] I had heard a good deal of his work in the east of London, and so I went to St Peter's close by us, where he preached this morning. I saw Lake among the congregation. The Bishop began by a startling picture of the shock it would cause if we could read for a single day all the thoughts of the people we lived with. I could not help looking at Flu and reflecting how very very few people in the world could stand the test of having her thoughts revealed so well as she could. She has been a little husky and looks worn; the London life is trying for her, though she rather likes it; I hope her teeth troubles are now over; they have been a great worry, and the time spent in visits to Truman a real tax. Last night we dined with Knowles—a pleasant party though too crowded at dinner; Huxley and Sir James Paget and Andrew Clark were there; Mrs Peel [2] came without her husband, who is so worn out by his week that he had to go to bed. Lord Stanhope told me he deeply feels the new position of not having the support of the Chiefs of the Opposition, on which, as well as on the support of the Government, he could formerly count; but Gladstone has burnt his ships and is desperate. I met W. H. Smith in the street today; he is ugly and common looking, but I am not sure he may not be going to prove a strong and valuable man for the present crisis. After the Knowleses we went to a large party at Mrs Evelyn's in Piccadilly, and then to another at Lady Stanhope's in Grosvenor Place; when we got to Lady Stanhope's there were plenty of people still on the stairs and in the refreshment room, but in the drawing room no one was left but her and Lord Stanhope. Nelly's pleasure in going about gives me pleasure too, but I long to have my quiet Cobham days again. I was down there yesterday, and found three Fox How daffodils in bud, to my great pleasure. The Walters cannot come, but I shall go to Gracechurch Street to have a look at Walter. Louis comes to supper tonight. I rejoiced for your sake at the defeat of the Ambleside bill; and I have heard since from the John Marshalls[3] that the railway station at Keswick is an intolerable nuisance: though I can hardly imagine it worse than the state of Ambleside in the tourist months under the present system. Last Monday we met the Wilson Foxes at dinner;[4] she is dreadful; he very good looking and very pleasant. She always talks of him as "the Master" and addresses him sometimes as "Master" sometimes as "Sweetheart." But in general the women are the best part of London society; I met two at luncheon the other day at Lady Blanche Hozier's, Mrs White, wife of the American Chargé d'Affaires, was one, and Lady William Compton was another, who were both of them quite charming in their different ways.[5] We go on all this week in our present courses; on Friday Nelly goes to Shropshire, but Flu and I dine and sleep at the Wards. How hospitable they are! they want to take in Fred & Lucy, with the nurse and baby, when they come to London. Now I must go home and hear the history of Flu and Nelly who have been receiving visitors all the afternoon. You can't think how well Nelly is looking; Andrew Clark was quite enthusiastic last night in his admiration of her. And so cheerful and good in the quiet of Cobham as well. Give me a good account of yourself—and I am always   your most affectionate

M. A.—

I send you a natural and touching letter from poor Carnegie, who has lost both brother and mother.

MS. *Balliol College.*

1. William Walsham How (1823–1897: *DNB*), at this time suffragan to the bishop of London (Temple), with the title of bishop of Bedford, was "widely known for his work with the poor in East End of London."

2. The wife of Arthur Wellesley Peel, speaker of the House.

3. John Marshall (d. 1894), Derwent Island, Keswick, and his wife (m. 1866) Ernestine Emma Wodehouse (d. 1929), a granddaughter of second Baron Wodehouse.

4. Son and daughter-in-law of the physician of the same name, a Lake Country neighbor who died in 1887 and whom Arnold of course had known.

5. Lady Blanche Hozier (born Ogilvy, 1852, daughter of the seventh earl of Airlie; m. 1878 Henry Montagu Hozier 1838–1907, K.C.B., of the Dragoon Guards, son of James Hozier) is listed in Kelly under her own name as living at 97, Cornwall Road, Westbourne Park, W.; Margaret Stuyvesant White (née Rutherfurd) was the wife of Henry White (1850–1927: *WWWA*), a career diplomat, who was in London for the International Conference; Lady William Compton, the former Mary Florence Baring, daughter and heiress of Baron Ashburton, was now the wife (m. 1884) of William George Spencer Scott Compton (second son of the fourth marquis of Northampton), who succeeded his father as fifth marquis in 1894.

To Charles Kegan Paul

Athenæum Club

Dear Mr Kegan Paul   March 28, 1887

We are at 3, Wilton Street, Grosvenor Place till Friday.

How kind of you to treat my cool request so favourably!   Ever truly yours

Matthew Arnold.—

MS. University of Virginia.

To Henry Reeve

3 Wilton Street, S. W.

Dear Reeve,   March 29, 1887

I wish I could accept your kind proposal, but my engagements for this year are made, and are as much as I have any hope of being able to meet.

Norton has sent me the book, but I have not yet read it. Carlyle is so distasteful to me that I do not promise myself much pleasure from the reading, but I am glad Goethe comes out well.[1]

I came to London with the best intentions as to dining at "the Club," but I have been perpetually engaged and am engaged today. I must come up from Cobham after Easter for an early Tuesday.   Ever truly yours,

Matthew Arnold.

Text. Notes and Queries, *116 (July 1971).*

1. Norton's *Correspondence between Goethe and Carlyle* (1887).

To Lucy Charlotte Arnold Whitridge

Athenæum Club, Pall Mall, S. W.

My darling child   April 2, 1887

We have had your telegram and are now beginning to reckon on you for the 16th or 17th of May. I am glad you are coming by the Aurania, as we all know it so well and think it so comfortable; and I am glad you are a little later on the sweet midget's account, as she ought to be weaned before start-ing. I wept, as you and I always do weep over these sweet traits, at your story of Katie's present to the baby and your intended present to Katie—I am sure you will not lose sight of that poor girl; I am quite interested in her myself, and hope with all my heart she will "get a husband," as I say to Nelly, and be happy with him. This is my last day in London; we gave up the Wilton Place house yesterday; it was a pretty little house and suited us perfectly; but Lady Maud comes in today in order to arrange for the sale of her furniture next week. Since I wrote I have made the acquaintance of a really charming American, Mrs White. I sate next her at luncheon at Lady Blanche Hozier's, and thought her less pretty than I had been led to expect but quite delightful; she seems good, too. She has written a pretty note begging me to come and lunch with her tomorrow in Grosvenor Crescent, but I cannot. Her White [*for* husband?] is very rich, and they have a pleasant life here; she told me she could not help preferring London to every other place. Dolly has written us a sweet letter about the midget; it is now going the round of the family but you shall see it some day; she was pleased with Fred, too, with the house, with everything. I say nothing of you, because that is an old story with her. He is so much disliked here,[1] that to be fêted must be a new sensation to him; I do not myself dislike him at all, though he is not good enough for Dolly. Mamma and I dined last night with Mary and Humphry, and slept there; I was next Lady Ribblesdale, a sister of poor Laura Lyttelton, and very nice. Humphry has given me a print of Sir Joshua's Nelly O'Brien, the face which I admire most in the world, I think; you will have it in the spare room. I saw Nelly off in the rain and sleet yesterday morning for Shropshire; this afternoon Mamma and I go down to Cobham, and before ten I shall take two young gentlemen a turn in the park, Miss Lu. Max has kept his health in London perfectly, but he has required, and received, a good deal of attention. Tomorrow I come up to sleep at George Russell's—with whom we had a quite pathetic parting, he embracing Mamma—and dine at Chamberlain's; Ld Randolph Churchill is to be there. I have promised to come up some day to meet Lady Randolph at luncheon at Lady Dorothy Nevill's. Politics here are extraordinarily interesting, as I need not tell you; Mrs White assures me that the best Americans are still anti-Gladstonian, just as I thought when I was in America; but of course she and the London Americans are a little swayed by the society round them here, and speak as they wish. Gladstone came to dinner at Grillion's the other night, and I was close to him—only Sir James Paget between us; the party was all Conservative as it happened, but very civil to him, of course. We put him in the chair, and he talked a great deal, but looked white, worn, and old, and his voice quite gone— husky and extinguished. Nelly has given great satisfaction in London and has much liked it; she wishes for another month, and would then, she says, be satisfied; but I doubt it. Dear Mamma has got her teeth all right at last, and I think will quite pick up now, though she has a little cold. We shall find the violets all out, and the primroses and daffodills coming; it is a beautiful moment in the country. The Wards were full of your coming to them if you had come now; they said they could take you all in; in the middle of May they are going for a month to Switzerland and Italy. We are much interested to hear of the prosperity of the firm; and of course the more so as these journeys home are expensive and the prosperity of the firm renders them easier. My love to Fred: I do wish we could have stayed in London till you came, taken you all in, and remained a fortnight with you there. I doubt your Aunt Forster letting Fox Ghyll beforehand for four or five weeks; it would destroy the chance of a summer let for three months, which she hopes for; but we will see. Ten guineas is quite enough rent I am sure. Ever, my own Lucy, your most loving,

Papa—

I send you a touching letter I have had from poor Mr Carnegie.

MS. Frederick Whitridge.

    1. Henry Yates Thompson.

To Henry Willett[1]

Athenæum Club, Pall Mall, S. W.

Henry Willett Esq.

Dear Sir   April 6, 1887

    I have to thank you for your kind letter and invitation, but I am declining all invitations to speak or lecture this year; I am only just free from a public service of thirty five years, and want to establish myself as altogether a private person.

    I hope we may one day meet, at Oxford or elsewhere; and I remain, dear Sir,   very faithfully yours

Matthew Arnold.—

MS. Sidney Coulling.

1. Henry Willett (1822/23–1905), of Arnold House, Brighton, friend and admirer of Ruskin, whose works are scattered with references to him, and named there as a collector of works by Turner and Ruskin. Allibone records one title by him, *Record of the Sub-Wealden Exploration* (1878).

To Arthur Howard Galton

Pains Hill Cottage, Cobham

My dear Galton,   April 7, 1887

I liked your paper in "Macmillan."[1] You have an excellent subject in Thomas Cromwell: it shows how ignorant I am, that when my wife said he was Lord Essex, I contradicted her—but she proved to be quite right. Do you not think that your dedication is a little strong, applied to one who could make such a blunder about your subject? I do, but I will not interfere with your freedom of action, if I have been of use to you and you wish to say so. We have a raging north wind here, and no flowers yet. We have just lost our dear dear mongrel, Kaiser, and we are very sad.   Ever truly yours,

Matthew Arnold.

Text. Arthur Galton, Two Essays upon Matthew Arnold with Some of His Letters to the Author, *pp. 110–11.*

1. "Perugia," *Macmillan's Magazine*, 55 (Mar. 1887): 366–70. The next sentence refers to Galton's book, *The Character and Times of Thomas Cromwell* (1887).

To Jane Martha Arnold Forster

Cobham

My dearest K   Easter Eve, [April 9], 1887

I have thought much of you this week, as you will believe; Flu wrote to you for your sad anniversary, but I have waited till the end of the week to tell you what I think will give you pleasure—the earnest way in which Ld Randolph spoke of William's effect, in these last years, in the House, and his impressiveness as a speaker. When I arrived at Chamberlain's last Sunday, the first thing he said to me was: "I am going to put you next Randolph"; I found him in good spirits and a very fresh and animated talker. But nothing which came from him struck me so much as what he said of the effect of William's speaking. He was talking of Balfour's speech, and his case for his Crimes' Bill; Balfour is his rival and he does not like him, but the case was clearly not well presented and the speech a failure. Then he went on to contrast it with Wil-

liam's speech and case for *his* Crimes Bill, and the praise he gave to the make
and presentation of the case, and to the energy and effect with which William spoke, was unbounded. He said that on this, and on one or two other
occasions of equal importance, William had been so powerful that in his
opinion no one in the House, except Gladstone himself, came near him. His
earnestness was so deep and burning, that it caught the House.[1] Gorst, who
was sitting near, confirmed what Ld Randolph said. I wish I had heard William when he had the stimulus of an earnestness of this kind; it must be ten
years since I heard him. Balfour has great ability and great nerve but he never
acquires, in speaking, the accent of conviction, and this is a terrible drawback
for a man in his position. Bright, of course, has this invaluable earnestness,
and magnificent voice manner and language besides; but then his case, if a
troublesome one, would not be got up with the care and fulness of William's.
Gladstone's of course would—and the union of the two things, command
of detail and earnestness in delivery, is what made Ld Randolph parallel Gladstone and William with one another.

Ld R. showed a great deal of interest about books, opinion, and style,
but nothing that he said about these matters had much value. He was much
impressed with the actual state of the H. of Commons—"the police kept
near, the old plan of the House governing itself by *consent* among its members
gone"; and of course this is serious. But we are in a crisis[2] out of which we
may emerge safe and sound, if things are fairly well and firmly managed;
and I think that all the important people on the governmental side, except
Balfour and perhaps Salisbury himself, are showing well. Of Hartington,
Chamberlain, Goschen and W. H. Smith, one may certainly say this. I saw
Goschen the other day, and found him animated and in good humour. The
latter part of his speech—the last speech—is said to have been uncommonly
effective. I have promised Knowles to give him an article for May with the
title "Up to Easter," and shall try to do what little good I can.[3] Morley
came and sate down at the table where I was lunching on Monday, and made
himself very pleasant; he said he was going to dine alone with his wife and
to read my poetry afterwards, as he constantly did. This could not but be
pleasant to an author, but I think his speeches full of the real Jacobin
temper.

When is Flo coming down here? Not that there is anything to see yet,
except a few daffodils—but we want to see *her*. I have asked Tom, but he
cannot leave Julia. Ethel is coming for a few days. I send you a note (which
may burn) from George Russell, whom you know; we have known him from
a boy, and the note will show you why we like him. I conclude with some
news which will give you all pleasure: Dick has got his promotion! I know

no particulars, but I have a note this morning from the Under Secretary at the Home Office to say that Dick is just promoted on Redgrave's recommendation. Redgrave is the Inspector in Chief.[4] Ever my dearest,   your most affectionate

M. A.

MS. *Frederick Whitridge.*

1. John Eldon Gorst (1835–1916: *DNB*; knt 1885; *VF*, 7/31/80), undersecretary of state for India; later, Conservative Member for Cambridge University and vice-president of the Committee of Council for Education.
2. The Crimes Bill, Criminal Law Amendment (Ireland).
3. "Up to Easter" (Super 11 : 190–209), *Nineteenth Century* 21 (May 1887): 629–43.
4. Unidentified.

To William Henry Milman

Pains Hill Cottage, Cobham, Surrey

My dear Milman   April 11, 1887

I am rather worn out, and am declining all public dinners and functions this year, except a Rugby dinner at the Mansion House from which there is no escape; so I must not accept your very kind invitation to the Sion College banquet.[1]   Most truly yours

Matthew Arnold.—

MS. *University of Rochester.*

1. Milman was now librarian of Sion College.

To Henry Thomas Mackenzie Bell[1]

H. T. Mackenzie Bell Esq.   Cobham, Surrey

Dear Sir   April 13, 1887

I have to thank you for sending me your sonnet; I shall forward it to my sister, Mrs Forster, who will be much interested by it.   Very faithfully yours,

Matthew Arnold.—

MS. *Pierpont Morgan Library.*

1. Henry Thomas Mackenzie Bell (1856–1930: *WWW*), poet and critic, on the staff of the *Academy*.

To Constance de Rothschild Flower, later Lady Battersea

Pains Hill Cottage, Cobham, Surrey

My dear Mrs Flower   April 15, [1887]

We left London on the 1st, and it was not till *yesterday* that I got your letter of the 4th. I did not hear of your dear mother's illness until she had got through it—but how frightened you must have been![1] Give her my love and tell her how I like to think of anything of mine giving her pleasure. The little paper on Tauler was really written out of charity to a poor man, a Mr Morell, formerly a Catholic inspector, who was dismissed by Lord Sherbrooke and is now living in poverty at Innsbruck; he appealed to me to help the sale of his translation by a notice, and I did it with reluctance as I always do a task which has not been set to me by myself; but I got interested in it.

Since I came back here I have been working at a political article for Mr Knowles, which *you* will agree with, I hope; though I have great doubts as to your mother's genuine sympathy with Cyril in his adhesion to the factious Old Man. Since I came down here I have had a bad attack of lumbago, but in this wind, who can wonder? Have you given up your foreign journey? poor Baroness Charles how I pity her if she loses the visit promised. If you stay on at Aston Clinton I must come down for a day, if you will have me, towards the end of next week. The white violets, too, are out, I suppose, or will be out by that time. At present I walk, or totter, like a man of ninety. With much love, especially to the dear ex-invalid,   affectionately yours

Matthew Arnold.—

MS. University of Kentucky.

1. Louisa de Rothschild (1820–1894), whose husband had died in 1886.

To Georgina Copley

Pains Hill Cottage, Cobham, Surrey

April 17, 1887

How charming of you to send me that flattering extract! If I were younger these things might be bad for me; but I am past sixty, and totter with lumbago just now, besides. Nelly . . . will bring you the first volume of Anna Karenine.[1]

MS. Henry Bristow Ltd., Cat. 203 (1973), Lot 12.

1. Included for the sake of the reference to Tolstoi's novel, about which Arnold was to write in his essay "Count Leo Tolstoi" (Super 11:281–304), *Fortnightly Review*, 42 (Dec. 1887): 783–99 (rptd *Essays in Criticism, Second Series*).

To Lucy Charlotte Arnold Whitridge

Cobham

My darling Lucy   April 20, 1887

I told Mamma I would write for her today—I have just finished and sent off an article on politics for the XIXth Century, and feel so relieved that I am ready to do whatever anybody asks me. I feel as if we ought not to be writing to you any more, though, and as if you ought to be on your way here; but that is because you so raised our expectations about the 3rd of this month. You would have had a shocking passage, I must confess, if you had come, and have found a cold east-windy world here; so I am glad you stayed. The weather has now changed, and the wind though still in the north has lost its harshness; it barely freezes at night, and the temperature goes up to 65 in the day. And with this an entire dryness such as we so seldom have in England, making walking delightful to your Mamma, who hates wet and mud. But to me the dryness is unnatural, and all the vegetation is suffering; however, for lilac and laburnum it will be a good year, and how I like to think of your arriving at the beautiful moment. You pleased me very much by saying you were beginning to share my feeling about a mild and moist air. We have day after day of sunshine, but nothing makes up for the want of moisture. Mamma and I are off today for Hastings, and we very much like the thoughts of the excursion—Your Aunt Fan is there, rather suffering; I have had a bad week with my old enemy, lumbago; lumbago and an article together are too much, and I said I thought it would do me good to try the sea for a day or two. Mamma and Nelly urged my going, but I said nothing would induce me to go without them; but Nelly was going to the Lushingtons for a Mansion House dinner, and thence to the Deacons, so Mamma and I are going tête à tête. You may conceive the pleasure of your poor Aunt Fan at the prospect. She is alone there: at least the Greenhills are her only resource; and that resource is not *riant*. We have the Leafs' carriage to Walton, go up by the 3.36 train to London, and down to Hastings, by the Express at ¼ to 5, which only stops once and brings us to Hastings in time for dinner, a little before 7. We go to the Queen's, and how I shall think of you darling children! We shall make an excursion to Hurstmonceau Castle, which we have never seen, and return home on Saturday, meeting our Nelly in London. She wrote an amusing account of her Mansion House dinner; she sate by next year's Lord Mayor,[1] who has taken her address and promised to invite her to I know not how many entertainments. I am getting better, but moving in bed is still painful, and keeps waking me at night. The young Lady Ellesmere—a very pleasant woman—who is now at Burwood, has the same affliction and we compare notes. But she, poor thing, has a clot also—a clot and eleven children. However, she has good courage and spirits. Mamma and I had tea there last night, Max sitting in honour and being much fed. The little children are sweet pretty little things; the elder girls plain, but beautifully brought up and mannered. Brackley is a very nice boy.[2] Poor Mrs Martin has just had another baby, which makes rather a cram in the lodge; Mamma went to see them yesterday, and says the infant is the prettiest she ever saw—she did not even except the midget. The eldest boy (16) has got a place in the Goods Station at Nine Elms, and leaves home today for the first time. Mamma has had a sad letter from poor Mrs Hutton this morning saying that they are left wholly unprovided for. Every one took advantage of dear little Dr Hutton as you may imagine. About the last thing he did was to attend Col. Learmonth in his last illness, going two and three times a day, and never taking a fee at all. I have said nothing about Kai, darling Kai, because I should have filled my letter with him if I had once begun with the subject. Mamma and I have often said how you would feel his death as the extinguishing of such a marked bit of home, though you did not love him much. Max has quite since his death fallen into the habits of an old man. He never urges us to go out after luncheon, as with Kai he used to; he goes to the kitchen and lies in his chair till he is called; then he is pleased enough to go out. He goes about with me much in the garden of a morning, this fine weather; I think he will go about with Annie and the midget. That sweet midget! she has lost one of the rivals Fred apprehended for her; we have all agreed, however, that Fred will catch it from you if he shows heartlessness about Kai's death. Mrs Brown Potter is in deep dejection, and will not go out in society; she plays to empty houses. We had Flo and Robin to dine and sleep the day before yesterday, and Admiral Egerton to meet them at dinner; it was pleasant. Love to Fred and many kisses to the midget—always my darling,   your own

Papa—

MS. Formerly, Mrs. Harry Forsyth.

1. Vernon Lushington (1832–1912: *WWW*), judge of the county courts for Surrey and Berks, a widower since 1884, was a neighbor at Pyeports, Cobham.

2. The eldest son, Viscount Brackley, courtesy title of John Francis Scope Egerton (1872–1944), later fourth earl (succ. 1914). In the next sentence, Mrs Martin has not been identified.

To Arthur Howard Galton

Hastings

My dear Galton   April 21, 1887

Your letter has been forwarded to me here, where I have come to try and get rid of a sharp attack of lumbago. I shall find the Hobby Horse, no doubt, on my return home.

I do not like to undertake anything as to contributing, for I have promised as much as I can well perform for this year. But if I can make anything of a little Horatian Echo, in verse, which has lain by me for years, discarded because of an unsatisfactory stanza, you shall have it.[1] But I repeat that I can *promise* nothing.

I shall be curious to see what Ruskin has done for you.[2] His is indeed a popular influence; I will not say that a contribution from me could do you no service, but it is not to be compared, as a help with the great public, to one from J. Ruskin.

Hard dry winds, and an aching back! but the sea is always inspiriting. Ever truly yours,

Matthew Arnold.—

MS. The College of Wooster.

1. "Horatian Echo," Allott, pp. 58–60, first published in *Cantury Guild Hobby Horse*, July 1887.

2. "Arthur Burgess," *Century Guild Hobby Horse*, 1887, pp. 46–53, with woodcuts (Ruskin's *Works*, 14:340–56).

To [?Messrs Spottiswood]

Athenæum Club, Pall Mall

Dear Sirs   April 23, 1887

In the last page of my article, please read, instead of "the *glowing* countenance of Sir Wm Harcourt," "the *genial* countenance of Sir Wm Harcourt."   Faithfully yours

Matthew Arnold.—

MS. Bryn Mawr College.

To Charles K. Tuckerman*

Pains Hill Cottage, Cobham, Surrey

My dear Mr Tuckerman   April 25, 1887

Your verses touch with feeling a matter of real and sad concern.[1]

We made acquaintance at Stockbridge with some relations of yours; one of them, Miss Emily Tuckerman, became quite a friend of mine, as we botanised together. I asked about you, and found you were abroad. I have sometimes talked of ending my days at Florence, but somehow when it comes to up-rooting myself from my Cottage and garden here, I cannot do it. But I think Florence the most beautiful place I know, and hope to see it again before long. You may be sure I shall not come there without endeavouring to see you and Mrs Tuckerman.

The Delanos are now in London, and I hope to call on them the first day I go up there.[2]

Lucy was not quite well informed as to the American rules for sending cards, but I am sure she has retained, as have we all, the pleasantest remembrances of our meeting with you, and would much like to meet you again. Believe me,   most truly yours,

Matthew Arnold.—

MS. University of Virgina.

1. The verses, unidentified, are alluded to again below, letter to Tuckerman of Oct. 28, 1887.

2. Whom Arnold had visited at Steen Valetje in New York in 1883 and again in 1886.

To George William Erskine Russell*

Pains Hill Cottage, Cobham, Surrey
My dear George   April 28, 1887

I am going to Aston Clinton on Wednesday 4th, and must return to my forsaken ones here on Friday 6th. Besides,——would certainly say, if I dined with you again, that it was because not a bone was left in the cupboard in Grub Street.

We have designs on you for a Sunday here, but Mrs Arnold will write.   Ever yours affectionately,

Matthew Arnold.

Text. Russell, 2:425.

To Charles Buckland

Pains Hill Cottage, Cobham, Surrey
My dear Charles   April 29, 1887

My brother Edward's son, Edward A. Arnold, is editor of "Murray's Magazine." You can write to him at Murray's in Albemarle Street. The editor of the Quarterly is Dr Wm Smith, who has a house in Westbourne Terrace, but whom you may also address in Albemarle Street.

I think my nephew will be down here on Sunday, and if so I will speak to him about you. You might also mention my name as an introduction if you write to Dr Wm Smith.

The pressure on the reviews and magazines is no doubt very great, but any man who has had your experience must have a special fund of interesting matter to draw upon, if he will use it.

I am sorry to hear of your loss of voice, but we are not so young as we were when we went to Laleham like your little grandson whom I met there the other day.   Ever affectionately yours,

Matthew Arnold.—

MS. Texas A&M University.

To Arthur Howard Galton

Cobham

My dear Galton   May 6, 1887

You could not have sent me a prettier and pleasanter present. The purple flowers are come out today, and I think the white ones will come out tomorrow. They are all beautiful.[1]

Stead seems to have promptly put on his head the cap marked "feather-brained."   Ever truly yours,

Matthew Arnold.—

You shall hear about Hans as soon as quarters are prepared for him.

MS. The College of Wooster.

1. The flowers were fritillaries, "Oxford fritillaries, consecrated to 'Thyrsis' and to Matthew Arnold's 'pastoral song'" (Galton, *Two Essays upon Matthew Arnold*, p. 112). In the postscript, Hans, a dachshund and Kaiser's successor, was also Galton's gift.

To Jane Martha Arnold Forster*

Cobham

My dearest K   May 12, 1887

Your last letter to me was a more cheerful one, but I am sorry to hear you are not at your best. I do wish you were more within reach; but I will certainly try to have two or three days with you before you leave Fox How. I was always fond of Tilberthwaite and Easdale, and now I shall be fonder of them than ever, because you found abundance of flowers there. I have just ordered a fly that we may take Fan to see a thoroughly good cowslip field, which I know she likes; we shall not take Max, for she does not like dogs, and I think she is never quite happy in a pony carriage with a lively pony, so probably the fly will be to her taste; at any rate it will enable us to go all four of us together, which in the pony carriage we could not have done. It is a beautiful moment, the pear and cherry blossom are abundant, and so will the lilac and laburnum blossom be in another week. But I wish it were brighter, or that we could have a few hours rain; it is dull and the wind is in the north; however, we had some rain on Saturday night, and we get so little in May generally, that we may be thankful for that. We are going on a road today where the nightingales sing continually; you do not know what you lose by living out of the hearing of nightingales. Fan is better, but not so disposed as formerly to be active or to be in the open air. I got a chill in going to Aston Clinton on Saturday, and have had a troublesome swelled face; however, it is better now; but it spoiled my enjoyment of one of the most beautiful days I ever saw, which was last Sunday. We drove to Chequers, a place in the midst of the Chilterns; hills crowned with beechwoods, with combes full of box, and pure green spaces here and there among the box; one of these, Velvet Lawn, belongs to Chequers, and is so beautiful that people come from a distance to visit it. The owner, a young Mr Astley,[1] is seventh in direct descent from Cromwell, his ancestor having married one of Cromwell's daughters, and they have many memorials of the Protector, his sword, his christening clothes, and the only authentic miniature of him—done by Cooper for his daughter. In spite of my swelled face I enjoyed Chequers. Cyril Flower who married Constance Rothschild was full of politics; he is likely to lose his seat for Bedfordshire if one of the Duke of Bedford's sons stands, and is working hard to keep up his influence, attending meetings and opening chapels of the Dissenters, who are strong in the straw plait district. Cyril is one of the Gladstonian whips, the other being Arnold Morley;[2] he has kept friends with Chamberlain, but says that the feeling against him on their side of the House is intense, and that his following is very small, the strong man being Lord Hartington. This is of course true, but I think the man with a future is Chamberlain. I have promised to go to the House one night with Cyril Flower, to dine there with him, and go through the whole thing; he says he can probably get me into the diplomatic gallery, where one is in comfort; it is years since I was in the House, and I should like to see the corps of Irish members as they now are. I hope they will not be always what they are now. Of course you are quite right in saying that local government with these men to administer it is no pleasant prospect; but I think if their violence and disorder were fairly confronted and broken, and at the same time good measures were introduced, there would be a change in them. However, very cautious proceeding is requisite. But the Castle and its system are as surely doomed as Protestant ascendency. Ld Emly has been greatly pleased with my article; he says the Pope is ready and willing to be dealt with, but the Govt must frankly deal with him. Now I must get ready for going out; my love to Francie, and congratulations on the success of St Ignatius.[3]   your ever affectionate

M. A.—

MS. Frederick Whitridge.

1. Bertrand Frankland Astley (born 1857), Chequers Court, Tring, Bucks, and Eaton Place, an Old Etonian, member of Marlborough Club (*County*). Samuel Cooper (1609–1672: *DNB*), miniaturist, perhaps England's finest.

2. Arnold Morley (1849–1916: *WWW*), barrister, Member for Nottingham, and later Privy Councillor.

3. Frances Arnold-Forster's St Ignatius has not been identified as such but it is probably related to her *Heralds of the Cross* (1883, 1885), a book for children.

To Charles Kegan Paul

Pains Hill Cottage, Cobham, Surrey
May 17, 1887

You are perfectly welcome to the lines you mention. I wish you had stuck to your intention on Sunday.

Text. Stewart Kidd (Cincinnati), A Catalogue of Autograph Letters *(1930).*

To Margaret Dyne Symons Jeune

Athenæum Club, Pall Mall, S. W.

My dear Mrs Jeune   May 18, 1887

I shall be in London the 23rd and will come to luncheon with very great pleasure.   Ever truly yours

Matthew Arnold.—

MS. Garrick Club.

To Mrs Manners [1]

Cobham, Surrey

My dear Mrs Manners   May 19, 1887

You remember what I said to you about my desire to fish the Lathkil[l] once more, before I get too old and too feeble to go anywhere beyond my garden. I am going to fish at Chenies on Monday and Tuesday, the 20th and 21st of June; and any days at the end of that week would suit me perfectly for the Lathkil, if you will graciously use your influence to procure leave for me. Forgive my thus boring you, and believe me,   ever truly yours

Matthew Arnold.—

MS. *University of Virginia.*

1. Apparently, Clara Gothard Manners (d. 1927), wife of William Posnette Manners (d. 1915), of the Old Hall, Netherseale, Burton-on-Trent (*Landed*), with possibly a recollection of the days of yore (see 1:248–49).

To Andrew Carnegie

Pains Hill Cottage, Cobham, Surrey

My dear Carnegie   May 22, 1887

We are very anxious to see you and to make acquaintance with Mrs Carnegie,[1] but at Whitsuntide we are engaged to pay a visit at Wotton in this county, and after that, a visit at Oxford. I suppose you will be coming to London, and then you and Mrs Carnegie must run down here for the day. We have got Lucy with us and her husband and baby; he goes back by the Umbria on Saturday, and Lucy goes down to Liverpool to see him off; then she returns here, and he joins her again in July and they stay till October. With love from us all I am   ever yours affectionately,

Matthew Arnold.—

MS. *New York Public Library.*

1. Carnegie married Margaret Whitfield, a New Yorker, in 1887.

To Frances Bunsen Trevenen Whately Arnold

Athenæum Club, Pall Mall

My dearest Fan   May 23, 1887

You are today on your way to Oxford, and I hope this will reach you there tomorrow morning. You behaved very ill in quitting Cobham prematurely, and in staying so much longer with Walter than you did with us. The little grand-daughter is too sweet; today her nurse has gone to see her relations near Epsom and the maids in general have undertaken the baby, who is a very sweet-tempered child. The attic really makes a very good nursery, there is far more space than I expected. Lucy and Fred go to London tomorrow, to a hotel; he has business which compels him to be the whole of every day in London. On Friday they go to the Dingle,[1] and on Saturday he starts by the Umbria; Lucy will probably stay over Whitmonday with Susy and will then go to the Dicks; how would it suit if I joined her at Manchester, and we then fixed a visit of three days to Jane? On Saturday Flu, Nelly, and I, go to Wotton till Whit-tuesday; but I could then join Lucy and take her to Westmorland for the rest of that week. The Rugby dinner was interesting, though the speaking was poor: the most sincere things I heard were the tributes to Papa from Waddington & Ld Derby: Ld Derby spoke tellingly and well; Waddington is a very bad speaker. Goschen's voice and mouthing are so unpleasant that really I would rather read him and not hear him. Temple's voice is horrid too. Vaughan was inaudible. Jex Blake was long and perfectly ineffective; the hum of conversation drowned his voice. I made the Ld Mayor's secretary laugh by forcing him to own that two speeches for literature were an absurdity, and telling him when he owned it, that I should leave Tom Hughes to make the one speech, because I knew he would like it. Not a word he said was audible. I went yesterday to the function in St Margaret's church;[2] Farrar gave me a splendid place, just between the front row of seats and the chancel steps: I was close to the Speaker, W. H. Smith, Gladstone, Hartington and Goschen; and also to the preacher. The sermon was a brilliant effort, but (I thought) without soul and sincerity; very inferior to the discourse I heard in Dorking Church. It was just what is called "Irish eloquence," dealing with surfaces, never with depths. But the scene was a striking one and I am glad to have seen it; and the church, which I had never seen since its restoration, is beautiful. Farrar's reading of the xiiith of Corinthians[3] was the best part of the performance. I have been pleased by a long message from Lady Iddesleigh[4] urging me to reconsider my determination not to write her husband's life; it appears he felt great interest in me and said in his last days that one of his great regrets was not to have seen more of me; but I adhere to the opinion that I am not the right person to write his life. It is curious how I am begged to write political articles; I have just been withstanding the editor of the Fortnightly. If you could but be with me this next week! the lilac and laburnum will be out. I saw Eds for a moment at the Rugby dinner; Oakeley I did not see. We had Mary and Humphry with us yesterday; Mary is, and looks, quite exhausted with brain-work. Tell my Tom it is better to be a lost Paddy and Papist, than a free-thought Londoner exhausted by brain work. Love to them all—special messages to poor Julia—your ever affectionate

M. A.—

MS. Frederick Whitridge.

    1. At the home of the Croppers, Liverpool.
    2. A Jubilee celebration, with a sermon by Boyd Carpenter, bishop of Ripon.
    3. Four days later Arnold wrote "xiiith of Romans."
    4. Cecilia Frances Northcote, countess dowager of Iddesleigh (born Farrer), whose husband, the first earl (cr. 1885), had died Jan. 13 and whom *DNB* calls "perhaps the most

pure-minded politician that has taken part in English public life since Lord Althorp." His life (1890) was written, though not by Arnold, at least by an Arnoldian, Andrew Lang.

To Mr Bonner [1]

Pains Hill Cottage, Cobham, Surrey

Dear Mr Bonner   May 24, 1887

We are coming to Wotton for Whitsuntide, and probably I shall be fishing on Monday. If I find the Wotton fishing bad, which I fear it is now, may I come on to Tillingbourne? I am emboldened to ask, because you were so kind about my fishing at Tillingbourne when I was at Wotton last. Ever truly yours

Matthew Arnold.—

MS. University of Kentucky.

    1. Unidentified.

To Victoria Lady Welby [1]

The Hon. Lady Welby.

Dear Madam   May 26, 1887

You will find the sentences at pp. 56, 101, and 117 of the little book which you have purchased. [2]

A book of mine, "Literature and Dogma," of which there is a popular edition, will give you more fully those views of mine which attracted your notice in the Nineteenth Century articles. But whoever has once grasped the idea that the natural truth of Christianity is its strength, may be trusted to work out this idea for himself in the manner best suited to his own nature and training.

I cannot forbear adding that in my opinion there is no writer more helpful to those who are working out for themselves the idea in question than a man whom the orthodox would claim for themselves—Alexandre Vinet. He is not much read in England except as an opponent of Church Establishment. But if you will get and read a little book of his called *Méditations Evangéliques*, I think you will find in it, as I have found in it, a line of religious thought which is of great service. Believe me, dear Madam, sincerely yours

Matthew Arnold.—

MS. York University Libraries, Ontario.

    1. Lady Victoria Alexandrina Maria Louisa Stuart-Wortley (d. 1912), maid of honour to Queen Victoria, was the daughter of Charles James Stuart-Wortley (1802–

1844), second son of first Baron Wharncliffe, and Emmeline Charlotte Elizabeth Manners (d. 1855), second daughter of the fifth duke of Rutland, married Sir William Earle Welby Gregory, fourth baronet, in 1863.

2. The sentences from Morell's Tauler are in Super 11:182: "They who have left sins and come to grace have more delight and joy in one day than all sinners have ever gained"; "But in order to be 'a thoroughly natural man' one who 'enters into himself, listens to the eternal word, and has the life full of ecstasy and joy,' a man must set aside all things and follow Christ. Christ is the everlasting aim of all men.'"

To E. Lloyd Jones[1]

Athenæum Club, Pall Mall

E. Lloyd Jones Esq.

Dear Sir   May 26, 1887

My engagements of other kinds are such, that I have determined not to lecture or speak at all during the present year.   Faithfully yours

Matthew Arnold.—

MS. Yale University.

1. Listed by Allibone as the author of *Satan's Guile and Satan's Wiles, or The Battle-field of the Two Worlds* (1883), and *Landed* records the Rev. Edward Lloyd Jones (1832–1918), Penyrallt, Llangeler, Camarthen, and of Folkestone, Corpus Christi College, Cambridge, M.A.

To Frederic William Farrar

Cobham, Surrey

My dear Farrar   May 27, 1887

An old Westminster teacher, a widow,[1] whose only son is in India, has asked me to get her sent out there by the S.P.C.K., to superintend or organise an English or native school there. I think very highly of the woman, who lost her place in Westminster from a remodelling of the schools which was necessitated by want of funds. But I am not going to trouble you with her case; only I want you to tell me, to whom I should write at the S. P. C. K. If you could mention some one of influence there, who is known to me or to whom you could give me a word of introduction, I would try and do something for Mrs Strong.

The function, for which you gave me so splendid a place, was interesting; but I did not think the Bishop so *edifying* as when I heard him before. However, he delivered a brilliant essay. What gave me most pleasure in the whole performance, was your delightful reading of the xiiith of Romans.[2] Ever yours affectionately

Matthew Arnold.—

I fear we cannot dine on June the 28th, having no sleeping place in London.

MS. Bodleian Library.

1. Unidentified (Society for the Promotion of Christian Knowledge).
2. Four days earlier he called it "xiiith of Corinthians."

To Mrs Manners

Pains Hill Cottage, Cobham, Surrey

Dear Mrs Manners   May 31, 1887
    Probably it is much better for me not to be struggling up Derbyshire dales; I am only sorry to have given you trouble, but I am the gainer in your charming letter to *me*.

    You must let me send you the third volume of my poems; it contains a Greek tragedy which you need not read, but one or two other things which perhaps you may like to have.[1]   Gratefully and sincerely yours,

Matthew Arnold.—

MS. University of Virginia.

1. *Poems by Matthew Arnold, Dramatic and Later Poems* (1885), with the first publication of *Merope* since 1858.

To Arthur Howard Galton

Cobham, Surrey

My dear Galton   June 4, 1887
    I send you the thing I promised—a relic of youth. It is quite artificial in sentiment, but has some tolerable lines, perhaps.[1]

    If you can bear to part with Hans, my son Richard will be ready for him on or after Monday fortnight, the 20th, at his new place of abode,

        Holly Bank,
        Audenshaw,
        nr Manchester.

Let me see a proof of the lines, and believe me,   most truly yours,
Matthew Arnold.—

MS. Yale University.

1. "Horatian Echo."

To Henry John Roby

Education Department, Whitehall

Cobham, Surrey

My dear Roby   June 13, 1887

When I resigned my inspectorship I was so beset with applications, as an educationist "en disponibilité," to make addresses and read papers, that to establish my liberty I resolved to keep silence from all such utterances[1] for one year at the very least, and to that resolution I must stick.

But I hope to be in Manchester, and to see the exhibition,[2] and to see *you*, in the course of the year, as my son has just established himself in a new house between Manchester and Ashton, and I must go and see it.

I had occasion lately to read again the report of the Taunton Commission—your Commission, and an excellent piece of work the Report remains even after the lapse of 20 years. In a paper I have written on Schools I have called attention to it, and hope to send a certain number of people back to read it, to their great profit.   Ever truly yours,

Matthew Arnold.—

P. S. I have the highest opinion of the Manchester Grammar School, and if I spoke anywhere would certainly speak there. But I have reached that age when, in the age of Faith, serious workers retired into a Monastery.

MS. John King.

1. With an echo of Psalm 39:3 in the *Book of Common Prayer*: "I kept silence, yea, even from good words."

2. The Manchester Art Exhibition in honor of the Royal Jubilee, opened on May 3 by the Prince and Princess of Wales.

To Arthur Howard Galton

Cobham, Surrey

My dear Galton   June 13, [1887]

Of course you may keep the Manuscript.[1]

I think I prefer the singular of Echo to the plural, in this case; but as you please.

Will you tell the editor that I received, and thank him for, his kind letter.

I shall be interested in seeing your Cromwell. You have taken, I repeat, a really excellent subject.   Ever yours truly,

Matthew Arnold.—

MS. The College of Wooster.

1. A "signed and dated autograph is among Yale Papers" (Allott, p. 58).

To Arthur Howard Galton

Athenæum Club, Pall Mall, S. W.

My dear Galton   June 15, [1887]

I have been looking at your letter again. If you make the title plural, you must not put *Echos* but *Echoes*. There speaks the ex school-inspector.

But speaking as a composer, I really think the singular is preferable. Ever yours truly,

Matthew Arnold.—

MS. The College of Wooster.

To Arthur Howard Galton

Cobham

My dear Galton   June 18, [1887]

I am going down into the north next week and will take Cromwell with me. You have so good a subject that it would be a pity you should waste it;—and it would be wasting it to employ it as "a bomb." However, from turning over the pages I hope that this expression of yours alarmed me unnecessarily. I will write and tell you what I think when I have read you.

Dick has not got into his house yet, though he hopes to do so next week. But perhaps it would be more comfortable for Hans to wait till they have settled in. I have told Dick to write and tell you just how things are.

The dedication makes me a little apprehensive, for fear it should injure the book. Strong praise provokes many people; and this praise is very strong, too strong. But if the book is good it will be able to stand even this dedication to a less than half popular author.   Ever truly yours,

Matthew Arnold.—

MS. The College of Wooster.

To Arthur Howard Galton

Fox How, Ambleside

My dear Galton,   June 23, 1887

I have read your book through. It has many errors of the press, and your meaning is not always made quite clear; but I have been greatly interested, and the summing up in the latter part of the volume I think thoroughly good. If I have done anything to help you to the acquisition of the temper and judgment there shown, I am glad. I still think your dedication may provoke people, and be somewhat of an obstacle; but men like Stubbs, and S. Gardiner,[1] and Freeman are the men whose judgment on the book it is important to have, and I cannot but believe they will be interested by it. I am only here for a day or two, and shall then return to Cobham.　　Ever yours truly,

Matthew Arnold.

MS. Arthur Howard Galton, Two Essays upon Matthew Arnold with Some of His Letters to the Author, *p. 115.*

1. Samuel Rawson Gardiner (1829–1902: *DNB*), an eminent historian, especially noted for his dedicated work on the Puritan revolution.

To Sidney Colvin

Pains Hill Cottage, Cobham, Surrey

My dear Colvin　　　　　　　　　　　　　　　　　　June 26, 1887

I finished your Keats yesterday—on a journey from Westmorland to London—I would not thank you for it until I had read it. You have got the Life rightly written at last—its story and personages made clear. It is not much of a story, nor are the personages great, but one is glad to have them right, for the sake of Keats and of our conception of him. The criticism all through the volume interested me extremely; you never gush, but the tone of admiration mounts in some instances too high for me—what is good in Endymion is not, to my mind, so good as you say, and the poem as a whole I could wish to have been suppressed & lost. I really resent the space it occupies in the volume of Keats's poetry. The Hyperion is not a poetic success, a *work*, as Keats saw, and it was well he did not make ten books of it; but that, of course, deserves nevertheless the strongest admiration, and its loss would have been a signal loss to poetry; not so as regards the Endymion.

And the value you assign to the Belle Dame sans Merci is simply amazing to me.

On the whole, however, it is long time since I have read any criticism with such cordial pleasure & agreement as this volume. The remarks on Spenser are excellent; my high pleasure began there. How true it is that one's first master, or the first work of him one apprehends, strikes the note for us; I feel this of the 4th Eclogue of Virgil, which I took into my system at 9 years old, having been flogged through the preceding Eclogues and learnt nothing from them; but "Ultima Cumaei," etc., has been a strong influence with me ever since. All the remarks on the diction of Keats, and indeed of others too, are good; it would be hard to beat, for truth and utility, the three or four lines at the bottom of page 147. Very good and just, also, is all you say about the sense in which Keats is & is not Greek; in fact, as you truly say, he is on the whole not Greek. "Loading every rift of a subject with ore" is not Greek;[1]

I had written *dangerous* against the phrase, & lower down in the page I found you calling attention to the danger. The extract from Landor's letter was new to me; it sums the matter up very well. If Keats could have lived he might have done anything; but he *could not have lived*, his not living, we must consider, was more than an accident. Once more, I thank and congratulate you, and remain,   ever *sincerely* yours

Matthew Arnold

I should say most pressingly, Come down for a Sunday, only we are crammed in this cottage at present by having with us my American daughter and her nurse and baby.

MS. Fitzwilliam Museum.

1. As Keats said to Shelley (echoing Spenser) in the famous letter of Aug. 16, 1820.

To Sidney Colvin

Athenæum Club, Pall Mall

My dear Colvin   June 28, 1887
    I shall not be in town on Friday, or I would most gladly have come to you.
    If Keats had left nothing but Endymion, it would have alone shown his remarkable power and have been worth preserving on that account: but when he has left plenty which shows it much better, I cannot but wish Endymion away from his volume.   Ever yours truly

Matthew Arnold.—

MS. Yale University.

To Sarah Emily Davies

Athenæum Club, Pall Mall

My dear Miss Davies   June 29, 1887
    I should be disposed to admit women to take degrees; but I have dealt so little with the subject of female education, that I do not consider myself entitled to sign a Memorial to the University of Cambridge upon the subject.   Most truly yours

Matthew Arnold.—

MS. Girton College.

To [?John] Deacon

Cobham

My dear Deacon   June 29, [?1887]

Do come here today, because we are expecting a nephew from Eton. Miss A'Court we hope to see here also.[1] We will come to you next time. It is perfectly delicious down here today, as you say.   Ever truly yours,

Matthew Arnold.—

MS. National Archives of Canada.

1. Neither the nephew from Eton nor Miss A'Court has been identified, though the latter was probably of the family (possibly one of the daughters) of the second Baron Heytesbury William Henry Ashe A'Court, later Holmes-A'Court.

To Arthur Howard Galton

Athenæum Club, Pall Mall

My dear Galton   July 1, 1887

I will put your letter into Macmillan's hands; I think he is of opinion that the sort of people who want my poems are people who do not mind a high price if they get a handsome book; and I leave the matter very much to him. I never have been broadly popular, and I cannot exactly bring myself to believe I shall ever become so.

But I ought none the less to thank you for your interest in my sale, and your kind letter.

I feel for you in parting with a friend like Hans. It is nothing to say that Dick will be very fond of him; but you may be glad to know that Dick is the sort of person animals like and are happy with.   Ever yours truly

Matthew Arnold.—

MS. The College of Wooster.

To R. H. Bouchier Nicholson[1]

Pains Hill Cottage, Cobham, Surrey

R. H. Bourchier Nicholson Esq.

Dear Sir   July 2, 1887

I never take a fee for lecturing in this country. In America, where it is fair that the Americans should repay me for pirating my books, it is different. All I shall ask of you is my fare to Hull and back.   Faithfully yours

Matthew Arnold.—

MS. *Princeton University.*

1. Unidentified.

To Arthur Howard Galton

Pains Hill Cottage, Cobham, Surrey

My dear Galton   July 4, [1887]

As I expected, Macmillan says he has of course often thought of a single volume, but thinks the time not yet come. The case of Tennyson, he says, is "somewhat different." He adds that he is certain the one volume edition would injure the sale of the 3 volume one, now good.

The judgement of Stubbs is really precious, and that of Gladstone, if it could be made public, would be the best of advertisements. I was sure, after reading the volume through, that you had done a good piece of work. In the fuller work which you promise, you must, above all, keep the specialists in view: their verdict is so important to a historian at his start.

I hear from my son today that Hans, to whom I long to pay my respects, has passed two good days and seems settling down in his new home. You must go and see him when you are anywhere in the neighbourhood—after you have given him time, that is, to accustom himself to his new friends. Ever truly yours,

Matthew Arnold.—

MS. *The College of Wooster.*

To Mountstuart Elphinstone Grant Duff

Pains Hill Cottage, Cobham, Surrey

My dear Grant Duff   July 7, [1887]

I hoped to see you and your wife at Bertram Currie's Indian party yesterday.

Your liking for my verse has always been precious to me; and it gets more & more precious, as one begins to apprehend, in every fresh thing one attempts, the flagging and failure of old age.   Ever yours affectionately

Matthew Arnold.—

MS. *British Library Oriental and India House Collections.*

To Isaac Wayne MacVeagh

Athenæum Club, Pall Mall

My dear Mr MacVeagh   July 8, [1887]

I am come to town for a horrid school function, and find your note. To think of your being here! Cannot you come down to us on Sunday? I must return home this evening as soon as my function is over, or I would come to your hotel. I cannot easily tell you what pleasure it gives me, and will give us all, to know that you and Mrs MacVeagh are over here.   Ever yours affectionately

Matthew Arnold.—

Write to *Cobham, Surrey*.

MS. David Moynihan.

To Arthur Howard Galton

Pains Hill Cottage, Cobham, Surrey

My dear Galton   July 9, [1887]

Very many thanks to you and to Mr Horne for the picture, which shows all Watts's power. The numbers of the Hobby Horse have arrived this morning—I hope, but can hardly believe, that my little bit of a thing may have been of some [service to you.   Ever truly yours,

Matthew Arnold.]

MS. The College of Wooster.

1. "A framed copy of the picture, which Mr. Watts gave to the January *Hobby Horse* for 1887." Herbert P. Horne (d. 1916, *WWW*), architect, editor of *Hobby Horse*, connoisseur, and author.

To Frank Harris

[?July 9, 1887]

Acts of mental judgment attempted in compliance with a sudden call like yours, are difficult and untrustworthy. I should not like to pronounce on the spur of the moment, what work or what passage, in prose and poetry, I think the best of those known to me. But independently of any such weighing, comparing, and judging as is needed for this, we have a positive test of the degree in which *passages* at any rate, have moved and pleased us, from the force with which such passages have lodged themselves in our mind and memory. Applying this test, I should say that no passages have moved and pleased me more than, in poetry, the lines describing the pity of Zeus for the horses of Achilles (*Iliad*, xvii. 441–447), and the famous stanza of Horace, "Liquenda tellus," etc; in prose, Bossuet's passage on St. Paul and Plato, quoted at page 72 of my *Essays in Criticism*, and Burke's tribute to John Howard, the prison reformer. . . . Passages from the Bible I leave out of account. Things like "Foxes have holes," &c., comply with the test mentioned as much as anything in the world, but in their case the conditions are somewhat different.

Text: Fortnightly Review, *47 (Aug. 1887): 297–316; Super, 11:380–81.*

1. In 1887 Guthrie records six (or seven, counting one to "Harris") letters from Arnold to James Thomas ("Frank") Harris (1856–1931: *DNB: VF*, 11/12/13), editor of the *Fortnightly Review*, 1886–94. The four parts of "Fine Passages in Verse and Prose" were in the *Fortnightly* Aug.- Nov. The passages cited are fully identified in the *Fortnightly Review* and in Super, 11:502.

To Isaac Wayne MacVeagh

Pains Hill Cottage, Cobham, Surrey

My dear MacVeagh   July 11, [1887]

Then I come on Friday; but I want you to come *here* and to keep Saturday free for that purpose. We cannot put you up for the night, because we have Lucy and her nursery; but you and Mrs MacVeagh might come down in the afternoon, in time for a stroll before dinner; and we would fetch you from the station and send you back. Keep Saturday open, and we will settle about trains when I come on Friday. You *must* come here; it is real rural England far more than Harrow.   Ever yours affectionately

Matthew Arnold.—

MS. David Moynihan.

To George Washburn Smalley

Pains Hill Collage, Cobham, Surrey

My dear Smalley   July 12, [1887]

I am engaged down here on the 19th,[1] so I cannot have the pleasure of meeting MacVeagh at your house. I know him; not many men so likeable are produced either in America or anywhere else.   Ever most truly yours,

Matthew Arnold.—

MS. University of Virginia.

1. "Terry's garden party" (Guthrie, 4 : 1744).

To ?

Athenæum Club, Pall Mall

My dear Sir   July 13, [1887]

Decidedly there is more Greek in the world than I had supposed. The day after I received your letter I met the great South American merchant, Mr Hucks Gibbs, and he quoted to me some Greek lines he has just written on that inexhaustible subject, Mr Gladstone.

The Latin and the verse of the epigram on Victor Hugo are good, but with the glorification of that "half genius half charlatan" as an immortal poet I never can sympathise.

The English poem tells a touching incident in a touching way.

I agree with you and Landor about Florence so entirely that I often think of moving my household gods thither; what chiefly causes me to hesitate is my doubt about fire-places and the Florentine winter—for I am very chilly. I remain, dear Sir,   Truly yours

Matthew Arnold.—

Thank you for your kindness to poor Kaiser.

MS. University of California, Berkeley.

To Lady Dorothy Nevill

Athenæum Club, Pall Mall, S. W.

Dear Lady Dorothy   July 13, [?1887]

I cannot be in London on Monday, but I do hope I may be able to come to luncheon with you once more before we all disperse.

I think you once asked me to meet Mrs Post; I was next her at dinner last night; what charming looks and manners![1]   Ever yours sincerely

Matthew Arnold.—

MS. University of Virginia.

1. At Mrs Eliot Yorke's (Guthrie 4 : 1744); Mrs Post has not been identified.

To John Duke Lord Coleridge

Pains Hill Cottage, Cobham, Surrey

My dear Coleridge,   July 19, 1887

I have read you with entire pleasure and agreement. Nor do I in the least disagree with you, probably, about the Irish landlords, but Gladstone's remedy of an Irish Parliament, a single Irish Parliament, seems to me the very height of unwisdom.

I ceded the MacVeaghs to you, as I happened to be lunching with them when your telegram came, and I felt how much more you had to offer than I. Wells is one of the things I have not seen and want to see; I have not seen Cheddar either, but I care much more about Wells.

Of course we desire and intend to come to Ottery. But Lucy returns to America at the end of September, and all our arrangements are made with a view to having that dear child's company till the last moment. I think Fred. Whitridge will very likely take Fox Ghyll, which is to let, and we shall be at Fox How—but all this is still uncertain; what is certain is that we hope to visit Ottery some time this autumn, that we all send affectionate messages to both you and Lady Coleridge, and that I am, my dear Coleridge,   Yours as always,

Matthew Arnold.—

MS. Lord Coleridge.

To William Knight

Athenæum Club, Pall Mall

Dear Professor Knight   July 20, [1887]

Mrs Shairp or her son wrote to me some time ago asking me to give my remembrances of my old friend in the form of a letter, to be used in his Life, and I answered, as I must answer now, and as I have also answered in the case of a like application concerning Theodore Walrond,[1] that it does not come natural to me to speak of my dead friends in this fashion, and that what one does not do naturally one never does well. Some day or other, and in some manner, I should like to say a word or two about both Shairp and Walrond; for each of whom I had a sincere affection; but when I shall feel able to do it, or how, I cannot say.

I am very glad you are preparing a Memoir of Shairp;[2] he was not only a loveable man in the time when I knew him best, but a very stimulative and inspiring one.   Ever truly yours

Matthew Arnold.—

MS. Pierpont Morgan Library.

1. Arnold had attended Walrond's funeral on June 20.
2. Knight's *Principal Shairp and His Friends* (1888).

To John Duke Lord Coleridge

Education Department, Whitehall

Cobham

My dear Coleridge   July 22, [1887]

The best thing I can do is to send you Perry's letter. He was a great friend of my poor brother Willy, and I should be really glad if you could help his son. The young man has great merit, and the father, besides having been a most successful tutor at Bonn, has made himself very useful in forwarding the establishment over here of Collections of Casts from the Antique—so usual abroad, so rare here.

You will tell me as soon as I may mention what you told me. The more I think of it, the more I am convinced that what I may call the ecclesiastical solution will not in general be felt at all.   Ever affectionately yours

Matthew Arnold.—

MS. Princeton University.

To Percy William Bunting

Percy Wm Bunting Esq.   Cobham, Surrey
Dear Sir   July 23, [1887]

There is no truth whatever in the report that I am preparing my reminiscences ⟨of⟩ or autobiography.

Some day or other I hope to write an article on a man very interesting to me, Alexandre Vinet; and that I will give you.   Very truly yours

Matthew Arnold.—

MS. University of Chicago.

To Andrew Carnegie

My dear Carnegie   July 23, [?1887]

I have only just had your note. I am engaged to lunch with a charming Swedish lady—a reader of my poor works.

We expect you on Saturday—train from Waterloo at 5.20—for *Cobham* Station on new line.   Ever yours affectionately

Matthew Arnold.—

MS. New York Public Library.

To Thomas Brower Peacock

Holly Bank, Audenshaw, Nr Manchester

Mr Peacock

Dear Sir   August 10, 1887

You seem to have now quite adopted literature as a profession. I am inclined to advise you to read the English authors of the last century rather than your contemporaries.

I will review your volume when it reaches me.[1] I am much better in health since I returned home, but we have had a summer of unusual heat for England.   Faithfully yours

Matthew Arnold.—

Text. Facsimile, Thomas Brower Peacock, Poems of the Plains, *3d edn, 1889.*

1. Peacock's *Poems of the Plains* (1889).

To Bernhard Tauchnitz

Holly Bank, Audenshaw, nr Manchester

August 10, 1887

I have often recollected our pleasant meeting the winter before last and hope we may some day meet again. I shall certainly not be at Leipsic without paying my respects to you.

I saw Messrs Macmillan before leaving London and find them strongly of opinion that the prose book of mine most suitable for your Library is my *Essays in Criticism*, a volume which has gone through several editions and has still a very good sale. Accordingly I have desired them to send you a copy of it, as I think it would probably do better for your Library than the volume of Prose Passages.[1]

Text. Der Verlag Bernhard Tauchnitz 1837–1912, p. 63.

1. See below, letter to Lucy Charlotte Arnold Whitridge of Nov. 15, 1887.

To Thomas Humphry Ward

Holly Bank, Audenshaw, Nr Manchester

My dear Humphry   August 11, 1887

If you could without inconvenience get for me the back number of the Times in which appeared the letter I wrote from America last August, and send it to me at Fox How, you would do me a kindness. I never saw the letter, and want to refer to it; I know from the American papers that it appeared.

The Guardian here takes a vicious line in politics, but Dick has not yet, as he ought, abandoned it for the Courier. We go to Fox How on Saturday. Tell Mary I have at last done my promised notice of Amiel. As a philosopher he is unprofitable, I think; but I find him a quite excellent literary critic. Ever yours affectionately

Matthew Arnold.—

I had never seen Millais's Somnambulist till I found it here at Manchester. How good it is!

MS. Yale University.

To William Gordon McCabe

Holly Bank, Audenshaw, Nr Manchester
My dear Mr McCabe   August 12, 1887
     Your letters have just reached me here, where I am come to see the Exhibition. And now from here I go on to pay visits in Yorkshire, Westmorland and Scotland, and shall not be at Cobham again till October. I wish I could shake you by the hand on board of the Umbria, but I go north tomorrow. My love to the Andersons;[1] what a traveller you are! Your short summer tour from Virginia embraces Russia and England! I am glad the Columbia opening is not closed; I feared it had been.   Ever cordially yours
                                                     Matthew Arnold.—

MS. University of Virginia.

     1. The Joseph Reid Andersons, with whom Arnold had stayed in Richmond, Virginia, in Dec. 1883.

To John Duke Lord Coleridge

Fox How, Ambleside
My dear Coleridge   August 22, 1887
     I sent your cheque to [?]Loring and waited for him to acknowledge it before I wrote to you; I have just heard from him; he tells me he has sent the receipt desired to you.
     We are fully bent on paying our visit to you and Lady Coleridge at Heath's Court; I think it will be some time in the first fortnight of October, if that suits you. Lucy and her husband sail from Southampton about the first of that month; they have been in Switzerland and are to arrive here today. Lucy must go and see her Aunt Forster and her brother Dick, and we shall not be able to spare her for any more absences, much as I know she and Fred Whitridge would like paying a visit to you. His firm is getting into very good

business; he has presently to run off to the Continent to see a new and very precious client, whom you probably know at any rate by name—Mr Gassett, the owner of the Ohio railroad.

I spared MacVeagh to you at Wells, because I knew it was for his happiness; but it was good of me all the same, as I have the greatest possible liking for him and wanted him to see my hut at Cobham. I have been very busy in the last month fulfilling promises to write "something," now that I am free, for this review and that; however I shall make no more promises of the kind for the next couple of months, and shall hope to draw my breath in freedom. I am quite sure we do not disagree as to the Land question in Ireland; if you look at the forthcoming number of the XIXth Century you will see the use I have made of a grand passage from Butler, in accordance exactly with your line of Horace—*Delicta Majorum*, etc.[1] As for Gladstone, my soul can find no pleasure in him. He never gives one anything for the mind and soul to rest upon; compare your favourite "Magnanimity in politics" with this platitude of Gladstone's, his last, which I copied down a week ago: "Bigotry is the native growth of a very narrow mind"![2]   Your ever affectionate
Matthew Arnold.—

Kindest regards to Lady Coleridge. My wife sends her love to you both; my sister sends her kindest remembrances to you; Nelly is in Yorkshire with the Deacons.

MS. Lord Coleridge.

1. "From Easter to August" (Super 11:246–64), *Nineteenth Century*, 22 (Sept. 1887): 310–24. (The Butler passage is on p. 261; the Horace quotation is from *Odes*, 3.6.1.)
2. "As for Matthew Arnold I will say no more than this, that I am delighted to find from your very kind letter that you are interested in him. I am not surprised that he occasionally annoyed and vexed you. I have admitted in my poor Epicedion that he, now and then, gave occasion to such feelings. But I know him as well as one man could know another, and of real irreverence I am sure he had not a trace. His was a reverent and religious nature, though he was at times very provoking. The famous 'three Lord Shaftesburys' he not only left out in his last edition but drew attention to the fact that he had done so, and gave his reasons for doing it" (Coleridge to Gladstone, Sept. 19, 1889, in Coleridge, 2:361).

William Drogo Montagu Duke of Manchester
to Matthew Arnold

Salutation House, [Ambleside]
August 23, [1887], 5.45 PM

My dear Arnold
We have just arrived after a most delightful round from Manchester, via Furness Abbey; & I find yr kind note.

We are quite unprepared for any dinner party or evening entertainment; but if your sister will let us come & take lunch with you on Friday we shall be most glad to do so; & then we can utilise the afternoon perhaps for some little excursion. We would be with you at 1.0 or 1.30. Believe me to be Your's sincerely

Manchester

MS. British Library.

To Andrew Carnegie

Fox How, Ambleside

My dear Carnegie   August 30, 1887

My daughter Lucy is claimed by her relations all the time till she returns to New York, and her mother and sister will not quit her till she returns: but I am not going to lose my visit to you if I can help it, as I don't know when I may be in the States again. Would it suit you and Mrs Carnegie if I came for a few days at the beginning of the week after next—that is, on the 12th or 13th of September?[1] I must be here till that time, and after that week I must return south.

With kindest messages from all of us to you and Mrs Carnegie, I am, always yours affectionately

Matthew Arnold.—

MS. New York Public Library.

1. He was at Kilgraston, Carnegie's property in south-east Perthshire, Sept. 13–16 (Guthrie, 4:1748).

To Charles Eliot Norton *

Fox How, Ambleside

My dear Norton   August 31, 1887

You will have received a little note from me, written to introduce a certain Perry, a devotee of casts from the antique: but that is no reason why I should not answer your letter just arrived. I am going to take Fred. Whitridge a turn upon Loughrigg: I wonder if you remember the Fell behind this house; it stretches for several miles and is the most delightful walking imaginable. The country is full of tourists—how many years is it since you came over here from Lowood?—but they keep on the roads and lakes, and you may wander over Loughrigg without meeting a soul. Ashfield is very pleasant to remember, and the newly bought hill where we found the creeping shallow and learnt the name of the Roman wormwood; also the long drive afterward, where the Trillium was found. I had some bad attacks of pain while I was with you, the worst I had in America, the worst I have ever had—but when they were not on I enjoyed myself, and your country, greatly. The streams I saw in that long drive with the Curtises[1] (remember me affectionately to them) were the most satisfactory and natural I saw in America; that drive was altogether beautiful. And how is your poor invalid, Mr Field? remember us most kindly to him and his wife.[2] We have had a long dry summer, but this county is as green as emerald, and never too hot. I have been for a week in Yorkshire, in Wensleydale—a county of purple moors and great Castles—Richmond, Bolton, Middleham. Why do you not come over more, and Curtis too? it is as you get older that you feel more and more the charm of this old civilisation and history. I heard of your eldest boy in Switzerland, but young America does very well at home and is sufficient to itself; it is men like you, and Curtis and MacVeagh (what a charming fellow he is!) who should come over. I am very much better, but have to be careful in going up hill; but directly I got on board the steamer and snuffed the Atlantic breezes I seemed to begin to mend, and have been mending ever since. I do not know whether I shall do any more poetry, but it is something to be of use in prose, and by coming out from time to time as the organ of "the body of quiet, reasonable people," I believe I do some good.[3] You will probably see the Nineteenth Century when you get back to Boston, and my remarks on Godkin's testimony. MacVeagh astonished Sir Charles Russell,[4] Gladstone's Attorney General and a very able Irishman, by boldly maintaining at a dinner party in London that nine out of ten of the men he himself habitually lived with thought Gladstone's policy wrong. Russell was at once astonished and furious. And now, you see, one of the Bunsens is speaking to the like effect from Germany.

Every one agrees with you as to Froude and Carlyle, but there is no doubt that one of the bad effects of Froude's extraordinary proceedings has been to tire people of Carlyle, and disincline them from occupying themselves any more with him—for the present, at any rate. Of Lily we can hear nothing. We all send love to you, Sally and the dear boys. My sister wishes to be most kindly remembered to you, and would be glad to see you here again. Lucy sails for New York at the beginning of October. Do not be in New York without going to see her.   Ever yours affectionately

Matthew Arnold.—

MS. Harvard University.

1. The George William Curtises.
2. John W. Field of Philadelphia, Norton's well-to-do, retired Ashfield neighbor, whom Norton had described at some length in a letter to Clough in May 1855 (Norton's *Life*, 2:127–28).

3. "Reasonable," a sort of continuo in "Up to Easter" and then in "From Easter to August," climaxes with "the body of quiet and reasonable people" in the latter essay (Super, 11:261, 264).

4. Charles Russell (1832–1900: *DNB*; *VF*, 5/5/83), Liberal M.P., Home Ruler of course, and, on the death of Lord Coleridge, Lord Chief Justice.

To ?

Fox How, Ambleside

Dear Sir   September 6, 1887

I daresay you know what I have said about the Puritans in my *St. Paul & Protestantism* and elsewhere. You know too, probably, that rhetorical statement of the case in their favour, Macaulay's essay on Milton. In Carlyle, too, there is a good deal about them to be found. But I think it is well, in preparing to speak on such a subect, to read carefully a single marking work, and for this purpose you cannot take a better book than the Memoirs of Lucy Hutchinson. If you want, in addition to this, a contemporary, or nearly contemporary, work on the other side, take Walton's Lives. I remain, dear Sir, Faithfully yours

Matthew Arnold.—

MS. Yale University.

To Annie Adams Fields

Fox How, Ambleside

My dear Mrs Fields   September 8, 1887

This is to introduce to you Mrs Dugdale, niece of Macaulay and sister to George Trevelyan, and whose son represents the family of the Dugdale who wrote the *Monastican Anglicanum*.[1] She is travelling with the Fergusons of Novar, very accomplished people; she herself is so bright and pleasant that I promised her an introduction to the most amiable and sweetest woman in Boston—a personage who, as everyone except herself must know, lives at No. 148, Charles Street.

I have so much got rid of the pain in my chest since I came home that my attacks at Stockbridge seem like a bad dream. But I cannot go up the mountains here as I used to, and I feel afraid of again trying a foreign country where the climate, in summer at any rate, seemed decidedly unsuited to me. But we shall see you over here someday and meanwhile with much love from all of us, in which we include Miss Jewett, if she is with you, I remain always affectionately yours,

Matthew Arnold.—

MS. Harvard University.

1. Alice Frances (née Trevelyan, d. 1902), who married William Stratford Dugdale (*Landed*), of Merevale Hall, Warwick, in 1872, had been a widow since 1882.

To Frances Lucy Wightman Arnold

Kilgraston, Bridge of Earn, N. B.

My dearest   September 13, 1887

I write for the early post at 1 o'clock, in the hope that this may reach you before you start. I had a capital journey, getting at Oxenholme into a good coupé, occupied by one man and a delicious Skye terrier, a little beauty about two years old. I read and looked out of [the] window to my heart's content: I noticed things on the journey which I had never noticed before— one being that from Solway Moss just before the Scotch frontier is crossed there is a truly magnificent view back upon Skiddaw and Saddleback. At Carlisle I got two sandwiches and a glass of beer, and carried a bun back with me over which I made great friends with the Skye terrier: his begging was too sweet. We had flying storms of rain and then fine again—the sky and the colours of the hills very grand. At Stirling my companion was joined by his wife who had been staying in Glencoe—and oh, Mrs Arnold[,] such a scene of rapture with the Skye terrier when his mistress got into the carriage; he is her dog, and she had been away at [*for* a] fortnight. At Perth it was getting dark, but John found me out on the platform and told me the carriage was waiting; in the carriage I found Miss Lauder, of whom you have heard from Nelly, and an American lawyer from New York who knows Fred, a Mr Holls.[1] They gave me the astonishing news that Mr and Mrs Carnegie were just gone off to Stirling where she has to unveil a statue, and had to proceed thence to Glasgow where he has functions today and tomorrow to which he has been engaged for months; they would not telegraph to me when my letter fixing Monday arrived because they feared if I was put off I would not come at all. But I send you Carnegie's letter which I found waiting for me here. Mr Holls had waited on purpose to see me—he sails by the German boat on Thursday; he is a pleasant man and had been presented to me at a reception at the St Botolphs' Club at Boston. The house is a fine one in red stone—just the house you would like, and I have a bedroom with an excellent dressing room, both looking south over the park to the Ochill [*sic*] Mountains which we should have shared had you come. I at first thought of returning today and joining you at Wharfeside; but the principals of Dundee and St Andrew's University have been asked to meet me today and tomorrow, it would be a slight to Miss Lauder, with whom I am at present tête à tête if I went away, and Carnegie,—who really could not give up these engagements,—would think I was offended. Besides, having come so far, I may as well stop and see the environs. It is very comfortable; at dinner there was champagne, a menu, and all you could wish; the Lauders engaged for them in Edinburgh before their arrival a Butler a housekeeper and a Coachman; the housekeeper engaged the servants of whom there are nineteen at this moment; only Carnegie will not stand *footmen*, so we are waited on by the Butler and a parlour-maid. All goes smoothly, Miss Lauder tells me, and the housekeeper is a treasure and goes with six servants from here back to New York, to start Mrs Carnegie in her new house. Mr Holls departed at 7 this morning; Miss Lauder and I breakfasted together at 9, and at 10 the gamekeeper arrived to know if I would fish or shoot. There is good partridge shooting; a man shooting here on Saturday killed to his own gun 28 brace; but I have given up shooting, and at 2 when the tide serves I am going with the keeper in a cobble on the Earn, to try for salmon. Love to my Fan and tell her to take care of herself; I had a sweet visit but then my visits at Fox How are always sweet. I miss the baby terribly. Mind you go first class. Ever, my own darling your own

M.

MS. *National Archives of Canada.*

1. George Frederick William Holls (1857–1903: *WWWA*), New York lawyer and author, later on important educational and reform commissions, "political orator in the English and German languages; extensive traveler in U. S. and abroad." Miss Lauder was one the two daughters of George Lauder, Sr, Carnegie's uncle in Dunfermline.

To Thomas Kelly Cheyne

Pains Hill Cottage, Cobham, Surrey

Professor Cheyne
My dear Sir   September 22, 1887
    I have just received your letter, having been travelling about till now. I will see that the Club Library gets your book, if it has not already got it; it is

sure to interest me.[1] As to my helping it, that is not much in my power; as to my speaking of it in print, if I can see my way to doing this seasonably, I will not miss the opportunity. Believe me   very truly yours

Matthew Arnold.—

MS. Bodleian Library.

1. Probably, *Job and Solomon, or The Wisdom of the Old Testament* (1887).

To John Duke Lord Coleridge

Pains Hill Cottage, Cobham, Surrey

My dear Coleridge   September 22, 1887

We are just come back here from the North, to see Lucy off from Southampton at the end of next week. Then we should like to console ourselves with a visit to you. Would it suit you and Lady Coleridge if we came— Mrs Arnold Nelly and I—on Thursday the 6th of October, to stay at Ottery with you till Monday the 10th, when we must go on to the Bensons in South Wales?

We are just going to drive over to Esher to see George Denman, of whom his wife gives us a melancholy account.

Kindest regards from us both (Nelly is at Manchester) to Lady Coleridge, and believe me as always, my dear Coleridge,   affectionately yours

Matthew Arnold.—

MS. Lord Coleridge.

To George Stovin Venables

Pains Hill Cottage, Cobham, Surrey

My dear Venables   September 22, 1887

On my way to pay a visit in Glamorganshire I want to turn aside and see something of the upper parts of South Wales which I have never visited. When I am in that land of rivers I shall want to fish; I know what public fishings are, and it comes to my mind that your sister in law,[1] when I had the pleasure of sitting by her at dinner at Fitzjames Stephen's a year or two ago, kindly said she would give me fishing in the Wye if I ever came that way. I daresay she has forgotten all about it, but you have been good to me as a brother Wordsworthian, and perhaps will bring it to her mind. We are going the week after next to stay with Lord Coleridge; on the 10th of October we shall be proceeding from him towards Gower, and I should like to let Mrs Arnold and my daughter proceed without me, while I turn off at Newport or Cardiff to see the upper Wye and if possible the Teifi and Lampeter. If there is any water, and the Wye is still open, will you give me fishing for one day? I am just come back from Scotland, and find you are out of London, so I write this line, which I hope you will not think bears traces of the transatlantic audaciousness of Carnegie, with whom I have been staying. Please send your answer here, and believe me,   ever very truly yours

Matthew Arnold.—

MS. *National Library of Wales.*

1. The second wife of the Rev. Richard Lister Venables, the former Agnes Minna Pearson (m. 1867).

To Arthur Howard Galton

Pains Hill Cottage, Cobham, Surrey

My dear Galton   September 24, [1887]

I have found your letter and magazines on my return here. I like both your articles, though perhaps you are a little hard on Macaulay—I have been a little hard on him myself. Such a wonderful correspondence between the man and his medium as there was between Macaulay and the age in which he lived and worked has hardly ever been seen; and what is provoking in him,—his cocksureness, his boundless satisfaction,—could hardly have been otherwise under the circumstances. After all, he pays a penalty heavier than any which our disparagement can inflict upon him—the penalty that he can hardly be of use to any mortal soul who takes our time and its needs seriously.

What you say of Gladstone is very interesting. He, too, has not a single true and [?]fruitful word for any son of Adam, as Carlyle might say. But his capacities for mischief are immense, if he has five years more of activity.

I am glad to hear what Gardiner says of your Cromwell; I hope you will make your monograph the nucleus for a large and solid piece of work.[1]

We start again visiting when we have seen our daughter off for America, and shall not be settled here much before the end of October.   Ever truly yours

Matthew Arnold.—

Hans is a perfect dear.

MS. *The College of Wooster.*

1. Unidentified (not in *Hobby Horse*).

To George Stovin Venables

Pains Hill Cottage, Cobham, Surrey

My dear Venables   September 30, [1887]

I waited to answer your very kind note until I could speak with some certainty of my movements. I will gladly and gratefully accept the hospitality of Llysdinam for one or two days if it suits you to have me on the 12th, by which day we must hope that some rain will have fallen. I leave Coleridge on the 10th and stay that night and the next near Usk, which will be very convenient for getting on to Builth the day after, and I shall see not only the Wye but the Usk. If I finish by Lampeter and the Teifi, on my way to Gower, that will be perfect. I don't know whether I like fishing because I so much like rivers, or like rivers because I so much like fishing, but I rather think the former; hardly anything gives me so much pleasure as to see a new and beautiful river.

On Wednesday, then, the 12th of October, unless I hear from you to the contrary. We are here till the 6th, when we go to Ottery. Pray remember me kindly to your brother and your sister in law, and say how kind I think it of them, as well as of you, to show such gracious willingness to receive me. Believe me,   ever sincerely yours,

                                                Matthew Arnold.—

MS. National Library of Wales.

To Edwin Lawrence Godkin

Pains Hill Cottage, Cobham, Surrey

My dear Mr Godkin   October 3, 1887

I am not sure whether it was in the Evening Post or in the Nation, and I am not sure whether it was in commenting on my article in the 19th Century for May 1886, or on my letter to the Times of the same date, or on my letter to an Irish Unionist in New York who wanted me to attend a meeting there. But if, with these indications given, you will make search, I think you will find what it was that lives in my recollection as having been said by you more or less to the effect of the words alleged as seeming to come back to me.[1]

I would not exactly copy the United States, but I would give Ireland precisely the self-government which England and Scotland enjoy; I quite agree with you that Ireland has never had this yet. But I would also break down the present state of refractoriness and defiance issuing in what is really a revolutionary condition—"hundreds of farms in Kerry on which no man dares lay his foot." The ideal would be a statesman like Stein, as detached in spirit from the landlords' interest as from care for the Parnellite vote, and bent simply on the public good. Gladstone is simply using Ireland for his party purposes, and the danger is that Balfour may do the same; as the Tories have done hitherto. But the best feature in the situation is that there is really a large number of men on the Conservative side determined not to throw in their lot with the Irish landlords and anxious to do what is right; and we must hope that the government will lean upon them for support.

Cobden said quite truly that the difficulty with Ireland lay in the impossible men the Irish sent to Parliament—and so it is still. How I wish you were at Westminster instead of editing even so good a paper as the Nation at New York!

Remember me most kindly to Mrs Godkin, and believe me,   very truly yours

Matthew Arnold.—

MS. Harvard University.

1. See above, letter to *The Times*, July 24, 1886, and Super 11:83, 408.

To Ernest Fontanès*

[Ottery St Mary]
[*c*. October 6, 1887]

Your letter has reached me here (Ottery St. Mary), where I am staying with Lord Coleridge, the Lord Chief Justice, who is a grand-nephew of the poet. He loves literature, and, being a great deal richer than his grand-uncle, or than poets in general, has built a library from which I now write, and on which I wish that you could feast your eyes with me . . . . The Church Congress has just been held, and shows as usual that the clergy have no idea of the real situation; but indeed the conservatism and routine in religion are such in England that the line taken by the clergy cannot be wondered at. Nor are the conservatism and routine a bad thing, perhaps, in such a matter; but the awakening will one day come, and there will be much confusion. Have you looked at Tolstoi's books on religion: in French they have the titles *Ma Religion, Ma Confession, Que Faire?* The first of these has been well translated, and has excited much attention over here; perhaps it is from this side, the socialist side that the change is likely to come: the Bible will be retained; but it will be said, as Tolstoi says, that its true, socialistic teaching has been overlooked, and attention has been fixed on metaphysical dogmas deduced from it, which are at any rate, says Tolstoi, secondary. He does not provoke discussion by denying or combating them; he merely relegates them to a secondary position.

Text. George W. E. Russell, Matthew Arnold, *pp. 260–61.*

To George Venables

Heath's Court, Ottery S. Mary, Devon

My dear Venables   Sunday night, October 9, [1887]

One line to say that I hope to come to you on Wednesday from Usk, following the programme kindly drawn out by your brother, and leaving Usk at 10 A.M. I am staying with Lord Coleridge, but hope to go to Usk tomorrow. Coleridge desires to be most kindly remembered to you; he is a raging Gladstonian, takes in the P. M. G. and says that he agrees with its politics. But I have had three very happy days here notwithstanding. If you will keep me Thursday and Friday, I think I shall give up Lampeter this time, for I must get down to the extremity of Glamorganshire on Saturday. But alas, the rain will not fall.   Ever sincerely yours

Matthew Arnold.—

MS. National Library of Wales.

To E. J. S. Smith[1]

Fairy Hill, Swansea

E. J. S. Smith Esq.

Dear Mr Smith   October 17, 1887

I have only just had your note, as I have been moving about paying visits. Thank you for the card but my absence from home, if no other reason, prevents my attending the meeting. I am glad the Homer is useful, and I remain,   Truly yours

Matthew Arnold.—

MS. Pierpont Morgan Library.

1. Unidentified.

To Thomas Arnold

Fairy Hill, Swansea

My dear Tom   October 19, 1887

Any friend of yours is welcome to shoot his work upon me. If it is rubbish, it shall be borne for your sake; if good, it shall for your sake be the more prized.

I have at last done what I have for more than forty years wished to do—

I have seen the Upper Wye. I have a passion for beautiful rivers in general, and for the Wye, that "wanderer of the woods" in particular.[1] Almost from its birth it has a bordering of forest, now rich with autumn colour; and I have caught a salmon in it too, though for fishing it is at present much too low. I have been staying with George Venables of the *Saturday Review* and his brother, who have jointly a fine place above Builth. I am full of desires to take some house still further up next summer, and to explore the lateral valleys; the tourist is still almost unknown in these blessed regions. If I accomplish my desire you must come and see us; the Wye is a river on the scale of the Tweed or the Tay, and there is all the difference between a river of this kind and our "becks."

Franklin Lushington was to arrive at Llysdinam (the place of the Venables brothers) the day I left it; does not that carry you back to old times? As to public affairs, Gladstone and his men do really seem on the way to break up the solid social frame of this old country; but a better turn will come at last, and men will lay to heart that profound truth of the *Imitation*: "Noli esse nimis liber!"[2]

I wish you could have given a better account of Julia, poor dear. Flu and Nelly send their love to you: we go to Cobham tomorrow.   Your ever affectionate

M. A.—

MS. Balliol College.

1. Wordsworth's "Lines . . . Tintern Abbey," l. 56 ("thro' the woods").
2. "Do not wish to be too free," *Imitation of Christ*, 1 : 21.1. Arnold refers to Gladstone's speeches and Irish policy and ultimately to the demonstrations in London at this time (including one on this very day) that led to "Bloody Sunday" in Trafalgar Square on Nov. 13. Arnold's words ("a better turn will come at last") might seem to suggest the opposite of what he in fact means, but he was no William Morris as the Latin words prove.

To Mr Elliot

Athenæum Club, Pall Mall, S. W.

My dear Mr Elliot   October 21, [?1887]

Very many thanks for your extremely interesting list. We all of us owe you a real debt of gratitude for reprinting it.   Most truly yours,

Matthew Arnold.—

MS. Texas A&M University.

To Alfred Austin

Cobham, Surrey
My dear Mr Austin   October 21, 1887
   I have just come home to work, and find your poem;[1] I see it is not one
to be glanced at, but to be read through, and as there is no chance of my
reading it through until I have discharged my present engagements, I thank
you for it at once, although that is a shabby way of making one's acknowl-
edgements in these cases. But then I have the sincerest intention of reading,
and hope to meet you in the spring and tell you I have read.   Ever truly
yours,

                                                    Matthew Arnold.—

MS. Yale University.

   1. *Prince Lucifer* (1887).

To Alfred Austin

Pains Hill Cottage, Cobham, Surrey
October 28, 1887
My dear Mr Austin
   If I carry out a plan I have of saying something about disestablishment,
you shall have it for the "National" in February or March.[1] Things are not
looking agreeably, but the growing moderation and openness of mind in
Conservatives is a ground for comfort and hope. Nothing has more contributed to this new growth than the generally excellent line taken by the *Standard.*— Of course I will read your November paper.[2] A paper can be read in
any mood or with any engagements: not so a drama.   Ever yours truly
                                                    Matthew Arnold.—

MS. Yale University.

   1. "Disestablishment in Wales" (Super 11:334−49), *National Review*, 11 (Mar.
1888): 1−13.
   2. Unidentified.

To Charles Keating Tuckerman

Pains Hill Cottage, Cobham, Surrey
Dear Mr Tuckerman   October 28, 1887
   Certainly I read your lines, and have now been reading them again.
There could be no possible objection to your reprinting them; they have a

spirit of moderation which innovators at present too rarely show, but which on these questions is invaluable.   Very truly yours

Matthew Arnold.—

MS. Rutgers University.

1. See above, letter to Tuckerman of April 25, 1887.

To Lucy Charlotte Arnold Whitridge

Pains Hill Cottage, Cobham, Surrey

My darling child   October 29, 1887

I missed last Saturday, but I do hope to write regularly to you every other Saturday. You do not give a very good account of either yourself or the midget; we have now all of us faded from that darling's mind, but I never go downstairs without looking up to her banisters, for the sweet little head smiling between them. We have perfect weather for the last day or two—more rain at night, which was much wanted, west wind and sunshine, thermometer at 55 and glorious colour. Mamma and I took your Aunt Forster, who is staying with us, round the open part of this end of St George Hill yesterday, and she was in raptures. Mr Max also liked it very much, but the moment he gets out into the road he is depressed, limping, and slow. Your Aunt and Francie go back to London today, and to Wharfeside on Monday. Mary's wedding was the day before yesterday; she was in famous spirits, and he looked, not young certainly, but a gentleman, and nice.[1] I took in to luncheon Meta Holland that was, now Mrs Reginald Smith[2]—a most lively young lady, who I thought, as I told her, was in bed in a splint, for she had a shocking accident in the hunting field lately; however she is about again and in high spirits, only she is to hunt no more. Mamma and I were asked by the Duchess of St Albans[3] to go and stay with her at Bestwood for three or four days next week, and if Nelly had been included we should have been compelled to go; but I have my Tolstoi article to write, and we have declined. Tolstoi is very interesting, but a new article, as you know, always makes me miserable—And then when I have done that, I have one on Shelley. We shall not go to London this winter or spring, as I am in doubt about our finances, and want to see how we really stand, and how far our mode of life is adapted to my income. Besides I am full of a plan for taking a house on the Upper Wye next summer—the most charming district in these islands—and having you and Fred and the midget there; Fred shall find the carriage and horses and you shall all stay with me. I had a pleasant visit at Llysdinam Hall, with the Venables family, and was so enchanted with the Wye and its tributaries that I have asked Mr Venables to look out for a house in his neighbourhood for us next summer. There are three or four neighbours, and no tourists but a river which is a dream of beauty. I caught one salmon, but the river was not in order owing to the obstinate drought, and nothing much was to be done in the way of fishing; the salmon could not get up from the sea. Then I joined Mamma and Nelly at Fairy Hill, which is only four or five hours from Llysdinam; the dear Bensons are so affectionate and pleasant that a visit there always goes easily. We went to a new place, Port Eynon, which I liked exceedingly. I am glad you have the Herschells to dinner;[4] I am sure to meet him at one of my Clubs on his return, and shall hear of you. It makes a great difference to have had you here this last time, all went so smoothly with the nursery arrangements that your coming must surely be an annual thing. Nelly is engaged in trying to separate Fred's part of Harding's bill from mine,[5] and when she has succeeded, Fred shall know what his share is. I do not remember the person and voice of Emma Lazarus, but all that I have ever heard of her is so interesting that I feel the greatest sympathy with her in her suffering: do tell her so in the kindest and most feeling words you can find, if she is able to see you again. Mamma has just heard of the death of Fanny des Voeux;[6] she died at Feltwell where she was on a visit to her sister Amy Newcome; she caught cold and it turned to bronchitis, and she died after a two or three days' illness. We have good accounts of the dear Dicks, who sent us your letter. Kiss my precious midget, and love to Fred—always my darling, your own

Papa

MS. National Archives of Canada.

1. Mary Emma Buxton, daughter of Charles Buxton of Fox Warren, Cobham, married Albert Osliff Rutson Oct. 27.

2. Wife of Reginald Abel Smith, she was the former Margaret Alice Holland, daughter of Viscount Knutsford.

3. The former Grace Osborne (daughter of Bernal Osborne), second wife (m. 1874) of the tenth duke.

4. Farrer Herschell (1837–1899: *DNB*; *VF*, 3/19/81), cr. Lord Chancellor and baron in 1886 as an unswerving Gladstonian, and his wife the former Agnes Adela Kinderley.

5. The allusion is not clear, but Arnold's share was £8.2.6 (Guthrie, 4:1763).

6. Frances Wood Des Voeux, widow of Arnold's former neighbor Col. Benfield Des Voeux.

To Sarah Knowles Bolton

Pains Hill Cottage, Cobham, Surrey.

Dear Mrs. Bolton   November 1, 1887

When I receive a volume[1] from you, my mind goes back to my visit to you in Cleveland and your kind interest in my lectures there. I hope you and yours are well and prospering. I have been reading your Emerson with pleasure; of many of your heroes your estimate is too "personal" for my taste: I mean that because they have been important in your own circle you make them of like importance absolutely. I have always felt that in England one had to be on one's guard against this, and one has, perhaps, to be even more on one's guard in America. Ask yourself what the Danish critic, of whose work an advertisement is wrapped up with your volume, would say to the dimensions you claim for your heroes one and all. In the majority of cases—not of course in those of Emerson and Hawthorne—he would simply throw up his hands. But I know I am objecting to the very quality which will make your book precious to the "good American."   Ever truly yours,

Matthew Arnold.—

MS. American Antiquarian Society.

1. *Famous American Authors* (1887).

To Stephen Coleridge

Pains Hill Cottage, Cobham, Surrey

My dear Stephen   November 3, [1887]

When I saw "Demetrius" at Ottery the other day,[1] the conviction flashed upon me that I had seen the book before; a copy of it came into my hands just as I was leaving home for a visit, I just opened it, and then laid it down again and departed. However, your father gave me the book, and I have since found my own copy at home, and, though late, must thank you for it—I have read the book through; it is a fine story; I remember looking at Schiller's "False Demetrius" years ago, but have forgotten all about his treatment of the subject. Your story is very well written; but I soon discovered that it had been composed as a play, and that the blank verse of the speeches, though not printed as verse, remained. This tantalised me; and I think it injures the effect of the book. The verse is good, and the prose narrative is quite particularly well written, so either the one or the other treatment would probably have in your hands been satisfactory, but the mixture of both treatments is not. I remember how the feats of Dickens, in the way of long pieces of disguised blank verse, used to put me out in some of his works.

The public abhor plays for the closet, so you should try a story, a fine story, in a sustained prose style, which is a very effective thing. I am sure you could do it well.

My love to your wife, and a kiss to that sweet little Johnny.   Ever yours affectionately

Matthew Arnold.—

I send this to Sussex Place, as I have not the address of your new house.

MS. Pierpont Morgan Library.

1. Stephen Coleridge, *Demetrius* (1887).

To William Knight

Pains Hill Cottage, Cobham, Surrey

Professor Knight

My dear Professor   November 4, 1887

I shall be glad to have your book, which I shall hope to find at the Athenæum when I go there.[1] In writing the life of Wordsworth you are filling a real gap. I looked at his nephew's two volumes again in the summer; they are impossible.   Ever truly yours

Matthew Arnold.—

MS. Pierpont Morgan Library.

1. Probably *Memorials of Coleorton* (1887). Christopher Wordsworth's *Memoirs* appeared in 1851.

To George William Erskine Russell*

Pains Hill Cottage, Cobham, Surrey

My dear George   November 10, 1887

Only imagine poor Sichel writing the whole Christmas number of the *World*; well indeed may he desire a change![1] I would sooner be body-servant to the Hyrcanian tiger. I remember Sichel perfectly, and wish him very well, but to get him into partnership with a publisher is a pure business matter in which I can be of no use at all; his lawyer or a business friend are the people to go to. A man called Butler has just left the Education Department to join Rivington, and my nephew was with Bentley—but how they managed it, I have no notion. Introduce Sichel to this and that publisher I can, but for the purpose of getting a book brought out, not of getting taken into the house. Ever yours affectionately,

Matthew Arnold.

Text. Russell, 2:430–31.

1. Walter Sidney Sichel (1855–1933: *WWW*), biographer, journalist, and barrister, out of Harrow and Balliol.

To Lucy Charlotte Arnold Whitridge

Cobham

My darling Lucy   November 15, 1887

Nelly had your long delightful letter yesterday; it [is] on Monday that we love to hear, it is a poor post on that morning, so that your letter stands out more by itself. We all agree that you must not wear yourself by writing too often; write us one of your long letters by the Cunard boat on the Saturday and we shall be satisfied. As for the midget I hunger and thirst for her; we were all charmed with the story about her repeating my *Baa*. We are a little disturbed about her foot; it is odd, but I dragged one foot and the leg got bent in consequence, and the very first thing I can remember in my life is being on the rug before a blazing fire at Carpue's[1]—the great authority on curvature of limb at that time—and an old gentleman with white hair pulling me about, and having a whip given me afterwards. I wore irons for a year or two, and got quite right as you know. The sweet midget! the maids are so delighted to hear any stories about her. I ought to have written on Saturday, but my Tolstoi article was pressing me so hard that I could not; I finished it yesterday and I think it will interest you. Today I go up to dine at the Grand Day dinner at Lincoln's Inn—no speaking and I shall return at night as Mr Justice Butt offers to drive me home from Weybridge.[2] By the 15th of December I have to furnish an article on Shelley, so I have only a few days respite before I fall to work again; I have Dowden's Life of Shelley to read through for the first time and all the Poems to read again, before I begin to write. Still it is a great thing to have this occupation, living so quietly as we do; it makes the days seem as full and busy as if we were living in the high pressure of London. It is more than a fortnight since I was there, and I am curious to see whether there is any perceptible difference in the appearance of the streets and squares from the habit of disorder which has grown up lately. Now I must stop and brush out my hair in the well known six partings. It is a glorious morning; a slight frost, the first we have had for more than a fortnight, and a blue sky and clear sunrise.—

12 o'clock. It has clouded over, but Nelly is starting for Poynters to lunch;[3] I shall not go up till the 5.7 train, I have so much to to. The Tauchnitz edition of my Essays has come[4]—a pretty book in 2 vols, but they will bind well in one. I am sending a copy to Bain to be bound in morroco for Beatrice Fearon who is going to be married.[5] It is a good marriage—a young Alexander, son of the bankers in Lombard St, and to be taken into the bank himself at the new year. The father has bought and furnished a house in Phillimore Gardens (he lives himself at Campden Hill) and given it to Beatrice as a wedding present. We are asked to the wedding, but shall not go; but I remember Margaret Fearon's birth, and the first sovereign I ever

had was given me by her father (who did not like parting with his sovereigns) when I went to school at Laleham at 8 years old. He is failing now in body and mind, poor man, and they hardly expect him to live through the year. You will all have been interested about the Crown Prince;[6] Nelly and I do nothing but swallow since we heard the details. He was charming—much more attaching than his wife, though I like her too. But he was *bieder* (Fred will explain) through and through; the best German I ever saw. The accounts of Mr Hayes are bad, and your poor Aunt Mary is worn and anxious.[7] Here we go on much as usual; I sate and thought of you last night at 12, before I went to bed and how you would have liked our evening; soup fish sweetbread and a bird for dinner; coffee cream and Marie Louise pears; we did not have Champagne though it was my Dick's birthday, because we knew he would so much prefer to drink his own health when he comes. Then after dinner two long chapters of Lorna Doone[8] (excellent) by the warm wood fire; then the Standard and not a wink of sleep, the accounts of the Crown Prince and of the London riots were so interesting;[9] then Mamma and Nelly to bed, and I read in George Sand's Letters till bed time. I have been planting and we have two new roses in the Standard bed which I hope you will enjoy—Sultan of Zanzibar and Violet Bowyer. A great many fresh bulbs are put in, but I fear they will be over, all except the narcissuses, when you come. Your house must be charming now. I am very glad you have dined Mrs Dugdale; I shall hear of you both from her and from the Herschells. We see nothing of our neighbours at Pains Hill, but the beauty of Miss Leonard[10] is admitted by common consent—she seems well disposed to enjoy it herself while it lasts. I sate at dinner the other night at the Deacons by Barbara Webb, and found her more pleasant than ever. She and her sister Sybil have been absorbed in Anna Karénine. I have been almost as much interested by his religious books and autobiography, though they are not so good. Keep up your reading: I know you have Ste Beuve, make a rule to read a volume of him in each year, as I do although I have read his Causeries all through once. I doubt whether I shall like Mary Ward's novel, although I shall try to. It is no reason against her that she has had little experience of life, for there is Miss Austen—who had no experience of it beyond a Hampshire village and a few months of Bath—and yet her books are as full of life as an egg is of meat. But this is just where the gift comes in, and I doubt whether Mary has it. My love to Fred, and do tell Emma Lazarus that I think of her. Say something kind for me to the Godkins when you meet them, and of course to the Butlers. Do not forget the Godkins, because I a little controverted him in one of my articles, though I am sure not viciously. Do you remember a rather terrible person at Boston, Col. T. W. Higginson? I have a touch at him in my Tolstoi article, not quite so [?]innocuous as what I said of Godkin; but he has been at me again and again, and is a vain goose.[11]

Now I must stop; the midget will have just waked up; at least she would have, if your time coincided with ours which it does not: Your ever, ever loving,

Papa.

MS. *Frederick Whitridge.*

1. Joseph Constantine Carpue (1764–1846), surgeon and anatomist (see Honan, pp. 11–12).

2. Charles Parker Butt (1830–1892: *DNB*; knt 1883; *VF*, 2/12/87), justice of the high court (probate, divorce, and admiralty division) since 1883.

3. Edward John Poynter (1836–1919: *DNB*; knt 1896, bt 1902; *VF*, 3/4/97), the famous painter, later director of the National Gallery and P.R.A.; his wife was the former Agnes Macdonald (sister of Georgiana Burne-Jones), and they lived at Albert Terrace, S.W.

4. He had sent a copy of the English edition to Tauchnitz in August.

5. Margaret Fearon (who married Daniel Robert Fearon in 1861; d. 1909) was one of the five daughters of Bonamy Price, who died in 1888; Beatrice, who married young Alexander, of the Lombard Street banking family, was presumably her daughter.

6. Frederick William, Crown Prince, who succeeded briefly as emperor of the death of his father on Mar. 9, 1888, had been stricken with cancer of the throat. ("Bieder" means upright or true-hearted.)

7. The date of his death is not known.

8. Richard Doddridge Blackmore's novel (1869).

9. Demonstrations on Nov. 13 for the release of William O'Brien, M.P., the Irish nationalist, in the vicinity of Trafalgar Square. "A series of struggles ensued with the police . . . and serious conflicts took place. . . . A large number of arrests were made, chiefly for assaulting the police." (*Annual Register*).

10. In the next few sentences, Alice Ethel Leonard, daughter of John W. Leonard, C.M.G., of Pains Hill, first married Alexander Cushny ("Cousin Alick," as we learn below) of Shanghai and Pains Hill, and then, widowed, entered another January-May alliance and became in 1906 the wife of Charles Combe, by now, like her first husband, well stricken in years and a widower (Kelly, *Landed*, *WWW*); Barbara Webb, also a neighbor, from Milford House, Godalming, was the second wife of Robert William Webb (b. 1831), J.P. and of a distinctly military cast, son of a colonel, at one time himself a lieutenant in the 37th Foot, member of Army and Navy Club (*County*, Kelly); Mary Ward's *Robert Elsmere* was published Feb. 24, 1888, and Arnold read it a few weeks later.

11. Super, 11:283 (also 364–66).

To James F. Clark[1]

Pains Hill Cottage, Cobham, Surrey

Jas F. Clark Esq.

Dear Sir   November 15, 1887

I am unable to accept your kind invitation. I hardly ever lecture in this country, and never for money.   Your faithful servant

Matthew Arnold.—

MS. *Pierpont Morgan Library.*

1. Unidentified.

To Arthur Howard Galton

Pains Hill Cottage, Cobham, Surrey

My dear Galton   November 15, 1887

Do not send me the Hobbyhorse, for I get it from the Editor. I liked better the Parish Magazine, and what you and Image had written there. I have been very busy, but over no employment so good as reading Tacitus and Thucydides.   Ever truly yours

Matthew Arnold.—

MS. The College of Wooster.

To Walter Sydney Sichel

Pains Hill Cottage, Cobham, Surrey

Dear Mr Sichel   November 15, 1887

I have no acquaintance whatever with Bentley, and therefore cannot introduce you to him. The only publishers I know well are George Smith (Smith & Elder) and Macmillan. Besides these I know slightly Murray and Kegan Paul.

I feel sure I have no power with any publishers beyond that of getting them to attend to a book or article offered to them.   Very truly yours

Matthew Arnold.—

MS. Balliol College.

To Isaac Wayne MacVeagh

Pains Hill Cottage, Cobham, Surrey

My dear MacVeagh   November 21, 1887

I have been reading with interest your discourse to the Yale students. "The State" is an unfamiliar conception to the American as to the English mind, but will have to be thought of. If there is one thing more certain than another it is that popular education will bring the question of the right distribution of wealth, and of the wrongness of its present distribution, into prominence. You have rightly seen that the American rich can no more escape this question than the European rich. Perhaps they can even less escape it than the English rich; because where wealth is associated with family and long descent it does no doubt appeal to the popular imagination (unless there has been crying misconduct in the holders, as in Ireland and in pre-revolutionary France) in a way that the wealth of the Vanderbilts and the Jay

Goulds does not. Perhaps even the beneficence of my friend Carnegie will hardly make "the people" regard his wealth with the same patience as they still regard here that of the Duke of Devonshire. But the whole question is full of interest, and has been much in my mind lately because I have been dealing with a very remarkable Russian, Count Tolstoi, who has been run away with by it.

—I hope you dined with my Lucy to meet Chamberlain.[1] And I wish you were here now! The thermometer at 35 on the lawn, at 55 in the hall, and at 65 in the sitting rooms; the grass still quite green and the ground workable; all the morning I have been seeing plants moved and planted. Now Mrs Arnold is going to hold that institution of the British village, a "mothers' meeting," while my daughter Nelly and I walk in the beautiful dry fir woods. Then I read Shelley's Life till dinner, as I have promised to write about him. At 8 we dine; then I read "Lorna Doone" aloud, then the newspaper to myself, and after that, George Sand's letters; to bed by 12, and up at ½ past 7. Such is my day here. You must not again miss coming here, though I let you off this year in consideration of the better things offered by Coleridge. But I should like to have you and Mrs MacVeagh down here very, very much. Mind you come back next year, and let me know when you are starting. Ever yours affectionately

Matthew Arnold.—

Kindest remembrances to Mrs MacVeagh and your daughters from all three of us.

MS. Formerly, David Moynihan.

1. Joseph Chamberlain was in the United States negotiating a treaty regarding North American fisheries.

To Louisa Lady de Rothschild

Pains Hill Cottage, Cobham, Surrey

My dear Lady de Rothschild   November 25, [1887]

Alas, for the first fortnight of next month I *must* keep quiet at home, for I have promised Mr Knowles an article on Shelley's Life and the article has to be written in that very fortnight.

We were prevented going to Bestwood[1] (where I much wished to go) by a like engagement *this* month; I cannot write an article anywhere but at home. The worst of all consequences of this is that I am prevented coming to see *you*; but it is some consolation to think that you, my most prized and best of readers, will read me and it is not on politics this time. Does not even

Cyril think that the inflating air is beginning to run out of the Old Windbag of his affections, and that a collapse seems probable?

We all send love; after Christmas I mean to boycott my Editors. Ever yours affectionately

Matthew Arnold.—

MS. *Evelyn de Rothschild.*

1. Bestwood Lodge, Nottingham, home of the duke and duchess of St Albans.

To Lucy Charlotte Arnold Whitridge

Cobham

My darling Lucy   Saturday, December 3, [1887]

I told Mamma I would write to you today, which suits her, as she is very busy about the nurse. I am busy too, as I have to make my Shelley article by the 14th; but I want to keep to the habit of writing to my Lucy every other Saturday. It is a delightful still morning, the thermometer at 50, no frost last night, and the grass nearly as green as in June; we had a pheasant feeding in the shrubbery this morning. All my planting is done, and I think you will say some improvements have been made; I am now at work pruning all the pear trees against the fence, in the hope of at last making them bear as well as the big ones against the stable. I have a new pair of nippers which work with wonderful neatness and force, and I am quite interested in using them; I have always till now used a common hand knife. Mr Max, for a wonder, chose to accompany me into the kitchen garden this morning, and stayed for nearly a quarter of an hour hunting about; I thought how the midget would have called out to him, and I thought, too, how I should have come across that darling little thing as I went and came in the garden; for the weather is such as to allow of her being quit[e] as much out as when she was here in the autumn. I have never so much felt the pleasantness of the soil climate and country here, for a winter residence, as since I have ceased to go up to town. We are not so secluded, however, as we shall be in Radnorshire, if we go there next summer; we had a dinner party here on Monday, the Combes' ball on Wednesday, a dinner at Fox Warren last night, and one at the Combes' tonight.[1] Next week we have Mary Wakefield down on Wednesday, and Henry and Mildred Whitmore, the Chinnerys, and Courtenay (one of the two bachelors who have taken the [?]Whim) to meet her. On Friday we dine with the Chinnerys. On Tuesday in the week following we go up to stay at the Coleridges' till Saturday, when we return here and the dear Dicks come to us. Then we shall all go to the Leafs together. It was pleasant meeting Mary [Rutson] last night; they have a shoot at Fox Warren today and much pressed me to join but I would not. Mr Ferg. Davie and Charles Lawrence were at dinner, without their wives; both pleasant. I made Mary laugh by telling her I knew it was Rutson's insane jealousy which prevented her going to the Combes' ball, and that it was ridiculous his beginning with it so early. I had to go to the ball because Mrs Combe and the girls made me promise I would; but Vernon Lushington took me home before 12 though Combe pursued me into the porch to stop me. But the standing about is dreadful; I pity the chaperons. It seemed to me that Mamma and Lady Ellesmere stood against the wall in one corner all the time I was there[.] I believe things got better for them afterwards, and that your Mamma had a long sitting at supper with a charming Mr Drummond Forbes, who cannot say enough in praise both of her looks and her manners. Nelly danced everything, and Dora Whitmore, who looked extremely well, got plenty of dancing too. Mrs Royle did not look well, nor (I thought) did the new beauty from Pains Hill, Miss Leonard; she was not well dressed and holds herself badly; but every one has been talking of her good looks, so she was surrounded; [?]Rory Combe danced incessantly with her. I shall see her better on Saturday, as she dines at the Combes. The eldest girl of the Ferg. Davies has grown up into a tall and very well looking girl with nice manners. Lady Moon looked very well; not so her daughter, who, you know, is said to be going to marry the widower Hankey at Fetcham. Mrs Terry was there with a picturesque granddaughter like Mme Moscheles. Susan Lushington enjoyed the ball greatly; it was her first, and her sisters would not go. And now I think I have told you enough about the ball.

You did not tell us enough of your Chamberlain dinner, but your letters are, as you know, *delightful*. Don't bother about the other steamers, but write regularly by the Saturday Cunarder; we all wish this, then we get your letters generally on Monday, and it makes the Monday post something to count upon for giving us pleasure. Poor Emma Lazarus![2] We have thought this week that the end was coming both for poor Mr Hayes and your Aunt Julia; but they are better again. Do not forget Mrs Delano, when she comes to New York; and do not forget the Carnegies. You are sure to see my Fortnightly article in New York, or I would send it; do you remember that rather dreadful Col. Higginson? he will not be gratified. I have had to read Dowden's Life of Shelley right through; very interesting but a great deal of it most unpleasant. Do not let Fred overwork himself; my love to him; also to Bessie Marbury whom you never mention. As for the midget, kiss her again and again and again for poor old baaing Grandpa. Carus Selwyn is standing for Uppingham School of which the headmaster, Dr Thring, died lately; I should think he had a good chance, and the change would be of advantage, there is so much against the Liverpool College. Mary Ward has been telegraphed to at Florence and is coming home to her mother; Humphry has been quite ill. Now I must stop my own precious darling child— your own

Papa

I hope Fred's father is better. His sister Bertha wrote your mamma a quite charming letter.

MS. National Archives of Canada.

1. In the following miniature of Surrey society (painted with the brush of Jane Austen), Mary Wakefield, who came to the Arnolds on Dec. 7 (Guthrie), is probably Augusta Mary (d. 1910) of the family at Sedgwick House, Kendal (*Landed*); Walter Moresby Chinnery (b. 1833), J.P., and his second wife, the former Alice Emily Wilson, were neighbors at Hatchford, Cobham (Kelly); Courtenay, unidentified, could have been John Edward Courtenay Bodley (m. 1891); Arnold had attended the wedding of Mary Rutson (*née* Buxton) on Oct. 27. William Augustus Ferguson-Davie (1833–1915), barrister and clerk of fees and principal clerk of the public bill office, House of Commons, was a neighbor at Stokeleigh, Weybridge (Kelly; *WWW*); Drummond Forbes and Dora Whitmore elude identification; Cicely J. Royle (*née* Snow) was the wife of Arnold Royle (b. 1836), army surgeon and, from 1884, clerk of the robes to the queen, from Esher; Ellen Moon (*née* Sydney, d. 1906) was the wife of Rev. Sir Edward Graham Moon, second bt, rector of Fetcham, Leatherhead, Surrey, and her daughter, Ellen Gertrude, married John Barnard Hankey, Fetcham Park, in April; Charlotte Terry (*née* Fellowes) was the wife of lt.-col. Thomas Henry Clarke Terry (b. 1810), J.P., of Burvale, Hersham, Walton-on-Thames (Kelly); Mme Moscheles was the wife of Felix Moscheles (1833–1917: *WWW*), London-born son of the famous composer; Susan Lushington was the youngest of the three daughters of Vernon.

2. Both Emma Lazarus and Bessie Marbury were among those saying farewell to Arnold when the *Servia* sailed from New York on Mar. 8, 1884. The Rev. Edward Thring, who died Oct. 22, was succeeded by Selwyn, Thomas Arnold's son-in-law.

To Lady Dorothy Nevill

Pains Hill Cottage, Cobham, Surrey

Dear Lady Dorothy   December 5, [1887][1]

I am rooted here till Christmas; it is the season when the firs and the hollies and the [?]Sundays are pleasantest. I never "run up."

Your friend "Joe" has been dining with my daughter in New York, and she was delighted with him.   Ever truly yours

Matthew Arnold.—

P. S. My letters have only just reached me from the Club.

MS. Bryn Mawr College.

1. Date confirmed in Guthrie 4:1754.

To Edward Robert Pearce, later Pearce-Edgcumbe[1]

Dear Sir,   December 15, 1887

Your idea is a good one, and what you say of my fitness for the proposed task is very kind; but I doubt whether the public would accept such a collection from me cordially, and at any rate I have not at present the courage or leisure to try.   Faithfully yours,

Matthew Arnold.

Text. Athenæum, *No. 4179, Nov. 30, 1907, p. 691.*

1. Edward Robert Pearce, later Pearce-Edgcumbe (1851–1929; knt 1895), barrister and banker, Member (Gladstonian Liberal) for various constituencies from 1886 (Kelly, *Landed*). In the *Athenæum* the letter is preceded by this explanation: "Mr. W. L. Courtney has just published, and not before it was wanted, the 'Literary Man's Bible.' It may interest you to know that in 1887 I wrote to Mr. Matthew Arnold suggesting such a book was wanted, and that he was specially qualified to prepare it."

To Lucy Charlotte Arnold Whitridge

Athenæum Club, Pall Mall, S. W.

My darling child   December 17, 1887

This is for your birthday—make the darling midget give you a kiss for poor old "baaing" Grandpa. You were a Christmas present indeed—and the midget is not a bad Easter offering. We like to hear all you can tell us of her; how she must keep the house alive with her calling and her crawling. We are going back to Cobham today—I get fonder and fonder of the place, the life so exactly suits me. But it is particularly beautiful at this time of year, with the slopes of Pains Hill visible through the leafless trees of the island. We have delicious southwest wind and sunshine—thermometer between 40 and 50 and not even frost at night; deluges of rain at night have filled the springs, made everything green and started the shrubs and trees I have been planting. We have had a pleasant three days at the Coleridges' they are so anxious we should do what we like and we have so much to do. The day before yesterday they had a dinner party of 22, among them Mr and Mrs Leaf and George Russell, as they thought we might like to see them. Lady Westbury[1] was on one side of Coleridge, Mrs Leaf on the other; he talked a great deal to Mrs Leaf, and was struck by her; indeed she is quite a clever well informed woman, when she is not in a fuss. We had Hannen and Lord Justice Lopes,[2] both excellent specimens of the Bench—and last night Mr Justice Kekewich brother of the man, now squire of Peamore, of whom with his pretty wife we saw so much at Birmingham, before you were born. Lady Coleridge improves in looks, though she was pretty to start with; and her amiable conciliatory temper makes friends for her all round. He had a nasty attack of spasmodic choking in Court the other day; he had a similar one at Oxford in the summer; he is getting stout and looks much older than he did; but he is wonderfully happy and she takes great care of him. Jowett is staying there, he too very much aged. Lady Kekewich's entire incredulity as to my being of the same generation with Coleridge and Jowett was very amusing; she would not even believe that I was not some ten years later than her brother in law the Squire, who is in fact three or four years my junior.[3] But the life at Cobham, and occupation that I like—first the Tolstoi and then the Shelley—has suited me and every one says how well I am looking. I would have sent you the Tolstoi twenty times over, but Fred expressly told me you got the English reviews in New York without the slightest difficulty. To be sure it is a pity to buy reviews, they accumulate so; but have you no lending libraries? I have been much interested in doing Shelley, but it is an odious story, that of his first marriage and his wife's death. I have treated Dowden his biographer (you remember him at Dublin) as gently as I can; but his sentiment, all in the wrong place, made me sick, and I have been driven to make one or two remarks he will not like. I have just heard that Carus Selwyn has got the head-mastership of Uppingham School; I am very glad, it is a thorough good school, and a far better position for him than the Liverpool College. Mary Ward and Humphry are come back improved in health; your Aunt Julia has a respite from pain just now, but is not really better. Mary's novel is to come out in January. Ted is doing very well with Murray, and will get an income out of it, I do believe; besides being *busy*, which he likes. Mary [May?] Wakefield at Cobham was very pleasant, and in her very best singing form. Your Aunt Forster is in a very feeble state of health, but she does not go the right way to be better. She is to be at Fox How for Christmas. Your Aunt Fan is not in good spirits either. Your Aunt Mary is gone off for a day or two to Arnold[4] at Caversham [Cavenham?]—a change she much needed; Mr Hayes is better. I wonder if you would care to have for your birthday the Tauchnitz edition of my Essays, which is just out in two volumes; it is a pretty book, and in England, at any rate, it is rather a curiosity, as it is not allowed to come in. The Dicks were to have met us at Cobham tonight, but he has a prosecution to conduct, and they cannot come till next week. The going to the Leafs is a bore, but perhaps I am the one who will dislike it least as a new county always interests me, and their county is a quite specially pretty one. I was very glad to hear of your dining at Godkin's; mind you remember me to both him and his wife. Do not neglect the Carnegies, nor Mrs Delano. I hope Mr Whitridge is better—why does'nt he try Europe? I am going now to see poor Fanny du Quaire, who has been quite ill with bronchitis, and whose affairs, besides, are in a bad state. The George Smiths are going to have a supper dance, which is a good idea and I daresay the thing will go off well; the people arrive at ½ past 8, sit down to supper and dance afterwards, thus avoiding dinner altogether. Nelly is asked, but will not go, I think. You are quite right about Curtis being very preferable to Lowell,[5] but I like you to see every body whom I also know, because I get the chance then of talking to them about you. Your talked of expedition to Stockbridge seems never to have come off; there is one view here, from Marshall Warner's gate,[6] which I would rather see again than any view in America. Love to Fred: his cheque came all right and I have paid Harding,[7] and Mamma has paid some smaller bills with the difference. Ever my own child   your fondly loving

Papa—

Fifty kisses to the midget, sweet thing.

MS. National Archives of Canada.

1. Probably, Mary Florence Bethell (d. 1901), widow of second Lord Westbury (d. 1875).
2. Henry Charles Lopes (1828–99: *DNB*; *VF*, 3/25/93), of Winchester and Balliol, judge of the court of appeal since 1885; cr. Baron Ludlow 1897; Arthur Kekewich (1832–1907: *DNB*; knt 1887), of Eton and Balliol, judge of the chancery division of the high court of justice and not an ornament to the profession ("expeditious judge, but his judgements were often reversed on appeal; strong churchman and conservative"); he married Marianne Freshfield in 1858, who died in 1923.
3. Arnold errs, apparently, for Trehawke Kekewich was born Jan. 23, 1823 (*Landed*).
4. Her son Arnold Hiley.
5. George William Curtis and James Russell Lowell.
6. Marshall Warner remains unidentified.
7. He paid (the unidentified) Harding £8.2.6 on Nov. 5 (Guthrie 4:1765).

To Henry Allon

Pains Hill Cottage, Cobham, Surrey

My dear Dr Allon   December 21, 1887

The sight of your handwriting carries me back to old times, when you and Mrs Allon were always so hospitable to me. With regard to the inspectorship, a formal application should be made to the Secretary to have your son's name placed on the list of candidates, and testimonials should be sent.

But the office is in the gift of the Lord President, and it will depend upon your means of making interest with Lord Cranbrook, more than on anything else, whether your son gets appointed. The number of inspectors is no longer being increased as it was formerly; I think Lord Spencer did not make one single new inspector; however, if any are made, it is the Lord President alone who makes them.

I am delighted to hear of your sound views on the Irish policy of Mr Gladstone; I fear a great deal of his strength comes from the support of the Nonconformist body. What mischief he has done, even if he fails to carry his dangerous plan of Home Rule!

With very kind remembrances to Mrs Allon, I am always, dear Dr Allon,   very sincerely yours

Matthew Arnold.—

MS. Dr. Williams's Library.

To George de Bunsen*

Pains Hill Cottage, Cobham, Surrey
My dear George Bunsen   Christmas Eve, 1887
I know by experience how trustworthy your information is, and I want to fortify myself with it in a matter where I am rather vague. The editor of one of the Conservative reviews has begged me to give him an article on Disestablishment in Wales. A number of the Conservatives are becoming very reasonable, and this editor thinks they will be willing to hear reason about the Establishment in Wales from me. The Liberal party has no idea beyond that of disestablishing the Church and secularising its funds, the old-fashioned Tories have no idea beyond that of keeping things as they are. I am anxious that the endowments should remain for religion, that the Episcopalians should keep the cathedrals, since in the cathedral towns the Episcopalians are in a majority, but that the Nonconformists, who are all of the Presbyterian form of worship, should have the Churches and endowments, for that Presbyterians form, where they are in majority, as in many of the country districts. I know what is done in France, but this will not weigh much with people here. But I feel sure that in Protestant Germany, Establishment follows population, if I may so speak—that is, when you come in Saxony, for instance, to a town which is Catholic, the Catholics have the churches and are salaried by the State, just as, also, they have the public schools. What I am not sure of, is the manner in which this is accomplished; who decides that the Catholics shall have the churches and the stipends, and

who satisfies this deciding authority that the Catholics are the majority? Tell me this, and you will do me a service.

As to appointment, I think I remember that the locality presents two or three names, and that one of these names is chosen by the Church authority—in Protestant parishes, at any rate. But who appoints where there are endowments left to trustees—or are there no such endowments?

Forgive my troubling you with these questions. Remember me most kindly to your wife, and to the daughter whom we have the pleasure to know, and believe me, dear George Bunsen,   ever affectionately yours,

Matthew Arnold.

A happy Christmas to you all.

Text. Russell, 2:431–33.

To Andrew Carnegie

Pains Hill Cottage, Cobham, Surrey

My dear Carnegie   December 27, 1887

The turkey has been eaten; it was superb. We have four turkeys sent us this Christmas, but no one of them is to be compared with your American bird; and we do not spoil him, as they do in America, with cranberry sauce.

The hickory nuts are a curiosity, but I suppose, like walnuts, they ought to be eaten while they will still peel. However, I am glad to have them and try them, as I had heard of the hickory nut all my life, and never seen one before, that I know of.

I received some time ago the photographs, which were a pleasant reminder of my visit to Kilgraston—that beautiful place, though the air, as Mrs Carnegie and I agreed, is not so bracing as the ideal Scotch air which one goes for in summer.

My love to Mrs Carnegie, if she will accept it, and love from all of us here to both of you. We have a beautiful bright Christmas, thermometer between 22 and 32, bright sun and no wind; the variegated hollies on the lawn shining like gold.

I should much like to see your new house, but it is not probable that I shall ever come to America again. I hope to see you and Mrs Carnegie regularly over here. Do not forget to see Lucy sometimes, and believe me, ever yours affectionately

Matthew Arnold.—

MS. New York Public Library.

To Lorettus Sutton Metcalf[1]

Pains Hill Cottage, Cobham, Surrey

Mr L. S. Metcalf—

Dear Sir December 30, 1887

I have to thank you for your kind invitation, but I am sure that what I have to say, unless it has been specially addressed to an American audience, is better and more freely said in one of the English reviews than elsewhere. Believe me, Truly yours

Matthew Arnold.—

MS. Texas A&M University.

1. Lorettus Sutton Metcalf (1837–1920: *WWWA*), formerly managing editor of the *North American Review*, now (1886–91) editor of the *Forum*.

To Lucy Charlotte Arnold Whitridge

Pains Hill, Cobham, Surrey

My darling Lucy December 31, 1887

This very morning I have had the photographs of the sweet midget. To say the very truth I do not like either of them so well as the one we have: they are not so much her unique little self, to my mind. Dick is of the same opinion, but Mamma and Nelly are quite satisfied, and I have no doubt I shall come round to the one they like best, the one in which the face is longest. In the other the eyes seem to me to be too light, and the look of seriousness and depth in the little face to be in great measure lost. On the other hand, the first photograph, which stands always in its red plush frame on the drawingroom table, I like more and more.

You need not be told how we thought of you on your birthday and how I looked at your initials joined to mine on the cake. Mamma will have told you of our not going to the Leafs: luckily we had any amount of Christmas stores to be consumed; four turkeys, a goose, a hare, six rabbits, three pheasants and three partridges; Mr Carnegie sent also with his wild turkey (excellent) a great bag of hickory nuts which he said in his note were piquant, like me; but I find them poor dry things, and very hard to crush; perhaps I am no better. Your oysters, or whatever is coming, we have not yet got; but perhaps they will come with the same ship which brought the photograph. I am sorry about the Tolstoi: of course I would send it you ten times over if necessary, but certainly Fred told me the reviews were got in New York with perfect ease, and so they surely must be; ask Gilder, or some one who knows about publications. Certainly they reprint the chief articles of the English reviews immediately; the Coateses at Philadelphia showed me one of mine. I have now got the Shelley out, the first part of it at least, but as I give a copy to the public library here I shall not send it you unless I find that really and truly, after making enquiry of people who know, you ascertain that the New York publishers do not get the reviews.

We have Ella and Dick with us, and very pleasant it is, though Ella has managed to dose herself into a bilious attack, and is keeping her bed today. When she arrived, she was looking better than I have ever yet seen her. Dick seems to be going on very well and is as affectionate and homelike as ever. He has brought Hans who is a great darling and gets on perfectly with Max. The change in dear old Max you will understand when I tell you that this morning Dick, wanting to take him to the park, had to take him in the chain; he would not follow of himself. Hans on the other hand is so lively and as ready for travel as dear K[ai] was. But I think Max will go on a long while, with quiet regular life. Your dear Mamma is wonderfully well, and takes exercise much more as if she was 40 than 60. She thinks nothing of going alone to Mrs Helme's and back, after having been to church in the morning. Mrs Helme has got another little girl—born yesterday: it is to be called Eleanor, after Nelly. The Terrys had a ball last night, but Mamma and Nelly did not go; they are keeping themselves for the Hatchford ball on the 5th.[1] Tonight we all five dine with the George Smiths; I am afraid the P. M. G. is a real obstacle to Dolly and Mr T[2] and George Smith is simply scared of the state of things. Stead has got a tight hold of Mr T, I imagine, and is not likely to let go. The baby of the young George Smith was a jolly boy but has become quite plain and ordinary looking. I have settled to take Mamma with me when I go north at the end of January to lecture at Hull and Bradford; she will go to the Dicks when I go to Hull, and I shall join her at Audenshaw from Bradford. She likes the prospect and the Dicks are enchanted. Nelly will go to the Deacons. I am afraid there is no chance of our going to London; our income will not stand it at present. I want to see what I can produce by keeping quietly at home and working regularly; since, if we go again to London, it can only be by the publishers' help. This is a stupid letter, but I have been harried, having begun arranging books and remained arranging them too long. Reggie Toogood[3] is going to be married—to a widow. My love to Fred and every good wish to your both, and to the sweet midget for the New Year.   Ever my darling child,

your own Papa—

MS. Frederick Whitridge.

1. Lt.-col. Thomas Henry Clarke Terry (1810–1897: *Landed*) and his wife Charlotte (1819–1900), *née* Fellowes, of Burvale, Walton-on-Thames, Surrey. (Hatchford has not been identified.)

2. Henry Yates Thompson.

3. No doubt the son of the Henry Toogoods, their old Chester Square neighbors.

To Lionel Tollemache [1]

[?1888]

I was glad to find you quoting Clough; some very little thing more in him, and he would have had all the public quoting him.

I consider myself, to adopt your very good expression, a Liberal Anglican; and I think the times are in favour of our being allowed so to call ourselves.

Text: Tollemache, Nuts and Chestnuts, p. 69. Second quotation from Mr and Mrs Lionel A. Tollemache, Safe Studies (4th edn, 1895), pp. v–vi; Russell, Matthew Arnold, p. 259 (American edition, p. 263).

1. Lionel Arthur Tollemache (1838–1919: *WWW*), an old Balliol man, second son of Lord Tollemache, later the author of several books, member of the Athenæum, and a Surrey neighbor.

To Frederic William Farrar

Pains Hill Cottage, Cobham, Surrey

My dear Farrar   January 4, 1888

You have made your request so charmingly that I cannot refuse it—but tell me of *what length* the discourse should be? [1] I suppose it should not exceed a quarter of an hour or twenty minutes; and that, in that case, it is better read than spoken?

We all send love and New Year's wishes to you and all yours. I hope Hilda is much better.   Ever yours affectionately

Matthew Arnold.—

I rely on your day not being earlier than the middle of February.

MS. Bodleian Library.

1. "Milton" (Super 11:328–33), delivered in St Margaret's Church, Westminster, on Feb. 28, 1888, was printed in *Century Magazine*, 36 (May 1888): 53–55 and reprinted in *Essays in Criticism, Second Series* (1888). Hilda was presumably one of Farrar's five daughters.

To Lady de Rothschild*

Pains Hill Cottage, Cobham, Surrey

My dear Lady de Rothschild   January 4, 1888

I ought not to come, for I have engaged to make a discourse at Hull, on the 31st inst., concerning "life in America"—a very ticklish subject—and I meant to compose my discourse during the week of the 27th.[1] But I *cannot* refuse you twice; so Mrs Arnold and I, who were going to Dick at Manchester on the 30th, from whence I shall go on to Hull on the 31st, will come to you on the 27th and go on from you to Manchester on Monday the 30th, if you will keep us till that day.

You know how I like to think of your reading what I write. In this article on Shelley I have spoken of his life, not his poetry; Professor Dowden was too much for my patience.

My love to Constance and Cyril, and believe me,   affectionately yours,

Matthew Arnold.—

P. S. We shall come by the ¼ to 6 train from Euston, unless I hear from you that that will be too late.

MS. *Evelyn de Rothschild.*

1. "Civilisation in the United States" (Super 11:350–69), delivered as a lecture at Hull Jan. 31, 1888, was reprinted in *Essays in Criticism, Second Series.*

To George de Bunsen*

Cobham, Surrey

My dear George Bunsen   January 8, 1888

What you have told me is very valuable. But, as you kindly give me leave, I shall add a question or two. Did the settlement at the Peace of Münster give the Church property to Lutherans and Catholics only—to Lutherans in the Protestant regions, and to Catholics in the Catholic? Was there no recognition of the Calvinist Church? And cannot the United Church, in which the late King and his father took so much interest, enjoy stipends which, until the new form arose, were belonging to the Lutheran Church only?

Did the settlement after the Thirty Years' War recognise provinces only as generally Protestant or Catholic, and make no provision for isolated localities when the religion was not that of the province generally? For instance, I think some one told me, as we passed Bautzen in the train, that it was a Catholic place, and that the Catholic Church was rich there; but it is in a Protestant province. Have its Catholics, then, no endowments or stipends from the State?

I understand you to say that the State has taken possession of the church property generally and pays stipends in lieu of it. But does not the Church, Catholic or Protestant, retain its property in some parts of Germany?

I was taken by Baron von Canitz near Gorlitz, to visit the pastor of his village, whom I had heard in church previously. How is such a pastor appointed? I know how a schoolmaster is, but am not sure whether the *Gemeinde* has any voice in the appointment of a *Pfarrer*.

You say that the existing religions were recognised after the Peace of Münster, although the majority cannot now alter the dispositions then made of endowments. But, at any rate the majority, the facts, determined those original dispositions. In England they never did; but the State devised a form supposed to be one in which all reasonable people could meet, and gave the endowments to that form only.

I am much interested in the reappearance of the name of Arnold in your son's family.[1] You must make me acquainted with that son when you next come to London,—and from London, I hope, to Cobham. Come soon, and believe me, with kindest regards to your wife and daughter, and with cordial thanks to you for letting me learn of you,   ever affectionately yours,

Matthew Arnold.

Text. Russell, 2 : 433–35.

1. "*R*eappearance" because of Bunsen's son Arnold, who had died in 1866 (*Life and Letters of Baroness Bunsen*, 2 : 360 – 61).

To Messrs James Veitch & Sons

Pains Hill Cottage, Cobham, Surrey

Messrs Veitch.

Dear Sirs   January 10, 1888

The Basket was returned; but I see that in your new bill just received it is still charged for. Be good enough to say whether you have received it, and whether you allow for returned baskets.   Faithfully yours

Matthew Arnold.—

MS. University of Virginia.

To John Oliver[1]

Pains Hill Cottage, Cobham, Surrey

Rev. John Oliver

Dear Sir   January 12, 1888

Actual Catholicism I think a lost cause, but I quite agree that a renewed and transformed Catholicism may have a great future before it—and not among the Celtic races only.   Faithfully yours

Matthew Arnold.—

MS. Howard J. Garber.

1. Unidentified.

To Lucy Charlotte Arnold Whitridge

Pains Hill Cottage, Cobham, Surrey.

My darling Lucy   January 14, 1888.

We have had your letter and I quite agree with Mamma that it is much better for the midget not to be single,[1] and that you had better come over here; if the event is in August you might quite well be at the Cottage with Mamma; Nelly and I should pay visits. If you were looking forward to the event happening in America, I am sure as the summer advanced and the climate got more intolerable your spirits would sink and you would fancy you never could get through; and such an event in New York in August would, I own, be pretty bad. But I should come over as late as was safe, in order to stay with Fred as long as possible; and why on earth, if all goes well, you should have to pass the winter and not be able to go back at the beginning of October, I do not see. Give Fred the thanks of all of us for the oysters: we do not all of us eat them but we all share the pleasure of having them to give away, a pleasure which is very great; we are sending to the Denisons, the Combes, the Cushings, Mr. Young, Mr Gage, old Bignold, Lyon and Richard Lee.[2] Now I want Fred to do something else for me. Farrar has made me promise to give a discourse in St Margaret's Church when a painted window in memory of Milton's "espoused saint" and her child, who are buried there, is uncovered; the window is given by G. W. Childs of Philadelphia, and the American Minister is coming. The Americans have given much in Westminster, both to the Abbey and to St Margaret's, and about this I must say something. This will give the discourse a connexion with America; I am constantly asked to write for American periodicals, but always answer that unless I am writing with an American audience in my mind's eye in some degree, I think it better to publish in the periodicals of my native land. But if Fred can arrange with either Gilder or Curtis to print this particular discourse,[3] I shall be glad. It will be about half the length of the Philadelphia address which Gilder printed the year we were with you. Farrar answers for keeping the reporters out of St Margaret's, so the thing will be fresh; it is to come off on the 18th of February, and I could post it to America just before that day. I do not want Fred to drive a hard bargain at all, so the task I am asking him to undertake will not, I hope, be an irksome one; he might choose which Editor he liked, it is all one to me.

The photograph grows upon me, but I still think it not so interesting and "marquant" as the other. I went up to see Perry and his wife yesterday on farm business, and she quite won my heart by the way she went on about the baby: it appears Annie took her up to the farm sometimes. There are two families of pigs up there just now, one of nine tinies, and the other of ten a little larger ones, that would delight her. They are of a very good breed, and perfect little beauties. I find Mr Cushing very easy to do with: I heard yesterday from Mr Leaf; he is very weak, having been outside the house only twice since the 18th of December; but the neighbours have all called, and Herbert has been much invited to shooting parties and luncheons, and has been out a good deal with the hounds. We shall go there about Easter; it is a paradise for the primrose and the wild daffodil. We have had a week of fog and gloom, but no frost, and the ground all green and workable. We dined last night at the Deacons, and Nelly has two dances this next week. Both she and Mamma are excellent about not going to London, but we really cannot afford it. Nelly will very much enjoy being with the Deacons while Mamma and I are at Aston Clinton and Audenshaw. The dear Dicks were all that is delightful here, and Ella wins and keeps golden opinions. I have been asked by Lady Anne Chandos Pole, whom I met with her very handsome daughter at Lucerne two years ago, to come and stay with her mother Lady Harrington near Tunbridge Wells and renew the acquaintance. Tunbridge Wells made me hesitate, I so love that country, but I have declined because I have so much work on hand. We are all three asked to go and *stay* with the Locke Kings[4] at Weybridge; she wrote a pretty note, you remember her at Harrow, the daughter of Sir Thos Browne, the Bp of Winchester's brother. We are not going there either: but all invitations to London I shall encourage Nelly to accept: Lady Emma Talbot asked her yesterday to come to them when they go up. Your dear Aunt Mary has made up her mind to sell Woodhouse, and she is quite right, for she has not income enough to live comfortably there, now she has to help both her sons so much, and I am sure, if Mrs [?]Hemich were to die, nobody else would give the price she offers. It

will be nearly £30,000 altogether. I heard from your Aunt Forster this morning: I am going there for a night or two between Hull and Bradford; she says
Flo is very strong and well, though thin. They have asked the Dicks to go
and pass a Sunday there. I shall like to see Aubrey. I am interested in all you
say of Charlotte Boyle; I always liked her. Say something kind for me to the
T. Wards, when you see them. I suppose the Brownings will soon be coming
back here.[5] I am glad she married him, but he is not interesting. I have sent
you Amiel, and the XIXth Century: I cannot bear your being troubled about
getting these things. But keep the XIXth Century and bring it over to me,
for I have no copy, having given mine to the Village library here. Love to
Fred and twenty kisses to the darling midget; I thirst for a sight of her, little
darling.   Ever your own

Papa—

Max sends his love, Miss Lu; he is going in the carriage to the Chatley Gate,
then to walk home through Pains Hill with his old master and his Miss Nell.
Mamma is busy about a new parish house; not an unpleasant labour to her.

MS. Frederick Whitridge.

1. Her second child, John, who died in infancy (Honan, p. 428).
2. Except for the Combes and Deacons, the Cobham neighbors in this letter remain
mere names.
3. That is, in the *Century Magazine* or *Harper's Weekly.*
4. Hugh Fortescue Locke King (1848–1926), barrister, J.P., and a member of the
Athenæum Club, and his wife Ethel (later, Dame Ethel), born Gore-Browne. He was a
nephew of the 7th Baron King (*County*, 1904).
5. Neither Aubrey nor Charlotte Boyle nor the Brownings have been identified.

To John Duke Lord Coleridge

Pains Hill Cottage, Cobham, Surrey
My dear Coleridge   January 17, 1888
     We *all* read your address in Macmillan a fortnight ago, and were de-
lighted with it;[1] I only wish we could have heard you deliver it. *Some* people
do not gain by being heard, but you do.
     It is a horrid story that Dowden tells, but Shelley's face, and certain traits
in his disposition, plead for him always with me. He has a strain of madness,
however.[2]
     I knew Tolstoi, the man, would interest you.
     I could not be in town yesterday, but the spring shall not pass without
my meeting you at one of the Clubs, and going back with you, if you will
let me, to sleep in Sussex Square.

But first I have a perilous discourse to give at Hull on "Life in America." With all my reasons for liking the Americans, and with all their good qualities, I find their braggadocio, I am sorry to say, more and more irritating to me.

Goldwin Smith is very good, as usual, in his paper on American Statesmen. Love from all three of us to you and Lady Coleridge, and I am always yours affectionately

Matthew Arnold.—

MS. Lord Coleridge.

1. "Sir Stafford Northcote," *Macmillan's Magazine*, 57 (Jan. 1888): 161–67.
2. Unidentified.

To George Lillie Craik

Pains Hill Cottage, Cobham, Surrey

My dear Craik   January 17, 1888

Let me have the 3 volume Globe Shakespeare, for I find Mrs Arnold is indignant with me for declining it. She says it is just what she wants, and like Macmillan she does not mind double columns in the least. But both she and Macmillan are wrong here.

It occurred to me as I walked away from Bedford Street, pleased with the sale of the little volume of my "Selections," to ask why for my Wordsworth volume we should have the ninepenny royalty, and for my own little volume the £50 per thousand. The latter is a good deal the more favourable arrangement to *me*; and I should have thought the sale of the Wordsworth at least equally sure, so that you run no greater risk with that volume. It may be, however, that you are at greater expense in producing it.

But my chief feeling, as to both volumes, is one of cordial satisfaction at their continuing to do so well.   Ever most truly yours,

Matthew Arnold.—

MS. British Library.

To George Lillie Craik

Pains Hill Cottage, Cobham, Surrey

My dear Craik   January 18, 1888

Very many thanks. Up to Midsummer /87 is quite sufficient.

I write at once while the account is before me to say that my difficulty as to the Byron continues. It appears that 5000 have been printed and that

1167 were left in June last. Ought I not therefore to have received the royalty on 833 copies! 3000 + 1167 + 833 makes 5000 copies.

As to the Johnson, I understood that the £50 I had was for furnishing the Notes. I am sure I should not have furnished them for the love of the task, which bored me extremely. Surely I have not received £50 on account besides? Forgive me if I am making a mistake, but your accounts will show and mine do not.   Ever yours most truly

Matthew Arnold.—

P. S. Will you kindly send a copy of my little Selections to the Bp of Rochester as from me, putting in a mark at the last poem, *The Future*. Palgrave quotes it in a recent article, and the Bishop declared the poem was not in his 2 vol. edition!

MS. British Library.

To George de Bunsen*

Pains Hill Cottage, Cobham, Surrey

My dear George Bunsen   January 19, 1888

I cannot enough thank you for the trouble you have taken and for the information which you have given me, and I promise that the two questions I am now going to ask shall be my last.

1. I find "es sollte der Besiz der kirchlichen Stiftungen, Kirchen, etc., der Religionspartei Bleiben welche sich l Jan. 1624 im Besiz befunden."

But you say that the majority's faith did not determine the disposition, but the ruler's faith. Surely the German words I have quoted seem to show that the *community* using the Churches was to keep them.

2. On the principle *cujus regio, ejus religio*[1]—how is it that the Protestants in Saxony have the endowments when the King is Catholic?

A postcard to your brother Ernest was put up with your letter to me, and I posted it to Ernest.   Ever yours affectionately,

Matthew Arnold.

P. S.—You see the point at which I drive is this: In Germany the persuasion of the community governs the disposition of the endowments. In Wales, or in a great part of Wales, it does not.

Text. Russell, 2:435–36.

1. "Cujus regio, cujus religio," *Augsburger Religionsfriede* (1555): "The religion of a sovereign should determine the religion of his subjects" (*OCGL*).

To George Lillie Craik

Pains Hill Cottage, Cobham, Surrey

My dear Craik   January 20, 1888

I knew I should hear from you today, and I answer both your letters at once.

—Your offer to put the Selections from Wordsworth and Byron, under certain conditions, on the same terms with my own little volume, is very liberal; but then you and Macmillan have always treated me well. I gladly adhere to what you propose.

—I now perfectly understand about the Byron sales.

—Since writing to you on the subject I searched for Macmillan's letter about the annotated Johnson and found it. It is as you say. And you call me a good man of business! I had read Macmillan so hastily till now I was under the impression that the £50 was for the Notes, and that the book was on the same footing as the unexpurgated Johnson.

I see in Macmillan's letter he says "Of course we should keep the present book on sale." But I have seen nothing about it in the accounts of the last year or two—The Civil Service Commissioners recommended the Six Lives, and one of the great Crammers told me the book was much used. For all but girls and young boys the unexpurgated book is the best. Might it not be well to append to it the Notes to the School Edition, making, of course, the necessary changes in the paging? The Notes are quite as much as either book requires.

—Let me have again the Statement as to the books which was enclosed with my letter to you.

—And now I will pester you no more, but remain, with renewed thanks to Macmillan and yourself,   most truly yours

Matthew Arnold.—

P. S. I have come to the conclusion that it is inexpedient to publish volumes of *mixed* essays, and shall do so no more. Sooner or later I hope to divide my Essays into volumes according to subject. But I have lately thought that a purely *literary* volume,—to go with "Essays in Criticism" and to be called "Essays in Criticism, Second Series,"—might do. I should like to include the Wordsworth and Byron prefaces, and the three Essays from Ward's book; then the Amiel, Tolstoi, two Shelley articles, and one or two more literary articles which I hope to produce this year. The volume to appear about Whitsuntide next year. What do you think of this?

MS. British Library.

A. W. [?]Nuffield to Matthew Arnold

Selsdon Park, Croydon
My dear Arnold   January 20, 1888
I am charmed by your kindness. But you must add to it by writing my name on the enclosed slip, which I will gum in. It will match the Wordsworth which you gave me.

Certainly the vol. is full of gems. Thyrsis is unsurpassable.   Ever yrs with warm regard

A W [?]Nuffield

MS. British Library.

To Alfred Austin

Pains Hill Cottage, Cobham, Surrey
My dear Mr Austin   January 22, 1888
What is the latest day in February on which I may send my MS to you?[1] I shall not be long—15 or at most 16 pages.

A horrid discourse at Hull, a horrid discourse in St Margaret's Church; and this paper for you—then I turn to Prince Lucifer!

I am glad you gave Byron a centenary article.   Ever yours truly
Matthew Arnold.—

MS. Yale University.

1. "Disestablishment in Wales" in the *National Review* in March.

To James Bain

Pains Hill Cottage, Cobham, Surrey
Dear Mr Bain   January 26, 1888
My daughter tells me you are kindly exerting yourself to get me Ward's Diary.[1] If you have got it, well and good: but if not, do not give yourself any more trouble about it, as Macmillan offers to let me have it to look at, and I am content if I can read it without being obliged to go to the Museum for that purpose.   Truly yours

Matthew Arnold.—

MS. Harvard University.

1. Possibly, John Ward, *Experiences of a Diplomatist, Being Recollections of Germany Founded on Diaries Kept during the Years 1840–70* (1872).

To George Charles Brodrick

January 26, 1888

I am just off for the North to make a horrid discourse about America at Hull and at Bradford; I have then to prepare a horrid discourse about Milton, and a horrid article on Welsh Disestablishment—all before the middle of February. . . . I should much like to come and hear you on Home Rule, instead of discoursing myself on America; you are sure to be good, and I know you speak without the least difficulty. Fortunate man![1]

Text. G. C. Brodrick, Memories and Impressions, 1831–1900, *p. 263.*

1. Brodrick, who had approached Arnold about the new professorship of English at Merton to no avail, was told that Arnold "heartily" disliked lecturing. He also said: "What Professor Max Müller well calls 'his Olympian manners' never repelled me, for I soon discovered that they were not in the nature of airs, and did not even [for "ever"?] conceal his warm and simple heart" (*Memories and Impressions*, pp. 262–63).

To Frederic William Farrar

Pains Hill Cottage, Cobham, Surrey

My dear Farrar   January 27, [1888]

The half past will suit me quite as well as three.

I have not yet thought about the Milton, being full of a horrid discourse about America for Hull & Bradford next week.   Ever yours affectionately

M. A.—

MS. Benjamin Franklin Fisher IV.

To Lucy Charlotte Arnold Whitridge

Wharfeside, Burley-in-Wharfedale, Leeds

My darling Lucy   [February 4, 1888]

We have not heard much from you lately—but we gather from Fred's addition to your last that poor Fanny Coddington,—about whom we were really in most distressed alarm, as she seemed dying,—is better, and going to live. Today's Cunarder will bring us, I hope, a longer letter from you, and tell us that you are more comfortable. I have given my lecture at Hull and Bradford, with much success; certainly I learned by my American experience to hold up my head and talk my lecture, instead of reading it with my eyes in the manuscript—and this is everything. Hull interested me much more than Bradford which is a one-horse sort of a place though very prosperous and growing; but Hull has been a borough ever since Edward I, the center of the whaling trade, with a Trinity House the only one in England besides those of London and Newcastle and a glorious old church. Jemmy Daniel[l] [1] is quite a personage there, as Secretary to the Hull & Barnsley, the great dock company, and at the same time educated at Harrow and Oxford; you know how he and his family feel about your Mamma and he quite put himself at my service and took me everywhere. Now I must give this lecture at Bristol, and perhaps in London—after that, I shall have discharged my promises and hope never to lecture any more. I have said the truth about the American newspapers; I hear the American consul,[2] who heard me at Bradford, admitted it was the truth and highly approved of its being said; but I shall not publish the discourse at present, partly because I want to have an unpublished discourse which I can use as a lecture if I must, partly because all the answerings and letters from the American newspapers would be a worry, and consume my time. We came into snow in the north, and at Manchester it was very cold and miserable, though the Dicks have improved their house greatly and do all they can to keep us warm; it was very cold here too when I arrived, but this house is kept quite warm, so one is not cold except outside the door. Now it has thawed, the wind is west, and the hills and fields have the first look of spring on them; the buds are showing on the lilac and ribes and the snowdrops coming out. From Limerick, which is wetter and far milder, the O'Briens have brought snowdrops and violets in full bloom, and we shall find them quite out at Cobham. Flo & Robin are here with their children; Aubrey is a perfect darling, and his robustness is pleasant to see, for Flo looks sadly small and washed out: nothing will induce Aubrey to call me anything but *Matty*—he had heard me much talked about as "Uncle Matt who was fond of children," and he shows his regard by dropping the *Uncle*. The baby is a dear calm little boy, rather an *ug*, Nelly would say, but he has such beautifully marked eyebrows and good skin that it is a pleasure to me to see him. I have left him sitting, as good as gold, on Mamma's knee; she notices the children very much. Aubrey is rather a handful. I don't think they manage him quite judiciously; Francie fidgets with him. Your dear Aunt Forster looks very worn, but I like to be with her; she can think really of nothing but the Memoir. Edith, wife of Eds, is looking very well, and quite handsome. I like her, and she has no affectations and mannerisms. You will be amused to hear that your Uncle Walter is giving a dance and has appealed to Nelly for her aid in a letter so charming that I must send it; she will have to go. Flo and Robin are going up to lodgings in London for a fortnight, leaving the children here; Mamma and I go back to Manchester (such a fine journey through the Yorkshire moors!) today: the dear Dicks have the Meade Kings to dinner to meet us; rather an event for them. Aunt Tiny has sent partridges, and I find the Champagne; then Dick has the wine Mr Leaf sent, and the dinner seems planned excellently—soup and fish (John Dorey), leg of moor mutton, partridges, orange jelly with cream, sardines on toast and dessert—nothing else; six of us at dinner, and only the little Welsh maid to wait. How I wish you and Fred were to make us 8! We go back to Cobham on Wednesday; we have a dinner with "the Widow Jenkins" in prospect, to which Nelly is asked—but every one will now be going to town. Kiss my sweetest of Midgets—and my love to Fred.   Your own loving

Papa—

MS. Frederick Whitridge.

1. James Whiteman Daniell (b. 1841), at Harrow during Arnold's years there, then St John's College, Oxford, barrister, and later Hull, and Boodles.
2. Unidentified.

To James Van Vorden
[Monogram]

Mr James Van Vorden   Cobham, Surrey
My dear Sir   February 8, [?1888]
      The line I sent you is unpublished, and has not yet got itself rightly fitted to a context.
      With every good wish to my namesake, I am   sincerely yours
                                                      Matthew Arnold.

P. S. I have long since left Oxford and ceased to be a professor.

MS. University of Virginia.

To Edmund Gosse

Pains Hill Cottage, Cobham, Surrey

Dear Mr Gosse   February 9, 1888
      Yes, "Alaric at Rome" is my Rugby prize poem, and I think it is better than my Oxford one, "Cromwell," only you will see that I had been very much reading "Childe Harold."   Ever truly yours
                                                      Matthew Arnold.—

I have been away in the North, and have only this morning received your note.

MS. Berg Collection.

To Frederic William Farrar

Pains Hill Cottage, Cobham, Surrey

My dear Farrar   February 11, 1888

Childs has given the window; have you any other gifts from Americans in the *Church*?

What are the gifts from Americans in the *Abbey*?

Was it not a fountain Childs gave to Stratford?

Is Whittier's quatrain good? will it be inscribed on the window? Is Lowell's on the Raleigh window? did the Americans give that, and the Caxton?

Just a word of answer to all these questions.   Ever yours

M. A.—

Did Milton ever actually live in the parish of St Margaret's?

MS. Bodleian Library.

To John Everett Millais

Athenæum Club, Pall Mall, S. W.

Dear Millais   February 13, 1888

A swell like you, can be no rule for a poor old recluse like me. I have got let in, through an old half promise, for one infernal address this year, and I have vowed to myself not to make another.   Ever truly yours

Matthew Arnold.—

MS. Pierpont Morgan Library.

To John Duke Lord Coleridge

Cobham, Surrey

My dear Coleridge   February 15, 1888

A window in memory of Milton's "espoused Saint" is to be unveiled in St Margaret's Church, Westminster, next Saturday, the 18th, at 3.30 P.M. I am to read a short address, and Farrar suggests that I should ask you to come, and Lady Coleridge of course too, if it will not bore her. The address is sure to be badly read, and will very likely be bad in substance as well; but I give you Farrar's message. Perhaps when I am delivering a discourse is the occasion when your companion[ship] affords me the *least* pleasure—but it affords me pleasure always.   Ever yours,

M. A.—

MS. Lord Coleridge.

To Robert Hawthorne Collins[1]

Pains Hill Cottage, Cobham, Surrey

My dear Sir Robert   February 17, 1888

I was afraid you had forgotten to send Ruskin's letter: many thanks to you for letting me see it. It is a beautiful letter, though a very sad one. I cannot think that either at the National Gallery or at the British Museum he would not meet the great consideration due to him; if he does not, it is too bad.   Ever truly yours

Matthew Arnold.—

MS. Yale University.

1. Robert Hawthorne Collins (1841–1908: *WWW*; *VF*, 1/14/93), K.C.B., a neighbor at Esher, comptroller of the household of the duchess of Albany, as also (until his death in 1884) of her son, Prince Leopold (d. 1884), of whom he had been the tutor. Several letters to Collins are in Ruskin's *Works*.

To Lucy Charlotte Arnold Whitridge*

Cobham

My darling Lucy   February 17, 1888

I had thought of giving up my letter for this week I am so busy with an article promised to the Tory review, the National, but I told Mamma that I found it would do me good to scratch a line to you, only it must be a short one. Well, my darling, and so we are to see you in April; and the midget too; how delightful! We imagine you are coming with the Brownings, which will be a good arrangement, and will also save the expense of having Dick over. I love to hear of the sayings and doings of my midget; I pity Fred for losing her, hardly less than for losing you; but he will know that you are both of you in a climate better for you than that of New York. It was very kind of Fred to telegraph to me about the Milton address; I will send it straight to Gilder tomorrow, after I have delivered it. I hate delivering things, and I hate to have a subject found for me instead of occurring of itself to my mind; still, I think the Milton will read pretty well in print. Last night we dined with Lady Ellesmere, and had only her sister in law Lady Sandwich, but she is a conversable woman, and we got through. Nelly is in London, with the Deacons; I shall see her at the function at St Margaret's Church tomorrow, where Mamma is going up with me. How I wish my Lulu was to be there too; my faithful follower at Brooklyn, the first time I succeeded in making myself heard. I have just finished reading the Pioneers[1] aloud to Mamma and Nelly; a good deal of it is boring, but it is wonderful how the topography and manners gain in interest by having been in the country; the country described in the novel is round the Otsego lake, in western New York; I cannot find it in the map, but it must be near Binghamton where I have lectured, and where I insisted, though they thought me mad, in going out in the awful cold, when I arrived just before dark, in order to see the youthful Susquehanna. I am reading to myself the latter volumes of G. Sand's Correspondence, and find them so interesting that I shall write an article on "the old age of George Sand." [2] We have regular March weather here; cold north and north east wind and sometimes a sprinkle of snow, but the thermometer never below 30, and up to 35 in the daytime. In the north of England they have had heavy snow and severe cold; thermometer at Fox How down to 6, the lowest I ever heard of there. Mamma and I are going this afternoon with Max, Miss Lu, to the promontory by the Mole in Pains Hill park; it is now white with snowdrops; you remember them, my darling: how you have laughed while we gathered them, or dug up bulbs, and how I love to think of you! I found at Hull and Bradford that my American experience had made it quite easy for me to speak audibly in lecturing; but I also found lecturing a great bore, and determined henceforth to give it up, having discharged my positive promises. We have a great dinner at the Lovelaces on Tuesday to meet the Judges; Nelly is asked. Lady Ellesmere will be there, but she goes in the afternoon and sleeps as she must not be out after dark; so she cannot take us. Later in the week Ada Wood [3] comes to stay here, and we have on Friday the Combe girls to meet her, and "Cousin" Lambart. A daughter of George de Bunsen is also coming to stay here, so we shall be kept alive though so many of our neighbours are in town. They will have told you that Miss Thynne is going to be married—to a well off man with a German name. Now I must stop, and if you knew how my article pressed me you would say, "poor old Papa it was not bad of him to write me even this stupid scrap of a letter." Mamma is sweet company, never dull for a moment; the nurse is an unfailing matter of thought; I believe Mamma is to be secretary now. At Grillions' breakfast last week Chamberlain came on for ballot and was blackballed; it shows how high party feeling runs. At the Athenæum Canon MacColl who is thought a creature of Gladstone's received 59 blackballs! [4] Love to Fred— always your own

Papa—

I send you two notes one of Froude one of Millais—because I think they may be useful to you as autographs, if you have autograph-collecting friends.

MS. Frederick Whitridge.

1. James Fenimore Cooper's novel (1823).
2. He did not live to accomplish this.
3. Probably, Adela Wood, younger daughter of Peter and Caroline Wood.
4. Joseph Chamberlain was admitted into Grillion's in 1890; Malcolm MacColl remained in outer darkness.

To Francis Gledstanes Waugh [1]

F. G. Waugh Esqre   Cobham, Surrey
My dear Sir   February 19, 1888
    Many thanks for the promised book. My letters have been forwarded from the Club, but not books and newspapers; I shall find them when I go up next week. From your description, it seems to me that your book will be a useful one. Believe me,   very truly yours,

                                    Matthew Arnold.—

P. S. Mrs Arnold remembers your mother quite well. I hope we shall meet at the Club.

MS. Bryn Mawr College.

    1. Francis Gledstanes Waugh (1846/7–1902), author of *History of the Athenæum Club from Its Foundation*, 1894 (of which this was apparently an early edition), after four years at Rugby School, went on to Exeter College, Oxford, in 1865, became chaplain to the British Embassy in Tangier, 1874–75, and then, invincibly mediocre, finally subsided into the vicariate of Moulsford, Berks.

To Mr Russell [1]

Pains Hill Cottage, Cobham, Surrey
Dear Mr Russell   February 21, 1888
    I have now read both of your papers, and both with pleasure. In that on Art, I am glad to find you quoting Hazlitt, who has certainly much that is unattractive, but who is unjustly neglected at present. But for that matter so too is a greater man—S. T. Coleridge.   Ever truly yours

                                      Matthew Arnold.—

MS. Boston College.

    1. Neither author nor papers have been identified.

To Florence Earle Coates

Pains Hill Cottage, Cobham, Surrey
Dear Mrs Coates   February 24, 1888
    We were all glad to hear of you. The weather here reminds me of our first visit to America, we are so wintry; not that we have more than two or three degrees of frost, but we have that day after day, and driving showers of sleet, though it does not lie, and a north-east wind which dries one up. How

kind you were to us both in winter and summer! My remembrance of our last visit and of your tulip-trees and maples I shall never lose.

I had a special reason for writing about Tolstoi, because of his religious ideas; in general I do not write about the literary performances of living contemporaries or contemporaries only recently dead. Therefore I am not likely to write about Tourguenieff, though I admire him greatly, and am going to read two of his novels this very year.

I think you will have been interested by a review I lately wrote of the *Life of Shelley*. I believe you get sight of the contents of the English periodicals not unfrequently, although my daughter in New York writes me word that there is difficulty about it, and begs me to send her any periodical I want her to see direct from England. And when are you coming over here? We are not likely to go again to America, the climate tried my heart too much the last time, so we are the more desirous that our friends should come over here.

We all three, Mrs Arnold, Nelly, and I, send affectionate remembrances to Mr Coates, Alice, and yourself; think of me when the tulip-tree comes into blossom in June, and believe me, dear Mrs Coates,   your affectionate friend,

Matthew Arnold.

Text. Russell, 2:438–39.

To Mrs Cumberlege[1]

Athenæum Club, Pall Mall, S. W.

Dear Mrs Cumberlege   February 27, 1888

I send the autograph you ask for.

I am glad to be free from the work of inspecting, but I often regret the friends I used to meet, you and Mr Cumberlege amongst the number.

My kindest remembrances to him, and believe me   sincerely yours

Matthew Arnold.—

MS. Yale University.

1. Unidentified.

To General Viscount Garnet Joseph Wolseley

Athenæum

Dear Lord Wolseley   February 27, 1888

A nice little nephew of mine wants to approach you about an article he desires to get from you for "Murray's Magazine" which he edits. He fears,

unless he has an introduction, he may get no answer if he writes and may be evicted if he calls; but I tell him that like all true heroes you are amiable.[1]
Ever truly yours

　　　　　　　　　　　　　　　　　　　　　Matthew Arnold.—

MS. Hove Public Library, Sussex.

　　1. No article on Wolseley appeared in *Murray's Magazine.*

To ?

Athenæum Club, Pall Mall, S. W.

Dear Sir　　　　　　　　　　　　　　　　　　February 27, 1888

　　I like this poem, too. But I cannot give any more opinions; besides, it is of no use; we must fight our own battle.　　　Truly yours

　　　　　　　　　　　　　　　　　　　　　Matthew Arnold.—

MS. New York University.

To Walter Sydney Sichel

Pains Hill Cottage, Cobham, Surrey

Dear Sichel　　　　　　　　　　　　　　　February 29, 1888

　　I have been interested in reading your political matter, and have looked through several of your papers on other subjects. "Time's footsteps for the month" is a good idea. I wish you success; I cannot write for you, my promises already extend much beyond my powers of performance; I do not even write for my nephew who edits "Murray."　　　Truly yours

　　　　　　　　　　　　　　　　　　　　　Matthew Arnold.—

MS. University of Virginia.

To Messrs R. and E. Clark

Pains Hill Cottage, Cobham, Surrey

Messrs Clark—
Dear Sirs　　　　　　　　　　　　　　　　　　March 1, 1888

　　I have been correcting the punctuation in the little volume of Selections from my Poems. At the end of the second part of *Tristram & Iseult* I have changed the word *flurried* into *startled*; but on further thought, I wish *flurried* to stand. Mr Craik will forward the volume to you.　　　Faithfully yours

　　　　　　　　　　　　　　　　　　　　　Matthew Arnold.—

MS. Yale University.

To Philip Archibald Primrose Earl of Rosebery

Pains Hill Cottage, Cobham, Surrey

My dear Rosebery   March 1, [1888]

Quite right to go back to that dear little girl; I hope she gets on.

It was not very amusing at Grillion's either, though your friend with the "cachinnus immanis"[1] was not there. I cannot come again next Monday, but on Tuesday week next I must dine at the Club. Come there.

What *was* pleasant was my evening at the Durdans.[2]   Ever yours sincerely

Matthew Arnold.—

MS. *National Library of Scotland.*

1. "Great loud laugh."
2. A Rosebery seat, at Epsom, Surrey, a few miles distant.

To Thomas Humphry Ward

Pains Hill Cottage, Cobham, Surrey

My dear Humphry   March 3, [1888]

I have a sort of hope that *you* carried off from here a book of Senancour—"Libres Méditations d'un Solitaire Inconnu," which has disappeared, and which I value: Did you?

You were quite right. Ethel Leonard is to marry Mr Cushny—"Cousin Alick." He came to announce it to us. Much indignation prevails—but I daresay it will do very well.   Ever yours affectionately

M. A.—

Tell dear Mary I hope to see her mother on the 9th, at Oxford.

MS. *Yale University.*

To Lucy Charlotte Arnold Whitridge *

Pains Hill Cottage, Cobham, Surrey

My darling Lucy   March 3, 1888

We have had your charming long letter this morning. I like to have you pleased with your warm house, but I wish you had not to write your pleasure in it from your bed, to which you are confined with a cold. I went over the other day to dine and sleep at the Durdans, Lord Rosebery's, and very pleasant it was—the house the warmest I have found in England. But they all had colds, and that pretty little Peggy, whom Millais painted, has inflammation of the lungs. Lady Rosebery says she doubts whether the warm houses are expedient in this climate, and Lord Rosebery declares that he has ascertained that furs do not [*sic*]. But it is a delightful house, and I found him very pleasant company—so pleasant that I did not regret having driven the five miles to Leatherhead in the teeth of a bitter east wind. We have none of us had a cold, so we can match you; we have Alice Benson[1] with us, which is very pleasant; and Nelly's London friends invite her so faithfully that she need never be at home if she did not like; but she is a very good girl; I don't think any father ever had two girls who were quite so good in going out walks with him as you and Nelly: you both do it as if you liked it. We have quite fallen back into our old way of using the park as if it were our own; we took Ally there yesterday and she was perfectly delighted; the lake is all frozen, but the ice is rotten. The weather has been curious; no rain and only a slight occasional flurry of snow which does not lie: the thermometer at about 30 in the night and 34 in the daytime; but a persistent north east wind. However, the glass is falling at last. I long to have the Midget here: I am quite sure the moderate cold will do her no harm—nay, will do her good if she is warmly clothed. I send you an absurd newspaper which sells much at railway stations, because I thought the Midget might be interested in the picture of me; Mamma thinks it very *weak* looking, but for my part I am well pleased to be made to look amiable. We have the young Locke-Kings to dinner tonight: you remember her at Harrow, one of the Gore Browne children. We have Mr Combe and Evelyn, and all our efforts fail to provide us with another man.[2] Nelly and Alice have left the house in the pony carriage, Nelly declaring that she will not return to it without a man. We have tried Sir Robt Collins, Mr Basley, young Money Wigram, Mr Helme, Mr Gaye—all in vain. We have a last chance in Mr Young—but Mamma thinks he, too, will fail us. I don't much care, but Nelly and Mamma think it very serious. Nelly has had a very nice judicious note from Ethel Leonard about her engagement to "Cousin Alick."[3] People express much disgust and horror; for my part, I think most of how pleasant it will be to have so good looking and so amiable a mistress of Pains Hill. Not that I do not find the Master amiable—I do. I am sure you will think the changes, which his amiability has enabled me to make, an improvement. I should not wonder if the marriage turned out well enough; the worst of him is that, though a fine big man, he is a valetudinarian. Old Mr Butler has sent me a nephew or grand-nephew or his, with a long letter telling me nothing of you, or Miss Butler, or Fannie Browning,[4] or anybody; I suppose after 85 one does put nothing in one's letters. But the Butlers have a real claim upon us, so I have invited the young man down here to dine and sleep. I think Alice will stay here a week or more; it is very pleasant having her. On Thursday I go to Bristol, to give my Hull discourse on America for the benefit of the Branch University at Bristol; on Friday I dine and sleep at Balliol, in order that I may go and see your poor Aunt Julia. She hangs on wonderfully; so does Mr Hayes. Frank Arnold is engaged to be married to a girl without a sixpence. Ted is doing well: the Murrays thoroughly like him, and have just taken him into the business as a coadjutor to young Murray: his manners please. Ld Rosebery, who as President of the Federation League saw them both, told me he thought Oakeley had "the worst manners of any young man he ever saw" but that Ted was "a dear little thing."[5] We must have them down here before you arrive, him and Minnie: they want to come. Your Aunt Fan is in London with Aunt Mary: Aunt Susy comes up next week. Lucy Ada has a little boy, and is going on capitally. Dick has a craze about business, and I feel sure will never rest till he tries it. It is a great risk, in my opinion, but John Cropper and Humphry Ward seem in favour of it. What does Fred think? My love to him; tell him this Swiss stick is the comfort of my life now, as his cane was in summer.   Your ever loving

Papa—

MS. Frederick Whitridge.

1. A niece, daughter of Henrietta and Henry Roxby Benson.

2. Arnold's pen but Jane Austen guided it! Evelyn was the second of the six daughters of Charles Combe (who also had nine sons). Wesley, Gaye, and Young have not been identified. Alfred Money Wigram (b. 1856), later chairman of Reid's Brewery and Conservative M.P. for Essex, and a resident of Eaton Square, had been married since 1882 (Kelly).

3. See above, letter to Lucy of Nov. 15, 1887.

4. Fannie Browning has not been identified.

5. Above, "people express . . . a valetudinarian" and, below, "I suppose . . . dine and sleep," "Frank Arnold . . . sixpence," "saw them both" and "Oakeley had . . . saw' but that" inked over by another hand.

Francis ("Frank") Arnold (1860–1927), seventh child of Thomas Arnold, later, a "medical man," married Anne Reed Wilkinson.

To Alfred Austin

Cobham, Surrey
My dear Mr Austin   March 5, 1888

Many thanks for the cheque, which I have also acknowledged to the "National Review" Office. Your reception of my article was very kind; it has been my great good fortune in periodical writing to be generally able to please my employers, whether I please the public or not.

I have read with pleasure Brodrick's article and George Curzon's, and also the short review of politics.[1]

I never go to London except by a late train which arrives just in time for me to dress for dinner; and after dinner I return here. So I have not yet read your defence of Dowden. But I have read your "Prince Lucifer" through, and with admiration for the facility and clearness of expression, vigour of thought, and feeling for nature, exhibited in it. My criticism would be that there is too much symbolism. Your preface treats "Prince Lucifer" as a poem "strictly objective," and describes objective poetry, in your sense, as "poetry which aims at representing the struggles, the pathos and the tragedy, engendered by the active antagonism of rival Creeds, rather than seeks [*sic*] to adjudicate between them." I admit that you do not seek to adjudicate; but I think that in really objective poetry the personages impose themselves on the imagination as concrete living beings, and that your poem loses something by its personages not being sufficiently of this nature, but rather symbolical manifestations of "the antagonism of rival Creeds."

But it is a great thing to be able to speak in verse nowadays with so much freshness and force as you exhibit in this poem. Believe me,   sincerely yours

Matthew Arnold.—

MS. Yale University.

1. George C. Brodrick, "Plain Facts about Ireland," George N. Curzon, "A Purified British Senate: the Status Quo," and "Politics at Home and Abroad," *National Review*, 2 (Mar. 1888): 87–102, 115–34, 135–41.

Louisa Lady de Rothschild

Athenæum Club, Pall Mall, S. W.

My dear Lady de Rothschild   March 6, [1888]

At the end of this week I have a horrid discourse at Bristol for the benefit of the Branch University there; next week is an interval of blessed freedom before I begin the second part of "Shelley," and it will be a delightful celebration of that happy interval to come to Aston Clinton at the close of it, on Saturday the 17th. It was too bad of Constance not to turn up at the Durdans the other day, but I can forgive her the easier as I am to see her on the 17th. My love to her and Cyril, and believe me dear Lady de Rothschild ever affectionately yours

Matthew Arnold.

We shall come by the 5.45 train from Euston, if that is not too late.

MS. Evelyn de Rothschild.

To Thomas Arnold

Pains Hill Cottage, Cobham, Surrey

My dear Tom   March 11, [1888]

I have read your little brochure through with interest this afternoon. I have a message for you from Lord Francis Hervey, a very pleasant and very intelligent fellow.[1] When you go again to Bury he would like to know, in order that he may meet you there and take you about. Of course he might be useful to you, as he and his family are the personages of that neighbourhood. So let me know when you can fix your time of going to Bury, and I will write to Lord Francis.

I gave a discourse at Bristol last week for the benefit of the University College there; and on my way back I stayed at Oxford to see poor Julia, with whom I sate for an hour and more. She has wonderful vitality, but the change in her since I saw her last is very great. She seemed much distressed about the uncertainty of your coming; I can quite understand the difficulty of getting another man to take your lectures, unless the doctors absolutely summon you home, but I think, if you will allow me to say so, I would be careful not to hold out a prospect of your coming on this or that day, and then, changing your plans, to put off your return; as these changes worry an invalid and the mind goes on disturbing itself with them.

Ethel was looking better than I expected. I wonder what you think of Mary's book; I mean to read it this week. Her power of writing is conspicuous; is the "roman" her line?   Ever your affectionate

M. A.—

George Bunsen's daughter is with us; a clever and striking girl. I can never see a Bunsen without interest.

MS. Balliol College.

1. Francis Hervey (1846–1931), son of the second marquis of Bristol, an old Balliol man, a barrister, who had been and was to be Conservative Member for Bury St Edmunds.

To Mr Bourne[1]

Athenæum Club, Pall Mall

Dear Mr Bourne   March 13, 1888

I cannot attend your meeting—I attend no meetings—although I have the pleasantest recollections of the kindness which I have always met with from your Committee and from its Secretary.   Ever truly yours

Matthew Arnold.—

MS. Cecil Lang.

1. Unidentified. Possibly, Hugh Clarence Bourne (b. 1858), an old Balliol man, formerly secretary of the Charity Organization Society, then a barrister, and later in administrative jobs in Trinidad, Tobago, and Jamaica (*WWW*, *Men-at-the-Bar*).

To Lucy Charlotte Arnold Whitridge

Cobham
My darling Lucy   March 16, 1888

    This will be my last letter to you before you sail, and will go out on the Umbria with the dear Dicks. How charming Fred has been about their coming; when they got the final telegram, they were both, Ella in particular, averse to causing so much expence; but Fred's second telegram made all smooth for them. Mamma and I should not so very much mind coming out with them, Dick is so pleasant a travelling companion. I had your delightful letter by the Umbria; you do not give a very good account of yourself but your letter was written in good spirits and was quite one of your most delightful letters; delightful they all are. Since it came we have had news of the terrible storm in New York and of the failure of the milk-supply; poor little midget, what did she do? Everything you can tell us about her is interesting—"Little sweet!" Mamma keeps saying, when she is mentioned. I hope her bruises will be gone when she arrives; she is at an age when she requires looking after. I shall be amused at seeing her meeting with Max, who is more tranquil and dignified than ever; I feel sure she will remember him. The garden will be full of interest after you come; nothing will be over except the snowdrops and crocuses. I have a beautiful glass of crocuses of all colours standing before me as I write. The weather shifts about but never goes below freezing now; things are backward, however, but fresh points push themselves up above the ground every day. Mamma is much pleased with the new nurse, Miss Edwards, who has been lunching with us today; unluckily she has just got a good offer to go and live with a lady, a former friend; £80 a year and all found, and she will go. I have suggested to Mamma that she should get her to stipulate for a month's leave from her next situation in August, to come and nurse you; Mamma likes the idea and is going to try it. We have been staying for two nights with the Leafs in London; their pleasure in having us is something pretty to see; Mr Leaf kept rubbing his hands and saying: "This is a red-letter day indeed;' and Mrs Leaf could not do enough for Mamma. But in going up there in a Hansom after dining at "The Club" I caught cold in my face, and have had one of my aching and swelled faces which you remember well; but this morning I have been able to lance the gums and am relieved. I gave satisfaction at Bristol and got much money for the College which I went to help; on my way back I dined and slept at Oxford, at the Master of Balliol's,[1] in order to go and see your poor Aunt Julia; I had not seen her since my return from America. She is terribly wasted, one arm a yellow skeleton, the other monstrously swoln and discoloured; but her head and brow have still something fine and deerlike about them. She liked my visit; I stayed more than an hour. Nelly is with the Deacons in London; tonight Mamma and I are asked to dine at Burwood, where Lady Sandwich, the Archie Campbells[2] and the Balfours are staying; but we refused on the plea of my swelled face. Tomorrow we go to Aston Clinton and shall take Eliza, as there is a party there and I see it will be a comfort to Mamma. On Tuesday we dine and sleep at the Teds' in London, to meet Mary Kingsley that was.[3] In Easter week I am going to Wilton; I could not resist it, for it is the place of Sir Philip Sidney and Arcadia; besides there is a trout-stream; also I like Lord & Lady Pembroke. Tell Fred if I did not fully thank him for what he did about the Milton discourse, I am a brute; the Times meant to report it in full and sent a reporter whom Fraser would not admit. The newspapers were angry with him, and he then covered himself by saying that I had promised the discourse to an American Magazine and did not wish it forestalled: but I really had nothing whatever to do with his excluding reporters. I sent it straight to Gilder, and ought to hear from him soon; I suspect he will send me £50, which is better than a report in the Times. Old Mrs Butler sent us a grand-nephew, a nice-looking youth, whom we had down here to dine and sleep. Mind the Dicks see old Mr Butler and Emily. I am reading Mary Ward's new book, and it interests me; it is not fated to please all the world, I expect the public will be interested in it: I am afraid she has nearly worn herself out in writing it, and is now looking for a great success, and that the book will probably not have. It is like "Tom Brown"; not the work of a creative novelist, but the experiences of a person who has been in contact with interesting people and tries to make them live again. This can never have the charm of real creative work like Miss Austen's or George Eliot's, but it is interesting if the experience has been interesting. And all that Oxford and clerical world is interesting to *me*; Mamma and Nelly do not care for the book at all.[4] The Wards have set up a brougham, and seem prospering in their affairs. Now I must go out with Max: I am keeping Mamma in the house, because she has a stuffy cold. My love to Fred and a kiss to the Midget. How you will like showing New York to the dear Dicks!   Your own loving

Papa.

MS. Frederick Whitridge.

1. Benjamin Jowett.

2. Of the many with this name, this one was probably a neighbor at Coombe Hill Farm, Kingston-on-Thames, Archibald Campbell (1846–1913), second son of the eighth duke of Argyll, a partner in Coutts and Co.

3. Charles Kingsley's third child, now Mrs William Harrison.

4. Three passages inked over in various degrees of impenetrability: "it is not fated . . . be interested in it," "and is now . . . probably not have," "Mamma and Nelly . . . book at all." The first one is guessed at on the basis of ascenders, descenders, dotted "i's" and crossed "t's," word length and context, and with the aid of digital imaging, a dermatologist's lamp, eyestrain, and faith. The second reading is much more reliable, and the third is virtually certain.

To Arthur Mills

Aston Clinton, Tring

Dear Mills   March 18, 1888

I was prevented coming to the breakfast yesterday, and I cannot come to the dinner tomorrow. Will you therefore, if you have not yet done so, kindly put down Lord Lytton's name in the Candidates' book for me?

I hear Lowell was blackballed; I wish your plan of withdrawing his name had been followed.[1]   Most truly yours

Matthew Arnold.—

MS. Texas A&M University.

1. Neither Lowell nor Lytton ever made the grade at Grillion's.

To Miss Barlow[1]

Pains Hill Cottage, Cobham, Surrey

Miss Barlow
Dear Madam   .   March 27, 1888

You are welcome to publish the words of "Requiescat," but as there are many settings of them, and I am no judge of music, it is better that your setting should not be dedicated to me, lest I should appear to adopt one setting in preference to others—a preference which I am not competent to establish.   Faithfully yours

Matthew Arnold.—

MS. University of Texas at Austin.

1. Unidentified.

To John Franklin Genung[1]

Professor Genung   Cobham, Surrey

Dear Sir   March 30, [1888]

I have read with interest your letter and Mr Ginn's Circular, but I cannot undertake any work for his Series, my engagements are already too numerous.

Pray remember me kindly to President Seelye and to any friends at Amherst who have not forgotten me, and believe me,   Truly yours

Matthew Arnold.—

MS. Amherst College.

1. John Franklin Genung (1850–1919: *WWWA*), biblical scholar and teacher of English at Amherst College. Edwin Ginn (1838–1914: *DAB*) was the famous Boston publisher and head of Ginn and Co.

To Thomas Arnold

Pains Hill Cottage, Cobham, Surrey

My dear Tom   April 9, 1888

Your touching and beautiful letter, which I shall always keep, crossed mine. I had hoped to come to dear Julia's funeral but it is the same day as Mr Hayes's, and you will have the old home, and Fan, and your own children, and I suppose John Cropper; Mary is left more solitary and I think I ought to go to her if I can only go to one.[1] If your Oxford service was at 11 or 12 on Wednesday I would come to it and go on from that to Woodhouse; but I suppose you must have the Oxford service very early in order to get down to Westmorland the same day. I shall think of you, my dearest old boy, on Thursday, you may be very sure. If by any chance the Oxford service should be put later on Wednesday let me know; otherwise do not trouble yourself to answer this; you must have many letters to write.

Fanny Lucy's dear love—   ever your most affectionate brother

M. A.—

MS. Balliol College.

1. Julia Sorell Arnold died in Oxford on April 7, was buried in Ambleside on the 12th; Robert Hayes, Mary Arnold's third husband, of whom so little is known, died on the same day, at the age of 49 (*Times*, Apr. 11, 1888, p. 1).

To Marion Margaret Violet Lindsay Manners Marchioness of Granby

                                    Pains Hill Cottage, Cobham, Surrey
Dear Lady Granby   April 10, [1888]
How amiable of you to have remembered of yourself my last year's application! I should like very much to go to the Lathkill some day in July; I
was at Wilton last week, and found myself fishing in a greatcoat amid snows-
torms, and that inclines me to put my fishings in prospect somewhat late in
the summer.

I am glad Lord Granby has come into Parliament.[1] If I were ever in
London I should come and see you, but weeks pass without my going there
though I am within twenty miles.

I wonder if you have seen my niece's novel, *Robert Elsmere*, and if so,
what you think of it.

I am always, dear Lady Granby,   very truly yours,
                                    Matthew Arnold.—

MS. University of Virginia.

1. The marquis of Granby (succ. as duke of Rutland in 1906), who had been Salisbury's principal private secretary, entered Parliament as Conservative Member for East
Leicestershire in 1888.

To Frances Bunsen Trevenen Whately Arnold *

                                              Pains Hill Cottage
My dearest Fan—   April 10, 1888
. . . We have since had a telegram from Fred to say they all went off
by the *Aurania* safe and well on Saturday afternoon. They can hardly be at
Liverpool before next Sunday evening. Both of them say the baby is more
fascinating than ever. We have a flock of sheep—Southdowns, with fine
black-faced lambs—in the paddock; what a sight for the Midget!

I had a pleasant visit at Wilton, which is a place of immense interest
and beauty. Goschen was in good spirits, as one might expect. I found Lady
Charles Beresford[1] enthralled by *Robert Ellesmere*, tell Mary; and Lady Hilda
Brodrick[2] has promised to introduce her to Mary. Goschen had read only
one volume yet. The rest at Wilton had not begun it, but were all meaning to read it. George Russell was here a day or two ago; he was staying at
Aston Clinton with Gladstone, and says it is all true about his interest in the
book: he talked of it incessantly, and said he thought he should review it for

Knowles.[3] They had it at Wilton that the book was by a sister of mine; by *you*, that is!

Now I must stop. The Bishop of Salisbury and Mrs Wordsworth dined at Wilton, and I had Mrs W. on one side of me; she spoke with warm affection of Lucy Selwyn—indeed of Mary too—but Lucy Selwyn in particular.[4]   Your ever affectionate

M. A.

Text. Russell, 2:441.

1. Born Mina Gardner, in 1878 she married Charles De la Poer Beresford 1846–1919: *DNB*; *VF*, 5/13/96, 1/3/95, 7/6/99), second son of fourth marquis of Waterford, Conservative Member for East Marylebone from time to time but currently fourth lord of the Admiralty (1886–88, promoted admiral 1906) and remembered for his colorful and forceful personality (Irish charm, Irish temper) in naval service and society.

2. Lady Hilda Brodrick, born Charteris (d. 1901), married Baron William St John Freeman Brodrick (1856–1922: *DNB*; succ. as viscount 1907, cr. earl 1920; *VF*, 5/6/76), of Eton and Balliol, currently Conservative Member for South West Surrey, later in several high government offices.

3. Gladstone's famous review, "Robert Elsmere and the Battle of Belief," was in the *Nineteenth Century*, 23 (May 1888): 766–88.

4. John Wordsworth (1843–1911: *DNB*), nephew of the poet, married to the former Susan Esther Coxe (d. 1894), daughter of Henry Octavius Coxe, formerly Bodley's librarian. Lucy Selwyn was Tom Arnold's daughter.

To George Washburn Smalley

4, Buckingham Gate, S. W. [London]

My dear Smalley   April 13, [1888]

I don't think the "nice" Americans ought to take to themselves what I say about shortcomings in the life of their nation, any more than the "nice" English what I say about shortcomings in the life of ours; but I was determined to say at some time what I thought of the newspapers over there and of the prevalent "greatest nation upon earth" strain; and I am not without hope that it may do good.

When I was in America your Tribune letter was always an oasis in the desert of the journalism there; not only from its matter, which of course interested me, but from its tone. I think you will end by judging this article of mine less unfavourably.[1]   Ever truly yours

Matthew Arnold.—

MS. Yale University.

1. "Civilisation in the United States," the lecture at Hull on Jan. 31, published now in the *Nineteenth Century*, 23 (Apr. 1888): 481–96.

To George William Erskine Russell*

[April 15, 1888]

S[malley] has written a letter full of shriekings and cursings about my innocent article; the Americans will get their notion of it from that, and I shall never be able to enter America again.[1]

Text. G. W. E. Russell, Matthew Arnold, *p. 19.*

1. Russell introduced this sentence with "On the last day of his life he said in a note to the present writer." Smalley's "Lampooning America" (headed "Mr. Matthew Arnold's Peevish and Splenetic Eruption" and "The Apostle of Sweetness and Light Casts Mud against His Former Hosts, and Abuses Americans Indiscriminately because They Will Not Write Themselves Down a Nation of Base Braggarts Living in a Fool's Paradise") had appeared in the *New-York Daily Tribune,* April 1, 1888, p. 1. An editorial on the subject, rather less acerbic, was printed on p. 4. The attack, obviously written in the heat of the moment, was dated Mar. 31; Smalley, withdrawing nothing, nonetheless printed an elegant amende honorable in a letter dated Apr. 17 (see his *London Letters and Some Others,* 1:289–302).

Frances Bunsen Trevenen Whately Arnold to Thomas Arnold*

Dingle Bank

My dearest Tom,   April 16, 1888

I hear they wrote or telegraphed to you to tell you of this awful blow that has fallen upon us. I cannot realize it. Indeed we are all stunned. Poor F[anny] L[ucy] is sometimes stunned sometimes agonized—sometimes quite natural. They were on their way to meet Lucy. They left here at 2.30 to catch the Tram. Just as they reached it, he swayed & fell. He was taken into a doctor's house close by but he must have died instantaneously, & without the least pain. They brought him back here, & then poor F L went to meet Lucy and the Dicks, & staid at the Hotel with them all night. Nelly came down in the night. Poor poor thing, it is an appalling blow. Never was a man more deeply beloved or more loving. Jane & Francie have just come. Dick has gone to Cobham to make preparations. Lucy & Ella go there tomorrow. On Wednesday Dick returns & takes his mother & Nelly with the coffin straight to Laleham, & he will be buried by his boys on Thursday. Thank you dearest, for your letter. I wonder if you will go, or stay for the funeral.

I am   Ever your loving sister

F Arnold

One grief comes upon another. May we feel really able to say, "Thy will be done."

MS. Pusey House (this text from William S. Peterson, Times Literary Supplement, Aug. 28, 1989, p. 188).

APPENDIXES

Appendix A: Additional Letters

To Thomas and Mary Penrose Arnold

Lower Continent Room

My dear Mamma and Papa   .   Friday, April 7th 1837

Do not disturb yourself at all about my Hand which is doing well: last night indeed no one sat up with me, which till now they had done, owing to my sleepless nights, and the great Pain of my hand which not only gave me no sleep, but was obliged to be bathed in Lotion every quarter of an hour to keep out the Fire. If Mr. Wickham had not been here at the time I should have lost my middle and forefinger, but he after putting my hand into Lotion, prepared some very strong kind of Powder which he put over my hand, which turned the Phosphorous into bone from which it is made. It [?]rose afterwards in a very large tight bladders all over the Palm of my hand and between my fingers, but they have been opened and I have Mr. Wickham's Authority for saying that it is going on well.

M. Arnold.

MS. Percival Library, Clifton College, Bristol.

To Laura Greenhill

Balliol

My dear Laura   Monday, [?1842]

I am afraid I cannot possibly come to you to morrow, as I dine with the B. Powells.[1] Believe me   your's affectionately

M. Arnold.—

MS. Roger Brooks.

1. Baden Powell (1814/15 – 1860: Foster), Savilian Professor of Geometry.

To Charles Wellington Furse (formerly Johnson)

Brimpts

My dear Johnson   Thursday, [July 6, 1843]

I hope you have by this time received a copy of my verses which I told Vincent to send you. I left Oxford in a hurry and was unable to send it myself. You will have heard that the Title Page carries a mis statement on the Face of it, in as much as Jelf's Unpopularity put a stop to the whole Exhibition. However I am very glad to have got the Poem to send you, and I hope you will read it in a merciful spirit.

But I must not delay any longer, for I am sure I have already delayed long enough, to express my real sorrow for the Carelessness whch has left your letter of last summer utterly unacknowledged, and to thank you most sincerely for the great kindness of it. I do so strongly feel that such Carelessness is inexcusable that I find it difficult to say anything more than that I am truly sorry for it: but I trust that I am overcoming, and late enough, that inveterate habit of laziness which interferes no less with other Duties than with Letter Writing. However I did honestly feel at the time the kindness of your letter, and the great difficulty of telling you how I felt it: it was one of those unlooked for kindnesses which make one feel very strongly how little one has done to deserve them. And above all, as my Father's influence seems generally to have been felt so much most deeply by those who have actually associated with him, more generally, I think than has often been the case with men like him; and as much that he thought has been so deeply misunderstood, I am half surprised, half delighted, when I hear of its having had an effect on those who have known him only thro: his character and his writings.

I was very sorry to hear yesterday from Hawker, thro: your brother, that you still suffered much in bodily health: I do really hope you will come to Brimpts and this miracle air of Hawker's, in which as a Devonshire man you are bound to believe, and try if you can bear this simplicity of Life as well as you could two years ago. I am sure one reading would still flourish, and it would be a great pleasure to see you. There seems to me to be a strange Melancholy which I dare say you have felt, in coming with a changed Party to the same Place and under much the same Circumstances that other People, who in their turn are changed, have inhabited and experienced at no great distance of time. One feels a familiarity with the old inhabitants and a longing to make the Place more natural by assembling them in it so far as one can, a second time. Meanwhile old Hawker passes amongst us for a stately Relic. I really hope you will come, and stay as long as you can. Ever, my dear Johnson, most sincerely yours,

M. Arnold.—

MS. Lambeth Palace.

To Richard Dowden

R. Dowden Esquire   London
Sir   July 21, 1849
    I am directed by the Marquis of Lansdowne to acknowledge your letter of the 14th instant, and to inform you that he will communicate the request contained in it to Sir George Grey, who accompanies the Queen: but he fears, from the short time the Queen will remain at Cork (only a few hours) the number of visits she will be enabled to pay will be very limited.
    I remain, Sir,   Your obedient servant

M. Arnold.

Text. Timothy P. Foley, "An Unpublished Matthew Arnold Letter," Notes and Queries, n.s. 45, no. 2 (June 1998): 219–20 (MS. Cork Archives).

    1. Richard Dowden (1794–1861), mayor of Cork.

To J. H. Beale

Education Department, Council Office, Downing Street, London:
Mr. J. H. Beale
My dear Sir   July 4, 1855
    Many thanks for your statistics, which will be both interesting and useful to me. I have read with pleasure the article of yours in the Banbury paper on the three Education bills. On the second Saturday in this month, I go to Dover, so that it will not be possible for me to have the pleasure of attending your meeting on that day.
    If the copy of the Minutes destined for your school has not yet been sent it will be sent very shortly.
    I hope to see you if all goes well in October, and to talk to you about last Xmas. Believe me,   faithfully yours

M. Arnold—

MS. Roger Brooks.

To J. H. Beale

Privy Council Office

Mr Beale
My dear Sir   November 15, 1860
    There is one point in your last letter which I did not notice. You said Riley had left you. I don't know what his intentions are, but you should let

him know that unless he continues at work till Xmas he cannot have a Queen's Scholarship, nor indeed any employment under it. His Indentures bind him till the 31st December 1860.   Truly yours

M. Arnold—

MS. Roger Brooks.

To Henry Peter Brougham

The Lord Brougham   Ipswich
My dear Lord   July 31, 18[61]
     Pray allow me to thank you for your kind note, and to assure you how grateful I shall be to you for any comments upon my account of education in France, if you find time to read it. Upon the general subject of popular education, you are the founder and leader of us all—and on the particular subject of France, there are few persons, if [an]y, in this country, with so much knowledge, and such means of judging any statements on French matters. Meanwhile, from the authorities in Paris, I receive the most agreable testimonies to the accuracy of my Report.

     I have asked Lord Lansdowne to say to Lord Clarendon how much I should like to complete my acquaintance with French education, by being sent to report to the new Public School Commission, of which Lord Clarendon will probably be Chairman, on the *Secondary* instruction of France. Although the Commission have not to deal with the question of Second Instruction generally, yet the present seems to me an admirable opportunity for obtaining information upon it; and, in France at any rate, full and accurate information on these matters is not easily obtained except by persons officially authorised to ask for it. If your Lordship should have an opportunity of strengthening this application of mine to Lord Clarendon by speaking to him upon the subject, I know no one whose recommendation would carry more weight, or whose exercise of it on my behalf would confer on me greater pleasure.

     I am at present going the Norfolk Circuit as Marshal to my father in law, Mr Justice Wightman, who I think is an old acquaintance of your Lordship's; but I hope to be in London, at No. 2, Chester Square, by the end of this week.

     Believe me to remain, my dear Lord,   Your faithful & obliged servant,

M. Arnold.—

MS. University College London.

To Lady Reay

Deanery
Westminster

Dear Lady Reay   Good Friday, [?March 26, 1880]

   The Dean will be most happy to see you at the Abbey at 11 on Wednesday, and there will be luncheon here at 1 o'clock, after the *Explorations.* Ever truly yours

Matthew Arnold.—

MS. Herbert and Rita Gold.

To Thornton Hunt

Woodford

Sir,   June 15, 1864

   I have desired Messrs Macmillan to send you a copy of some considerations on Middle Class Education which I have just published, and I take the liberty of begging you to give them, if possible, a moment's attention. Allow me to explain why I venture to take this somewhat unusual step of writing to you. I have written to the Editor of no other newspaper; but I have observed that the *Daily Telegraph* has from time to time, with regard to State intervention in social matters, held language quite different from the ordinary English commonplaces on this subject, and from the language held by the great majority of newspapers. As long ago as in February of last year I came across these words in the *Daily Telegraph*—their immediate occasion was, I believe, some proposal for registering changes of name: "No measure would more tend to rally the whole of the population in all its sections to the *conservative influences of the Empire*, than one extending a public enrolment which would *increase the numbers personally connected with the State, its traditions, royal sanction, and long-enduring institutions.*" The idea of the State and of its influences which is at the bottom of that is I believe perfectly sound, and familiar to the best political thinkers, but it is so at variance with the usual commonplaces talked everywhere in England on this subject, and repeated for ever in our newspapers, that I took the words down, and resolved, if ever I made any effort in the direction to which they point, to try and obtain your assistance.

Text: Edmund Blunden, "Leigh Hunt's Eldest Son," Essays by Divers Hands Being the Transactions of the Royal Society of Literature of the United Kingdom, New Series, ed. R. W. Chapman (1942), pp. 71–72.

To Samuel Davidson

October 31, 1876

When I saw your book advertised, I marked it for purchase, but I shall be extremely glad to have it as a present from yourself. Your work in the region of Biblical criticism has been unique of its kind in England, and of the greatest value: I am, therefore, deeply gratified by your praise. My task, so far as Biblical criticism is concerned, has been rather that of a populariser than anything else; for such work to do good it will always be necessary that more solid and complete work should be behind it. I will certainly suggest to the editor of the *Contemporary Review* to call attention to your volume when it appears; the critic should, I think, be a specialist, which I am not.

If you have time, I wish you would look at a suggested origin for Matt. xvi.18, in an article of mine in the forthcoming number of the *Contemporary Review*. The article is my farewell to theology.

Text: The Autobiography and Diary of Samuel Davidson, D. D., LLD, *Edited by His Daughter (Edinburgh, 1899), p. 122.*

Appendix B: The Chicago Hoax

Mr. Arnold in Chicago
His Observation of Society
A Solid Basis of Philistinism—A Varnish of Culture

London, April 5, 1884

Mr. Arnold begins the publication in The Pall Mall Journal of a series of papers embodying some of his impressions of American life. The first paper deals with Chicago, and will undoubtedly provide the inhabitants of that city with much food for reflection.

> I remember reading in *The Saturday Review* some ten years ago a statement to the effect that in Chicago might be seen "the concentrated essence of Americanism." This remark happened to coincide with the opinion which I had already formed from other considerations which I have made during my recent visit to America have only gone to conform [?confirm] its justice. For this reason I have chosen Chicago as the subject of the first of a series of articles in which it is my intention to record the impressions received while in the United States. Many of these impressions are of a fleeting, and all of them of a fragmentary character, and yet I have thought that they might throw a few rays of light upon the intricate problem presented by the civilization of the largest of English colonies, and that from them there might perhaps follow one or two of those leading principles of which criticism is ever in search.
>
> "If we would really know our hearts, let us impartially view our actions." I trust that I shall not too far tax the forbearance of Mr. Frederic Harrison by once more quoting from that most estimable of writers, Bishop Wilson. That which most impressed me during my stay in Chicago, as well as in other American cities of the larger sort which I visited, was a certain assumption of culture, which upon close observation I found to be very superficially varnished over a very solid basis of Philistinism. This affectation of concern for the things of the spirit, which may very easily be seen to be nothing more than an affectation, is chiefly observed in its aesthetic aspect. Of ethical culture there is hardly any pretence. From sheer stress of habit the members of the

clergy dispense from the pulpit their weekly modicum of diluted mo-
ralities, and from sheer force of fashion the more respectable classes
of the population give apparent heed to what is said to them. But it
would be safe to say that the condition of the trade in tinned meats, or
in pork or in grain has the largest share of their thoughts even during
the hour of ostensible devotion. The inevitable curse of the money-
getting spirit is writ large, as it were, in the action of this population
of half a million souls. It is an easy matter to know the heart of such a
community as this, when its actions are so open to the view of all men.
As an illustration of the slight extent to which Englishmen of reputation are generally known in America, I may mention an amusing incident which happened in Chicago. I was conversing with an intelligent
gentleman of commercial pursuits, and in the course of what I said I
took occasion to remark that Mr. Herbert Spencer had lately been in
America. My friend seemed a little surprised at first, and then said:
"Oh, yes, he came back from Europe last summer." I learned upon
further inquiry that reference was made to a Mr. Hibbard Spencer,
who is a Chicago tradesman, engaged, I believe, in the iron business,
and who had recently made a summer trip to Europe. I trust I may be
pardoned if I relate also in connection with this a little thing about
myself which I found quite as amusing as the one just mentioned. I
was conversing with a lady who was kind enough to tell me that she
had read my works and greatly admired them. I expressed my gratifi-
cation at learning that the ideas of sweetness and light of which I have
humbly endeavored to become an exponent had been so kindly received in this distant place, and ventured to ask which of my works she
honored with her preference. A little to my surprise she mentioned
"Tom Brown at Rugby" and "The Light of Asia."

But to take the matter more seriously, I gave myself the pains to
ask a large number of the apparently cultivated people with whom I
came in contact, whether they had read "Obermann." As the result of
these inquiries I must state the melancholy fact that to all but one of
those questioned, the name was wholly unfamiliar, and this one understood me as referring to a gentleman of that name who is the proprietor of a chemist's shop in Chicago. I do not know of any other
little thing connected with my stay in America which gave me such
a sense of the crudeness of American culture. What another alchemy
was that of the author of "Oberman," than the art practised by the
Chicago chemist in his daily dispensations!

During my stay in Chicago I attended a very pleasant little reception given by the Literary Club of that city. I call it the Literary Club

because that is the name by which it is known, and not in any way to imply that in so large a city as Chicago there is but one society of that character. I should judge, indeed, that there must be many similar nuclei of persons who are sufficiently released from the demands of the pushing business life of the city to be thus drawn together by the bonds of culture, and as far as my recollection serves me, the greater number of the persons of literary pursuits whom I had the pleasure of meeting were not included among the members of the particular association of which I am speaking. This evening afforded me a curious illustration of what combination in the person of the individual, or business ability and cultured tastes which I so often had occasion to note while in the States. A pleasant little paper on the subject of Philistinism was read, and as the subject is one in which I have taken some interest, I naturally gave it close attention, for which I felt fully repaid. Wishing to learn the profession of the gentleman who had so intelligently handled the subject, I made inquiry of a friend who informed me that the essayist was the owner of a large grocery business. I learned also upon making further inquiry, that besides members of the clergy and of the legal profession, whom I should naturally expect to find in such a society as this, there was a very large element consisting of successful tradesmen, such as mercers, iron-mongers and packers, which latter term is applied to dealers in the class of food products derived from the hog.

I was especially interested when at Chicago, as I was throughout my stay in America, in observing the various religious bodies, and in trying to get some insight into their spiritual life. It is quite unnecessary to say that in a country where there is no established church, there can be no such demarcation between the Dissenters and the members of the Church of England as exists in our own country. The mode of worship of the Dissenters has about it that bareness which is noticeable in England, but this may be seen to an almost equal degree in the bodies of non-dissenters. I attended one Sunday morning the chapel in which services are conducted by one of the most popular of the dissenting members of Chicago. The chapel was really nothing else than the large hall in which most of the more important concerts and lectures are given, and in which I had myself lectured but a few nights before. The audience in attendance upon this service seemed to be made up of a well-to-do and intelligent class of people, and I afterward learned that regular attendance here stands in Chicago as a sign of cultured tastes. So when afterward I tried to put my recollections together in some sort of order, I came to the conclusion that from all I had heard I should be justified in assuming the tone of these services to be fairly typical of the ideal of culture prevailing in Chicago. Here, I must confess, I was disappointed. I heard so much of the language of culture in the higher classes of Chicago society, that I was almost prepared to admit that I had been unjustly prejudiced in the statements which I have made from time to time concerning America. But if the discourse to which I listened on the morning of which I speak stands in any way as an expression of the Chicago ideal of culture, that ideal is, I regret to say, a low one. I shall venture to say that it is chiefly lacking in definition of aim, and yet, alas, know how little right I have to indulge in such a criticism, for have I not been accused of being sadly to seek, myself, in "a philosophy with coherent, interdependent, subordinate and derivative principles." There was something quite pathetic to me in the thought that this discourse, with its dreary waste of unctuous commonplace, its diluted rhetoric and its judgements, many of them so ludicrously misconceived, should be to such an audience as I saw about me the embodiment of cultured thought, and from time to time I could not help thinking that Philistinism in its frank English expression was a less unpleasant sight than was afforded by the thinly-disguised Philistinism which was here imposing on itself and making pretense of culture.

Chicago, I should say, though no one could be more painfully aware than myself of how inadequate were my opportunities for observation, had just reached that stage of its development at which the incompleteness of the commercial ideal of life is beginning to make itself keenly felt, and is somewhat uncertainly groping in search of the larger and finer things whose existence it dimly apprehends. But it has not yet reached the stage of clear discernment and is easily satisfied with the appearance of culture, even if the substance be wanting. Its great commercial success has given it, moreover, a certain impatience of temper which makes it incapable of going to work in the right way to acquire that of which it is just beginning to feel the need. A society that has lived in the flesh, so to speak, for so long, cannot at once and naturally come to live in the spirit. The change of heart which is the condition of the working out of such a change of life, must be a gradual one. The prevailing attitude of Chicago towards things of culture has about it an air of patronage. It seems to say: "These things are desirable, and we will make them the fashion." All that need be done is to build costly chapels, to purchase expensive pictures, to make the concert and the opera places of fashionable resort. How different is this from the humble attitude of one who recognizes the real significance of culture and who knows that to be genuine it must grow up silently with the life. "The kingdom of God cometh not with observation." Nor, I fear, will the sweetness and light of the cultured life come to Chicago at the beck of the rich man.

Yet it would be ungracious of me to close these random observations without saying that the general aspects of society in Chicago, as it appeared to me, are very far from being aspects of much of the individual life with which I came in contact. Were I to base my criticisms upon the delightful friends whom I made while there, or in their charming homes, my picture would be a very different one.

Text. New York Tribune, *Apr. 6, 1884 (rptd Leonard, pp. 336–40).*

Index

Note on cumulative index: Matthew Arnold (MA throughout index) addressed his correspondents with the assumption that they understood the context. Thus, when he discusses politics, there are few details; what appears are more like sidelong references to, and opinions on, the situation. The best ways for the reader to access these discussions are through the various key players (e.g., for politics, look at the entries for Gladstone) and through his comments on his various writings (e.g., for politics, *Irish Essays and Others*). Arnold's prose and poetry are listed in the index by their titles. Women's names are either listed under both maiden and married names or cross-referenced from one to the other. Places he visited in America are listed under their specific states (e.g., Massachusetts). Places in England are listed under their own names (i.e., "Cambridge" is Cambridge, England, not Massachusetts). Page numbers are in the form of volume number followed by page number; "n" indicates a note; italicized page numbers indicate illustrations; boldface page numbers indicate biographical notes.

Arnold, Mary Penrose (MA's mother)
(*continued*)

2:476–77, 2:478–79, 2:482–84; letters to (1866), 3:2, 3:7–9, 3:11, 3:12–16, 3:17–18, 3:19–20, 3:22–23, 3:26–27, 3:30–33, 3:36–39, 3:44–45, 3:47–48, 3:50–52, 3:54–55, 3:56–57, 3:58–59, 3:60–61, 3:62–63, 3:64–65, 3:67–69, 3:71–72, 3:83–85, 3:87–88, 3:89–90, 3:91–94, 3:95–98, 3:99–100; letters to (1867), 3:102–3, 3:104–9, 3:110–11, 3:112–13, 3:114–17, 3:118–20, 3:126–30, 3:132–34, 3:137–38, 3:148–49, 3:150–51, 3:154–55, 3:157–58, 3:159–60, 3:163–64, 3:165–66, 3:167–69, 3:172–73, 3:182–83, 3:186–87, 3:190–91, 3:193–94, 3:195–97, 3:198–99, 3:201–2, 3:206–7; letters to (1868), 2:236–37, 3:212–13, 3:216–17, 3:220–21, 3:223–24, 3:226–27, 3:230–31, 3:233–34, 3:239–40, 3:241–42, 3:242–43, 3:247–48, 3:255–57, 3:258–59, 3:260–61, 3:263–64, 3:265–66, 3:268–69, 3:273–74, 3:276–77, 3:283–84, 3:287–88, 3:295–96, 3:300–301, 3:303–4, 3:305–6; letters to (1869), 3:307–12, 3:313–14, 3:315–17, 3:319–20, 3:323–24, 3:329–30, 3:337–38, 3:340–41, 3:342–44, 3:346–47, 3:348–50, 3:351–58, 3:361–62, 3:364–65, 3:366–68, 3:369–71, 3:372–73, 3:374–75, 3:377–80, 3:382–83, 3:384–86, 3:389–92, 3:394–95, 3:397–98; letters to (1870), 3:400–401, 3:403–4, 3:417–18, 3:421–23, 3:425–26, 3:428–29, 3:433–34, 3:435–36, 3:438–39, 3:444–48, 3:450–52, 3:453–55, 3:456–59, 3:460–62; letters to (1871), 4:1–2, 4:3–4, 4:6–9, 4:10–12, 4:13–14, 4:16–18, 4:19–20, 4:22–23, 4:25, 4:26–27, 4:28–29, 4:30–32, 4:36–37, 4:39–40, 4:42–44, 4:46–52, 4:54–55, 4:58–60, 4:61–62, 4:64–65, 4:67–69, 4:72–

73, 4:75–77, 4:80–81, 4:82–83; letters to (1872), 4:88–90, 4:92–93, 4:95, 4:97–98, 4:102–3, 4:105–6, 4:108–9, 4:111–12, 4:137–38; letters to (1873), 4:151–53; on MA's childhood, 1:xlviii; mentioned, 1:1, 1:67, 1:81; remembered, 4:176–78, 4:220–21, 5:467, 6:124; *On the Study of Celtic Literature* sent to, 3:149; travels of, 1:23–32; visits with, 2:258–59; Wordsworth family and, 1:63–64. *See also* Fox How

Arnold, Matthew ("Crab"): accidents and injuries of, 1:32–34, 3:202, 3:206, 3:221, 3:227, 3:264, 3:308, 6:197, 6:198n, 6:367; autographs of, 2:472, 3:47, 3:230, 5:387, 6:124, 6:289n, 6:351; Cambridge degree for, 5:202–3, 5:204; characteristics of, 1:lii–liii, 1:lvi–lx; clothing of, 4:85, 5:353–54, 5:374, 6:92, 6:97; committee testimony of, 2:321; death of, 6:364; education of, 1:35; elocution lessons for, 5:236n, 5:328, 5:331, 5:338, 5:348, 5:457, 5:459; haircut for, 6:121–22; handwriting of, 1:xxii, 1:xxvi, 1:*lxxii–lxxv*, 4:280; health/illnesses of (1822–50), 1:20, 1:24–25, 1:31, 1:139; health/illnesses of (1851–55), 1:289, 1:297; health/illnesses of (1856–60), 1:337, 2:4, 2:46; health/illnesses of (1861–65), 2:57, 2:59, 2:61, 2:62, 2:93, 2:97–98, 2:118, 2:151, 2:261, 2:383, 2:384, 2:424–25; health/illnesses of (1866–70), 3:35, 3:37, 3:45, 3:84–85, 3:104, 3:106, 3:111, 3:254, 3:255–56, 3:300, 3:301, 3:311, 3:313, 3:363, 3:375, 3:400–401, 3:403, 3:418, 3:421–22, 3:428, 3:458; health/illnesses of (1871–75), 4:11, 4:48–49, 4:129, 4:133, 4:265; health/illnesses of (1876–80), 4:331, 4:332–33, 4:380, 5:21, 5:92; health/illnesses of (1881–85), 5:137, 5:230, 5:237, 5:361, 5:363, 5:364, 5:368, 5:371, 5:438, 5:449, 5:461, 5:470, 6:36–37, 6:38, 6:41, 6:47, 6:64, 6:100; health/ill-

2:187; publication of, 2:166n, 2:175n,
2:191–92, 2:207, 2:332; responses to,
2:212, 2:213, 2:215, 2:217, 6:10;
writing of, 2:204

Euripides, 3:437

Evans, Samuel H., 1:248

Eve, Henry Weston, 4:13

Evelyn family, 6:228, 6:269

Evelyn, Frances Harriet Vaughan, 5:161,
5:162n

Evelyn, John, 5:220

Evelyn, William John, **3:45n**; invitation
from, 4:39; marriage of, 5:162n; on
memorial, 4:413; mentioned, 3:45,
3:127, 3:352, 3:460, 4:43; quoted,
4:207

Everard, Charles Hugh: letters to (1876–
80), 5:18

Everett, Charles Carroll: letters to (1881–
85), 5:350; writings of, 4:324

Everett, Edward, 1:198, **1:202n**

Every, Frederick: letters to (1871–75),
4:170

Every, Henry, 4:170

Every Saturday (journal), 3:10n

Evesham, description of, 1:312

Ewald, Georg Heinrich August von,
1:115n, 4:158n; biblical commentary
of, 1:115, 4:386, 4:387, 5:229, 6:39,
6:83; *Literature and Dogma* sent to,
4:157; quoted, 5:220; Renan's work
reviewed by, 2:240, 2:241n

Ewart, William, 2:327

Examiner: on "The Bishop and the
Philosopher," 2:178, 2:179, 2:180n,
2:182; editors of, 1:261, 1:262n,
4:432n; Edward's articles in, 1:498,
1:499n, 2:124n; on *Essays in Criticism,*
2:393; on Irish situation, 1:109,
1:111n; on Louis Philippe, 1:91, 1:92n,
1:93; on *A Manual of English Literature*
(T. Arnold), 2:184, 2:185n; MA's portrait in, 5:72; on "My Countrymen,"
3:17, 3:18n; on *Poems* (1853), 1:283;
on "A Southern Night," 2:110,
2:111n; "To the Hungarian Nation" in,
1:153; on volunteer rifle corps, 1:508n

Exeter, bishop of. *See* Phillpotts, Henry
(bishop of Exeter); Temple, Frederick
(later, archbishop of Canterbury)

Exposition Universelle, 1:436, 1:438n,
4:414n, 4:419–20

Eyre, Charles Wasteneys, 1:24, 1:32n,
1:43

Eyre, Lucy Dorothea Foulis, 1:24, 1:32n,
1:199

Faber, Frederick William, 1:51, **1:53n**,
1:381

Faber, J. D. B., 6:8

Fabre, Jules, 3:178n

Faed, Thomas, 3:329, 3:331n

Fairchild, James Harris, 5:379

Fairchild, Mrs James Harris, 5:379n

Fairchild, Lucius, 5:384n, 5:392, 6:255n

faith, reflections on, 3:388

Faithfull, Emily: letters to (1861–65),
2:195; mentioned, 2:110, 2:215,
2:227; publishing by, 2:101n, 2:111–
12n. See also *The Victoria Magazine*

Falconer, Edmund, 2:180n

"Falkland" (MA): mentioned, 4:354n,
4:401; proofs of, 4:357; publication
of, 4:359n; references in, 4:177n

Falloux, A. de, 1:193, 1:194n

family: children's possessions, 1:1–2; do-
mestic details of, 1:xxv–xxvi, 1:xxviii;
education's role for, 1:lviii–lix; home
for, 1:xlvii–xlix; nicknames in, 1:1–
2n, 1:18; relationships in, 1:188–89,
2:91; values in, 1:xlv–xlvi. *See also*
Byron House (Harrow); Chester
Square house; Fox How; Pains Hill
Cottage (Cobham, Surrey); *specific
individuals*

Fane, Ethel, 6:26

Fane, John, 2:205n

Fane, Julian, **2:458n**; family of, 6:14n,
6:26; mentioned, 2:457, 2:460, 3:13,
3:14, 3:42, 3:124

Fane, Julian Henry Charles: introduction
for, 3:28–29; letters to (1866–70),
3:28

Fane, Priscilla Anne (Lady Westmorland),
2:204, 3:13, 3:14

Ruault, Jeanne Henriette Alice (later, Bourne), 4:240n

Ruault, Lena, 4:11, 4:12n, 4:388

Ruault, Pierre Marie Gustave: family of, 4:12n; letters to (1871–75), 4:96–97

Rubens, Peter Paul, 1:288, 1:462

Rubenstein, Anton Grigoryevich, 6:85, 6:86n

Ruble, Zulema A.: letters to (1881–85), 6:79

Rückert, Friedrich, 2:451, 2:452–53n, 2:475–76

Rugbeianism, 1:60n

"Rugby Chapel" (MA): editions and reprints of, 5:100, 5:174n; responses to, 3:168, 3:169n, 3:202; reviews of, 3:173

Rugby School: attitudes toward, 1:xlvii; Budge at, 2:368, 2:371, 3:100, 3:103, 3:107–8, 3:165, 3:206, 3:208, 3:267n; day pupils and, 2:470n; dining at, 1:241–42, 6:275, 6:285; events at, 1:6, 1:35; examiners at, 1:21–22n; fees of, 3:111, 3:119, 3:122, 3:227; founding of, 1:7n; headmastership at, 1:48n, 1:158, 1:161, 1:165n, 1:168n, 1:211, 3:373, 3:380, 3:383, 3:386, 3:392, 3:395, 3:396n, 3:462, 4:169n, 5:33n; move to, 1:18; remembered, 3:299; scholarships at, 1:50; sporting events and, 3:350, 3:354; students at, 1:3, 1:34n; Temple recommended to, 1:364, 1:365; Temple's tenure at, 2:62, 2:63n; traditions of, 2:81; visits to, 3:390, 3:391

Rush, Richard, 1:88n, 1:89

Rushout-Bowles, George (Lord Northwick), 3:357, 3:358n

Ruskin, John: acquaintances of, 2:58n, 3:156n; form and, 2:53; Gothic architecture and, 1:503, 1:506n, 1:518; on home, 1:xlvii, 1:xlix; lectures of, 3:405; letters from (1876–80), 4:375; letters to (1876–80), 4:375–76; on list of academicians, 6:263n; MA compared to, 2:234, 2:235, 2:236, 5:143n; MA's relationship to, 4:376n; mentioned, 1:222n, 2:214, 3:73n, 3:90,

4:70, 4:339, 5:328, 5:429, 6:31, 6:348; opinion of, 2:43, 4:5, 4:385, 5:55; on Paris, 1:421n; references to, 2:319; on Wordsworth, 5:119; writing of, 1:332–33, 1:336, 6:279

Russell, Mr (unidentified): letters to (1886–88), 6:350

Russell, Arthur John Edward, 3:204, 5:88n, 5:150, 5:161, 5:231, 6:17

Russell, Lady Charles: family of, 3:185; mentioned, 3:356, 3:457, 4:16, 4:92, 4:103, 5:220; roses of, 6:228; Tom's care and, 3:290; Tom's death and, 3:296, 3:314

Russell, Lord Charles: acquaintances of, 3:327; family of, 1:xvii, 3:362n, 4:143; gifts from, 3:372; Irish issues and, 6:304, 6:305n; mentioned, 3:350, 3:356, 3:447, 4:175; Tom's care and, 3:290; visits with, 3:343

Russell, Lord Edward, 3:343, 3:344n

Russell, Francis Charles Hastings, 3:136

Russell, George William Erskine: background of, 1:xvii–xviii; education of, 3:185n; on *Essays in Criticism,* 1:xiv; family of, 3:204n, 3:362n; letters to (1886–88), 6:253, 6:280, 6:318, 6:364; MA letters published by, 1:xviii–xxi, 1:xxv–xxx, 1:l; mentioned, 2:49, 4:143, 5:414, 5:430, 6:26n, 6:265, 6:271, 6:274, 6:327

Russell, George William Francis Sackville (marquis of Tavistock): fishing and, 6:36, 6:40, 6:147; letters to (1881–85), 5:205

Russell, Gertrude Louisa (later, Harris; Charles's daughter), 4:186

Russell, Henry, 3:362

Russell, Lord John: on Arnold's poetry, 1:266; educational issues and, 1:336–37n; electoral franchise and, 1:108, 1:110n, 1:194; family of, 1:xvii, 1:336, 2:418n, 2:422n, 3:257n; mentioned, 1:195, 1:384n, 2:462, 3:31, 3:197n; positions held by, 1:266–67n; Reform Bill and, 3:24n; resignation of, 3:52n; second wife of, 5:65n

Russell, John, Earl, 3:18, 4:159, 4:160n

VICTORIAN LITERATURE AND CULTURE SERIES